METAPHILOSOPHY

HENRI LEFEBVRE

TRANSLATED BY DAVID FERNBACH

EDITED WITH AN INTRODUCTION BY STUART ELDEN

VERSO

London • New York

Cet ouvrage publié dans le cadre du programme d'aide à la publication bénéficie du soutien du Ministrère des Affaires Etrangères et du Service Culturel de l'Ambassade de France représenté aux Etats-Unis. This work received support from the French Ministry of Foreign Affairs and the Cultural Services of the French Embassy in the United States through their publishing assistance programme.

This English-language edition published by Verso 2016
Originally published in French as *Métaphilosophie*
© Editions Syllepse 2000
Translation © David Fernbach 2016
Introduction © Stuart Elden 2016

1 3 5 7 9 10 8 6 4 2

Verso
UK: 6 Meard Street, London W1F 0EG
US: 20 Jay Street, Suite 1010, Brooklyn, NY 11201
versobooks.com

Verso is the imprint of New Left Books

ISBN-13: 978-1-78478-274-0 (PBK)
ISBN-13: 978-1-78478-273-3 (HBK)
ISBN-13: 978-1-78478-276-4 (UK EBK)
ISBN-13: 978-1-78478-275-7 (US EBK)

British Library Cataloguing in Publication Data
A catalogue record for this book is available from the British Library

Library of Congress Cataloging-in-Publication Data
A catalog record for this book is available from the Library of Congress

Typeset in Minion by Hewer Text UK, Ltd, Edinburgh
Printed in the US by Maple Press

Contents

Introduction: A Study of Productive Tensions

Stuart Elden

While he is best known today for his writing on cities, everyday life and the production of space, Henri Lefebvre's work covered a vast range of topics. *Metaphilosophy*, a book he wrote in his sixties but which counts as a mid-career landmark, is an essential part of that story.[1] The book pre-dates all of his major texts on urban questions, including *The Right to the City*, *The Urban Revolution* and *Marxist Thought and the City*.[2] It comes several years before *The Production of Space*, and almost twenty-six years ahead of his final book *Elements of Rhythmanalysis*.[3] It appeared shortly after the second volume of

---

1   Henri Lefebvre, *Métaphilosophie*, second edition, Paris: Syllepse, 2001 [1965]. For Lefebvre's career, Rémi Hess, *Henri Lefebvre et l'aventure du siècle*, Paris: A. M. Métailié, 1988, is invaluable. English studies of Lefebvre include my own *Understanding Henri Lefebvre: Theory and the Possible*, London: Continuum, 2004; Rob Shields, *Lefebvre, Love & Struggle: Spatial Dialectics*, London: Routledge, 1999; Andy Merrifield, *Henri Lefebvre: A Critical Introduction*, London: Routledge, 2006; and Łukasz Stanek, *Henri Lefebvre on Space: Architecture, Urban Research, and the Production of Theory*, Minneapolis: University of Minnesota Press, 2011.

2   *La droit à la ville*, Paris: Anthropos, 1968, translated and edited by Eleonore Kofman and Elizabeth Lebas as 'The Right to the City', in *Writings on Cities*, Oxford: Blackwell, 1996, pp. 63–181; *La révolution urbaine*, Paris: Gallimard, translated by Robert Bononno as *The Urban Revolution*, Minneapolis: University of Minnesota Press, 2003; *Marxist Thought and the City*, translated by Robert Bonnano, Minneapolis: University of Minnesota Press, 2016.

3   *La production de l'espace*, Paris: Anthropos, 1974, translated by Donald Nicholson-Smith as *The Production of Space*, Oxford: Blackwell, 1991; *Eléments de rythmanalyse: Introduction a la connaissance de rythmes*, Paris: Syllepse, 1992, translated by Stuart Elden and Gerald Moore as 'Elements of Rhythmanalysis: Introduction to the Understanding of Rhythms', in *Rhythmanalysis: Space, Time and Everyday Life*, London: Continuum, 2004, pp. 1–69.

Critique of Everyday Life, and in the same year as his *La proclamation de la Commune* and his study of the Pyrenees.[4] Lefebvre regularly stated that there were, for him, three key thinkers: Hegel, Marx and Nietzsche. *Metaphilosophy* clearly demonstrates this threefold debt, but it also brings a number of other figures into the conversation.

In his earliest writings, dating back to the 1920s, Lefebvre was already under the spell of Hegel. He was part of a small group that founded the journal *Philosophies*, along with Georges Polizer, Norbert Guterman, Georges Friedmann and Pierre Morhange. Their work was partly orientated as a challenge to Henri Bergson, and under the influence of Léon Brunschvicg, whom Lefebvre references a couple of times in this study. They wrote a manifesto of which excerpts were published in the *Philosophies* journal and then in its successor, *L'esprit*.[5] Politzer translated Friedrich Schelling's *On the Essence of Human Freedom* and Lefebvre contributed a long introduction.[6] Lefebvre read Edmund Husserl around this time, and while he would continue to have an interest in phenomenology throughout his career, later reproached himself for his 'juvenile presumptions' towards what would become known as existentialism.[7] It is important to underline that little of Husserl was published at this time, and it pre-dates the publication of Martin Heidegger's *Sein und Zeit* in 1927. Lefebvre and his colleagues worked for a while with the surrealists, and then discovered Marx. Together with Guterman, Lefebvre founded the journal *La Revue marxiste*. Marx's important 1844 manuscripts had been published in

---

4 *Critique de la vie quotidienne II: Fondements d'une sociologie de la quotidienneté*, Paris: L'Arche, 1961, translated by John Moore as *Critique of Everyday Life Volume II: Foundations for a Sociology of the Everyday*, London: Verso, 2002; *La proclamation de la Commune*, Paris: Gallimard, 1965; *Pyrénées*, second edition, Pau: Cairn, 2000 [1965].

5 On this period of his career, see Bud Burkhard, *French Marxism between the Wars: Henri Lefebvre and the 'Philosophies'*, Atlantic Highlands: Humanity Books, 2000; and the work of Michel Trebitsch, including his introductions to the Verso translations of the *Critique of Everyday Life*.

6 'Introduction: Le même et l'autre', in Friedrich Schelling, *Recherches philosophiques sur l'essence de la liberté humaine et sur les problèmes qui s'y rattachent*, translated by Georges Politzer, Paris: F. Rieder, pp. 7–64. For an English translation of Schelling's book, see *Of Human Freedom*, translated by James Gutmann, Chicago: Open Court, 1936.

7 See *L'existentialisme*, second edition, Paris: Anthropos, 2001 [1946].

German only in 1927, and it was a considerable coup for the journal to publish the first translations of these, made by Guterman, in the first and second issues, in 1929.[8] Lefebvre joined the French Communist Party, the PCF, that same year. In 1934 Lefebvre and Guterman followed this work with a collection of Marx's writings, spanning his entire career, and in 1938 produced a collection of Hegel's work and a translation of Lenin's notebooks on Hegel.[9] But not simply serving as editors, Lefebvre and Guterman wrote an important introduction for each book and also collaborated on *La conscience mystifiée*, published in 1936.[10] Shortly before the war broke out, Guterman, Jewish and with suspect papers, left France for safety in New York. Further collaborations were therefore limited, though he and Lefebvre kept up a long correspondence over multiple decades.[11] This early period had a profound impact on Lefebvre's work, especially on analyses of the relation between Marx and Hegel, a major theme of his career.

Opposing the prevailing political atmosphere in Europe, Lefebvre also wrote two stinging critiques of right-wing politics: *La nationalisme contre les nations* in 1937 and *Hitler au pouvoir: les enseignements de cinq années de fascisme* in 1938.[12] While the first has gone through three editions and is widely available, the second is hard to find today, though it was recently translated into Italian.[13] But, in terms of

---

8   Karl Marx, 'Travail et propriété privée', *La Revue marxiste*, no. 1, February 1929, pp. 7–28; 'Notes sur les besoins, la production et la division du travail', *La revue marxiste*, no. 2, June 1929, pp. 513–38. The *Revue* also published important texts by Engels. A few years later Lefebvre and Guterman published Marx's 'Critique de la dialectique hegelienne' in their new journal *Avant-Poste* in two parts: no. 1, June 1933, pp. 33–9, and no. 2, August 1933, pp. 110–16.

9   *Morceaux choisis de Karl Marx*, Paris: Gallimard, 1934; G. W. F. Hegel, *Morceaux choisis*, Paris: Gallimard, 1938; *Cahiers de Lénine sur la dialectique de Hegel*, Paris: Gallimard, 1938.

10   Henri Lefebvre and Norbert Guterman, *La conscience mystifiée*, third edition, Paris: Syllepse, 1999 [1936].

11   Guterman's papers are archived in the rare books and manuscripts room of the Butler Library of Columbia University, and contain letters and manuscripts from Lefebvre, among other materials.

12   *Le nationalisme contre les nations*, second edition, Paris: Méridiens Klincksieck, 1988 [1937]; *Hitler au pouvoir: les enseignements de cinq années de fascisme*, Paris: Bureau d'éditions, 1938.

13   *Hitler al potere: Cinque anni di nazismo in Germania*, translated by Cristiano Casalini, Milano: Medusa, 2012.

Lefebvre's longer-term work and the direct antecedents to the present book, two books published in 1939 are perhaps most important: *Dialectical Materialism* and *Nietzsche*.[14] The former, one of his first books to be translated into English, develops a clear and nuanced appropriation of Hegelian–Marxist thought, using the same title but opposing Stalin's work on the topic.[15] While *Dialectical Materialism* could be seen as consistent with some kind of orthodoxy, Lefebvre's reading of Nietzsche from a Marxist standpoint, especially in 1939 when Nietzsche was being praised by the Nazi regime in Germany, ran counter to the traditional line. Nonetheless, these two books give a very good sense of the philosophical-theoretical influences Lefebvre would continue to work with throughout his career. Their afterlives diverged: *Dialectical Materialism* went through multiple editions and was widely translated; *Nietzsche* had to wait sixty years before a re-edition in France, while first editions remain hard to find.[16] This is partly because it was proscribed and burned by the occupying Germans, along with Lefebvre's book on Hitler and other early studies.

During the war, Lefebvre left Paris and spent most of his time in the Pyrenees. The exact nature of his involvement with the Resistance is unclear, and it seems he worked more as a theorist and writer than as an active agent. He made use of the time in exile to go through local archives, which later formed the basis for his doctorate on peasant communities in the region.[17] This work, which led to his postwar career as a rural sociology researcher at the CNRS, and a range of small publications, was important to Lefebvre. The story of this later research lies outside the more philosophical one to be told here, but Lefebvre's rural work, which drew his interest to the industrialization and urbanization processes he saw taking place in his beloved Pyrenees and elsewhere, directly led to his more famous urban writings.[18]

---

14   *Le matérialisme dialectique*, sixth edition, Paris: PUF, 1971 [1939], translated by John Sturrock as *Dialectical Materialism*, London: Jonathan Cape, 1968; *Nietzsche*, Paris: Sociales Internationales, 1939.

15   J. V. Stalin, 'Dialectical and historical materialism', in *Problems of Leninism*, Peking: Foreign Languages Press, 1976, pp. 835–73.

16   *Nietzsche*, second edition, Paris: Syllepse, 2003 [1939].

17   *Les communautés paysannes pyrénéennes: Thèse soutenue en Sorbonne 1954*, Navarrenx: Cercle Historique de l'Arribère, 2014.

18   Many of the essays on rural communities and the transformation they

Immediately after the war, books came thick and fast. Between 1946 and 1958 Lefebvre combined production of introductory works on Marx and Marxism – *Logique formelle, logique dialectique; Marx 1818–1883; Pour connaître la pensée de Karl Marx; Le marxisme; Pour connaître la pensée de Lénine; Problèmes actuels du marxisme* – with a range of other studies.[19] Some of these other works concerned the great men of French letters – Descartes, Diderot, Pascal, Musset and Rabelais.[20] Others were on aesthetics or the painter Edouard Pignon.[21] One, perhaps best forgotten, was a PCF-inspired attack on the philosophy of the moment – existentialism and especially Jean-Paul Sartre.[22] Many of these books are perhaps only of historical interest today. But buried among them was the first volume of *Critique of Everyday Life*, which appeared in 1947 and then again with a very long preface in 1958.[23] This book, whose radical nature today is easy to overlook, helped to inaugurate what became known as cultural studies.

Though his writings on the subject would not be collected into a book until much later, in the late 1950s Lefebvre also began to engage with the emerging interest in structuralism.[24] We can see three of Lefebvre's main arguments about structuralism in the present book.

---

experienced are collected in *Du rural à l'urbain*, Paris: Anthropos, 1970. For a more extensive discussion see Elden, *Understanding Henri Lefebvre*, 2004, chapter 4; Stuart Elden and Adam David Morton, 'Thinking past Henri Lefebvre: Introducing "The Theory of Ground Rent and Rural Sociology"', *Antipode*, vol. 48, no. 1, 2016, pp. 57–66.

19 *Logique formelle, logique dialectique*, second edition, Paris: Anthropos, 1969 [1947]; *Marx 1818–1883*, Geneva and Paris: Trois Collines, 1947; *Pour connaître la pensée de Karl Marx*, Paris: Bordas, 1947; *Le marxisme*, Paris: PUF, 1948; *Pour connaître la pensée de Lénine*, Paris: Bordas, 1957; *Problèmes actuels du marxisme*, Paris: PUF, 1960 [1958].

20 *Descartes*, Paris: Editions Hier et Aujourd'hui, 1947; *Diderot ou les affirmations fondamentales du matérialisme*, second edition, Paris: L'Arche, 1983 [1949]; *Pascal*, Paris: Nagel, two volumes, 1949–54; *Musset*, second edition, Paris: L'Arche, 1970 [1955]; and *Rabelais*, second edition, Paris: Anthropos, 2001 [1955].

21 *Contribution à l'esthétique*, second edition, Paris: Anthropos, 2001 [1953]; *Pignon*, Paris: Edition Falaise, 1956.

22 Lefebvre, *L'existentialisme*.

23 *Critique de la vie quotidienne I: Introduction*, Paris: L'Arche, second edition, 1958 [1947]; translated by John Moore as *Critique of Everyday Life Volume I: Introduction*, London: Verso, 1991.

24 *Au-dèla du structuralisme*, Paris: Anthropos, 1971; *L'idéologie structuraliste*, Paris: Anthropos, 1975.

The first is that form, function and structure are all significant, both in Marx's work and more generally, but to privilege only one of them is ideology, an ontology which becomes an 'ism': formalism, functionalism or structuralism.[25] The second is that the relation between the diachronic and the synchronic is equally significant: by privileging the latter, structuralism denies history and becoming. The third is that content and form must be examined together in linguistics and semiology: *la langue*, language, must not take precedence over *la parole*, speech.

The year 1958 was crucial for Lefebvre: it was the year he was finally expelled from, or left, the PCF: the record is unclear.[26] In retrospect, it is astonishing that he lasted so long – that he was prepared to see works such as the proposed sequel to *Logique formelle, logique dialectique* and *Méthodologie des sciences* censored, or *Contribution à l'esthétique* delayed because of party strictures.[27] Lefebvre wrote so many books on literature in the late 1940s and early 1950s in part because they were easier to publish without the censor's involvement. But the death of Stalin and Khrushchev's subsequent denunciation of his regime led to the final break. Lefebvre was in East Berlin on 25 February 1956, when Khruschev delivered his famous speech during the Party's Twentieth Congress. He recounted having stayed up all night reading the report. Still it took two years before he was suspended from the Party, in June 1958. In July he published two pieces in *Les Temps modernes* stating his case, and left the Party later that year.[28] His parting shot was the massive, untranslated *La somme et le reste*, which ranges widely across

25   See also *Au-dèla du structuralisme*, p. 22; *Key Writings*, edited by Stuart Elden, Elizabeth Lebas and Eleonore Kofman, London: Continuum, 2003, pp. 38–9. For a reading of *Capital* in this light, see *Au-delà du structuralisme*, pp. 215–18. See *Sociologie de Marx*, Paris: PUF, 1966, p. 94; *The Sociology of Marx*, translated by Norbert Guterman, Penguin: London, 1968, p. 111.

26   For Lefebvre's version of the story, see *Le temps des méprises*, Paris: Stock, 1975, pp. 94–7.

27   *Méthodologie des sciences: Un inédit*, edited by Rémi Hess, Paris: Anthropos, 2002.

28   'L'exclu s'inclut', *Les Temps modernes*, no. 149, July 1958, pp. 226–37; 'Réponse au camarade Besse', *Les Temps modernes*, no. 149, July 1958, pp. 238–49. His important piece 'Le marxisme et la pensée française' appeared the previous year: *Les Temps modernes*, no. 137–8, 1957, pp. 104–37.

his interests and ambitions.[29] Not only does it criticize the PCF for its unrepentant Stalinism, it also rails against its weakness in opposing the war in Algeria and the strength of Gaullism. *La Somme et le reste* was quickly followed by a second volume of the *Critique of Everyday Life*, the *Introduction to Modernity*, the publication of his secondary thesis on rural sociology, two volumes of Marx's collected writings and yet another introduction to him.[30] All this before *Metaphilosophy* – enough of a career for almost anyone, and, while the date of Lefebvre's birth is disputed, by 1965 he could have been 60, 64, or even 67. But Lefebvre would go on publishing for another two and a half decades, including many of his most cited works.

PHILOSOPHY BECOMING WORLD: WORLD BECOMING PHILOSOPHICAL

In *Metaphilosophy* Lefebvre does nothing less than try to work out, in some detail, the implications of Marx's thought for philosophical engagement. Lefebvre continually insists that he is not trying to make Marx into a philosopher, but to suggest that there is a philosophy in his thought.[31] In a parallel way he insists that 'Marx is not a sociologist, but there is a sociology in Marx.'[32] The same assertion might be applied to Marx's contributions to rural and urban studies, fields with which he likely would not have identified. The crucial theme in this book, though, is the relation of Marx to philosophy. As Lefebvre stated in the first volume of the *Critique of Everyday Life*: 'The fact that economic science and political action had superseded or subsumed [*dépassaient*] speculative philosophy fostered the false conclusion that Marx had abandoned any conception of the philosophical world.'[33]

---

29 *La Somme et le reste*, Paris: Meridiens Klincksieck, third edition, 1989 [1958].

30 In addition to the works already cited, see *Introduction à la modernité: Preludes*, Paris: Les Editions de Minuit, 1962, translated by John Moore as *Introduction to Modernity: Twelve Preludes,* London: Verso, 1995; *La vallée de Campan: Étude de sociologie rurale*, Paris: PUF, 1963; *Karl Marx: Oeuvres choisies*, Paris: Gallimard, two volumes, 1963–6; *Marx*, Paris: Gallimard, 1964.

31 *Pour connaître la pensée de Karl Marx*, p. 46.

32 *Sociologie de Marx*, p. 17; *The Sociology of Marx*, p. 22.

33 *Critique de la vie quotidienne*, vol. 1, p. 190; *Critique of Everyday Life*, vol. 1, p. 177.

The nature of Marx's engagement with the world remains to be seen. While the eleventh thesis on Feuerbach is of course well known, Lefebvre was fond of quoting a phrase from the preparatory notes to Marx's doctoral thesis: 'The world's becoming philosophical is at the same time philosophy's becoming worldly, that its realization is at the same time its loss.'[34] Lefebvre and some of his contemporaries, notably Kostas Axelos, saw this as a crucial formula. In the realization of philosophy, its becoming real, its becoming world, it is transcended, superseded, overcome. How and why does philosophy disappear, or, to adopt the language often attributed to Marx with regard to the state, how must philosophy wither away?[35] To answer this we need to consider both what process is at stake and what is being overcome. Full answers to these questions must be sought in Lefebvre's work, and there is no better place to begin than *Metaphilosophy*.

With regard to the 'world', this is a book in which the vocabulary of *le monde, le mondial, le mondain* – the world, the worldwide, the worldly – and the term *mondialisation* appear continually. For consistency, especially with the *State, Space, World* collection, we have tried to keep to 'world'-based words. In English we tend to slip between 'world' and 'globe' very easily, and with all the talk today of globalization it is easy to miss the significance of what is going on here. Lefebvre, together with thinkers associated with the journal *Arguments*, including Axelos, was developing a new conceptual vocabulary which long pre-dates the English use of these terms. '*Le mondial*' – the worldwide – was not the same as 'the total', or '*le global*', which in most instances simply means 'the general'. In modern France '*globalisation*' and '*mondialisation*' are frequently seen as equivalents, or the latter as simply the French

---

34   Karl Marx, *Writings of the Young Marx on Philosophy and Society*, edited by Lloyd D. Easton and Kurt H. Guddat, New York: Doubleday, 1967, p. 62 (translation amended).

35   Marx suggests that the 'political state disappears [*untergehe*] in a true democracy' (*Early Writings*, London: Penguin, 1975, p. 88), but the term 'withers away' is actually from Engels: *Socialism: Utopian and Scientific*, Peking: Foreign Languages Press, 1975, p. 94. In a 1964 essay Lefebvre provides his fullest account of this idea: 'Les sources de la théorie marxiste-léniniste de l'Etat', *Les cahiers du Centre d'études socialistes*, nos 42/43, 1964, pp. 31–48; *State, Space, World: Selected Writings*, edited by Neil Brenner and Stuart Elden, translated by Gerald Moore, Neil Brenner and Stuart Elden, Minneapolis: University of Minnesota Press, 2009, chapter 2.

translation of the Anglophone word. But for Lefebvre, and even more so for Axelos, it was important to stress the 'world' element. Rather than the ugly 'worldization', we have left the French term untranslated. For Lefebvre and his colleagues, the process of what we today call globalization is made possible by the grasping of the world as a whole, and the extension of phenomena across it, i.e. '*mondialisation*'.

Lefebvre frequently uses the term '*dépassement*' here, often as a translation of the German '*Aufhebung*'. The terms relate to the verbs '*dépasser*' and '*aufheben*'. None of these words are straightforward to translate. The German, used by Hegel and developed by Marx, has a well-known range of meanings, including the seemingly contradictory ones of 'lift up', 'negate', 'preserve', and 'annul'. The term is thought to capture dialectical thought and processes, which is why Marx adopted it, even as he turned the process to stand back on its feet. 'Supersede' is a frequently suggested English-language equivalent, and it is used here. Yet as some of the remarks Lefebvre makes here and elsewhere indicate, the French term '*dépassement*' also captures for him the Nietzschean notion of '*Überwindung*' – 'overcoming'.[36] This was a term Heidegger would seize upon in his work seeking to overcome metaphysics, a theme which explicitly arises out of his engagement with Nietzsche. Heidegger's lectures on Nietzsche, originally conducted in the late 1930s and early 1940s, were published in abridged form as a two-volume book in 1961. Though not cited explicitly, the final volume contains a considerable amount of material that directly speaks to Lefebvre's concerns here.[37]

For Lefebvre, Nietzsche's arguments about *ressentiment* can be related to his own interest in alienation. Given his stress on the importance of Hegel and early Marx, it is not surprising that Lefebvre puts so much emphasis on the notion of alienation or estrangement – *Entäusserung* and *Entfremdung*. Lefebvre, against Althusser's interpretation of a break between early and late Marx, shows how

---

36   *De l'Etat*, p. 171.
37   Martin Heidegger, *Nietzsche*, two volumes, Pfullingen: Neske, 1961. The bulk of this study appears in *Nietzsche*, translated by David Farrell Krell et al., four volumes, San Francisco: Harper Collins, 1991, but some of the essays most relevant to Lefebvre's concerns appear in English in *The End of Philosophy*, translated by Joan Stambaugh, London: Souvenir Press, 1975.

alienation remained important to Marx throughout his career: 'The theory of fetishism demonstrates the *economic, everyday* basis of the *philosophical* theories of *mystification* and *alienation*.'[38] What this means is that alienation is significant both when it appears in late Marx – such as in the *Grundrisse* and the *Theories of Surplus-Value* – and when it is embedded in other terms such as reification and fetishism.

These, then, are the key figures being discussed in this book. Lefebvre is explicit in multiple places that while Marx's work is essential, taken alone it is insufficient.[39] In the first rank, then, are Lefebvre's trinity of Marx, Hegel, Nietzsche. His fullest discussion of these three comes a decade later in the 1975 book *Hegel, Marx, Nietzsche ou le royaume des ombres*,[40] but there is much analysis in the current volume. In the second rank, for Lefebvre, are his contemporaries: above all Heidegger, Sartre, Axelos. While Lefebvre was strongly critical of Heidegger in *L'existentialisme* (1946) and elsewhere,[41] there are multiple places where he treats Heideggerian themes, including everyday life, the Greeks, dwelling and space. After Hegel and Marx, Heidegger is the third most discussed thinker in *Metaphilosophy*, above even Nietzsche. One of the key aspects of his relationship to Heidegger is Lefebvre's attempt to build on Heidegger's work on ancient Greek concepts such as logos, aletheia and physis and do related work with praxis, techne, mimesis and poiesis (p. 69).

This is also the book that features Lefebvre's most extensive discussion of Sartre's later work, notably the *Critique of Dialectical Reason*. Lefebvre's initial take on Sartre was profoundly critical, coining the term 'excrementalism' in his PCF-inspired takedown of the movement.[42] But Sartre's massive attempt to reconcile the individual

---

38 *Critique de la vie quotidienne*, vol. 1, p. 193; *Critique of Everyday Life*, vol. 1, p. 179 (emphasis in original).

39 See, for example, Henri Lefebvre and Leszek Kolakowski, 'Evolution or Revolution', in Fons Elders (ed.), *Reflexive Water: The Basic Concerns of Mankind*, London: Souvenir Press, 1974, pp. 201–67.

40 *Hegel, Marx, Nietzsche ou le royaume des ombres*, Paris: Casterman, 1975. The book has not been translated into English, aside from a brief excerpt in *Key Writings*, pp. 42–9.

41 See, for example, *Hegel, Marx, Nietzsche*, pp. 51–2; *Key Writings*, p. 49.

42 Lefebvre, *L'existentialisme*, p. 30.

philosophy of existentialism with his turn towards Marxism in *Critique of Dialectical Reason*, especially in its theoretical introduction 'Questions of Method', brought him much closer to Lefebvre. In that introduction Sartre praises Lefebvre's grasp of dialectics as 'beyond reproach'.[43] He was especially inspired by the regressive-progressive mode of analysis, which Lefebvre outlined most fully in his work on rural sociology.[44] This mode was a means of combining descriptive sociological methods with historical understanding, moving back and forth between the two to continually deepen and extend the analysis. Lefebvre, of course, believed that he was simply describing what Marx himself had done. But here he sees Sartre's project as a 'titanic effort' to reconcile history and the individual lived experience, '*le vécu*', which is here translated simply as 'the lived' (p. 70).

Axelos is mentioned in only two notes here, but Lefebvre elsewhere is much more explicit about the debt he owes to Axelos's work. The crucial book in their initial discussions, which is important for the argument here, was Axelos's 1961 study of Marx as a 'thinker of technology'. This was a Heideggerian reading of Marx that saw modern-day alienation not just in economic processes, but in cultural life and technology as well. Axelos's primary thesis was partnered with a secondary thesis on Heraclitus, which Lefebvre also references here.[45] Axelos's major work on the Heidegger–Marx relation would be published the year after Lefebvre's *Metaphilosophy*, in German, though it largely combined texts which had been previously published, many of which related to texts in French.[46]

---

43   Jean-Paul Sartre, *Critique de la raison dialectique précédé de Questions de méthode, Tome I: Théorie des ensembles pratiques*, Paris: Gallimard, 1960, p. 51n; *Search for a Method*, translated by Hazel E. Barnes, New York: Vintage, 1963, p. 52 n. 8.

44   *Du rural à l'urbain*, pp. 73–4; *Key Writings*, p. 117.

45   Kostas Axelos, *Marx penseur de la technique: De l'aliénation de l'homme à la conquête du monde*, second edition, Paris: Editions de Minuit, two volumes, 1974 (1961); translated by Ronald Bruzina as *Alienation, Praxis and Techne in the Thought of Karl Marx*, Austin: University of Texas Press, 1976; *Héraclite et la philosophie: La première saisie de l'être en devenir de la totalité*, Paris: Editions de Minuit, 1962. Lefebvre reviewed the first book in 'Marxisme et technique', *Esprit*, no. 307, 1962, pp. 1023–8.

46   Kostas Axelos, *Einführung in ein künftiges Denken: Über Marx und Heidegger*, Tübingen: Max Niemeyer, 1966, translated by Kenneth Mills as *Introduction to a Future Way of Thought: On Marx and Heidegger*, edited by Stuart Elden, Luneborg: Meson Press, 2015.

Marx used the term 'praxis', Lefebvre suggests, to avoid the 'confusions' of the contemporary word 'practice', though 'it did not avoid contamination' (p. 6). He is interested in the way that the term can be used to capture a range of social activity, specifically concerning relations between humans. The turn to 'praxis' is significant, but Lefebvre stresses that 'poiesis' is similarly important as a creative impulse, and that 'mimesis' equally needs to be understood (pp. 68–9). 'Poiesis' is a mode of making, and if 'praxis' is directed towards other humans, 'poiesis' is concerned with the material world outside. As he notes, 'not all creation is "poiesis", but all poiesis is creation' (p. 8). He suggests that modern technology operates within a field outside of poiesis, but equally that 'poetry' is too restrictive a definition. Mimesis is, for Lefebvre, not imitation, but representation or expression, a mode that is a type of praxis and can be seen in relation to poiesis.

Conclusion

Metaphilosophy as an approach is therefore a metamorphosis of philosophy, turning the resources of previous thought towards a programme of radical change. Marx's famous eleventh thesis on Feuerbach is important here, but Lefebvre did not take this to mean that interpretation was no longer necessary. It was interpretation that made possible change, perhaps especially when it came to the issue of the 'world'. Philosophy is that which needs to be overcome, to be superseded: the dual sense of *aufheben* and *überwinden* that is implied by Lefebvre's use of *dépasser*.

Metaphilosophy is frequently a work in which earlier themes are embedded in a more philosophical context. One example is his work to extend Marxist analysis to the everyday aspects of modern life, rather than simply the economy or politics. Lefebvre uses three linked terms: *la vie quotidienne, la quotidienne* and *la quotidienneté*: everyday life, the everyday, and everydayness. Lefebvre is interested in the double sense of 'everyday' – something being mundane, ordinary; and something happening every day, the question of repetition or, as he would later say, rhythm. Though *Rhythmanalysis* is sometimes seen as the informal fourth volume of the *Critique of Everyday Life*, it is in the third volume that Lefebvre suggests that he is providing 'a metaphilosophy of the everyday'.[47] In places here, Lefebvre is also beginning to anticipate the concerns addressed in his last major work, the four-volume *De l'état*.[48] *Metaphilosophy* is thus a book that makes possible Lefebvre's later work on the everyday, and his inquiries concerning space, the state and representation.[49]

Metaphilosophy lies at the very core of his overall project. So many of his themes come together here that it is surprising that it has not appeared in English before. But now, in a fine translation by David Fernbach, anglophone audiences finally have access to this important work. In the postface to this book, Georges Labica suggests that it is an important volume, perhaps the most important in Lefebvre's *oeuvre*, a turning point crucial to his later work.[50] A philosophical text that seeks to leave philosophy behind, it is a study of productive tensions.

NOTE ON THE EDITION AND TRANSLATION

The original *Metaphilosophy* was published in 1965, in the *Arguments* series edited by Kostas Axelos at éditions de Minuit. It was re-edited in 2001 with éditions Syllepse. In the original, the book bore the subtitle *Prolégomènes* – 'Prolegomenas' – but this was removed for the re-issue.[51] Instead, 'Prolégomènes: Avertissement' has been assigned as a

---

47   *Critique de la vie quotidienne III: De la modernité au modernisme (Pour une métaphilosophie du quotidien)*, Paris: Editions de Minuit, 1981, translated by Gregory Elliott as *Critique of Everyday Life Volume III: From Modernity to Modernism*, London: Verso, 2008.

48   *De l'Etat*, Paris: UGE, 1975–8. For a sample of its arguments, see *State, Space, World*.

49   In addition to the texts already referenced, see *La présence et l'absence: Contribution a la théorie des représentations*, Paris: Casterman, 1980.

50   Georges Labica, 'Marxisme et poésie', in *Métaphilosophie*, p. 7; current volume, p. 329. This text appeared as a postface to the 2001 edition of the text.

51   The other two books Lefebvre published in the *Arguments* series had related subtitles: *Introduction to Modernity* had the subtitle 'Preludes', whereas *La fin de l'histoire* (Paris: Editions de Minuit, 1970) bore the neologism *épilégomènes*. See Rémi Hess, 'Note de l'éditeur', in *La fin de l'histoire*, second edition, Paris: Anthropos, 2001 [1970], p. v.

title to the first section, in place of 'Avertissement et tableaux'. Two other chapters have their titles amended in the table of contents: 'Inventaire de l'héritage' becomes 'Ouverture du testament: Inventaire de l'héritage' and the final chapter gains the subtitle 'Poièsis et méta-philosophie'. Both changes mean the second edition's table of contents better accords with the chapters as actually presented. The numbering is also different between editions. The chapters appear in the same order, but in the original the 'Avertissement' does not bear a number, with the remaining chapters I–VII. In the re-edition, the chapters are all numbered 1–8. While we have followed the second edition for this translation, these changes are important in terms of cross-references. We have given English references wherever possible in the notes, which has involved a lot of work with Lefebvre's frequently incomplete and sometimes inaccurate references. We have tried to provide references to all quotations by Lefebvre, many of which he does not give himself. We have largely followed existing English translations, but made a few modifications to accord better with aspects Lefebvre is himself emphasizing. Notes are by Lefebvre unless indicated. We have erred on the side of caution with explanations in notes, and hope that readers will find those that are there helpful.[52]

---

52 My thanks to Sebastian Budgen and Stathis Kouvelakis for their comments on an earlier draft of this introduction.

CHAPTER 1

Prolegomena: Notice to Readers

The reader is advised to cast a glance at these tables before consulting the main text, and finally to return to the tables, which will then acquire their full meaning.

If the said reader believes that he notices contradictions (in the main text or the tables), he is asked to take a second look at them, for he may be confusing contradictions in things and men with incoherence on the part of the author. If careful examination convinces him of such incoherence, the author would be grateful to hear of it.

TABLE OF FORMS, SYSTEMS, STRUCTURES

Preliminary comments
This table, which certainly needs further completion, seeks above all to show the *uneven development* of forms, systems and structures, that is to say, the entanglement between ends and beginnings, 'de-structurings' and 're-structurings', that history offers us. The forms, systems and structures considered are either products of praxis, or works of poiesis. It is important not to disassociate the two aspects of creative capacity. This table seeks to show how works and products have been deposited (secreted) by activity throughout its historical trajectory, and how they break up or dissolve. We could cite here a well-known text of Engels:

> The family represents an active principle . . . Systems of consanguinity, on the contrary, are passive; recording the progress made by the family at long intervals apart.

And Marx adds that 'the same is true of the political, juridical, legal, religious, and philosophical systems in general'.[1] We leave aside the living body as network, system of systems, hierarchy of self-regulations, as well as the cortex, organ of accumulation, experience and memory. Just as we neglect the earth as an ensemble of self-regulations (atmosphere, precipitation, climate, soil, etc.). We take certain propositions as established. These stabilities exist and constitute the 'real'. A vast and conflictual (dialectical) becoming pervades them, which philosophies call 'cosmos' or 'world', 'God', 'divine providence', 'spirit', 'life', 'will', and so forth. At each level of stability, this becoming seems exhausted. It seems reduced to a 'residue'. Then contradictions resurge: becoming recommences. It breaks or dissolves the stabilities. If we grasp creative capacity in human history using the terms 'praxis' and 'poiesis', we are not seeking to construct an ontology under this cover. We must not 'ontologize' history.

A. *So-called archaic systems.* These arise in precapitalist societies, particularly agricultural ones. Cosmogonies and mythologies of which several survivors remain: symbols, proverbial expressions (modified by the act of writing, the predominance of signs over symbols and, today, of signals over signs).

The signs of the zodiac (and astrological cosmogony);
The symbolism of the elements (earth, fire, air, water);
Languages and objects (flowers, precious stones, the ring);
The symbolism of dreams;
Mythological systems (in particular the symbolism of Mother Earth, Greek mythology, etc.);
Temporal and spatial cycles (governed by the number 12, number of the circle and the sphere);
Qualified space–times (represented and structured according to the

---

1   EN: Though the passage that Lefebvre attributes to Engels is indeed from *The Origin of the Family*, it is in fact a citation from Lewis Morgan that Engels endorses. The Marx quotation is taken from the same source: *Origins of the Family, Private Property and the State: In the Light of the Researches of Lewis H. Morgan*, in Karl Marx and Frederick Engels, *Collected Works*, vol. 26, London: Lawrence and Wishart, 1990, chapter 2, p. 141; Lewis H. Morgan, *Ancient Society, or Researches in the Lines of Human Progress from Savagery, through Barbarism to Civilization*, New York: World Publishing Company, 1963, p. 444.

numbers 2, 3, 4, 5, 6 and 7, according to cosmogonies and societies).

B. *Transitional systems*, attached to biological, physiological and territorial determinations, then broken by industrialization, but not without leaving survivors and traces. These are above all *systems of objects*:

Systems of dress (determined by sex, age, caste or group, region, nation);
Systems of food (according to the use of a staple: wheat, rice, maize, fat, oil, butter, etc.);
Systems of kinship (reduced by simplification to the conjugal family);
Systems of ludic objects (ball, football, board game, tarot, playing cards, etc.).

C. *Major constituted forms*. These forms, issuing from urban life, have more generality than the previously mentioned systems:

Origin	Brief description
Greece	Form of knowledge and knowledge of form: theory of Logos (denotations); grammar, syntax, form of discourse; formal logic, coherence of discourse; geometry (defined and homogeneous space), 'perfect system' (*teleion sustema*): homogeneity of octaves in music.
Greece and Rome	Rhetoric: practical use of discourse; political use of discourse; theory of figures of rhetoric (code of connotations).
Rome	Formal law (governing equivalences: exchange, contracts, transmission of goods).

13th century	Codification of rituals and customs (love, etiquette, etc.).
15th century	Formalization of spatial and temporal perception (perspective, standardizing of time).
16th and 17th centuries	Homogeneous and infinite space-time (Galileo, Descartes, Newton).
18th century	Developed tonal system (Rameau). Combinatory conception of intelligence (Leibniz, Condillac, etc.). Civil code (promulgated at the start of the 19th century, following earlier development with various interpretations of the law: generalized rules of exchange of goods and 'fair' contracts based on the equivalence of goods and properties).

D. *Ruptures, dissolutions, de-structurings (in Europe)*

Renaissance	Systematization of the dominant theology.
15th to 19th century	The peasant community.
17th and 18th centuries	The extended patriarchal family (lineage and household) with its system of kinship: cousinage, neighbourage.
19th century	Formal logic (attacked by dialectical thought, made flexible by the findings of science).
19th century	Dogmatic and systematic philosophy (critique by Karl Marx of the Hegelian system, the *teleion sustema* of philosophy).

End of 19th to early 20th century	Competitive capitalism (with its blind and spontaneous self-regulations: under the double pressure of monopolies and the working class).
End of 19th to early 20th century	Language, logos (fetishized and corroded, attacked by the image, etc.).
Around 1910	Classical perspective (reference to the horizon line); tonal system (reference to the tonic); absolute space–time (reference to Euclidean dimensions, the circular clock); system of nature (reference to mechanics, vital spontaneity); 'real' and solid perception; art (fetishized and in the process of dissolution, like language – process of destruction and self-destruction: Dadaism, surrealism); shift from signs to signals.
20th century	Local and national systems of objects (clothing, furniture, food) and situations (trades, functions and roles).
1945	Collapse of philosophico-political systematization on a biological basis (racism) or territorial basis (fascism).
1953–6	Collapse of philosophico-political systematization on a class basis ('socialism' as constituting a completely autonomous system in full development, and the 'capitalist system' another system in full degeneration).

Second half of 20th century	Virtual or complete explosion of the city. Possible explosion of the planet (perspective of the 'nuclear' death of the Earth).
E. *New constitutions*	
20th century	Everydayness (functionalized and structured in the disassociation of work and habitat, private life and leisure). The world of the image (audio-visual; the world made spectacle). The car (with its demands, pilot object in the 'world of objects': prestige, destruction of cities; with its codification, the 'highway code', perfect system of the modern age). Technicality (technological objects) and its social base (techno-bureaucracy). The system of survival (survival as system).

PRAXIS: PRELIMINARY COMMENTS

The Greek word 'praxis' was reintroduced by Marx to avoid the confusions of the current word 'practice'. It did not avoid contamination. Today 'praxis' encompasses several different meanings. It can denote any social activity, and thus human activity (including technology, poiesis and also theoretical knowledge). It can also be contrasted with pure theory and knowledge, or that which claims to be so, which then brings praxis close to *practice* in the current sense. Finally, it can denote specifically social activity, that is to say, relationships between human beings, distinguished by legitimate abstraction from relations with nature and matter (technology and poiesis). It is the final meaning that we are seeking to discern and define. Is this not also the sense of the word in Greek? *Pragmata* are affairs in general, things treated or managed by human beings in their active relations.

We shall develop the thesis of a multiplicity of possible analyses of praxis. The analysis of the Greek thinkers (determinism/chance/will) does not seem to us incompatible with the distinction between the dominated and non-dominated sectors, even in history, nor with the difference between *repetitive praxis* and *revolutionary praxis*. The point of view of growth (technological, economic) and that of (social) development are complementary.

The concept of praxis denotes this as determined and yet open onto the possible, as inexhaustible in the face of analysis. This concept also denotes praxis as site and origin of concepts. Praxis in the precise sense would then be the human 'real', on condition that it is separated neither from history and historical tendencies, nor from the possible. All praxis is situated in a history; it is a creator of history. Total history would thus be a history of praxis; it would tend (at the extreme) towards complete knowledge of human development. We shall simply give here a few stages and *moments* of it:

1. *Division of labour.* Inequality of labour. Growing split between groups labouring on matter (pastoralists, farmers, artisans, workers) and groups operating on other human groups (warriors, priests, administrators, traders, educators, etc.). Inequality of functions and struggle for the relative social surplus product (in penury).

2. *Exchange and trade* (trade in men and trade in goods). Money, market and language. The generalization of the commodity and logical rationality (social use of the *concept*).

3. *From powers to power* ['des pouvoirs au pouvoir'], from social functions to the state of functionaries, notables, chiefs and kings. The political and the statal [*l'étatique*]. The political use of discourse (as a means of action).

4. *Classes and their struggles* as major groups independent of territoriality. Challenges and combats of groups and classes. Tactics and strategies, the instruments of combat (including ideologies).

5. *From logical rationality to analytical rationality and dialectical reason.* The grasping of society as a whole (in social labour, at the moment of its advancement as concept and revolutionary reality; in the state at the moment when, at its apogee, its withering away is glimpsed).

6. *Constitution and consolidation of everydayness* (which presupposes the extreme division of labour, corresponding to a praxis of analytical reason; functionalization and general functionarization, etc.). Ambiguities of the everyday.

7. *Technological and bureaucratic praxis.* Society as a network of self-regulation.

POIESIS

We use this term for human activity insofar as it *appropriates* 'nature' (*physis*) around and within the human being (his own nature: sense, sentience and the sensorial, needs and desires, etc.). *Poiesis* is thus the creator of works [*oeuvres*]. It includes foundations and decisions with consequences that are unlimited despite being sometimes unperceived for long periods. Not all creation is poiesis, but all poiesis is creation. The word 'poetry' restricts the meaning of the term. A further remark: technology and technological invention will remain for us outside the field of poiesis. If it is true that technologies master 'nature' (the outside world), if they are therefore necessary, they do not suffice for the appropriation by human beings of their own nature. A distinction essential for determining the limits of technology in modernity and for correctly defining technological alienation.

1. *Foundation of the village* (generally attributed to women, including: sedentary agriculture, fixed habitation [the home], pottery, weaving, basketry, the beginnings of education of the young, etc.).

2. *The city in general* (as spontaneous creation of social, religious and political participations, including: sites of gathering, monuments gathering masses around them (ceremonies, processions); excitement or, rather, *catharsis* obtained in the course of a gathering, etc.)

3. *The Greek polis* (foundation of the agora, site of free assembly).
4. *The Roman urbs* (foundation of the forum, an assembly marked by prohibitions).
5. *The* (Platonic) *idea of absolute love* (the unique love of one single being for another, in thirteenth-century Western Europe).
6. *The mediaeval city and the project of accumulation* (of objects, goods, wealth, technologies and knowledge, a process of accumulation gradually extending into the constitution of capital).
7. *The foundation of ethnic groups, people and nationalities* (large groups attached to a territory, to the possession of this territory, to fashions of clothing, food, etc.).
8. *The proposition of the total man*, overcoming the division of labour (Fourier).[2]
9. *The unity of negations* to constitute the new totality (Marx), the working class as bearing within it radical negativity.
10. *Psychoanalysis* (as projecting a new catharsis founded on a transparency of individual consciousnesses, a direct communication between equal human beings, without involving magical operations, means of prestige and influence, opaque symbols and concepts with hidden implications, thus including an elucidation of conflicts).
11. *The decision to change everyday life.* The programme of taking up 'moments' or 'residues', art ceasing to be an end in itself, or a specialized and autonomized activity, to become a means for transforming the everyday and an instrument of 'real' life. Thus constitution of 'total', 'worldwide', 'planetary' man.

Restitution of the completed moments into their pre-eminent 'reality' and force. Creation of new moments (or, if you'd like to put it this way, new situations).

Declaration of war on the cybernanthrope,[3] as parody of total man (constituting a single and indivisible *poietic* act which should then

---

2   EN: See *Actualité de Fourier: Colloque d'Arcs-et-Senans sous la direction de Henri Lefebvre*, Paris: Anthropos, 1975.

3   EN: This is Lefebvre's term for technocrats, understood as a human in symbiotic relation with a machine, or a system. It is explored most fully in his book *Vers le cybernanthrope: Contre les technocrats*, Paris: Denöel/Gonthier, 1971.

be integrated into praxis, with the elucidation of practical consequences).

MIMESIS: PRELIMINARY COMMENTARY

The concept of mimesis does not coincide with that of imitation. Mimesis is not a psychic fact but a sociological one (enveloping the psychic but overflowing it). In this sense, mimesis can be defined as an aspect or level of praxis. But it needs to be founded, created. Standing between repetition and overturning (revolutionary) invention, it has a relationship to poiesis. It is the mixed notion par excellence, or the notion of the mixed, mean, intermediate, mediator, middle – along with language as such, or rather discourse. We ascribe to mimesis all activity that proceeds according to a form, and that moreover adds to its form. It depends then on an initial grasp, perception or intuition of the form. Subsequently it conforms to a greater or lesser extent. It may well give rise to a formalism that can distort the use and function of the form. It can also give rise to a conformism, apogee and paroxysm of mimesis. Contrary to widespread illusions, individualism in no way excludes mimeticism and the mimic as aspects of mimesis. On the contrary. In the 'human sand', each grain imitates the other grains, believing itself to be alone and separate.

The form that mimesis follows may be logical, juridical, ceremonial, gestural, ritual.

Mimesis, therefore, is not reducible to imitative repetition. It is inherent to educability, that is to say, to the relationship of teacher [maître] and pedagogue with disciple and pupil, the relationship of parents and children. It makes possible exemplarity, filiation and affiliation. It is also inherent to the relationship of legislator and citizens, the prince and his subjects, or gods and their worshippers. Fashion is simply a minor aspect of mimesis. Shall we say that it secretes structures? That it deposits systems as concretions along its way? Yes, on condition that we do not separate mimesis from praxis and poiesis, and keep in mind the uneven, obstacle-ridden and conflictual character of becoming.

1. *Initial grasp of an 'imago mundi'*, model of the city, temple, houses, perhaps clothing (round or spherical form, rectangular or grid form). Use of these forms thus perceived.

2. *Influence of partial systems of meanings* (semiological systems): formulae of politeness, legal formalities, formalisms of polite society, formulas of love, etiquette, ritual, conventions, procedures.

3. *General form of the re-production of objects*, situations, activities. Thus, form of accumulation of things that have become commodities, wealth, procedures and technologies.

4. *Formation of the 'human reality'* studied by the sciences of this reality: roles, attitudes, functions. Growing importance of models (*patterns*).

    Conformism and conformity.

    The reign of idols.

5. *Simulation and the simulacrum as method of thought and life.* The rise of a new kind in the human species, antagonist of total man: the *cybernanthrope* (caricature, simulacrum, parody, inverted image of total man).

IRREDUCIBLES

Every activity that becomes autonomized tends to constitute itself into a system, a 'world'. In this way, it constitutes, expels and defines a 'residue'.

In the course of an analysis that will seek to grasp the relationship of the terms considered (the systems – forms, functions and structures – of praxis, poiesis, mimesis) in the sketch of a total human history, we shall have the occasion to demonstrate these irreducibilities. By the same token, we shall show that each residual element (residual from the point of view of the power constituted into a 'world') contains something precious and essential. We shall end with the foundational decision on an action, a strategy: the gathering of the 'residues', their coalition in order to create poietically in praxis a universe more real and more true (more universal) than the worlds of the specialized powers.

Power [*puissance*]	Residue
Religion	Vitality (natural, carnal).
Philosophy	The non-philosophical (the everyday, the ludic).
The political	Private life (privation of everything that the political takes hold of).
The state and the statal [*l'étatique*]	The singular and singularities. Liberty.
Centralization	De-centralizations (ethnic, national, regional, local).
Mathematics (number and measure)	Drama.
Structure	Time. History, Dialectical movement. The tragic.
Technology and technocracy	The 'unusual'. The imaginary.
Cybernetic	Desire. Subjectivity.
Art (become culture, food for mass consumption)	'Creativity'. Style. (Mastery of the everyday and its metamorphosis.)
Bureaucracy	The individual.
Organization	The deviant. The original. Moments and situations.
Reason and rationality (technical or pragmatic). Adaptation. The notion of 'normal'.	The 'irrational'. The natural. Character. The non-mimetic.
Mimesis.	Poietic capacity.
Language and discourse.	Speech. The unsayable and the unsaid.
Meaning (sign, signifier, signified)	The insignificant.
The nuclear danger.	The state of survival. Possible life beyond the gates of death.

CHAPTER 2

The Superseding
of Philosophy

The many passages in Marx that question philosophy are dispersed in different texts and for a long time were neglected. Only recently have they been brought back to light. They appear both in editions of his so-called philosophical works and in exegeses.[1]

People are astonished today that Marx's declarations could have fallen into oblivion and been considered negligible. This oblivion would only have been excusable if philosophers had maintained subversive positions all along the line, trading in offending and offensive concepts. But this was not the case. Philosophy became an 'intellectual [*spirituelle*]' distraction or an ideologico-political justification. Only a return to Marx can restore the acute and trenchant character of these blunted concepts. We shall not dwell on the propositions that his earliest works contain. *'The becoming-philosophy of the world is at the same time the becoming-world of philosophy. Its realization is at the same time its loss.'*[2] This formula in the writings appended to Marx's thesis has become well known. Likewise his declarations in the 'Contribution to the Critique of Hegel's Philosophy of Right':

---

1   Cf. *Marx philosophe*, Paris: PUF, 1964, and the works of K. Axelos and F. Châtelet. [EN: Given the time of writing, it is most likely that Lefebvre is referring to Kostas Axelos, *Marx penseur de la technique: de i'alienation de l'homme à la conquête du monde*, Paris: Editions de Minuit, two volumes, 1974 (1961); translated by Ronald Bruzina as *Alienation, Praxis and Techne in the Thought of Karl Marx*, Austin: University of Texas Press, 1976; and François Châtelet, *Logos et praxis: recherches sur la signification théorique du marxisme,* Paris: Société d'Edition d'Enseignement Supérieur, 1962.]

2   EN: Karl Marx, *Writings of the Young Marx on Philosophy and Society*, edited by Loyd D. Easton and Kurt H. Guddat, New York: Doubleday, 1967, p. 62.

'Philosophy cannot be made a reality without the suppression of the proletariat, and the proletariat cannot be abolished without philosophy being made a reality.'[3] This assertion acquires an unexpected prominence in the present situation, that of philosophy in both the capitalist and socialist countries, that of the working class in different countries. If philosophy is not realized, this is because nowhere has the proletariat genuinely superseded the proletarian condition (although its economic, social and political situation differs greatly from one country to another).

The texts of 1844 follow from the earlier ones while adding a deeper meaning:

> Hegel's *Encyclopedia*, beginning as it does with logic, with pure speculative thought, and ending with absolute knowledge – with the self-conscious, self-comprehending philosophic or absolute (i.e., superhuman) abstract mind – is in its entirety nothing but the *display*, the self-objectification, of the *essence* of the philosophic mind, and the philosophic mind is nothing but the estranged mind of the world thinking within its self-estrangement – i.e., comprehending itself abstractly. Logic is the currency of spirit.[4]

We may express some reservations about this last formula, brilliant but somewhat facile as it is. Marx underestimates formal logic in reducing this to the *analogon* or speculative homologue of money. Is the *analogon* not rather to be found in language? It is quite correct, however, that the content of this logic is the pure abstract thing: stability in general. Its reign extends with that of commodity production, with the domination of the privileged form that is exchange-value.

> The *philosopher* – who is himself an abstract form of estranged man – takes himself as the criterion of the estranged world. The whole

---

3   Karl Marx and Frederick Engels, 'Contribution to the Critique of Hegel's Philosophy of Law', in *Collected Works* [cited below as *MECW*], vol. 3, London: Lawrence and Wishart, 1975, p. 187. [EN: Some translations have been amended adhere more closely to Lefebvre's French rendering.]

4   'Economic and Philosophic Manuscripts of 1844', *MECW*, vol. 3, p. 330.

history of the alienation process and the whole *process of retraction* of
the alienation is therefore nothing but the history of the production
of abstract (i.e., absolute) thought . . . Hegel's standpoint is that of
modern political economy. He grasps labour as the *essence* of man –
as man's essence which stands the test: he sees only the positive, not
the negative side of labour. Labour is *man's coming-to-be for himself*
within alienation, or as *alienated* man. The only labour which Hegel
knows and recognizes is *abstractly mental* labour. Therefore, that
which constitutes the *essence* of philosophy – the *alienation of man
who knows himself*, or *alienated* science *thinking itself* – Hegel grasps
as its essence; and in contradistinction to previous philosophy he is
therefore able to combine its separate aspects, and to present his
philosophy as *the* philosophy. What the other philosophers did – that
they grasped separate phases of nature and of human life as phases of
self-consciousness, namely, of abstract self-consciousness – is *known*
to Hegel as the *doings* of philosophy.[5]

Here we discover another notion that has been left in shadow.
Philosophers, according to Marx, knew and recognized, within alienation, *moments* of human life and activity. There is a philosophical
alienation, the *extremum* of real alienation and its denunciation; Hegel
pushes philosophical alienation to absurdity and at the same time, or,
rather, by the same token, he rends it asunder and shows what it
contains: on the one hand, what 'real' men have done, and on the other,
what philosophers have done and how. Alienation, and specifically
philosophical alienation, then becomes the common measure of both
philosophers and other men – a measure as well of that philosophy
which saw itself as measure of man and the world. With knowledge of
philosophical alienation without general alienation being finally
recognized, there is a start to the superseding of philosophy, compris-
ing the knowledge and recognition of *moments*.

Here we see how consistent naturalism or humanism is distinct
from both idealism and materialism, and constitutes at the same
time the unifying truth of both. We see also how only naturalism is

5   Ibid., pp. 331, 333.

capable of comprehending the action of universal [*universelle*] history.[6]

In order to conceive the production of man by his activity, to attain total history, it is necessary to start from being and nature, the primary moments. It is necessary to attain its successive moments in their formation: divided and organized labour, logical discourse, knowledge, mastery over nature.

There are 'moments' of the historical movement that are not singular historical events: religion, art, labour, law, morality, family, civil society, state.

> In their actual existence this *mobile* nature of theirs is hidden. It appears and is made manifest only in thought, in philosophy. Hence . . . my true *human* existence [is] my *existence in philosophy*.

In order for praxis and consciousness, taken in the succession of their historical moments, to appear according to their truth, it is necessary first of all to cast aside this illusion, philosophical existence, taken to its culmination by Hegel and so perfectly expressed that it becomes intolerable. It is necessary then to redeem and deploy the moments that it contains:

> The man estranged from himself is also the thinker estranged from his *essence* – that is, from the natural and human essence. His thoughts are fixed mental forms dwelling outside nature and man. Hegel [in his *Logic*] has locked up all these fixed mental forms [*fixen Geister*].[7]

Here we are in a position to make explicit the *moments* of philosophy, those that it has revealed and recognized, those that it has traversed, the 'fixed mental forms' laconically indicated by Marx, who did not develop his thought on this important point. The term *moment* has a double meaning. It denotes both periods (epochs) in time and elements in the content of representation.

---

6 Ibid., p. 336.
7 Ibid., p. 344.

This double determination of the *moment*, in becoming and in actuality, will form the subject of our reflections. We shall return to it at length. For the moment, we focus on the conclusions of the critical analysis that Marx inaugurated.

Marx and Marxism fundamentally criticize *philosophy*, that is, system, speculative thought, ontology, metaphysics (systematized conception of the world and 'being'). Philosophy as such is classed among ideologies, even if in a specific sense, not aligning it either with vulgar and banal representations or with the principles of law, aesthetic efforts and works, and so forth. Marxist critique starts with an examination of the Hegelian system viewed as the apogee of philosophy. Marxism does not criticize philosophy in the manner of positivism and scientism. It does not abolish it in the manner of an error of the spirit in an epoch that today is in the past. Despite speculative abstraction, philosophy was never completely external to praxis, if only in its struggles against religion and its conflicts with the state of the ruling classes (even though it developed in a relationship with religion and the state). The first and final aims that philosophers fixed for knowledge and action, which were Liberty, Justice, Truth, the Good (enjoyment and fullness of human beings), the advent of true (authentic) relations among men by the full and reciprocal recognition of their free consciousness – these aims are acceptable. They are the aims of revolutionary action. Neither philosophy nor philosophers can attain them by the forces of theory (of spirit). Only the action of the proletariat in the course of an effective (practical and theoretical) critique of the existing society makes it possible to bring them to life and realize 'social truth'.

Philosophy and its history therefore have an importance that is hard to overestimate, even though they do not coincide, as Hegel thought, with the history of being and knowing. This does not make the critique of philosophy any less radical – that is, penetrating to the roots. The works of Marx's youth, which have too often been taken, and are still taken, as 'philosophical works', contain precisely this radical critique. Philosophy must be superseded. It realizes itself by superseding itself and abolishes itself by realizing itself. The *becoming-philosophy of the world* gives way to the *becoming-world of philosophy*, revolutionary realization and superseding of philosophy as such. Each philosophical notion, inasmuch as it enters into the 'real' (into praxis), becomes world, it is accomplished. Inasmuch as it is accomplished, every philosophy is superseded. And philosophy as a whole, as a system entering into the world, has to be superseded. One might say, in a rather crude fashion, that the philosophers discovered and developed *homo sapiens* but ignored *homo faber*. Marx discovered *homo faber* and determined his implications and demands. For him, *homo faber* did not cease to be *sapiens*. On the contrary, he accomplishes (by superseding) man one-sidedly defined as *sapiens*.

In the second place, there was a historical connection between that state and philosophy, a connection that the Hegelian system illuminates by revealing its contradictions. The state develops towards an ideologico-juridico-politico systematization; it tends towards a practical system that seeks to be complete and without fissure. Philosophy developed towards the perfect theoretical system. Despite their conflicts, despite the attacks of philosophical reason against the principle of authority and *raison d'état*, philosophy and the state underwent a comparable development that culminated in Hegelianism, a perfected philosophical system and a complete political philosophy (justification of the modern state). The shattering of the Hegelian system, accordingly, signified both that of philosophy as a theoretical system and that of the state as a practical system. On the one hand, philosophical *representations* manifest their abstraction, their one-sidedness; on the other hand, political *representations*, that is, realities 'represented' politically (these 'representations' being entrusted to specialized groups) equally display their abstract and one-sided character, fixed and consecrated in the state. The state is not content to sanction the one-sidedness and mutilations of the human beings who compose it and whom it fixes in their narrow and limited conditions. To this alienation in civil society it adds specifically political alienation: the duplication between the real and its 'representation', between concrete activities and the deceptive perspectives that the 'representations' reveal above the practical, fragmented, narrow, stifling reality.

The radical critique of philosophy, which brings its social and practical truth, is therefore bound up with a radical critique of the state. The state has to *wither away* in order for philosophy to be realized and its objectives attained in praxis, starting with liberty and totality (total man). The revolutionary proletariat needs to organize itself as the ruling class; it has to break the existing state so as to be able to change the existing society that this state consecrates and consolidates. It therefore has to constitute its own state, that of the *dictatorship of the proletariat*. This state, Marx asserted (and Lenin after him), must wither away, and immediately so. The proletariat in power only needs a state that is withering away. Dictatorship of the proletariat, the power of the majority over a tiny minority (the 'representative' and active elements of the previously ruling class), a deepened and realized democracy, withering away of the state – these go together in the thought and historical perspectives of Marx and Lenin.

If the proletarian and socialist revolution follows the course proclaimed by Marx and accomplishes a total transformation of society (that is, going towards a concrete totality, freed from the contradictions and limits of bourgeois society), then the state withers away and philosophy is superseded by realizing itself. There are concrete, simultaneous realizations of the formal aims of philosophy (freedom, truth, good, etc.) and of the formal representations of the modern political state: liberty, equality, fraternity, justice, and so forth. The proletariat, putting an end to a dispersed and contradictory totality, resolving contradictions, superseding one-sidednesses, abstractions and 'representations' bound up with these contradictions, creates a new totality. Independent (speculative) philosophy loses its conditions of existence and gives way to the study of actual praxis, as well as to the transparent (non-ideological) reflection of revolutionary praxis. If the proletarian revolution does not follow the course proclaimed by Marx, if the proletariat does not (temporarily or lastingly) show itself capable of accomplishing its historic mission, then the state does not wither away; it continues. Philosophy likewise continues, but it is doomed either to a relatively ineffective critique, or to an apology for the existing state. It thus remains at the level of Hegelian systematization or falls back below this, to before Hegelianism. Its abstraction is aggravated. It risks becoming empirical, pragmatic, instrumental: an ideology in the service of politics, a dogmatism constituting the abstract knowledge specific to a political bureaucracy, a selection criterion for its institutional cadres, a justification of the state and its apparatus. Only a connection of philosophy with the state and the bureaucracy can assure it a certain effectiveness, and public honours for the philosopher.

With the state remaining instead of withering away, philosophy withers away instead, albeit while perpetuating itself. It regresses to a sociology of knowledge, as well as a political sociology studying the cultural or state institutions of which it itself forms part.

In a situation of this kind, other forms of investigation, starting from a radical critique and aiming to detect or create the authentic, the new, the 'true', may arise and replace the failing philosophy.

We are only too familiar with this. The first possibility of a theoretical alternative has not been realized. Nor has history exactly realized the second. In an unpredictable fashion it has taken an intermediate way, which we could already call a third way.

Let us spell this out. The world revolution is continuing, but by other paths than those proclaimed and envisaged by Marx: more complex, more contradictory, more dramatic. We are still too close to the reasons and causes to be able to see these clearly. They crush us, overwhelm us, blind us. It is certain that the split in the workers' movement, the separation between reformist ideology and revolutionary phraseology, the bureaucratization of political parties, are among these causes and reasons. For Marx, the revolution was to constitute a historic moment, a leap into freedom, the end of alienations. We know that this will take a long time. In general, the state has been consolidated on the world scale (except in Yugoslavia); new countries achieve national independence and economic growth only by the constitution of vigorous states. We do not at all intend to put on the same level – in the same bag, so to speak – bourgeois and imperialist states, the socialist states that issued from revolutions (in countries where the principal problems were agrarian, those of accumulation and industrialization, etc.) and have not withered away, and finally the recent states more or less bound up with a national bourgeoisie. It is likewise not our intent to contest the changes brought on in the modern world, the economic and cultural growth of the 'socialist camp' and the 'third world'. That said, the state in general continues, which does not mean that it is eternal. Why should it consolidate itself to the point of escaping the future that gnaws away that which exists and leads it towards destruction at the heart of its apparent triumph?

Philosophy also continues, but its status is either shaken or only too fixed. Its relations with science and technology, with politics, with religion, or quite simply with the university and the philosopher's craft, are either too uncertain or far too certain. It finds itself either enslaved or floating, instrumental or inconsistent. How could philosophers and philosophy engage afresh in great theoretical battles by themselves alone? Either the struggles that they wage are not their own, or they wage struggles without the means of combat. An old historical situation for philosophy, from Socrates to Descartes, recurs in aggravated form, with an increased risk of abstraction arising from the distance in relation to praxis, a distance proportional to the independence of the philosopher.

Given this situation of philosophy, several opinions and options are mooted among philosophers, and several hypotheses confront one another. For some people, philosophy is finished because this or that system is definitively true, adopted by them and adoptable by those who desire a philosophical truth: Cartesianism or Hegelianism, eighteenth-century materialism, dialectical materialism, Thomism, and so forth. For others, philosophy has failed as philosophy, swept away by science or technology. Dogmatism is opposed by scepticism. Still others believe that philosophy is undergoing a productive crisis and reconstituting itself. And finally, there are those for whom it is investigations of a new and still poorly determined type that will replace traditional philosophy.

The superseding of philosophy, therefore, signifies neither its abolition pure and simple (the positivist or scientist thesis) nor the continuation, under a more or less renewed form, of traditional, speculative, systematic thought (the 'philosophizing' thesis). The superseding of philosophy opens a way that neither positivism nor philosophism, neither a philosophically systematized materialism nor idealism, suffices to determine. The word *dépassement* [i.e. Hegel's *Aufhebung*] indicates a more complex movement, leading to a higher complexity of thought:

> To *sublate* [*dépasser*] and being *sublated* [*dépassé*] constitute one of the most important concepts of philosophy. It is a fundamental

determination that repeatedly occurs everywhere in it, the meaning of which must be grasped with precision and especially distinguished from *nothing*. – What is sublated does not thereby turn into nothing . . . '*Aufheben*' has a twofold meaning in the language: it equally means '*to keep*', 'to "preserve"', and 'to cause to cease', 'to put an end to' . . . The term '*dépassé*' *is at the same time* something preserved, something that has lost its immediacy but has not been destroyed for that . . . For speculative thought it is gratifying to find words that have in themselves a speculative meaning . . . Something is sublated only in so far as it has entered into unity with its opposite; in this closer determination as something reflected, it may fittingly be called a *moment*.[8]

It is in these terms that Hegel, in the first chapter of *The Science of Logic*, introduces the concept of *dépassement* [i.e. *Aufhebung*].

It is clear that this concept does not have the simplicity, clarity and distinctness that the habit of Cartesian thought leads us to seek in concepts. At the origin of an essential notion, what is it that we find? A play on words, an untranslatable pun – nothing formal and perhaps nothing that can be formalized in a perfectly coherent discourse. The French *dépasser* is a poor rendering of the German verb *aufheben*, with its double meaning.[9] It is hard for the concept with this dual determination to make its way into our language.

'*Dépasser*' [*Aufheben*] means at the same time to abolish and to raise (take to a higher level). The concept denotes an act, and the double determination of this act. Denoting a creative activity, the noun '*dépassement*' [*Aufhebung*] does not so much bear on the 'real' as on a realization, that is to say, a becoming. Between the two determinations (abolishing, raising) there is indeterminacy, openness: the possibility of realizing through an action, a project.

---

8 G. W. F. Hegel, *The Science of Logic*, translated by George Di Giovanni, Cambridge: Cambridge University Press, 2010, pp. 154–5. [EN: Many of Lefebvre's references to Hegel are to the collection he co-edited with Norber Guterman, *Morceaux choisis de Hegel*, Paris: Gallimard, 1939. We have provided references to standard English translations.]

9 TN: Likewise the English 'supersede', but the choice has been made here to use 'supersede/superseding' as the best rendering for Lefebvre's '*dépasser*/*dépassement*'.

In this sense, '*dépassement*' denotes a becoming that cannot be adequately formalized or exhausted in a discourse. We would rather say that the 'concept' of '*dépassement*' indicates what in living (productive, creative) activity does not pertain to the concept as such. Why? Because this creative power cannot be completely defined, and thus exhausted. It requires both a spontaneity and a project, a natural maturation and a reflected action. As we shall discuss shortly, a praxis and a poiesis. Only speech indicates the way of *dépassement*. Coherent and formally rigorous discourse, the discourse pronounced by writing and for writing, is not enough. *Dépassement* involves a risk, a possibility of defeat at the same time as accomplishment, a promise, a wager if you like, common features of all creative action. In *dépassement*, and inasmuch as there is *dépassement*, discourse and *logos* (discursive intelligence, logical and analytical reason) are forced to catch up with becoming by analysing it, describing it from different perspectives and points of view, formalizing it in every possible fashion. They never manage to do so completely: becoming shows itself inexhaustible, despite being actual and present. In the face of operations of understanding and discourse, a residue always persists.

For Hegel, the tree of knowledge, this tree with marvellous and maleficent fruit, which in the Christian tradition makes man both into man and into the rival of God – this tree of science becomes man himself. Man is no longer the demon gardener or the divine farmer who maintains this fine tree among others. He identifies himself with this privileged work. Knowledge and existence coincide (as Marx would denounce). Hegel, who dominated romanticism (too much, perhaps), forgot the warning of the Romantics and Goethe. Grey is theory, but green is life. The tree of knowledge is not the tree of life.

With Hegel, however, we soon perceive a poetic image: a word. On the cross of time grows the Rose of the World; the person who knows will pick it. The flower of the world is born from time, and the universe is a flower that seeds eternally.[10] It is not accidental that Hegel goes on to present Reason, the Concept and the Idea as flowers of the world

---

10   EN: Lefebvre references *Histoire de la philosophie*, vol. 3, p. 615, but the passage actually appears in the *Elements of the Philosophy of Right*, preface, p. 22; and in *Lectures on the Philosophy of Religion Volume II: Determinate Religion*, edited by Peter C. Hodgson, New York: Oxford University Press, 2007, p. 248 n. 45.

(or, to follow the image of the tree, as fruits). Hegel seeks to perfect Logos: philosophical discourse as such. He wants to grasp the totality, which includes life. This is his aim. For him, the word makes itself not flesh but systematic discourse, a system completed and presented as such: a circle that imitates the great circle of the universe, the idea returning to itself after its manifestations (externalizations). Philosophy forms a circle.[11] A non-systematic philosophy is only a contingent manner of feeling. What is true of the totality is equally true of its elements. Each part of a philosophical system is a whole and forms a circle.[12] Each 'moment', each circle, thus forms a partial system. There are several systems: the system of needs, the system of laws, the system of practical knowledge and the system of power. Each phase of history, each stage in consciousness, constitutes in its way a systematized or systematizable whole. Philosophy is thus a circle of circles each of which constitutes a moment, with the result that the philosophical system totalizes them and attains the totality of the Idea, which rediscovers itself in each partial totality.

Hegel scathingly criticizes the reflexive and analytical understanding that determines and perseveres in determinations. He sees this at work in earlier philosophies: 'The *reflection* of the understanding seized hold of philosophy . . . what is meant by this saying . . . [is] an understanding that abstracts and therefore separates, that remains fixed in its separations.'[13]

Turned against dialectical reason, which dissolves the determinations of the understanding and produces in this way the (concrete) universal, this understanding behaves like common sense. If dialectical reason is abandoned, as is possible when the understanding prevails, then the concept of truth is lost. Knowledge falls back to the level of opinion. Knowing is then simply reflecting in the sense of a second thought (discourse on discourse, discourse that though written is simply the reflection of immediate and familiar discourse).

---

11 Hegel, *Elements of the Philosophy of Right*, §2, addition, edited by Allen W. Wood, translated by H. B. Nisbet, Cambridge: Cambridge University Press, 1991, p. 26. [EN: 'Philosophy forms a circle' is actually a quotation from Hegel.]

12 Introduction to *The Encyclopaedia Logic*, translated by T. F. Geraets, W. A. Suchting, and H. S Harris, Indianapolis: Hackett, 1991, p. 39.

13 Hegel, *The Science of Logic*, p. 25.

Hegel, therefore, limited the claims of the discursive understanding despite ceding it a very wide place. It is the understanding that posits distinct determinations, which subsequently it maintains in division and separation. It thus intervenes as a historical and theoretical 'moment'. What is posited as different is an essential moment of the concrete, which in its becoming thus founds itself. Everything that is posited and determined has passed through the understanding. Philosophers previous to Hegel were 'correct' to note the determinations carefully (those of consciousness, of knowledge). Their failing and mistake was to preserve these in their separation. By this operation, which keeps to the middling level of thought (between empirical and dialectical), determination changes into indeterminate generality, into abstract theory. The partial determinations are unduly raised up as such (that is to say, separately) to the rank of attributes or predicates of the absolute. This is the fundamental operation of traditional metaphysics. These predicates are: existence and essence, being and nothingness, the one and the many, the simple and the composite, the in-itself or thing in itself and the for-itself or pure consciousness of self, the empirical and the conceptual, object and subject, determinism and freedom, matter or content and form, cause and effect, and so forth. All this is not to ignore the true and the false, which understanding fixes one outside the other, wanting this or that existing philosophical system to be accepted or rejected en bloc. When Kant tried to recapture a unity between the categorical determinations, in the unity of the self-consciousness that thinks them, what did he do? He listed the different forms of judgement as he found them in ordinary logic, obtaining them by an empirical procedure. With Kant, therefore, the connection remains external.

As discursive and logical (only logical) understanding, thought denies itself. That is one of the essential points of logic itself. It cannot resolve its own contradictions, and consequently resorts to dialectical reason that resolves these contradictions in another form. This movement of thought is essentially no more than the return of thought on itself and to itself, a return that does not take place without the danger of a 'misology': an attitude which sees the Logos as foreign and hostile.

Dialectical reason does not see understanding as separate from itself. This understanding, whose function is to posit, to determine, to distinguish, is posited by reason in its difference, but then it dissolves this difference. As a negation of that which posits, of the *positive*, it gives it back mobility. It thereby rediscovers identity with itself across differences, oppositions, contradictions. This movement is the absolute method and the 'immanent soul' of the content. This dialectical negativity goes still further. It recognizes and proclaims the force of discursive understanding, this action that posits and separates determinations.

The 'labour' of the understanding (Marx would observe ironically that Hegel, who knew human activity and labour in general, ended by recognizing only this labour of the understanding that was familiar to him) is 'the most astonishing and the greatest power, or rather the absolute power'. Dialectical reason, in effect, by introducing the negative, discovers the negativity specific to the understanding, which in appearance and for itself is only positive (thetic: positing determinations). By positing outside of itself different and distinct determinations, maintaining them in separation, the power of the understanding is none other than that of death, which is also that of movement and pure thought.

> But that an accident as such, detached from what circumscribes it, what is bound and is actual only in its context with others, should attain an existence of its own and a separate freedom – this is the tremendous power of the negative; it is the energy of thought, of the pure 'I'. Death, if that is what we want to call this non-actuality, is of all things the most dreadful, and to hold fast what is dead requires the greatest strength. Lacking strength, Beauty hates the Understanding for asking of her what it cannot do. But the life of Spirit is not the life that shrinks from death and keeps itself untouched by devastation, but rather the life that endures it and maintains itself in it. It wins its truth only when, in utter dismemberment, it finds itself . . . Spirit is this power only by looking the negative in the face, and tarrying with it. This tarrying with the negative is the magical power that converts it into being.[14]

---

14   Hegel, *Phenomenology of Spirit*, Oxford: Clarendon Press, 1977, p. 19.

Really terrible, this power of negation! Need devours its object; it destroys it. Man produces in order to consume. The work uses up the tool and the worker. Practice, in order to dominate nature, dissociates it, analyzes it, ravages it. Life that spends itself in time contains from birth the principle of death. History destroys everything that passes. Dialectical reason, by fortune or by chance, dominates this gigantic devastation. It discovers in it *moments*, their succession, and their supersession [*dépassement*].

Hegel, with his customary strength and dogmatic authority, posed a problem that we can formulate in modern terms: the understanding is concerned with stabilities; it constructs and maintains equilibria, structures. Time destroys these. What is the relationship between the understanding and the time in which and against which it struggles? What is the exact relationship between time and a higher form of thought than analytical understanding – in other words, dialectical reason?

> It is remarkable that this understanding which is surprised to note the complete difference and even contradiction that exists between the way in which it comprehends and employs the categories, and the categories such as they are produced in the Idea, does not wonder whether there might be, and indeed are, a different manner of thinking than its own, and that to put oneself in relation with this thought it is necessary to abandon the old habits of thinking.[15]

Hegel's position here is simple and authoritarian. Dialectical reason overcomes and encompasses analytic understanding as the infinite encompasses the finite, movement encompasses rest, concrete determination encompasses abstract determination, and the unity of contradictions encompasses logical identity. That said, Hegel relegates the understanding (which he knows is at work in the sciences, in mathematics and formal logic) to the old habits.

Hegel's line of argument has many defects, which today we perceive only too readily. Is it an argument at all? It is a decree, a philosophical

---

15   The 1827 preface to the *Encyclopaedia*. [EN: Lefebvre's reference appears to be incorrect.]

diktat. The first and most important of its weaknesses is that Hegel does not know, and does not want to know, that to understanding there corresponds a praxis. Whether cause or effect, or both, this is its foundation. Analytical thought discerns, distinguishes, determines objects. It names them; it contributes to producing them. The understanding and the hand go together, as likewise does the tool. Like the hand and the tool, the understanding separates objects and then stabilizes them. From the day that a man held in his fist a pebble removed from the becoming of nature and hammered into a tool, analytical understanding existed as a potential, with its characteristics of an active abstraction, defined determinations, and concepts fixed in language. Formal logic has a content: stabilities.

It is easy for the philosopher to criticize the mathematical method, so as to substitute for it his own method (intuition or concept). Hegel was not immune to this, having in mind Spinoza and the Cartesian school, aiming also at mathematics itself as a rival of philosophy in the domination of knowledge:

> In mathematical knowledge, discovery is an activity extrinsic to the object.

The mathematician, instead of starting with the triangle, breaks it up and then reattaches it to other figures, giving birth to construction.[16] This construction imposes itself without necessity. The proof follows a path that aims at an external goal. Which, according to Hegel, puts mathematical demonstration as true demonstration – that is, leading to a truth – in question.

It is easy, therefore, for the philosopher to relegate a method that does not suit him to the old habits, and enjoin all thinking people to repudiate it. This philosophical diktat risks having no result and giving rise, by reaction, to philosophies of mathematical reasoning (of reflection on the procedures of mathematical thinking). If we look closely, by these reactive shocks the diktat casts discredit on the procedure of

---

16   Cf. Hegel, *Phenomenology of Spirit*, p. 24 ff. Marx takes up this line of argument in the letter to his father of 1837. *MECW*, vol. 1, p. 12. [EN: The Hegel quotation can be found on p. 25.]

speculative philosophy, on its dogmatic decrees. Promulgating knowledge as absolute, it takes up a position external to the 'real' process of
knowledge, that of knowledge of the 'real'. By proceeding in this way,
philosophy as such (and not only philosophical idealism) makes itself
into a parasitic excrescence on the tree of knowledge. It abdicates the
right and capacity to define knowing. At the same time, it both abso-
lutizes and dissolves it.

Despite all the precautions that he took (or, more ironically, because
of them), Hegel pressed logos – analytical and discursive understanding – to its limit. A strange situation: he led to its implacable end term
the notion and theory of positive understanding (analysis, discourse,
chain of 'thetic' assertions), while showing at the same time the mortal
character of this *positive* understanding. The understanding that
knows bears within it both death in general and its own death, as well
as its condemnation as pure 'positivity'. Now, according to Hegel
himself, all philosophy is born from the understanding; every metaphysics separates, extrapolates and takes to the absolute an isolated
determination. Thus Hegel inaugurates the critique of philosophy; he
proclaims its end and supersession by denouncing the essence of
philosophical discourse. At the same time as he prepares the succession (Marx), he constructs the perfect system of understanding.

True, Hegel never renounces orienting discourse according to the
demands of a higher meditation: dialectical, temporal, poetic. However,
if he sees the time of the world as that of a plant which produces flowers and fruits, he also sees it after the image of a cosmos whose
hierarchical degrees are carefully preserved. Dialectical negativity,
which recognizes itself already at work in the non-dialectical understanding, protects what the understanding has posited in its place and
moment. The devastations of the negative only ravage the accidental
and circumstantial. What is essential (essences, moments) is preserved
in the total system, which comprises the totality perfect in its perfection. Marx would not allow this conservative side of Hegel's
systematization and speculation to escape. His critique was directed
against this above all. The system, like a puzzle of extraordinary scale,
brings into play the elements and aspects of the universe according to
a double structural schema: temporal (historical) and spatial (progres-
sion from matter to absolute spirit). It is a fine work of partition and

activation that gives rise (or believes itself to give rise) to the perfect discourse, total, totalizing and coherent. Truth, for Hegel, is an *automaton* that moves itself and demonstrates itself (Marx).

As latent and undeclared contradiction, ambiguity reigns in the Hegelian system. Philosophical discourse, logos, pursues its implacable trajectory. It follows a well-defined line, formally correct and well traced. But speech constantly intervenes in the form of humour (a humour that is quite heavy of its kind: a celestial constellation has no greater importance than a skin complaint), irony (often deep), poetry, play on words, including the famous pun on *aufheben* (abolish, preserve, raise, overcome, supersede). The line constantly trembles and deviates, like the straight lines and curves drawn by a great artist, which are without beauty when imitated by ruler and compass. This is the charm of Hegelianism (only appreciated by those who have practised it a great deal). Its images – the Rose of the World, the owl of the twilight wisdom of philosophers, the tree that organically produces its branches and its fruits – these images orient its discourse in a kind of beyond of the discourse, superseding it. Between the unique word and creative image on the one hand, and the rambling speculative discourse to which Hegel succumbs, there are many intermediaries and mediations.

The system, by its own admission, is born from a *magical* operation that transforms into absolute positivity, accomplished, finished and perfected, the uncertainty of becoming and the terrible power of death that haunts becoming. It is not that becoming understands itself according to being, but rather that becoming metamorphoses into 'being', grasped, determinable and determinate: metaphysical. By this magic, becoming vanishes and the historical evaporates. By the stroke of a speculative sorcerer's wand, the determinate is lost and fixed, each determination in its place, its degree. Man is born in pain and the seriousness of the negative. But the maieutic is pursued and completed in full certainty and positivity. The modern Socrates has nothing to fear. The system is the total man. After this, having been consumed, real men will have no more to do than contemplate and imitate, as disciples, the portrait of the total man by the Master.

And yet, the system never manages to close. Listen to Hegel:

The circle that remains self-enclosed and, like substance, holds its moments together.[17]

The moving eternal, however, is a process of completion and disappearance that itself never arrives or disappears:

> The True is thus the Bacchanalian revel in which no member is not drunk; yet because each member collapses as soon as he drops out, the revel is just as much transparent and simple response.[18]

The circle (vicious, infernal) of the system, which closes itself and seeks to enclose us in its magical operation, changes into the dance of the Bacchantes and Fauns, inspired by Dionysus. At the highest accessible or inaccessible point, rest and movement coincide in identity, with becoming and return-to-self, like music and light in certain ancient cosmogonies, like creation and repetition.

Between the poetic image that projects ahead of itself in anticipation its element taken in *Physis*, and *Meta-Physis*, a strange, alienating and alienated relationship is established, but one by which philosophy continues to overflow the philosophical logos, and poetic speech to overflow discourse.

The shattering of the system would follow the lines of cleavage, the fissures, left within the systematization by a discourse that wants to yet does not succeed in completing itself as such: in giving itself an immanent structure. Dialectical reason, bound by a deep and intense link with creative speech, traverses it with its breath deeper, and its risk higher, than any certainty. For the certainty of consciousness in its relationship with a 'thing' that is produced, determined, held and possessed, thus finite, is never more than provisional. This is the fundamental theme of the *Phenomenology*. Philosophy, which can be defined as the investigation of things by thought, as exploration of the relationship between men and things,[19] does not allow any certainty to subsist, whether palpable, practical, experimental, moral, political, religious,

---

17   Preface to Hegel, *Phenomenology*, p. 18.
18   Ibid., p. 27.
19   Introduction to the *Encyclopaedia Logic* [pp. 24–5].

sentimental or scientific. It shakes them all (in their principle and their foundation, by a diabolical, radical critique) so as to arrive at the true. And it is in this that philosophical freedom consists. If it comes to a halt, if it immobilizes itself in a certainty attained and possessed, philosophy is untrue to itself; it destroys itself. It falls back into something else. Yet systematic philosophy does come to a halt, becomes certainty, becomes the perfect Thing and is therefore unreal. The System is the truth, and it is the end and death.

Let us express the same propositions differently. With Hegel, or rather according to him, everything has taken place in discourse. It was not enough for him to bring to language determinations that were discovered or buried. He formulated, wrote, described them all. Nothing resisted the power of logos, neither nature, nor consciousness, nor being. Everything was said. And that is death: no more substantiality, no more residue. And yet, the Hegelian Idea symbolizes the inexhaustibility of 'being', of the sources of existents.

Philosophy, which set out to be totally dis-alienating, thus becomes, as metaphysics, total alienation. And yet the project of dis-alienation does not disappear. It shines through. It is the transparency of this system that closes itself over the opacity and hardness of its certainty.

The Hegelian system, as formulated in the *Philosophy of Right*, paradoxically intends to be a system of freedom (of free will, freely giving itself laws). Paradoxically, that is, contradictorily, Marx exploded the system by starting from this contradiction.

The system of freedom is the state. The state and rational right correspond in practice to what the Hegelian system is in philosophy. Right, in the rational state, realizes freedom and renders it present, like the philosophical system that corresponds to it. The system of freedom has a double determination: philosophical (the philosophy of Hegel) and political-juridical (the state). Law is realized freedom: *Dies, dass ein Dasein überhaupt, Dasein des freien Willens ist, ist das Recht* [Right is that existence in general should be the existence of free will].[20]

Hegel gave a sketch of a theory of praxis. In actual fact, the concept of praxis is *already* there in the *Philosophy of Right*, already elaborated in its scope and complexity and contradictions. No aspect or level of it

---

20 EN: Hegel, *Elements of the Philosophy of Right*, p. 58.

is neglected: labour, organization of labour, production in the widest sense (objects and works), individual and social needs, education, family and familiarity, narrow praxis and wider praxis, politics and history. Praxis is supersession, opening up to realization and the effective presence of freedom. The theory of praxis is here. And yet, it is not here: the whole of praxis is attached to speculation, and finally absorbed in the state.

The falsification that the understanding, according to Hegel, operates on determinations by fixing them in their reciprocal aspects as qualitative and separate differences 'is based on forgetting what is for [the understanding] itself the concept of these moments'.[21] Each one is itself only in *supersession*, the movement within which none of the terms has the advantage of a positive and absolutely affirmative existence:

> The finite is no longer superseded by the infinite as a force existing outside of it: it is its infinitude to supersede itself of its own account.[22]

Dépassement [*Aufhebung*] is indeed the fundamental concept that recurs throughout, that must be grasped with precision and in particular distinguished from nothingness.

What happens to the declarations of the *Greater Logic* on the subject of the state and right, or apropos the system? Hegel gives the lie to them by an assertion that corresponds to the magical operation of the metaphysician: *Das Recht ist etwas Heiliges*. Right is holy in the context of the canonized state. The task of philosophy is to construct the concept of right and of the state.[23]

It was all in good conscience, then, with an inconsistency Marx found 'repugnant', that Hegel developed his theory of the state, the finished synthesis of the system of needs and civil society, of property and morality, of particular interests and the general interest – in short, the God descended to Earth that must be worshipped as such: *als Irdischgöttliches verehren*. The state sits on top of a conceptual pyramid

---

21   EN: Hegel, *The Science of Logic*, p. 116.
22   EN: Ibid.
23   Hegel, *Elements of the Philosophy of Right*, pp. 26–8 (§ § 2–3).

built of successive triads, following the static schema of 'thesis-antithesis-synthesis'. Above all the appearances of right and morality, above subjective and objective, the family and civil society, there is the state, a living eternity.[24]

In the state, and in it alone, man (individual and social) attains total satisfaction. In it he becomes totality (total man) in the plenitude of his moments. His history (that is, history), his birth and his self-production lead up to and terminate in the rational state. Freedom, in and through the state, is accomplished for all members of this state, individual and groups (family – particular 'estates', that is, trade guilds – communities [cités] – classes – civil society as a whole). As supreme need, need of needs, the state organizes, crowns and perfects the system of needs. It encompasses and perfects all partial systems, including philosophy. It thus perfects ethics, since it is the actuality of the ethical idea and combines in its synthesis right and duty, demonstrating their previously concealed identity. The state, as reality (actuality) of concrete freedom, institutes and consecrates the free and mutual recognition of needs, in free consciousnesses that express themselves in their activities, labours and works. The synthesis of the real and the rational, subjective and objective, is consummated in it. The state is therefore the unconditioned arising from the totality of conditions. Virtually, within the Idea that it embodies, it pre-existed history; invisible, it drew this towards it from the start; it hoisted man to its level. The state is the insurmountable, the inescapable. In a word, the un-supersedable [indépassable]. Unlimited creative capacity, attributed to freedom, is exhausted in the state. Being and Self-Consciousness, combined in a reciprocal belonging by the Idea, pass entirely into their manifestation. They fix themselves in it or exhaust themselves in it. No creative reserve exists in the power named Freedom [Liberté]. (Freedom of what? Of whom? The metaphysician does not say. Or rather he does say. The only freedom, both substantial and active, is that of the state that accomplishes its destiny. How? By

---

24 Texts from Guterman and Lefebvre (eds), *Morceaux choisis de Hegel*, in particular fragments 166 to 191. EN: These selections are on the theme of 'Man and History'. Guterman and Lefebvre present multiple short passages under each theme and taken from a wide selection of Hegel's works, though here they are predominantly from *Elements of the Philosophy of Right*.

the supreme test: war.) The metaphysician takes freedom to the abso-lute and denies it by the same magical act. The freedom of the philosopher slips away. The disciples of the Master, in a philosophy that has become public and servile service, will join the state bureau-cracy by conviction. No relationship is abolished, neither that of master and slave, nor that of self-consciousness with the perfect Thing. All are promoted to the higher degree: philosophico-political. The conditions and situations described, analysed, integrated into the development (in the form of partial systems: needs – labour and division of labour – family, 'estates', civil society, etc.) were definitively only preparations for the state, stages of the Idea clearing the ground, being progressively embodied in the legal and political constitutions of the state. The final pages of the *Phenomenology* that declare the end of time and history thus acquire their meaning: a self-destruction. The prose of the world has killed poetry. The Rose, for its part, is either plucked or perished. Time (the world) is terminated, thus dead. The dead grabs hold of the living [*Le mort a saisi le vif*].[25]

Marx extracted from Hegelianism a kernel that was inseparably both rational and real (without the real and the rational being non-dialectically reconciled, that is, without conflict). First of all, he took from Hegel the concept of praxis: production in the broad sense (of man by himself), labour, works [*oeuvres*]. He rejected the husk of the system, ugly and rigid, that enveloped this germ of concrete thought, restoring it to its integrity; he refuted the inversion by which Hegel destroyed what he had won and killed his own conquest. Praxis ceased to appear as invoked and inspired by the state (by the Idea), as the set of its conditions. The conditions are grasped as such, the earlier no longer being explained by the later. If Marx places the emphasis on *homo faber*, while Hegel pressed to the limit the image and concept of *homo sapiens*, this is only one aspect of their differences. With Marx, time reappears, inexhaustible, and with it, unlimited creative capacity in praxis. The Rose of the World is not yet born. And the world (time) will perhaps bear many unexpected flowers. Man, finally free, will pluck these living flowers, and in no way will the dried flower of

---

25   EN: '*Le mort saisit le vif!*' Marx uses the phrase in the 1867 preface to *Capital*, MECW, vol. 35, p. 9.

philosophy or the false flowers presented by religion hide the world's chains. In other words, the creative power (present in praxis) is no longer fixed by a representation and completed in a synthesis. The notion of *dépassement* regains vitality and rigour. It is no longer frozen in the Hegelian synthesis. Becoming no longer falls into the abstract frame of 'thesis-antithesis-synthesis'. When writing his so-called philosophical works, Marx sought to determine, that is, to limit, the import of the philosophical concepts taken from Hegel; he began the critical inventory of the philosophy that in Germany, in German culture, and for reasons specific to Germany, played the role of first fiddle. This inventory includes on the one hand recognition of the 'positive' elements, and on the other hand a radical critique. What does the 'positive' element bequeathed by Hegel consist of? According to us, the notion of praxis. By accepting this, clarifying it, developing it, Marx immediately attacks the divine-right theory of the state. Civil society is not an emanation of the Idea, destined to serve the State. It is defined by praxis. The state can be defined neither as the crown of civil society nor as its cement. Institutions and constitutions are 'super-structures' (the word is not yet there, but the concept is born there). The middle class is not the universal class; the bureaucracy does not play the essential role in society, it is no more than an excrescence, with its own system: *the system of practical knowledge*. This real and central 'system' of state society has two aspects: technical competence and bureaucratic ontology (philosophy). A state bureaucracy determines 'being', that is to say, *its being*, as it sees fit and wishes it. This 'system of practical knowledge' has greater real importance in the society that Hegel theorizes, and that Marx criticizes, than the 'system of needs' and the real needs of men. The bureaucracy justifies itself by 'qualities' reserved for bureaucrats. The interest referred to as 'general' becomes state interest (*raison d'état*) and interest of the state bureaucracy. The system of [practical] knowledge, the justification of bureaucratic qualities by and for the bureaucracy, always has the look of a pleonasm and a tautology.

Hegel, in his construction of the rational state, simply took the features of the existing state to the absolute. In actual fact, in historical time, the state changes with its preconditions, its practical 'base' in civil society. It will change again. It could even disappear. Genuine

democracy, perfected democracy, presupposes the end of the democratic state itself as power and constraint. It was the French who
discovered and proclaimed this historical truth.[26]

The state and society, therefore, must be grasped starting from praxis
and not according to the demands of a philosophical systematization.
The exposition of the state, of society, of the corresponding constitutions,
becomes knowledge by becoming critique. Moreover, contemporary
praxis of society based on industry shows itself *open* to possibilities, to
considerable changes. It is *historical* in a double sense: situated in history
and creative of history (and thus revolutionary).

We should not flinch from emphasizing right away the originality
and novelty of the notion of praxis. In order to understand it, we have to
abandon certain routines of reflective thought. We are accustomed to
thinking that the well-determined is closed and fixed, that what is open
is poorly determined. Praxis, however, is both determined and open. It
is inexhaustible without, for all that straying into indeterminacy. Analysis
of praxis, whatever its method and aim, must not lose the guiding thread
that Hegel passed on to Marx. Society does not exist without men, individuals, groups, classes. It is nothing without their products and their
works. It is their work (institutions included). But the works and products of human beings escape them. They tend to acquire an autonomous
reality, without ever completely managing to do so.

Marx conceived with unmatched depth the relationship between
man and his works. By the word 'conceived', I mean the fact of having
brought to language and the concept relationships that until then had
been real but indistinct in praxis, and having 'problematized' what
seemed clear and understood because of being familiar. By 'man' or
'human being' (social man), I mean the man of praxis grasped as a
whole (with his contradictions, in depth, with groups and classes).
And by 'works', I include also (but not on a single level or plane) the
material products of the hand, tool and machine, and the effects of
action on human beings, both the results of social acts and those of
individual activities, both institutions and culture, both art in general

---

26   Cf. the Molitor translation of Marx's 'Critique de la philosophie de l'État de
Hegel', vol. 4 of *Oeuvres philosophiques*: for the bureaucracy and the 'system of
practical knowledge', p. 97ff. [*MECW*, vol. 3, p. 45ff.]

and the city or the nation. This means, in other words, poiesis as well as techne and praxis – both that which relates to determinism and fate and that which arises from chance or mischance, or is born from desire and from embryonic freedom.

No human reality exists without works, but no works exist without productive human activity. Works are, nonetheless, the 'being other' of man; he maintains a double relationship with them: alterity, alienation. Marxist investigation, bearing on the relationships between man (social man, the man of praxis) and works, cannot be said to be economic, psychological, sociological or philosophical. Following Hegel in a complete and concrete fashion because of having started from praxis and returned to it, Marx showed the double determination of the relationship between man and his works: he realizes himself in these, and he loses himself in these. Products and works escape him, but tendentially, never completely. Otherwise these multiple products and works would change into things pure and simple, petrify by losing all ambiguity, all indeterminacy, all flexibility.

Philosophy offers a privileged example of this double-sided relationship: realization in alterity, alienation in the abstract thing. Sometimes, to increase the complexity of the movement, what seemed a gain turns out to be a loss, and vice versa. On a historical scale, man realizes himself in certain favourable conditions, sometimes as an individual, sometimes as a group. He loses himself in certain conditions that capitalism exacerbates, by the sole fact that in this system the economic becomes determinant, and socioeconomic fetishes (the commodity, the market, money, capital) tend to assume an autonomous and automatic operation, constitutive and self-regulating of society (up to a certain point). Under capitalism, consequently, the development of material productivity posits the foundations for a higher realization of the human; at the same time it bears the loss of the human that risks undermining its preconditions. The realization of the human is accompanied, unevenly but deeply, by an alienation. There is dialectical unity and essential conflict between these two aspects of historicity. The fundamental project, issuing from philosophy but superseding it by definition, would thus be formulated as follows: how to enable man to dominate his own works, to fully appropriate these works that are both nature in him and his own nature?

Marx thus raised a lasting if not permanent question, which is in itself neither economic, sociological nor political, but encompasses all these determinations and levels. The economic, the sociological, the political as such, as fragmented realities or fragments of reality, each make up a part of the works of social man in praxis. Investigation bears on a totality (broken, fragmentary, contradictory). Besides, it is neither external to the 'real', nor located above or below what the philosophical method contributes. It bears on the 'real'. The fundamental question and the corresponding realities are reconsidered according to propositions (possibilities or impossibilities) that are always new. The double determination of the relationship leads to a double critique: that of man and men (individuals and groups) by works, and that of works by the human and by men.

This double critique itself presupposes a dialectical thought bringing language and the concept to bear on praxis, thus grasping in its unity a fragmentary and contradictory totality. Without this, reflection would not rise above either triviality (commonplace observations and recriminations) or a vicious circle (endless reference of man to works and of works to human beings, considering them simply as relating externally to one another). It is hard for the traditional philosophical method to cross these limits: triviality, circle. It knows how to transform a fatality into a virtue: triviality passes for realism; vicious circle, round robin [*tourniquet*] and pleonasm acquire the comfortable guise of a System.

Products, works and human groups, therefore, play for one another the role of 'realities' analogous to those of nature, to things. They introduce for one another determinism, necessity, chance, fate. That is history. The set of actions and interactions is praxis.

In order to grasp praxis, we shall have to introduce concepts posterior to Marx, for example those of tactics and strategy, programme or project, decision and choice, and so forth. But we shall also have to reject other modern concepts: those that pertain to pragmatism, the purely and simply 'operational' and, as we shall see, structuralism made into philosophy.

By way of Hegel, Marx's thought holds all philosophers within it: the project of man proposed by each, the moment of project proposed by philosophy as a whole. History, for its part, is the natural history of man, and the prehistory of his finally human reality. It is the story of his laborious and painful birthing, with its detours and errors, its alienations. The idea of 'maieutic' emerges from philosophy and extends to history as a whole. It acquires a new meaning, as a function of the power of man over nature.

> History itself is a *real* part of *natural history*, of nature developing into man.[27]

But the animal only produces itself, while 'man reproduces all nature'.[28]

We shall emphasize at many points the problematic (and not just categorical) nature of these propositions, the inexplicit character of the notion of 'nature' that they encompass. The critique of the philosophical system and the state, intimately connected, shows that abstract spiritualism is simply abstract materialism, and that abstract materialism (philosophical materialism, different from the rehabilitation of the sensible, of the senses and physical nature) is simply the abstract spiritualism of matter. Are not philosophical spiritualism and materialism, each as abstract as one another, the frameworks and categories of bureaucratic reflection?

The Marxist superseding of philosophy (and of the state, religion, bourgeois right, etc.) raises a number of questions. First of all, what exactly did Marx mean by the 'superseding of philosophy'? How can philosophy be superseded in the name of concepts that are incontestably philosophical in origin, and bear the mark of philosophy: that of alienation, even that of praxis? In order to answer this question it is necessary to re-read Marx, bring to light neglected texts and arrange these by inserting them into the development of Marx's thought–something that we have already partly done.

Secondly, what is the import of this theory? Is it only the thesis of a certain Karl Marx, a nineteenth-century thinker, who had and still has a certain influence but was mistaken on certain points, in particular on the state and on philosophy, since these two condemned items today flourish more than ever? Has Marx been 'superseded' by Marxism

---

27 'Economic and Philosophical Manuscripts', *MECW*, vol. 3, pp. 303–4.
28 Ibid., p. 276.

itself, given that there is an official Marxist philosophy and states that pay allegiance to Marxism? Must we accept, in the name of contemporary history, what has happened – the perpetuation of philosophy and the state, among other things – and even consider as useless and negligible the restitution of Marx's real thought on philosophy and the state? Is this not what is done by many major thinkers (by J.-P. Sartre, for example), who think about philosophy as political realists, challenging neither the official 'Marxist philosophy' nor the justifications of the 'socialist' states in terms of Marxism, and instead propose to complete them?[29]

Incidentally, if the superseding of philosophy is recognized as a necessary and fundamental theoretical procedure, where does this lead us? Has it already been achieved? Does the word 'superseding' fully contain it? Or does it not have wider consequences, in the method of thinking and even in action? These lines of questioning demand a double response as far as philosophy and its superseding are concerned.

---

29   EN: Sartre's *Critique of Dialectical Reason* is discussed in detail in the next chapter.

CHAPTER 3

Philosophy in Crisis

At a level close to the empirical, understanding the words 'crisis of philosophy' simply implies the desire to *see clearly* at last into this activity that traditionally has precisely assumed the privileged role of *seeing clearly* into the human and the world. These words express the intention of casting a beam of clarity onto something that claims to bring light and yet whose face remains in shadow. They presuppose that this or that philosophy cannot be entirely satisfactory, and that the confrontation between various philosophies leaves zones of shadow between them, behind them or within them. These words will have no sense for the dogmatic, whether they are materialists or idealists, Marxists, Husserlians, Kantians, Thomists, and so forth.

For every dogmatism and for every dogmatist, if there is a crisis it is that of other people or other philosophies. Or else it is a fruitful crisis that will enable their philosophy and philosophy in general to advance, to bring itself up to date, to reach the level of a certain scientific discovery or technical innovation. Dogmatists always start from a definition of philosophy posed and proposed by their philosophy. They believe that they possess this precious treasure: the very concept of philosophy. But they do not. Here as elsewhere, the concept is only attained by comparing the elements of an ensemble and the terms of a multiplicity. Conceptual abstraction relates to a concrete history, an actual confrontation.

In his preparatory studies for *Capital* (*A Contribution to the Critique of Political Economy* and the introduction to this critique), Marx explains how the concept of (social) labour could only be born and formulated in certain historical conditions. It was necessary for the division of labour to have reached a high degree, and for fragmented labours to constitute in practice a vast ensemble, that of social labour itself. Previously, men (slaves, peasants, artisans) laboured. But this was not officially known, it was scarcely taken into account in philosophy or discourses on man. The invention of the first machines (and not just tools) made it possible at the same moment to glimpse the distant possibility of an emancipation of man in relation to labour, with machines doing the work. The concept of labour went together with the preconditions for non-labour. In an analogous manner, it is in their current dissolution that we grasp what the town and the city were. Hegel saw admirably this negative side, destructive and destroyed, of 'becoming conscious', which is so often taken as positive and only positive. Isn't this how it is with philosophy – that is, with the concept of philosophy?

The history of philosophy has drawn all past philosophies from oblivion, with ever more refined methods. Alongside the imaginary museum of world and universal art, the perfect discotheque and cinema, we have the imaginary museum of philosophies. Philosophy is entering into culture, even in those countries and universities where it has the greatest difficulty acclimatizing: the Anglo-Saxon countries committed to empiricism and pragmatism. It is conquering the world at a giant's pace. It receives cultural and political support. Made official, it is in power in a large part of the world. The great ideological battles are waged on its ground. Isn't this the moment when its concept is determined and, as a consequence, according to dialectical thought, negated? In Marx's time, only the total revolutionary project, insepara-ble from the critique of the perfect system – that of Hegel – put philosophy in question. Today, as a global success, an effort towards cultural unity, philosophy has completed itself in its concept. Does it found *a single* life, *a single* praxis? Is it not rather a *reflection*, and thus a justification, of existing *praxes*? Philosophy is no longer content with being a conception of the world. It becomes genuinely worldwide. It also becomes worldly, a centre of cultural radiation. It becomes world as philosophy. It worlds itself [*se mondialise*]. There is more than ever a 'philosophical world', not in the Marxist sense of a realization of philos-ophy, but in the traditional sense in which the world of the philosopher – of each philosopher – is asserted to be sole and true, solely true. Is this not the moment when this world dissolves? When its alienation leaps to the eye? When philosophy puts itself in question?

We presuppose a basic lack of satisfaction as far as philosophy is concerned. In the nascent state, empirical and psychological, this dissatisfaction was bound up with the confrontation between several philosophical systems, that is, with the concept of philosophy, without which there is neither a history of philosophy nor a critique of philosophy. Born with the classic and inevitable confrontation of philosophies, the state of unease and discontent built up towards the confrontation between philosophies and practice (between 'conceptions of the world' and the everyday, between the philosophy of socialism and socialist praxis, between Catholic philosophy and the practice of the church and religion, and so forth).

We propose here to elucidate the concept of philosophy and the dissatisfaction, nascent or mature, that necessarily accompanies every philosophy. We shall explore this dissatisfaction. Philosophy will be illuminated in its crisis. Nothing reveals an essence more than its dissolution.

The defender of philosophy will put forward a preliminary objection here. Philosophy as such is supposed to appear and be judged. Before what tribunal? That of common sense? The philosopher rejects this. For knowledge or philosophical wisdom, common sense is identified with unreason. Several times already, philosophy has appeared before good sense and common sense; several times it has been condemned; it only emerged in better shape. Philosophy cannot accept the judgement of the non-philosophy that opposes it. The philosopher accepts only the judgement of his peers, after deliberation without a timeframe fixed in advance, and reserving a right of appeal. Philosophy, as such, answers only to itself. Assuming that a sentence condemns it to death, it continues with greater strength. Socrates is immortal. To condemn philosophy is still to philosophize.

This preliminary objection disappears in the name of the concept of philosophy itself. This concept envelops that of philosophical need, an educated and cultured need that is not without a double dissatisfaction:

> For on the one side we see man imprisoned in the common world of reality and earthly temporality, borne down by need and poverty, hard pressed by nature, enmeshed in matter, sensuous ends and their

enjoyment: mastered and carried away by natural impulses and passions. On the other side, he lifts himself to eternal ideas, to the realm of thought and freedom, gives to himself, as *will*, universal laws and prescriptions, strips the world of its enlivened and flowering reality and dissolves it into abstractions . . . But for modern culture and its intellect this discordance [*Zweispältigkeit*] in life and consciousness involves the demand that such a contradiction be resolved.[1]

One aspect of this double dissatisfaction involves, on the one hand, reality such as it is and common sense, and, on the other hand, abstraction as already developed, including ideas already circulating and philosophies. The philosopher rejects common sense, because from its origins philosophy challenges the 'reality' that common sense, as robust champion of the real, ratifies and with which it rests content.

Dissatisfaction, the principle of philosophical invention, turns sooner or later against philosophical ideas. If the essential thing about philosophical research and its initial act consisted in a challenge to and a judgement of the 'real', this critique casts a light on philosophy considered 'real', that is, as entering or having entered into the 'world'. Philosophy is thus summoned before the fundamental demand resulting from the split between the real and the idea. It is impossible for the philosopher to reject this instance and appeal, without already denying himself. On the other hand, pursuing the same metaphor, convocation before this tribunal already contains themes that will lead to condemnation. Philosophy cannot resolve the split from which it starts. It can only explore endlessly and bottomlessly the philosophical need. In fact, it responds to the split with representations born from the division (split) between the real and the representation. To put it another way, man cannot expect plenitude from philosophy, since philosophy expresses directly or indirectly the dissatisfaction of man and the internal split of his existence.

Along the way, we pass from circumstantial symptoms (those of the present crisis) to more serious difficulties (those of philosophy as a

---

1 Hegel, *Aesthetics: Lectures on Fine Art*, translated by T. M. Knox, vol. 1, Oxford: Oxford University Press, 1975, p. 54.

whole). Criticism can define these difficulties as 'aporias' or 'antinomies' of philosophical reason. These aporias are not, it seems, those of speculative reason, but rather those of philosophy as such, including critical philosophy that does not proceed to its end point – that is, the critique of philosophy.

We are reaching the root [*fond*] of the question. Let us not go too quickly. Let us not jump over the linkages and mediations. The slightest error has its consequences.[2]

FIRST APORIA: THE DOMAIN

Either the philosopher and philosophy possess a specific domain, or they do not. If the philosopher has his domain, whether in knowledge, in wisdom, in being or, finally, in the effort to draw from the particular sciences a picture of the universe, this domain is reserved for him. Entry into this domain demands a preliminary procedure: an epoche, a distancing that situates the philosopher outside of everyday life, outside of praxis. This procedure involves ascesis and separation (split). Reflection changes into wanting a philosophy, into the desire to philosophize, into philosophical culture. From this point on, the philosopher is established in his private domain – house, castle, fortress. He is isolated and becomes a private philosopher. His relationship with knowledge (if he wanted to know) or wisdom (if he wanted wisdom) is disturbed. He will force his intimate concerns to take the form of philosophical dignity. His knowledge and wisdom will only have a sense within the philosophical world constituted by

---

2   A few years ago, a philosopher not content with philosophy, J.-F. Revel, published a pamphlet: *Pourquoi des philosophes?* [Paris: Éditions Julliard, 1957] Observers were amazed by the success of this little book, brilliant and light. Revel had touched on sensitive points: the isolation of the philosopher, the ridiculousness of little philosophical chapels with their idols and passwords, the inconveniences of a reflection in no way linked with praxis. In itself, Revel's pamphlet increased the confusion that it claimed to elucidate. It confused three theses without the least trace of analysis: the end of philosophy, the continuation of philosophy and the superseding of philosophy. In fact, he ignored the last of these almost completely, amalgamating it either with the end pure and simple, or with the continuation. He was content with a positivism expanded to cultural phenomena, hence many illusions and errors.

his retreat. Let us now assume that the philosopher does not possess a private domain; then he falls into the public domain. Philosophy becomes above all a matter of teaching, pedagogy, general culture, or perhaps rhetoric. Anyone can enter it, on condition that they do not bring their own flowers, as in the garden of Tarbes.[3]

Philosophy soon becomes public service, affairs of state. The philosopher and philosophy die after a long period of poverty [*misère*], as they no longer have anything of their own. They perish from cold and hunger.

Do we need a long illustration of this antinomy by recalling the opposition between Hegelian philosophy and the thought of Kierkegaard? For Hegel, the philosopher was in the state, part of the state, a servant of the state, an apologist for the state. According to Kierkegaard, philosophy is a private and secret business. In both cases, philosophy perishes. If we want to escape this impasse, that is, the contradiction between private and public, by going beyond it, we have to discover a different form of thought than the philosophical.

SECOND APORIA: PRAXIS

The philosopher may grant that there are no specifically philosophical problems, but rather human problems: cultural or social problems. In this case, there is no privileged regard or particular right to speech. Everyone may say their word, formulate their opinion and their appreciation, propose their solution to these problems. The philosopher's opinion is simply one opinion among others, perhaps better presented and better argued, but in no way distinguished from others as truth is from error or approximation.

Or the philosopher maintains that he is a man for problems, or the man of problems, and that he has problems that are his own particular ones: a problematic. He will draw up a list of these problems: soul and body, being and thought, essence and existence, immanence and transcendence, theory and practice, knowledge and action, consciousness

---

3 Cf. Jean Paulhan, *The Flowers of Tarbes: Or, Terror in Literature*, Champaign, IL: University of Illinois Press, 2006.

and reality, subject and object, and so forth. Thus he will have beneath his eyes, stuck to his wall, his table of categories, his panoply of problems, his list of 'pertinent oppositions'.

This being the case, these differences (between being and thought, and so on) may be posed as real differences in man, in practice, in being, with these terms denoting splits, conflicts. Then the splits have to be overcome in order to resolve the problems. To reach difference in unity, unity has to be realized or rediscovered. And only a real, practical energy can resolve actual problems. Only an active, poietic (creative) thought, a form of energy that is practical and based on a praxis, can cross the point at which differences, contraries, oppositions, contradictions, confront one another and rigidify in an endless confrontation.

> The resolution of the *theoretical* antitheses . . . is by no means merely a problem of understanding, but a *real* problem of life, which *philosophy* could not resolve precisely because it conceived this problem as *merely* a theoretical one.[4]

From this point on, subjectivism and objectivism, spiritualism and materialism, activity and passivity, lose their existence as contraries to make way for practical energy.[5] Alternatively, these differences (between being and the knowledge of being, and so forth) are themselves abstract; they exist only for representation. In this case, a new abstraction and an improved philosophical representation may claim to resolve them, by attaining (but only in the abstract, in representation) unity and totality. And philosophy continues as abstract representation, sinking into reflexive abstraction and representation.[6]

---

4   Karl Marx, 'Private Property and Communism', *MECW*, vol. 3, p. 302. [EN: Lefebvre has 'real oppositions' in place of 'theoretical antitheses'.]

5   EN: Lefebvre references the passage above here; though he has moved from quotation to paraphrase.

6   This is why we speak and shall speak of questions, demands and questionings rather than 'problems' – and of meditation or poietic thought, rather than 'reflection'. The reflective in the broad sense includes all 'second degrees': discourse on discourse, desire for desire, art about art, poetry about the poet, love of love, meaning of meaning, and so forth. It is thus not unrelated to circle, pleonasm and round-robin

THIRD APORIA: UNIVERSALITY

The philosopher proclaims his need for universality, his desire for the universal. Philosophical thought calls itself universal and seeks to be so. Let us leave aside, for any philosophy, the obstacle of other philosophies. Let us consider only the non-philosophical world. In the first of two possible interpretations, philosophy declares that it has already absorbed the non-philosophical world, the entire world, and that the system is complete. Universality is attained only at the price of an assertion that is hard to maintain: the whole world is occupied by philosophy; philosophy coincides with the world; being is exhausted; time now will be filled only by the contemplation of the finished system, of completely revealed being.

'Spirit necessarily appears in Time, and it appears in Time just so long as it has not *grasped* its pure Notion, i.e. has not annulled Time . . . Time, therefore, appears as the destiny and necessity of Spirit that is not yet complete,' Hegel peremptorily decrees in the final pages of the *Phenomenology*.[7] And he goes on to add that history is simply the becoming of spirit completed in time.[8] The universal system, in completing time, filling it, thus also terminates history. By filling accomplished time, it leaves open the time to come.

Therefore either the universal, along with truth, is found at the beginning of philosophy, in the principles and premises of a deduction, in presuppositions. In this case, philosophy is closed and completed right at the start. Or else, the universal reveals itself along with the true; it is found at the end; it is reached by being realized. Or else again, philosophy cannot remain philosophical. The non-philosophical world persists in the face of philosophy and the philosophical world, whether as determined adversary and tenacious reality, or as a residue hard to reduce ('lived experience' or 'the empirical'). In this case, the universality attained is only fictitious. The conflict between the philosophical world, philosophy that seeks to be world, and the non-philosophical world will not proceed without damage to

---

[tourniquet]. Cf. infra.

7 Hegel, *Phenomenology of Spirit*, translated by Parvis Emad and Kenneth Maly, Bloomington and Indianapolis: Indiana University Press, 1988, p. 487.

8 Ibid., p. 492.

philosophy and the philosopher. To escape from this and resolve the conflict, there is only one way: for philosophy to become world, not as philosophy, but as a project that is realized in the world, denied by its very realization as this supersedes it. Then the philosophical world and the non-philosophical world will lose their one-sidedness and will both be overcome. The realization of philosophy will make simultaneously for its grandeur and its loss. Time will continue, fertilized by philosophy and in no way destroyed by it.

FOURTH APORIA: TOTALITY

First aspect of the philosophical difficulty: the notion of *totality* imposes itself. It is indispensable. Without it, knowledge is dispersed; it accepts the fragmented division of labour without challenging it, without the hope of dominating it. It falls to the rank of pure and simple statement of facts. It is faced with a chaos, the dust of empirical facts. In the human sciences its importance is still greater, if that is possible, than in the natural sciences. Moreover, no revolution is possible if totality is not put in question in *praxis*, on the basis of a challenge or negation that, to start with, can only touch on part of the ensemble. Ensembles, groups, forms, moreover, are facts just as much as are individual phenomena, the fragments and parts.

Yet, if we start from totality, and as soon as we do start from it, reflection deduces or constructs arbitrarily instead of studying the facts. It systematizes. There is always a great risk of passing from the partial to the total, concluding from the part to the ensemble. Dogmatism is the least danger for reflection of this kind. When it is accompanied by action and command, it can go as far as totalitarianism, under the cover of realization of a social fact or a total humanity. Besides, is not the concept of *totality* one of the least utilizable today? Nothing guarantees the immanence of totality (of what totality – consciousness, being?) in each partial assertion or each negation of each compartmentalized reality. Totality, to the extent that there can be a question of such, reaches us only in fragmentary form. The 'real' human totality of our day is neither capitalism (as in Marx's time), nor a state that is both ideal and real (as with Hegel), nor socialism (as the dogmatic claim, constantly presenting socialist society as accomplished or close to being so), but a broken totality. Culture itself (which has been substituted without warning for *style*) is dissociated. Despite the claims of culturalism, it becomes a 'mosaic-culture'. The technical and social division of labour, the compartmentalization of research and perspectives, fragment it. It no longer constitutes a unity, but a juxtaposition of domains, sectors, points of view, techniques, art and knowledge mixed together and yet broken. How can there be a coherent discussion of totality except by putting the concept in question?

But on the basis of what? Of consciousness? 'For me, consciousness develops and expands with the blossoming of intelligence. It is equal to the universe, or more exactly constitutes this, asserting at the same time its own value as subject and the value of its objects', Léon Brunschvicg declared in a memorable debate at the Société française de Philosophie, on 24 February 1921.[9] For J.-P. Sartre, totalization is also accomplished starting from the thinking 'I', that is, from the philosopher. We shall see how Claude Lévi-Strauss rejects this assertion, once the philosopher seeks to attain history and constitute it into totality. Yet he makes the same claim for his own part, starting from the intellect and a limited representation, the structure. We reject here both these symmetrical attempts.

Philosophy seeks to be the totality of human experience or of human knowledge. Yet it can no more attain totality than it can universality. Knowledge discovers the new. The totality reached and formulated cannot claim to be definitive. Either it denies the creative discovery of the new, or it determines this in a way that destroys it. The experience of the philosopher, or the philosophical experience, cannot coincide with the entire human experience.

The philosopher conscious of these difficulties will subtly emphasize a more dynamic concept: *totalization*. If there is always new totalization, imposing itself as such, of the new in knowledge or lived experience, a totalization always repeated and recommenced, nothing guarantees the philosopher that this totalization will be philosophical. It may for example be religious, or political. The state is also by nature totalization. The

---

9 EN: Léon Brunschvicg et al., 'L'intelligence est-elle capable de comprendre? Séance du 24 février 1921', *Bulletin de la Société française de Philosophie*, vol. 21, nos 3–4, 1921, pp. 35–67.

church likewise, as a religious form of state. The philosopher will either let philosophical totalization be identified with political or religious totalization, or he will protest against this in vain. If praxis makes itself totalizing outside of philosophy, pragmatically, without philosophy, then the philosopher will again protest – in vain. Today, technology seeks to be totalizing. It is so. It projects a totalitarian control into praxis, a control of praxis. It seeks to automatize the whole of human life. The notion of totalization is thus more dangerous than ever.

Final point: the moment when philosophy renounces totality to take refuge in a totalization (which it admits to be always incomplete, always repeated), it is perhaps a totality that effectively expresses the 'being' to which man aspires. Does he not seek to live totally? Can his abandonings and disappointments bear on totality? Does he not continue to always seek, through trials, through empirical limitations, to become total man? Does he not obscurely reject whatever denies this totality, a rejection that bears its chance, which is our only chance? Though he seems remote to us, broken as we are by specialized work and compartmentalized specialisms in the sciences of human 'reality', total man is close. He is what is closest of all. We are already this possible totality: matter and spirit, consciousness and being, life and lucidity, play, work, love, rest, knowledge. 'Become what you are!'[10] Is not the command precisely to construct in praxis, through praxis, a new totality that will no longer be that of philosophy as such, no longer thought and reflection, but act? For want of this, if it proved impossible, the philosopher would triumph; he would continue his 'totalizing' exploits and undertakings on the ruins of man and human being, among the debris of a life and culture in pieces, under cover of a technicality that he either accepts or fruitlessly challenges. 'Totalization' would permit philosophical eclecticisms that are pleasing and inconsequential.

In this sense, metaphilosophical thought does not reproach the philosopher, in the vulgar way, for speaking of everything, but, on the contrary, for not being able to speak of everything: for not posing

---

10   EN: This phrase appears in Nietzsche's *Thus Spoke Zarathustra*, in *The Portable Nietzsche*, edited by Walter Kaufmann, New York: Viking, 1954, part IV, p. 351 ('The Honey Sacrifice'); it is also the subtitle of Nietzsche's *Ecce Homo* (in *On the Genealogy of Morals* and *Ecce Homo*, translated by Walter Kaufmann and R. J. Hollingdale, New York: Vintage, 1967).

all the 'problems' that he should pose, those of totality. For reasons that are already clear but that will subsequently appear ever more in their imperative clarity, we shall substitute for the concept of *totality* that of world and *worldness* [*de monde et de* mondialité]. The claim of philosophy, which sought to start from totality and, by a reverse and reciprocal movement, arrive at the total, can no longer be sustained. It confused the total with the universal, whereas our planet is only a point in the universe and a relatively stable figure in infinite nature. The earth is our world, and what extends to the whole earth worlds itself [*se mondialise*]. Totality, or rather partial totalizations (since totality conceived systematically has shattered), is defined by *mondialisation*. Thus technology worlds itself.

At all events, we have to guard against abuses of this concept. If everything is needed to make a world, this is not made with just anything. It is possible to 'world [*mondifier*]' this or that: scarcity or abundance, work or leisure, art in general or one art in particular, or else a particular work. The increasingly frequent use of the term shows that it is imposing itself. At the same time, it is used in a mystic and arbitrary manner. People talk of a 'world' in connection with no matter what painting, novel or poem. The nascent concept of *worldness* is transformed into a figure of rhetoric, a subjective impression, an emotional attitude that exalts the undetermined.

We have to attach the concept to the description and critical analysis of well-determined processes, or ones by which a 'reality' (for example, technology or the state) becomes worldwide. Between the 'worldwide', the 'terrestrial', the 'planetary', there are close links but also differences that we shall have to emphasize. Only in this way will we have superseded the speculative difficulties arising from 'totality' conceived with too great a lack of precision. We will have located the metaphilosophical meditation.

FIFTH APORIA: INDIFFERENCE

What does 'being a philosopher', 'having a philosophy', mean in everyday language? 'People see philosophers as curious beings, remarkable in either a good sense or a bad, as people who are not like them', a contemporary thinker noted, one of those who seek to rescue philosophy, with a heroism worthy of another age.[11] 'Being philosophical' means attaining indifference. If this is how popular wisdom judges philosophical wisdom, with envy and severity, are not philosophy and philosophers to a certain degree responsible? The masses (without having to spell out the meaning of this term, so often abused to exalt or deprecate the reality it denotes) are not always right. It could be that they are not entirely wrong in their spontaneous verdict on philosophy. It could be that the philosopher, even when he does not believe himself indifferent, even when he is far from disinterested, even passionately interested, in political problems, remains somewhat indifferent to the masses, who for their part have their 'problems', those of everyday life for example, which they perceive and seek to resolve otherwise than by philosophical reflection. Apropos several philosophers (Spinoza, Schelling and Schopenhauer, for example), critical analysis rapidly detects an oddness about speculation. This posits sooner or later a principle that it calls Absolute, substance, *causa sui*, *Grund* or even *Urgrund*, if not *Ungrund*, in-itself, Idea, Being, and so forth.

Such a principle, prior to its manifestations, implications or consequences, is as a principle indifferent to them. Philosophy, from start to finish, swings between two responses to the question 'What is being?' Its first response is to converge this with human consciousness: it personalizes it; the principle ceases to be posited and posit itself with indifference to its consequences; it loves, it desires; it is a god that is touched by human fate; but then it falls into finitude; this humanly satisfying principle, one even agreeable and comfortable, the object of various sentiments and sentimentality, bears the human imprint. Philosophy falls into anthropomorphism and magic. In the second response, the principle is posited and posits itself at an infinite distance; man reaches it only by determining it, that is to say, negatively – by denying it and denying himself. This satisfies contemplative and speculative thought, while its principle becomes inhuman. It is indifference (*Gleichgültigkeit*), with its attributes of superabundant creation, cruelty towards beings cast into existence, waste, absolute play with being and nothingness.

---

11   E. Weil, *Logique de la philosophie*, Paris: Vrin, 2000 [1950], p. 12.

Philosophy has never been able to choose, and cannot choose, between the dog as barking animal and the dog as celestial constellation, in the images, symbols or metaphors invented by Spinoza. It can only hesitate or swing between two poles: magic that brings being closer by evoking it so as to identify with it, and speculative purity that takes its distance and loses it by losing itself.

How could the principle posited by the philosopher not react on philosophical consciousness? Here we see it with its hard kernel of indifference, incorruptible but insensible. Those who say indifference do not say innocence.

Our project here is not to organize a dialogue, following the guise and mode of dialogues between philosophers and non-philosophers. It is not to vindicate the common opinion against philosophy. It is to *supersede* this contradiction, by showing that what escaped the philosopher and assumes the face of ordinary (everyday) man is no less precious. The irreducible *residue* resulting from the philosophizing attitude (suspension of the everyday) is a deserving object of reflection.

SIXTH APORIA: SUBJECTIVITY

In our day, the philosopher likes to proclaim himself defender and spokesperson of subjectivity against the hard objectivism of the sciences and technologies and the impersonality of dogmas. It is all too true that subjectivity has need of defenders to speak for it and protest in its favour. The institutional world works flat out to prune subjectivity and cut off whatever tries to supersede. On one side and another, in one way or another, with very varied techniques, subjectivity is overwhelmed, exploited, utilized, denied. Propaganda, journalism, means of mass communication, all bear down on subjectivity, masking its own exaggerations and its own failure. The *reification* of a great number of human relations, alienation in objects taken to an extreme, leads to deceptive protest and demand —deceptive as it soon forgets that the operations effected on subjectivity from outside use subjective means: myths, symbols, images. As a result, by claiming its freedom and right to existence, subjectivity scarcely escapes what affects and alienates it.

If it believes itself to be moving in a dimension of its own, or an appropriate one, it loses its way. The image as deployed in our culture, the image of photography and television, is particularly ambiguous and deceptive. It seems a fact and it contains dreams and myths, memories and illusions. It seems a given and it leads into a 'world of images'. It seems objective and it releases the illusions of subjectivity. This is only pursued and believed to be attained in a world that is itself subjective: reflection of reflections, a pileup of images. From this point on, it does not constitute itself as a free being; it simply loses itself in the labyrinth of a subjectivized objectivity (images) and an objective subjectivity (alienated and externalized relations).[12]

In praxis, defence of subjectivity can no longer take the philosophical form. It has a domain and a precise meaning: defence of the individual against over-organization, productivism, bureaucracy. This defence of the individual can only be conceived in new terms, and no longer in terms of individualism or philosophical '*prise de conscience*'.

When the philosopher sets himself up as the defender of subjectivity (of individual consciousness, the for-itself, etc.), he puts forward his own subjectivity. That is what he is speaking of, explicitly or not. Philosophy becomes the *egology* of the philosopher, with his 'I' and his 'ego' constituted by this initial detachment, the philosophizing attitude. Even when he speaks and is not satisfied with just discourse, other people do not recognize themselves in the words of the philosopher; they find in them neither their complaints, nor their tumults, nor their silences – neither their abstentions, nor their acceptances, nor their refusals. Philosophical subjectivity does not coincide with human consciousness; it is a subjectivity of its own: a subjective world, that of the philosopher as such, described 'phenomenologically' and constructed to the measure of man. No one understands this rather vain speech, but many believe that they understand it, given that they find themselves in an analogous situation: rather solitary, rather detached, rather overwhelmed by the world outside. The philosophical absence comes to fill by illusion the non-philosophical (yet only too real) impression of absence.

---

12   Cf. Daniel J. Boorstein, *The Image: A Guide to Pseudo-events in America*, New York: Vintage, 1992 [1961].

The result is that, in order to grasp the situation of subjectivity today, with its appeals and aspirations, we have to emerge from philosophy as such, supersede philosophical subjectivity, regard what is happening and what is not happening within the dark bosom of a consciousness immersed in actual social practice, with its myths, symbols, images and signs. A sociological study is indispensable, but one that overspills the narrow horizon of specialized science and technology, following the demands of a thought freed from traditional philosophical frameworks. Let us strongly emphasize this point. Defence of subjectivity and individuality is freighted with subjective illusions by recourse to a subjective philosophical absolute in which it is as easy to lose one's way as it is on the side of the object. We have first of all to escape from the abstract dialectic of 'object-subject'.

SEVENTH APORIA: ALIENATION

Philosophy and the history of philosophy have bequeathed us, among other concepts, that of alienation. In a mystic or metaphysical form, by way of obscure visions or images (failure, fall, dereliction, decadence, etc.), the concept of alienation runs through human thought from its origins up to Hegel and Marx. How can we grasp human reality today without this concept? How can we determine it and open it onto the possible?

And yet the concept often embarrasses those who wish to use it, and its use is not without its questions.

The immoderate (ontological) use of the concept of alienation returns either to a mystical vision or to a metaphysical speculation. As with Hegel, for example, where becoming results from the alienation of the idea, where alienation is higher and deeper than contradiction, since it creates it. The concept abandons human reality; it makes it possible to soar over it and deny it ideally by seeing it as only the abstract alienation of an abstract general principle. According to Marx, this abstraction did not prevent Hegel, in his *Phenomenology* and elsewhere, from attaining the human concrete, conditions, situations, dramas. It could be that, after Hegel and Marx, a speculative wielding of alienation no longer has this merit. In a manner both contrary and analogous, official Marxist thought, once more become systematic – fallen back into a philosophy of nature – has difficulty accepting the concept of alienation. If we remain on the terrain of philosophy, then either we attempt a philosophy of consciousness (and how would the pure transparency of consciousness alienate itself? It has a relationship with the 'other', but this relationship is not alienating) or we try a philosophy of nature (and how would there be alienation of nature?). Thus either philosophy as such tends towards a philosophy of alienation, or it tends to eliminate the concept because it is dependent on other principles. As a consequence, we either release this concept from philosophy, or return to its abstract use. But what happens if it is released from philosophy but remains caught in the architecture of systems?

We have recently seen alienation become a literary and fashionable theme. In Italy, in particular, there are seasons and festivals of alienation. While philosophy that calls itself Marxist accepts this concept only with the greatest reticence, confining it to the history of Marx's thought, there is an abundant and fairly inoffensive literature of alienation in the capitalist countries. Fortunately, some serious and seriously critical work has arisen from this concept. When David Riesman, in *The Lonely Crowd*, distinguishes between 'inner-directed' and 'other-directed', he describes man as alienated in present-day capitalism. He makes the concept of alienation an instrument of critical knowledge, if not of action. If we want to understand the situation of women in contemporary society, it is hard to dispense with alienation and not seek where women are in alienation and dis-alienation. But sociology is hardly enough. Does not the condition and situation of women contain both paradox and confusion, extreme ambiguity and extreme contradiction? Are women not at the same time nature and facticity, the finest creation and the depth of being? To understand this, philosophy is no more sufficient than is sociology or psychology. The study of films, the press, novels, and above all study of the actual condition of women in everyday life is more interesting than the themes of philosophy. What does this study of alienation lead to? To reforms that are minimal, even if of 'positive' interest (half-time work for women, continuous working-day, provision of crèches and kindergartens, etc.), or to the project of a radical transformation of the everyday? In these two perspectives, which moreover – in terms of reforms and the revolutionary project – are not mutually exclusive, what role does the concept of alienation play when the question is to envisage a praxis? It leads to the demand for a creation. It does not go further forward.

In other words, use of the concept of alienation can only be critical; this critique is either radical, or falls back into apology for the status quo. The concept of alienation has its limits. It beats a path, but is not enough to say what lies at the end of the road. Taken in isolation, it does not make it possible to discover solutions to the problems raised by alienating and alienated praxis. It does not supplement poiesis. Taken separately, it risks getting lost in considerations of detail (alienation of women, young people, work, etc.), and finding a content and points of application only in the domain of specialized sciences (sociology, psychology, etc.). Specialists, moreover, often of positivist inspiration, accept only with reticence a concept taken from philosophy. Wielded without precaution, it can be emptied of content and revert to a speculative use. Taken generally, as access to a total conception, it borders on this speculative use. The question is all the more intricate when we come to *alienations of the second degree*: no longer just by the 'thing', but by the gaze at the thing; no longer just by the 'real', but by the image of the 'real'; no longer by subjective illusions on objectivity, but rather those of subjectivity. The critical use of the concept is all the more urgent, with a parallel increase in precautions, so as to avoid the dupery of a redemption by the concept, that is, by philosophy.

The difficulty is all the greater, given that reflection in philosophy, or outside of philosophy, has brought to light a connected theme: the relation with the *other*. After Hegel and Marx, consciousness is no longer self-sufficient for philosophers. Even for those who, in the manner of phenomenology (Husserl) or existentialism (Sartre), still find the starting point of their philosophical reflection in consciousness, this consciousness is no longer defined by the strictly Cartesian *cogito*; it is relationship, intention, signification, hence connection with the *other*: the object, the thing, the work, the other person, or again and more remotely the foreign and the foreigner, the fascinator. The theme of alterity has invaded philosophical thought, and the ambiguous character of this theme – sometimes concrete, often abstract – conceals the difficulties of philosophy as such. We know already that Marxist thought does not propose as its central theme the relationship of individual consciousness with the 'other' (the object, the other subject, etc.). This relationship, or rather the various types of this relationship, fall rather to psychoanalysis, to sociology. Marxist thought meditates in a broader and more critical fashion on the relationship between social man, the man of praxis, and the products and works of his activity. There is a dialectical movement, that is to say, a contradiction, between these two aspects of activity – alterity and alienation. If alterity, or relationship with the other, is realized, alienation wanders and is lost. The two aspects of activity, its two poles, are mingled and confused. Philosophy, because it 'philosophizes', scarcely feels the need to discern these two aspects, to grasp their dramatic becoming. It thus leaves the ground open for the speculative use of the concepts, a ground that is uncertain, but where it feels itself at ease. It should get down to examining, in praxis, the relationship between men and works, this 'being-other' of social man. It prefers to transpose this dramatic and always concrete relationship into speculative relations between the in-itself and the for-itself, between essence and existence. The 'alienation quarrel' has never been able to illuminate and give rise to reasoned discussions, as it challenges too many acquired attitudes and accepted representations, including the philosophical attitude and the representations made commonplace by philosophy. No one has been interested in enlightening these concepts – neither philosophers nor specialists in the social sciences, who prefer to confine themselves to an 'a-critical' positivism.

Linked with these difficulties are those arising from the relationship between philosophy and politics. The philosopher has two choices: one is to leave political action, the political state, out of his thought; he refuses to take responsibility for political questions. His thought then no longer conceives and instead lets escape the totality; it distances itself from praxis, suffering all the more from this in proportion as it seeks to be more philosophical. If the philosopher rests content with an eclecticism that is barely coherent or systematic, if he more or less mistrusts politics as such, then he will accept existing political practice; he will bow down to the state and power; he will lack gravity and seriousness (negativity, in Hegelian terms). The philosopher's other alternative is to enter into political life, that is, bring politics and the state into his philosophy. He then must immediately make the painful choice between two paths, neither of which is philosophically satisfying. Will he produce a philosophy of power, given that all state power demands a philosophy, every bureaucracy seeks a theory of 'being' that justifies it? Will he move towards a system that, by encompassing the state, legitimates *raison d'état* and hands it a philosophical certificate of good conduct and good manners? Will he move towards a pluralism that leaves him with free hands but is philosophically no more than an intellectual game? Will he build the system of the future, the image of the ideal state?

The difficulties become destructive when we have a state issuing from a revolution. Up to this point, traditional philosophy and the traditional philosopher could maintain themselves, and maintain their freedom, in the sphere of a moderate criticism of the state and politics (as was the case with Alain; his formula of 'the citizen against powers'[13] consecrated the political in the citizen and demanded that political powers should be equitable towards citizens). But the victory of a socialist revolution in a barely industrialized country, leading to the strengthening of the state, forces a choice. The philosopher either changes into an executive agent, now that political power has a philosophy, or else he keeps silent as a philosopher. In the first case, philosophy triumphs (officially) and disappears. In the second, it withers away in the silence and impotence of the philosopher. A third option is scarcely any better: retreat into pure thought. Philosophy then dies of dehydration. Its philosophical alienation is absorbed into the total alienation of both philosopher and man.

To escape from this, we have to follow in Marx's line, taking up the concepts of state, politics, and thus *political alienation*. Political theory must aim at the superseding of politics. On the basis of radical criticism, thought can study political acts and techniques, like any other technical activity, connecting them to another modern form of alienation: technological and technocratic alienation. By restoring them

---

13   EN: Alain, *Le citoyen contre les pouvoirs*, Paris and Geneva: Stathine Reprints, 1979 [1926].

into the context of praxis, critical thought can judge them. Effectively or not? The question here is a subsidiary one. The revolutionary project rebounds. It takes back its fundamental character: to change the world and life. We are no longer in philosophy, but beyond it.

EIGHTH APORIA: POETRY AND POIESIS

Philosophy as reflection and systematic elaboration develops an attitude, spelling out an initial position. What lies at the start of philosophy in general, and of every particular philosophy? An intuition? A vision? A concept? Or rather an act, a poietic word?

Greek philosophy constituted itself as such by separating itself from poetry and the sciences – and from praxis. But no separation within creative activity can be complete and make a division. Formerly, before this split, before this division of labour and this specialization, philosophical speech and poetic speech were not distinguished. They remained bound up with praxis. And praxis was dominated by poiesis, by creative speech and act. The poet-philosopher knew the laws of the city. He could decide on them. He was political. Subsequently, praxis (pragmatic action on men, empirical management of human affairs, justified by ideologies) was established and prevailed. Philosophy, rejecting the specialized knowledge of the compartmentalized sciences, proclaimed itself knowledge and even absolute knowledge, but not without using fragments of knowledge borrowed precisely from these compartmentalized sciences. In an analogous way, it could never separate completely from poetry. Philosophical discourse formalized and developed its initial speech according to the rules of discourse (rhetoric and syntax). This speech introduced into discourse images and symbols, which do not escape discursive rigour but palpably shape it. Seeing itself expressly as truth, as accomplished truth about what has been accomplished, making itself mimesis without knowing it (imitation of what has already been said and done), philosophy could not however dispense with poiesis, that is to say, with a project. It projected an image of man. Consequently, philosophical discourse never consistently attained its formal aim: becoming purely discourse, purely philosophical. There is within philosophy and in its relationships with the world outside both ambiguity and misunderstanding: a fortunate ambiguity, the chance of a misunderstanding. Discourse passes from master to disciples, not *despite of* but *on account of* these ambiguities and misunderstandings: on account of words that underlie discourse and images or symbols that give impulse to concepts. In the belief that they are receiving concepts, hearer and reader also receive images and symbols. Systematization conceals an attempt; but the attempt (of human forces, of the maieutic taken to a conclusion) inspires the system. The conclusion is happy and revivifying, and has to end up with a return to poetry and a new alliance between discourse and speech, concepts and the imagination.

In Descartes, accordingly, running through his rationalism, we find a number of dominant images that are very familiar: the tree of science, the great book of the world. In Spinoza, the happiness of contemplative knowledge. In Leibniz, the harmony in the combinations, the vast symphony of the monads. In Kant, the idea of free choice in the absolute (the intelligible) through which the individual constitutes himself as such and creates the very thing that he believes himself to experience, and actually does experience, in the phenomenal and empirical, in space and time. And was not even the weighty and forceful Hegel, the man of perfect philosophical discourse, an initiate of the Rosicrucians? The cross signifies time, the crossroads of the present in a becoming between past and future, between action and passion, between the contradictions that move it. It is on this painful cross that the Rose of the World grows, the flower of time that man must pluck and that the philosopher is the first to enjoy.[14] Is not the image of the owl of Minerva, of a twilight wisdom, equally expressive and meaningful? Does it not express the culmination of philosophy and of a world, the world that gave rise to philosophy? Does it not already signify, beyond this heavy and obsolete Hegel, the superseding of philosophy?

Either philosophy continues to isolate itself from poiesis and from praxis, or else it rediscovers and recognizes, lucidly, the link that was

---

14 See the preface to Hegel's *Philosophy of Right*; also *The History of Philosophy*. [EN: As Chapter 2, note 10 indicates, the second reference is more likely to be the *Lectures on the Philosophy of Religion*, vol. 2, p. 248 n. 45.]

never completely broken. Then it supersedes itself in the name of a new project and a new poetic word, a creative word that has to be found, by restoring poiesis into praxis and above it.

NINTH APORIA: PROOF AND DISCOURSE

Philosophers, as logicians and founders of systems, have formulated with great rigour the theory of *proof*. This has been studied principally in structures of mathematical discourse, in a discourse that probably represents the perfection of discourse once this has replaced words with signs and perfectly defined operations. Following this, philosophers transported into philosophical discourse the absolute requirement of proof, or the requirement of absolute proof: demonstration. The effort not to accept anything that has not been formally declared, the effort to show the validity of procedures step by step, has characterized philosophical thought ever more clearly. The quest for philosophical proof could be defined, from Spinoza on, by this demand for rigour in a domain that does not self-evidently allow for rigorous deduction or formally rigorous construction.

The result is somewhat unexpected. The philosopher, in fact, prisoner of his own intention, abuses his rights; he takes the exercise of his speculative thought for rigour par excellence. The concern for rigour, devolved on philosophy, yields a style of rigour, a project of rigour, though not genuine rigour: proof. This infinitely precious proof indefinitely escapes philosophy. It suffers not only the torment of Sisyphus (always starting again, always climbing the same steep slope, hoisting the materials of the system to the top), but combined with it the torment of Tantalus: thirst for reality, hunger for proof.

Each time that the philosopher (or someone else) seriously examines his premises, he discovers there presuppositions that are not explicit, that is to say, a content, direct or indirect borrowings from history: from praxis. The quest for proof is duplicated. On the one hand, the philosopher has vowed to make his postulates explicit, but he discovers that analysis and explanation can be infinite or indefinite. The question of proof then becomes that of the ultimate and unchallengeable foundation: last instance, last fact or act at which it is possible to stop. The philosopher has to stop, but he cannot. The foundation is constantly under scrutiny; it is questioned without cease. On what side, then, is proof to be found? In coherence. The system proves itself by being coherent and compact. Logic prevails over the foundation, and form over content. The system, speculative analogy of God, is *causa sui*, and its truth is demonstrated by exhibiting it: *verum index sui*. This sufficiency is evident in the systematic form.

The philosopher, accordingly, installs himself in rigour: in a rigour of appearance, apparatus, and apparel [*rigueur d'apparence, d'appareil et d'apparat*]. He despises empiricists and practitioners with their externality. He inhabits rigour; he makes it his dwelling, a rather cold one, with a pale dry light. But the power that decrees rigour and establishes itself there can also emerge from it by decree. Anyone who puts this or that in parentheses (this or that in the world, or the world as a whole), keeping only a fragment of it, but keeping it well and not admitting anything not elucidated on the basis of a will to rigour, finds out sooner or later that he has broken, or has finished breaking, the world as totality. He has broken the connections, replacing them with rigorously defined articulations. Yet he continues. In the name of rigour, he will have suspended rigour.

Explanation turns out to be infinite: and yet a stop must be made. The first word of metaphysics is also its final word. The *alpha* and *omega* coincide. The circle closes. There is a circle, that is to say, a system. But what is there in this circle as such? Nothing. There is nothing. Not even the 'nothing'.

How could the philosopher have stayed for so long in the icy desert of a philosophical project reduced to the pure state, the pure form? He leaps from moral rigour to postulate without proof: the faith of Jaspers, the mystery of Gabriel Marcel, or, even with Husserl, a reprise of the metaphysical problem in transcendental phenomenology. Rigour changes into its opposite, once the philosopher perceives that he can neither provide the proof announced, nor suspend an 'existence' that proves itself until its end, death. Extreme formal and rational rigour is transformed into absence of rigour in the silence of reason.

The philosopher and philosophy may still find a refuge: *logos* – not this or that specialized language, but language itself. Philosophy proclaims itself *logology*, without smiling or fearing pleonasm. The philosopher becomes a man of language in general, discovering in it the citadel [*investissement*] of truth. But he is besieged from all sides. The logician leads the attack, specialist in formal rigour and coherent discourse. He wants a language that is universal, demonstrative, usable by machines, based on a general semantics, axiomatized and formalized after the model of mathematics. The most violent assault is waged by the champions of structuralism, the information and cybernetics theorists. They seek to occupy the sphere of discourse, to expel the other inhabitants, and from this point conduct raids and assaults on the neighbouring domains and states. But the philosopher is also attacked by the writer, who wants a genuine tongue and language of his own, irreducible to discourse even at the price of a destruction of discourse, its structures and its laws. Is philosophy to be a kind of metalanguage? Yes, inasmuch as the philosopher has his own vocabulary and substitutes his own discourse (on discourse) for spontaneous discourse. Yes, inasmuch as the philosopher uses metaphor in his own manner (replacing a customary term with other terms) and likewise metonymy (replacing an everyday word with a less current word, moving from the part to the whole, the relative to the absolute), which constitutes a jargon and risks, as we know, establishing a pathological state by making a break and division between elaborate discourse and everyday discourse. And yet, no. Only the logician, the semanticist and the semiologist can constitute metalanguages or, if they can manage to, the universal metalanguage.

The structuralist and cybernetic offensive is justified from this specialized point of view. Against the extension of traditional philosophy, a technocratic positivism or neopositivism can profit from the lacunas in this thought in order to proclaim itself the new philosophy. Classical philosophical discourse sought to be completely meaningful. But philosophers did not see very well that the informational and meaningful exist only in relation to a redundancy. The meaningful is the surprising, what is unforeseen in the use of the signs of the repertoire. Redundancy is intelligibility, and intelligibility is rigour. The desire for total meaningfulness and the desire for complete rigour, simultaneously present, confer on the discourse of philosophers a sometimes unbearable tension. Without knowing it, they seek to eliminate redundancy. Redundancy, that is to say, repetition, the already known, takes its revenge. Philosophical discourse, when it is no longer redundant but surprising, often ceases to be intelligible. Seeking intelligibility, philosophers wager on redundancy without knowing this.

The philosopher of today seeks to establish himself in language. Yet he cannot be content with everyday discourse. If he adds nothing to this, he denies himself. Below language there is silence, a certain silence (in the region that is called by philosophy pre-perceptive, pre-cognitive, pre-reflexive, or again 'infra-linguistic'). Above language there is another silence. It would be witty to say that a 'sleeve of silence' envelops language. Above language, there is also the cry, the call, the poetic speech. Where is the philosopher to establish himself? In the silence below or in the silence above? In the infra-linguistic or the supra-linguistic? In the region of larval acts and impulses that await communication? In cries? In poetic speech? On the one side he encounters psychoanalysts, on the other side many people: mystics, poets. Doubtful associations that cannot fail to disturb and compromise him.

There remains ordinary [*courant*] language – discourse that is non-philosophical, by hypothesis – with which, by hypothesis, the philosopher cannot be satisfied. Philosophy then becomes what it has always been, revealing itself in its essence: discourse on discourse, second-degree discourse. The philosopher *reflects* on first-degree discourse. He *reflects* it. Perhaps he implicitly operates on the most general model of discourse: the paradigm of reflexive discourse, the quintessence. In praxis, ordinary people speak among themselves; as a function of their work, their social activities, they have such and such opinions (*doxai*). The philosopher reflects on these opinions formulated in everyday discourse. He substitutes for them reflected judgements and ripened concepts, freed from the incoherencies of practical discourse. He seeks out true opinion, which understands and dominates the diversity of empirical opinions and behaviours. He wants coherence.

Unfortunately, second-degree discourse, discourse on discourse, if it does not constitute a particular terminology and transform itself into jargon, refers to everyday practical discourse as its source. It imitates everyday discourse and aims in this imitation at a total and totally coherent discourse. It is mimesis. Reflection is imitation and imitation reflects what it imitates. Philosophical discourse as the quintessence of commonplace discourse always risks offering only a weakened image or echo of real discourses after having purged them of some of their contradictions, their incoherencies, and consequently their richness. The mirror does not have all the dimensions of what it reflects, nor does imitation have those of what it imitates.

As discourse on discourse, it ceaselessly and endlessly pursues its foundation and its proof. It risks transforming the world of discourse, entirely detached from praxis, into a philosophical truth, in which each person says whatever he likes and soliloquizes, without for all that meditating in solitude.[15]

It is here that a path opened by Heidegger has its point of departure: If 'all ways of thinking, more or less perceptibly, lead through language in a manner that is extraordinary,'[16] if language is more than a means of communication, if it is the dwelling place of Being, then can philosophical thought not draw indications for a renewal from a very attentive examination of language?

This suggestion is very worthy of consideration – all the more so as Heidegger supports it with admirable studies of logos, aletheia, physis, and so forth, which stimulates us to study in the same fashion praxis, techne, mimesis, poiesis, and so forth.

Such work shows the point at which living language, caught in total historicity, supersedes the mechanics of discourse and also overflows the sociologism and historicism that would attribute certain meanings and words, at a certain period, to country people, and certain different meanings to people already gathered in a town, which is not wrong but remains trivial. Language followed these mutations from rural life to the life of the city. Up to a certain point, it made them possible. It could not fail to contribute to creative acts (to foundings and foundations) either as reason or effect. Yet despite this, Heidegger does not escape the difficulty (*aporia*): if certain human works, for

15   This antinomy of discourse was demonstrated by Yvon Belaval with both seriousness and humour; cf. 'Les deux langages' in *Les philosophes et leur langage*, Paris: Gallimard, 1952, pp. 150–61.

16   Martin Heidegger, 'The Question Concerning Technology', in *The Question Concerning Technology and Other Essays*, translated by William Lovitt, New York: Harper & Row, 1977, p. 3.

example a city, a law or a constitution, are only founded when named and spoken, it is hard to posit in truth that it is words that do things. If truth is poetry and poetry truth, what is their common source? Language alone? Language intervenes in all creation as a level of praxis. Does it constitute all creative activity? No. Not even in the original and poetic period of creation, naïve and fresh.

Why not appeal to the pre-Socratic thinkers in order to shape the new investigation, metaphilosophical thought, by restoring their words?

Poetry clearly passes into language; but does it derive from language alone? And besides, if poetry has to be included in the superseding of philosophy, can we expect the realization of philosophy from language alone? The critical study of praxis and its contradictions, as well as of technology, must be included in the renewal of a meditation that would no longer be simply reflection and mimesis but, once more, act and poiesis.

Heidegger wrote that philosophy is stumbling. It drags along far behind the problems of modernity and current praxis. He was right. It is not only far behind the problems of technology and nuclear danger, it is behind all along the line, along the whole front. To make up for this delay, do we not have to deliberately break the framework of this thought, expressly rejecting its limits and faults?

TENTH APORIA: LIVED EXPERIENCE AND HISTORY

Jean-Paul Sartre, in the *Critique of Dialectical Reason*, makes a titanic effort to resolve a problem that could already be glimpsed in his previous works, emerging from traditional philosophy still half-concealed. What problem is this? That of the confrontation between the lived [*le vécu*] and history. This problem encompasses that of language, since language gathers both the results of the everyday and those of history. Yet it is located on a different scale from customary exchange between interlocutors. Praxis has, among its other aspects, the repetitive and the creative, or the lived and the historical. These two sides of praxis do not go well together. They do not correspond. Neither 'reflects' the other. There is little that the *lived* can be reduced to: it is a philosophical name for everydayness. One of the aspects of existentialism was the description of the everyday in its triviality, using terms that were still philosophical; this concealed the object and paralyzed the critical procedure that could have proposed both to understand the everyday and to overcome it. The mediocrity of the lived, this immediate work of Freedom, shattered the philosopher of free consciousness. Philosophical amplification and transcription failed to metamorphose the shabbiness of the lived. What is the lived: nausea. And bad faith. And unease. And embarrassment or torment under the gaze of the Other. Now, well below and well above these wretched undertakings of freedom, there are the great undertakings of history. For history is grandiose. More: it is spectacular. Perhaps it is still something else, as people do not make history innocently; but from the standpoint of the philosopher, when he perceives it, unfolding well above what he writes and describes, history has grandeur. On the historical stage, great actors perform great tragic plays. Is the philosopher going to deflate history, tear the banners in which history covers itself and show the histrion in the tragedian? He may try. History resists; it is not easy to get rid of *homo historicus*, his grandeur and his misery.

How then to diminish the gap between the lived and the historical? There are many possibilities for doing this. In the name of a programme to transform the lived, one can show its richness and the demands hidden beneath triviality. One can also show human alienation within the historical. One can move towards a total history that does not relate events in terms of their apparent grandeur or men in terms of what they have said of themselves, but reconsiders events and men in a different perspective of the *undergone*. One can posit anew, as fundamental demand, the reduction of the gap between the everyday and the state, that is to say, between the experienced and the historical. In other words, we can demand that the 'lived' should lose its trivial character separate from the historical and that the historical should cease to be practically separated from the experienced on account of being dominated by blind forces, by state and political powers.

Sartre, however, blocks off these paths, because of his philosophical origins. He started out from the Cartesian *cogito*, from the separation between *res cogitans* and *res extensa* (which with him becomes an abyss between the for-itself and the in-itself, with the in-itself taken as 'being' and the for-itself as truth, this tremendous fissure being peopled with 'concrete' existences that appear to be philosophically conceived but are in fact recorded empirically). No doubt Husserl took the same path. Fichte as well. The *cogito* opens onto the object, onto the other. The intentional seeks to bridge the distance and aim at the object. The method of description of consciousness is perfected. It approaches formal rigour. It classifies assiduously the problematic, the categorical, the thematic. It teaches the philosopher to put this or that in parentheses (the fragments of a world buried in its fragmentation), to the point that Sartre himself for a long while put history in parentheses (in *Being and Nothingness*). The philosopher knows what describing and spelling out means. Yet the speculative relationship between object and subject remains the central theme of this philosophy, which starts from (individual) consciousness. It forbids itself both access to being (natural or social) and access to history, the two things moreover being connected, if it is true that history is the history of (human) being.

Lévi-Strauss quite easily had the upper hand when he declared that the 'supposed totalizing continuity of the self' is simply an illusion maintained by a certain social life.[17] 'Political' life, too, we may add. Today Marxists – political men of action who use the Marxist vocabulary – make history. They operate with a summary ontology (materialism) which they need to justify themselves ideologically, and with a method sufficiently flexible to pass from pedagogical dogmatism to a dialectical subtlety close sometimes to the sophistic. This gigantesque historicity manufactured with the aid of a mediocre philosophy obsesses the excellent philosopher that Sartre is. No matter how degenerated, official Marxism still has enough striking force to shake a philosopher convinced of his rights. The positions that he adopts in the *Critique of Dialectical Reason* have a manifold interest, both for diagnosing the exact point reached by the general crisis of philosophy and to locate the difficulties of a particular philosophical tendency, that which starts from the '*prise de conscience*' of the accomplished fact. The criticism of this

---

17 Cf. Claude Lévi-Strauss, *The Savage Mind*, Chicago: University of Chicago Press, 1966, p. 256.

non-critical criticism will enable us to make clear the notion of metaphilosophical thought.

It is quite true that institutional Marxism has left aside questions relating to the individual. The attempts made by certain Marxists in this direction have been rejected by the official ideologists. There are also objective reasons for this rejection. The problem of the individual is a practical problem: that of his full and entire realization. Realization of the individual and realization of philosophy go together. The socialist societies, not being ripe for the superseding of philosophy, cannot tackle the problems of the individual in their praxis. Between the level of individual life and the totality of praxis, between the lived and history, Marxist thought has left an abyss that Sartre seeks to fill by restoring the *mediations* (in particular, intermediate groups). Problems then arise that are unresolved, posited badly or not at all. How do individuals participate in history? How can individual consciousness, that of the actor in the event, that of the witness who is or claims to be privileged (philosopher, historian, sociologist), accede to the total? How do action and comprehension become possible, that is to say, how and why does history become acting consciousness on the one hand, knowledge on the other? This problematic forms part of the requirements of a total history.

In his intention to accomplish this programme, Sartre contributes intuitions that are sometimes striking. It is true that most often he does not proceed to develop the intuition as far as the concept. He lets it drift. Thus he takes as his starting point *need*.[18] Subsequently, with Sartre as in Dionys Mascolo's earlier book *Le communisme*, the dialectical movement of need remains below the sketch offered by Marx in the *1844 Manuscripts*.[19] Need is essentially defined as lack and scarcity, whereas Marx indicated its transformation (by the mediation of productive labour) into capacity for work and enjoyment, a need both individualized and socialized. It is no less interesting that Sartre introduces need into his presentation of *practical ensembles* on the basis of

18   Cf. Jean-Paul Sartre, *Search for a Method*, New York: Vintage, 1968, pp. 14 ff. [EN: The more literal translation of the title would be 'Questions of Method'.]

19   EN: Dionys Mascolo, *Le communisme: Révolution et communication ou la dialectique des valeurs et des besoins*, Paris: Gallimard, 1953.

individual lived experience [*du vécu individuel*]. Just as he indicates a dialectical movement of alienation (alienation, dis-alienation, new alienation in this dis-alienation, and so on),[20] but the basis (not to say the foundation) of this dialectical movement does not go beyond a certain speculative narrowness, since the text mentioned has to do with the dialectical movement 'question–questioner–questioned'. In the wake of this, alienation for Sartre is almost always reduced to alterity (to perception of 'the other').

Similarly again, we have the idea of a 'presence' and of the possible in the project.[21] The reader may regret that this idea is not developed or actualized in a genuine theory of the possible, at least in Volume 1. This regret presupposes an encounter with a productive idea. On the way, Sartre restores mediations, particularly those of intermediate groups (family, town, gatherings, etc.). But he scarcely goes further than interpersonal relations. Is he able to go further? His philosophical concepts (consciousness, for-itself, in-itself) impede him from what he is seeking: access to the general. Until a new order, he remains with the partial while believing himself to be heading for the totality. At this level, he explains in an extremely intelligent fashion certain aspects of praxis, those that relate to the most conscious activity and that may be attributed to 'totalization' by a conscious ego: mediations between individuals, between the individual and the historico-social. The mediation privileged in this way then tends to attenuate the contradictions in the dialectical movement itself. Seeking to fill the lacunae left in knowledge by official Marxism, Sartre ends up falling into sociologism and psychologism. The general anthropology to which he wants to make a decisive contribution is not always clearly distinguished from culturalist and structuralist anthropology. We already know why, and we will know this increasingly profoundly. These scientific tendencies have a division in common with the philosophy of Sartre. They separate human activity from nature and so mutilate praxis by reducing it to consciousness or to culture.

Already in Sartre's introduction (*Questions of Method*), the reader notes that the author accepts under the label of 'Marxism' the

---

20 Sartre, *Search for a Method*, pp. 178–80.
21 Sartre, *Search for a Method*, pp. 128, 163, 180 ff.

historical development of this thought; he accepts in this way the historical; but if he examines and criticizes it, he does so in a non-historical fashion, philosophically. Knowing full well that Marxism has changed into dogmatism, Sartre seeks the origin of this dogmatism in the philosophy of Marx (and consequently in a philosophy that he attributes to Marx without investigating any further):

> The source of this dogmatism lies in the basic problem of 'dialectical materialism'. In setting the dialectic back on its feet Marx revealed the true contradictions of realism. These contradictions were to be the very substance of knowledge, but they have been concealed.[22]

By rejecting the Hegelian identity of being, doing and knowing, and consequently of history and truth, Marx according to Sartre promulgated a 'dualist monism'. He was 'dualist because monist'.[23] Marx, therefore, only established between being and knowing a 'problematic' connection, instead of their metaphysical identity as with Hegel. But this is not quite exact. If Marx broke the Hegelian systematization (or rather if he noted its rupture), he grasped what Lévi-Strauss correctly calls the 'essence of change',[24] while challenging the validity of this concept. Sartre views Marxism philosophically; he defines it, following Hegel, as a philosophically problematized Hegelianism. Right from the start, he brings it into the categories of philosophy. He leaves aside the radical critique of philosophy as such, the theory of the practical superseding of philosophy, the theory of praxis.

Marx saw political economy as the science of *economy* (in the sense of someone 'being economical'). He criticized it while showing its awareness of the division (one that continues to the present day to be spontaneous and non-conscious) of labours and of goods in poor societies, dominated by castes and classes who demand abstinence from other groups, and sometimes from themselves. Right [*le droit*] sanctioned and still does sanction this unequal and unjust division. The superseding of economics, that is to say, the end of penury, will go

---

22 Jean-Paul Sartre, *Critique of Dialectical Reason*, vol. 1, London: Verso, 2004, p. 21.
23 Ibid., p. 25.
24 Lévi-Strauss, *The Savage Mind*, p. 256.

together with the superseding of this ancient and solemn right. Marx frequently alludes to societies that are already historical but not in the sense of economic growth under capitalism, and still less so in the sense of a development that is at last conscious (known, mastered, thus genuinely historical) in socialism. He did not develop his theory, particularly that of the 'Asiatic mode of production', but he clearly showed its scope.

Outside of the process of accumulation, on a base that had remained close to nature and the archaic community, vast political edifices (empires) were constructed, destined to collapse by stagnation or the regression of their base, if not by external conquest. In these societies, a certain surplus labour and a weak surplus product could be tapped by the dominant groups, appropriated for their leisure and their works. These dominant groups, who were not yet classes, still had to justify their privileged existence and activities (those of war, administration, ideology) to a community from which they were not completely separated. Among their works, one particularly stood out, on which we have already focused several times: the town, the city. We have to understand the double aspect of these societies: the reign of violence, but also creation in art, symbolism, style, culture, wisdom and finally philosophy. It is in this way alone that we can understand, not only those groups recorded by ethnography, but also the great imperial societies of Asia, pre-Colombian America, Greece and Rome. In some brilliant passages,[25] Sartre starts from need and discovers the 'world of scarcity'. Having changed scarcity into world, he lets its contradictory aspects escape. They are only explained by the dialectical movement of need, reproduced by our thought through to the conditions in which desire is distinguished from need and becomes desire for creative work, for refined enjoyment, in violence or cruelty, in wisdom or grandeur. Hence the problem posited and not resolved by Marx: what is there to interest us in the works of these great social groups that established or maintained themselves by force, appropriating in penury the weak social surplus product? What is the source of the durable character of these works of art, of thought, 'superstructures' of societies that are outdated and often ferocious?

---

25 Sartre, *Critique of Dialectical Reason*, vol. 1, p. 79ff.

Is the question of the depth of archaic works not bound up with that of Desire? Do these works not address a deep desire, that for a style of life, a style of desire itself? Marx glimpsed this line of questioning: what becomes of art, wisdom and philosophy, these forms of nostalgia and hope, when penury disappears?

Because Sartre wants to avoid a systematized philosophy of nature (dialectics of nature), yet still thinks in terms of philosophical systemization, he ends up purely and simply effacing the existence of nature. It has no place in his philosophy. Where do trees, animals, children fall, between the in-itself and the for-itself, being neither one thing nor the other? Along with nature, it is perhaps the essence of need and desire that escapes, which is rather more serious than not knowing where to locate the mere living being in the philosophical picture of the world. And so the philosopher carries through to the end the implications of any philosophy of consciousness, which can rigorously rediscover the 'object', but not physis or 'being'. Nature manifests itself, according to his dialectical reason, as the ontological sector[26] of the anti-dialectic: the inert, the practico-inert. This qualification replaces the 'in-itself' of *Being and Nothingness* without great advantage, despite the attempt to insert it into praxis and history.

It is true that there are 'things' with stability, structures and 'beings' in this determined sense. Can we reduce them to a 'world of things', to pure inertia? This table is a thing; its wood is dead, or nearly so. To make the table, a tree has been killed. To the extent that the dead wood of this table continues to change, is not fixed in its death, the table changes and decays. It is true, therefore, that human labour often operates on the practico-inert: on the stable. It makes it inert. It stabilizes. It fixes. That said, we humans also deal with living trees; there are people who work to cultivate them, to produce fruit, and also to cut them down, to saw them, to shape them. The wood of a living tree is not absolutely different from the dead wood of this table, and yet it does differ. Besides, the table is a thing, perhaps a work of art that has a certain beauty.

---

26 Sartre, *Critique of Dialectical Reason*, vol. 1, p. 43. [EN: The second edition of Lefebvre's text references p. 1326 of Sartre, which is incorrect. The original edition provides the correct reference to p. 136. The English uses 'ontological region' instead of 'sector'.]

Apropos the tree, we can say with Hegel, and with Engels: 'The tree negates itself in the fruit; the negation of this fruit in the earth, negation of the negation, gives rise to another tree.'[27]

This is not wrong. One may wonder, however, if such statements add to our knowledge of trees. Besides, do they reproduce a genuine dialectical movement? What we have here is a cycle, thus a repetition, rather than a becoming, and it is hard to see contradictions at work, except very vaguely (the earth and the fruit, and so on). The question of dialectics in nature is thus raised. We may believe this is an acceptable hypothesis that, like all hypotheses, has to prove itself by its productiveness and not by the systematic interpretation of provisional facts and results of the sciences. Scientists can construct *dialectical models* for natural processes, and use these models. Nothing more. They do not have the right to change a model into an 'ontological' truth. This remark is as valid for the waves and particles of quantum physics as for the tree and the fruit. That being so, it is curious to refuse concrete existence to nature by reducing it to a single dead thing, to the collection of things. That really is extending a hand to the most summary materialism, that of the raw and isolated thing.

Nature, that is to say, 'being', resolves itself for Sartre into anti-dialectics, inertia. Neither the tree nor the animal – neither growth nor decline – finds a place in his philosophy. In contrast to Heidegger, he has not meditated on the physis of the ancient Greeks. He remains imprisoned by these categories: the mechanism of nature juxtaposed with the finalism of consciousness. This gives his thought a surprising aridity. Sartre reflects on things, stabilities, structures, as on the bones of a skeleton. This is the inert; these bones would have to be covered again with flesh, with living and conscious activity. Which is true. But he omits an important fact: the bones were born at the same time as the flesh, in organic growth. The bones were also living. The death that abandons them inert, when the fleshy life has disappeared, raises a question for us. Many questions, in fact, among which is that of

---

27   EN: This does not appear to be a direct quotation. See G. W. F. Hegel, *Philosophy of Nature: Part Two of the Philosophical Sciences (1830)*, translated by A. V. Miller, Oxford: Clarendon Press, 1970, §348. Engels develops these ideas in *Anti-Dühring: Herr Eugen Dühring's Revolution in Science*, and *Dialectics of Nature*, both in *MECW*, vol. 25.

analysis, which kills and which knows. When we pick up a dead shell from the beach, this shell has a structure. It makes it possible for us to classify the shell in a genus and a species. And yet it was the work of a living 'being', active and yet soft and barely structured. The dead wood, the dried-up vertebra, the empty shell, that is Sartre's *being*. Can we reply to questions concerning living being in terms of nothingness and death, that is to say, structures that life abandons and leaves behind?

A great absence pervades Sartre's thought. Along with nature and being (reduced to the 'in-itself'), poetry disappears. As distinct from Heidegger, Sartre's thought destroys poetry as style and word, poiesis as concept. He thinks of 'doing'; he does not meditate on production or creation. His philosophy tends towards a pure discourse that is too conscious and too organized. His dialectic becomes a dialectic internal to a consciousness opposed to the Thing (inert).

We know that Sartre starts from consciousness as act, as prototype of reality and intelligibility. And this even though he rejects transcendental consciousness. He conceives consciousness as existing in the act, not as 'metaphysical'. And yet, from the fact that he conceives it as act, by itself, is it not still and always metaphysical? Consciousness according to him is no longer absolutely and originally closed, as in the Cartesian school (the *cogito*, the monad). Yet it is relatively closed, being determined and limited on the one hand (subjectively) by lack, and on the other hand (objectively), on the side of the object, by the thing, the inert that it has to deal with. This inert is simultaneously before consciousness and within it. That is how it determines consciousness. Consciousness opens towards the inert, and the inert encloses it.

This consciousness, initially individual, rebounds in its struggle against its limits and its obstacles. In its relations with others, it becomes effervescent and beats against the obstacle: the inert. We then have an interindividual sociological process tending towards the historical. This is how the 'group' is constituted, an important mediation,[28] both mediated by an event, immediate reality for the participants, and mediation towards something else in time.

At each step, with each leap of consciousness, the inert reappears within it. Each form of the inert accompanies a consciousness both

---

28   Sartre, *Critique of Dialectical Reason*, vol. 1, p. 343ff.

vis-à-vis and face-to-face with it: counter-finality, counter-group, anti-human, field of inertia, repetitive series, structures, sociality of inertias, and so forth. At each step, consciousness (the conscious dialectic or the dialectic of consciousness) experiences its limits anew and shatters them [*les faire éclater*]. In a series of explosions or effervescences, it constitutes ever larger ensembles, including those that make history – in particular, classes. To illustrate our criticism, let us take the city. Sartre cannot consider it as a work, created by poietic acts that founded a city, promulgated its law, defined its frame, incorporated its institutions or those of society into monuments, and did so in relation to a praxis. For Sartre, the city can only be the inert frame in which effervescences, disturbances, revolutions are produced when the conjuncture is favourable.

It is in this sense that Sartre tackles the study of classes and class relations. For him, class reality and class consciousness are not discovered on the basis of the economic level of capitalist society; he relegates the economic to the inert, and more precisely to the scarcity of things, the anti-human world. Nor is the consciousness of a class born against another class, so that contradiction appears only within a constituted consciousness, which presupposes its constitution. It is not created in a historical struggle, among complex forms of consciousness (ideologies, social consciousness, conscious fragments of praxis). It is created against the inertia that it contains: the demands of the practico-inert field. This constitution is produced within the group consciousness. Gatherings – and likewise classes – become groups by way of their internal tension.

The class struggle is defined as *superseding the inert of the collective towards dialectical groups of combat*[29] – a formula that, by reducing the collective to the inert, delegates class struggle to the most conscious representatives of the class, to acting minorities and finally to restricted groups. Are these parties, or simply activists and shock troops? Whatever the case, the outlet towards history is narrowed. Inevitably so, since by starting from consciousness and its effervescences, it is

---

29 Sartre, *Critique of Dialectical Reason*, vol. 1, p. 805. [EN: The second edition references p. 741 of the French, which is incorrect; the first edition provides the correct reference, p. 744.]

only possible to arrive at very conscious but restricted groups. And the real basis of these groups is forgotten. If we take the Paris Commune of 1871 to illustrate the analysis, what do we find in action? Small groups? No. The whole city with its organic elements: the *quartiers*. The city as ensemble, with its great social categories: artisans, workers, women – and then ideologies.

The state appears up till now only in the *manipulation of inert seri-alities*.[30] It would be more interesting to tell us how the state renders active groups inert by manipulating them, transferring their activities to itself by taking hold of them. The works and products of human activity are defined at all levels by inertia alone. At each level the thing reappears in consciousness, at the same time as *for* and *before* it.

Never, in our opinion, does Sartre grasp human activities in the movement in which they alienate themselves, going to the point of losing themselves in the work or the product (until they are reified). That is what prepares and heralds superseding. But is this dialectical movement not what is essential in *Capital*? Sartre takes the thing and consciousness face-to-face; they arise together and rebound together. He presents them in an ambiguity between empiricism and ontology, between observation and speculative construction. And the transition, the passage from one aspect to another, is always missing, hence the dialectical contradiction and the dialectical movement themselves. He leaves aside the fundamental problem: the historical relationship between social man and his works.

The wide programme that Sartre set himself would be acceptable on condition of being elucidated, completed, put back on its feet. It is fated to attain only one part of history: the 'moments' of high conscious-ness, those of effervescence. What we need, however, is not to subject praxis to the categories of a philosophy, but rather to resume the criti-cism and superseding of philosophy by deepening the study of praxis (distinguishing repetitive praxis and creative praxis, following the dialectical movement of the latter in history conceived totally).

The question is not to provide a philosophical certificate for accom-plished history by starting from the lived or the existential, but rather to also criticize history as fait accompli on the basis of a reprise of

---

30 Sartre, *Critique of Dialectical Reason*, vol. 1, p. 640.

critical and dialectical thought. In this sense, with appropriate methods and concepts (without ruling out methods and concepts taken from philosophy, but transforming them), it is possible to envisage a new insertion of theoretical thought in creative praxis. A condition sine qua non is that the theory of the withering away of the state again returns to the agenda. If politics remains the key to the situation, this theory remains the key to Marxist political thought. It is free for those who so wish to reply that this theory is out of date, that Marx's authentic thought – and the restitution of this thought – has only an anecdotal interest. It is also free for them to assert that dialogue must be established with Marxism as it has historically become (and not with Marx, with the thinkers of ancient Greece and other interlocutors). But then let this be said explicitly, that is, theoretically.

In the form that it is presented, Sartre's programme risks failure. He attempts a philosophical summa, heroically pursued, without any criterion to distinguish the important from the accidental: without anything to indicate *what concerns us* by distinguishing it from what does not. In his own manner, with his presuppositions, he attempts a total history. Yet these same philosophical presuppositions prevent such historicity.

We could judge still more severely the fact that this work, like any speculative construction, is content with a few tautologies, which take up a great deal of space without ever making clear what they actually are, being concealed beneath dialectical pseudo-movements. Here is one of these underlying tautologies: 'For there to be reification of activity, there have to be things.'[31] This is not untrue. But a proposition of this kind, almost a caricature, gives rise to illusions. The reader believes he has thought, advanced, understood, learned something. He repeats a tautology. He is in a state of redundancy, of mimesis. He imitates more or less his philosophical master, who himself repeats an outrageous and trivial proposition. The real problem is to grasp at its particular level the movement of alienation that tends towards its structural limit: reification. It is to grasp a transition that Sartre's discussion leaps over by taking as essential the bare, dead result, at bottom tautological. This makes for an identification

---

31   EN: This does not appear to be an actual quotation.

between structure and the inert, an identification in the name of which Sartre seems to us to bypass the problem of structures, equilibriums and stabilities, their relationship with becoming, in all the dimensions of praxis.

He runs a strong risk of treating the categories of Marxism metaphysically: need, praxis, revolutionary action. He takes them; he separates them; he hypostatizes them and 'worlds [*mondifie*]' them.

The *Critique of Dialectical Reason* attests to the profound difficulties with which philosophy is struggling. By virtue of his philosophical preoccupations (that is to say, those concerning philosophy), Sartre is close to official Marxism. He is also closer than he thinks to a theological philosophy of history and evolution, of which Teilhard de Chardin's doctrine offers us a fairly successful example. These are ambiguous neighbours, and dialogues are therefore very natural. We persist here in asserting that they are based on a fundamental misunderstanding concerning philosophy.

Maurice Merleau-Ponty rubbed shoulders with Marxism from the start of his career, whereas Sartre only encountered Marxism after attempting an earlier systematization (*Being and Nothingness*). Merleau-Ponty accepted, later to reject them, the terms of the philosophical debate that substituted for the superseding of philosophy. He believed at the time that he could attain a total, exhaustive discourse, starting from a logical-ontological dilemma: either the primacy of being (material, natural), or the primacy of thought (spirit, consciousness). The philosopher soon came to see this dilemma as untenable. It was a choice between two attitudes, two postulates, two philosophical traditions – object and subject – that were equally unsustainable. For Merleau-Ponty, the pure thing and the pure consciousness were both impossible and inconceivable. The philosopher cannot start from two impossibilities, two abstractions, placed face-to-face.

Merleau-Ponty believed he could situate his ontological principle between the two, between being and consciousness, the in-itself and the for-itself. As distinct from Sartre, what he sought was an ontological principle and not a starting point of a totalizing knowledge in the act of consciousness. He believed he had found this principle in the ambiguity between the two terms. He accordingly replaced the dilemma with a formula that he supposed – not without reason – to be more dialectical: neither one nor the other, but the two together. Neither being nor mind, neither the thing nor consciousness, but between the two – a position that effectively satisfied the requirements of dialectical thought: 'yes and no', if this position had not also required the superseding of philosophy itself. Merleau-Ponty thus grasped something essential in Marx's thought: the fact that the products and works of the human being *tend* towards autonomous being, without ever completely arriving at it. But he does not seem to have grasped the other side of this dialectical movement. For critical analysis, systematized philosophies and the categories of ontology no longer fit the purpose.

On the other hand, the failure of proletarian revolution in an advanced industrial country, France, after the Liberation, led Merleau-Ponty to draw the conclusion of the ambiguity of history.[32] The thesis of ambiguous history is strongly linked to an ontology of ambiguity. The philosopher took two ontological impossibilities (on the one hand, isolated things, the thing pure and simple; on the other hand, pure consciousness, the pure act of isolated consciousness). These two impossibilities he denied, both separately and together, basing himself on a phenomenological psychology of behaviour and perception, in such a way as to constitute a 'mixture' that he attributed to the body itself, the corporeal existence of the human being in his natural and social milieu. And then to historicity:

> instead of grasping, apropos 'things' and 'consciousness', the 'in-itself' and the 'for-itself', the difficulties of metaphysics and its categories as such, Merleau-Ponty sought to rescue traditional ontology in favour of ambiguity – a debatable procedure. It perceives the problems, up to a certain point, only to bypass them or shift them. Then they lose their edge. Difficulties and contradictions are attenuated in ambiguity. The confrontation between lived experience and the historical falls into a kind of shadow. Was this deliberate chiaroscuro not a refuge, a manner of eluding the crisis of philosophy?

---

32 EN: See *Adventures of the Dialectic*, translated by Joseph Bien, Evanston: Northwestern University Press, 1973.

Merleau-Ponty's theoretical position was not very sustainable. It was situated neither in being nor in knowing, neither in the object nor in the subject, neither in the in-itself nor in the for-itself, not even in their conflict (as Sartre had attempted), nor beyond these philosophical determinations. A kind of nostalgia for Being predestined Merleau-Ponty to bury ontology. In his last book, *Eye and Mind*,[33] we see him confusedly orienting himself towards Heideggerian thought, that is to say, towards a philosophy of Being – very much towards a vision, since he is dealing with pictorial art – of Being as conceived philosophically. Sadly, he died well before the end of this trajectory. Undoubtedly, like Sartre and like Heidegger himself, he had two philosophies or two ways of tackling philosophical problems, but (as distinct from the other two) the second of these was more philosophical than the first.

ELEVENTH APORIA: FATHER AND SON. MASTER AND DISCIPLE

How should we understand Nietzsche's saying 'God is dead'[34] – a saying with immense resonance, genuinely poietic? We encounter certain weak versions. One version is that of the traditional philosopher, rationalist or empiricist: 'Nietzsche strongly criticized traditional thought, which situated the true in the supra-sensible. The Platonic theory of ideas marked Christian philosophy and theology. This had long been shaken, but Nietzsche gave it the coup de grâce. What died was an abstract conception of transcendence.' To this commentary we could add that the rehabilitation of the practico-sensuous and of all the meanings of *sense* had been effected by Marx, and that Nietzsche, thus interpreted, is of little interest. The version of the materialist and atheist philosopher is opposite to this, but equally facile: 'Superstition disappeared although the power of the church survives both faith and superstition. Religious alienation as such is attenuated; belief is reduced to an individual attitude, a kind of poetry that can be tolerated if it no

---

33   EN: *Eye and Mind*, translated by Carleton Dallery, in *The Primacy of Perception*, edited by by James Edie, Evanston: Northwestern University Press, 1964, 159–90.

34   EN: Nietzsche, *The Gay Science*, translated by Walter Kaufmann, New York: Vintage, 1974, sections 108, 125, 343, pp. 167, 181–2, 279–80.

longer has any political weight. There is no God. That has at last been perceived. A secular, lay, humanist morality can then be constituted.' In sum, Nietzsche condensed into a vigorous formula the materialist philosophy of the eighteenth and nineteenth centuries. The resonance of such a summary might well be surprising. The believer replies: 'In the modern world, even if the church and churches maintain themselves as institutions, even if we are moving towards a certain ecumenism, faith grows blurred – and with it, morality. With morality, taboos, sanctions and fears disappear. Immoralism triumphs, values collapse. No values without God! We come into anxiety, an insufferable nihilism. As proof, Nietzsche himself and the consequences of his theory, the results of his cry of revolt and despair.'

Is it by chance that these versions, in their platitude, are *philosophizing* or theological? Let us now venture the strongest and most dangerous hypothesis, observing that, if it frees the imagination, permitting a kind of poetic exploration of the impossible, or of a beyond of the possible, it cannot take itself without irony. Irony teaches us not to take entirely seriously half-dreamy and half-conceptual investigations. It teaches us to *play* with the most disturbing truths and the most dangerous errors. We shall therefore permit ourselves a few moments of philosophical irony. It is up to the reader to read these pages with the same irony. A more obscure version than the others, and certainly more poetic, attributes to Nietzsche the surprising doctrine that '*God did exist. He has died.*'

Let us make the attempt. Divinity has been the lived [experience] of humanity since its birth. Religion, accordingly, was not just an institution based on human weakness, or a projection by men of their own powers onto the screen of the clouds. The sacred and the divine (and perhaps the accursed and the diabolical) cannot be reduced to superstructures, ideologies, a play on primitive fears that is still short of systematic.

Someone or something (neither completely someone nor completely something) sought to arise. From the infinite universe, the consciousness of an infinite being sought to be born. Theologies attest to this, as before them do cosmogonies and mythologies, each in its own fashion. Christian theology breaks the unity of God by trying to account for this genesis: is the Father not the universe, nature? Is not the Son, as Word, the arising consciousness, with the result that Logos, son of God, is also son of man? As for the ultimate reconciliation, the Spirit, this intervenes only as virtual, horizon of horizons.

This infinite consciousness of infinite being, disseminated ever since it first arose, soon had to yield before the *law of the world*: finitude. What is born in the world and out of the infinite world (universe) is always finite. What arises in the infinite becoming always possesses a determination, and therefore limits. The presence of the sacred and divine in history, surrounding human birth, shows a God . . . who sought to be. God was (and remains) attempt and temptation, with its counterpart the diabolical and accursed.

God did not die a good death. He had to be killed – an act that is properly inconceivable (this side of conception, or beyond it). In order to be, to proclaim himself, man had to kill God. We still do have to kill him, perhaps at every moment. What could the divine be? Absolute spontaneity, the pure birth of what arises, the paradisiac encounter, or the chance of such an encounter, between man and nature. The divine suppresses struggle and action. It does not go into praxis; it does not insert itself into this. It implies the suspension of praxis. Who is responsible for the murder of God? Philosophy and the philosopher. They did not succeed. The task was far better accomplished by religions themselves. By instituting and institutionalizing the divine, they destroyed it. They fixed it in rituals and dogmas. Yet the death of God does not put an end to him. Many people still serve God, or believe that they do. They kill him and carry his corpse. Among these murderers of the divine, we still live the death of God. And Christ?

He is the dead God, ritually killed each day by those who admit his presence, for whom he is deemed to die and who believe that they live in him, which confers on Christianity an unexpected meaning. In order to know the divine and its place in human historicity, history must go back beyond Christianity, towards the cradle of religions in the East. The Greeks already experienced the decline of the divine. Did the words 'Pan is dead' not mark the end of human youth along with that of the divine? The history of religions, accordingly, could be considered in its literality, instead of being translated into rationalist language – which does not rule out radical criticism. In the same way, the history of philosophy, like that of religions, forms part of the history of being and consciousness. Religion took its stand on transcendence; philosophy wagered on immanence. For religion, man contained in himself neither the reason of his being nor the reason of his reason, nor the meaning of his life. Philosophies proclaimed that man contained in himself his raison d'être. Yet they never managed to escape the dilemma raised by religion: 'Man does not have his being in himself. And this is why there is the being of man, human being. Between man and being there is a split, duality. Therefore, either man submits to being, or he rebels. Either he is attached to being, or detaches himself from it and condemns himself to nothingness, to defeat, to nihilism.'

In order to escape this dilemma, philosophy has itself to wither away, its properly philosophical concepts (immanence and transcendence, among others) have to be simultaneously discredited, and the situation of man conceived otherwise than in terms of these concepts. If the future of man is determined by the *appropriation* of his being, 'nature', the representation that separates man from his being must first be refuted; it is refuted in praxis. The split is superseded in action. Religion and philosophy disappear, with their conflict never resolved. What dies? – a serious question to which it is both easy and hard to respond. What dies? Everything that has lived. Everything that exists. The totality gathered under the concept of end.

Many philosophers have represented ending and death in terms of a biological or physiological pattern, borrowed from a relatively undeveloped representation of nature; death results from a natural or historical process, from becoming in general, placed by some at the highest degree of both reality and thought, and by others at the lowest. Among these thinkers, let us class Hegel and even Marx, although with them more than one thought overflows this pattern. From this time on, during the period of the withering of philosophy, death has been brought into relationship with the human condition, with being or the consciousness of man. Man is familiar with death. He knows that he is going to die. Art, and knowledge itself, resulted from the effort to escape death, to create something durable. Philosophy included both this effort and a long meditation, always recommenced, on ending, on death, and on their meaning.

Is meditation not still needed on accomplishment and end in relation to the works of man (neither man viewed as a being of 'nature', enslaved to 'processes', nor man viewed outside of this marvellous mechanical nature)? Works are neither nature as such nor men as such. Yet they are not to be understood outside of a relationship between man and the world and 'nature'. Works are never 'someone', image of their creator or of the Creator. And yet they have an originality close to that of human beings. They vary with the person or the individual. They are never completely 'something', no more than those magisterial 'realities' that are also creations and works: society, the city. Even the commodity and money, which *reify*, are not completely things, but relations pulled onto the path of things. It is important not to conceive them in terms of crude reification and objectivity. Works are also born, they live and die. They exist. It seems that they fall into determinable sectors or domains (religion, art, philosophy, politics, etc.), despite interferences or connections. It also seems that they all experience a rise, an apogee, a decline (or again, in 'natural' terms, a youth, a maturity and an ageing).

What is it that dies? First of all, that which defined the human – that defined him by something else. Along with God, there perish Truth, Beauty, Good, the three absolutes. Beauty, which proclaimed itself immortal, also dies. As likewise does being, the Being of theologians and philosophers, accessible to man *hic and nunc* even though beyond his grasp, Being that was simply being, being without nothingness, the infinite without finitude, as again that which founded (or seemed to found) authority over men, and that which defined (or seemed to define) perfection, happiness, joy, ideas and values.

Along with God, too, dies Justice. Far more than guarantor of the True, possessor of the Good and protector of the Beautiful, God was the Just and the Judge. He promised the final reversal, the redressing of wrongs, the end of lies and violence in the world. Justice and injustice basically lose their meaning along with the just and the last judgement. The arbitrariness of power has replaced justice and injustice. Injustice was formerly compelled, out of fear of the Judge, to cover itself with the mask of justice, thus to conceal itself and lie, to take on the appearance of justice, and so accept compromises and not break out into open daylight. Now, arbitrariness is unmasked. Justice is no longer anything but the decision of force. There is no more injustice. It has been suppressed. However, justifications fall together with judge and judgement, with justice and injustice. With the justification of force revealing itself, force ceases forever to be justified.

With the alienation of man, therefore, there falls that which defined man. God is dead – all is permitted. Nothing any longer limits cruelty, violence, arbitrariness. All is permitted – all is possible. And so man becomes possible. He advances in the desert where the death of God abandons him; he walks in the cosmic solitude through which he still bears on his shoulders the corpse of his God. He discovers his terrible availability.

By rendering himself capable and guilty of the murder of God (act and proof of freedom), man obliges himself to be. He is obliged, before Being, to attain Being. He redeems himself or releases himself from external being (other in relation to him), setting out on the hard road that leads him towards the possible: his free being.

The death of God signifies the murder of God. The murder of God signifies the end of the world, the divine, and the end of a moment of man. The end of an alienated moment of man indicates the birth of man to himself (or rather: the continuation of ends and births, worlds in formation, moments, successions, forms).

Birth and death go together. *Supersession* includes both these terms. Someone or something (always neither totally someone nor totally something) is born and dies. On the mortal side, what is born loses something: being, presence. It distances itself, emerges from being and loses it by arising. But it also wins something: and first of all itself.

Hence the necessary and difficult use of the concept of *alienation*. Becoming-world (world in becoming and becoming of the world) is at the same time alienating, alienated, dis-alienating – realizing and de-realizing. That which alienates in one sense, in another sense realizes and dis-alienates by making possible realization or actualization. The combat against alienation can reveal itself to be the path of a deeper alienation. Alienation, therefore, is never defined either by one of the terms in presence (in conflict in their reciprocal presence) or by the possibly productive pain of the conflict, but rather by a halt to superseding (the blockage of the possible).

How could a dialectical development be otherwise determined? The pattern of becoming by way of a single feature, one-sidedly, by rise and perfection, comes from Aristotelian metaphysics. It ends up in a facile rationalism, naïve optimism, the theory of continuous progress, bourgeois materialism, linear evolutionism. If there is dialectic, then development cannot fail to encompass gain and loss, fall-back and rise, growth and decline, death and birth.

Man is born as species by dying to the Universe (to the infinite). He falls from the infinite into the finite. He appears therefore in the light, on earth, at the end of a becoming without assignable limits in the past and in space, a cosmic, physical, organic becoming with the not entirely false appearance of a finality; for he indeed 'is' the end of what reflection calls: evolutionary process, evolution.

In order to come to the world, he dies to the world: to the inexhaustible power of cosmic forces, to the divine spontaneity of life, animal naivety and innocence. However, the world continues to surround the human species, and spontaneous life does not abandon it. This first birth continues for a long time. The world keeps a meaning; if it did not, then the sky and the sea, the earth and the light, would no longer have a *presence* for us. Yet the world affects people in two ways: by the bitter struggle to which it compels them, and by its gentle and favourable presence (the two aspects mingling in the imagination, in praxis, in reflection).

Analytical examination of the material conditions of organic life, or of its transition to consciousness, or of historical conditions (in particular, labour), translates into an exact language, that of reflection, the poetic description of the totality. This poetic description of totality links up with and rediscovers the immediacy of the lived (birth, etc.), which authenticates it. Would poetic description not attain the 'empirical universal', on condition of having been purified by reflection and superseding this reflection? The effective exactness of scientific knowledge coexists with other truths, on other levels, at another level, on another scale.

Man is born as individual by dying to the maternal world. This is the second moment of the individual, his second birth. For his birth turns out to be multiform (in reflexive empirical terms: biological, physiological, social, sexual, etc.). By way of a singular contrast, the individual human being, this product and term of an immense becoming, is born prematurely; he comes into the world incapable of sufficing for himself. This condemns him to dependence and plays a great role in his formation. He traverses his maternal world, which plunges into the depths of cosmic and animal life, which extends into childhood and longer still in images. In order to be born to himself, the individual cannot dispense with living – through many conflicts – the collapse and death of the maternal world. During this test, he takes charge of his being (his body, his sexuality, his faculties and aptitudes, his environment and his time) and his absence of being (his availability, his uncertainties, his growing consciousness); in sum, his individual and social aims, his tasks, his possibilities. He traverses an ambiguous experience: end and beginning, death of the cosmic, archaic, primitive, infantile, imaginary world – accession to freedom.

Is this *all*? No. What other births, and what other deaths, does the human take responsibility for on the journey to himself, that is to say, towards his possibility and his being-free? What moments does he traverse by living the necessary collapse of a partial world lived as total?

Nietzsche discovered this: man must also traverse the death of God (of the sacred and the accursed, the divine and the cunning, of beauty and ugliness, etc.), that is to say, the death of the Father. Why not add to these moments, distinct yet bound together and mingled – the cosmic, the maternal, the paternal or the divine – other moments, other tests? Such as:

> *philosophy* (which, like God, defined man through alienating him
>   by way of another truth);
> *economics and its history* (until worldwide communism);
> *politics and the state* (same remark: they define the human from
>   outside and from above);
> *art* (which defines man by striking illuminations, and the human by
>   exceptional instants, thus still external and alienating in the
>   effort towards deliverance).

If beauty proves to be moral, how could we believe in the eternity of the work, the divinity of art? Has not each great epoch of art been a funeral feast in honour of a departed moment?

Each form or 'structure' conquered by history and civilization thus contains both a victory and a vital degradation.

Should not each of these 'worlds' be lived as a test, and thus through to the end: to its term, its collapse? It follows from this that each of them collapses only by making itself explicit, by deploying *all* its virtualities, and only when it has fulfilled *everything*, summoned everything to itself: when it has proclaimed itself totality on the human (and thus finite) scale. In the course of this deployment, and only after this illusory and extravagant proclamation, the negativity that this world always already contained within itself asserts itself, gives it the lie, dismantles it, shatters it. Only an accomplished totality can reveal that it is not the totality. That is how the law of the world (the dialectical relationship between the infinite and the finite) shows itself. Each of these moments or each of these worlds is thus 'worlded [*mondialisé*]' or will be so [*mondialiser*].

Before man can complete his traverse, arrive at his own encounter, perceive himself face-to-face, each of these worlds will have to detach itself, absolutize itself, fetishize itself, generalize itself and claim to be 'worldwide'. In this sense, the history of religion illuminates world history: it contains the index of theoretical struggles (Marx). Every criticism commences and recommences with the criticism of religion; but every radical criticism illuminates the historicity of the human, that is to say, the totality of the trajectory: destiny – the destiny of freedom. After the criticism of religion comes the criticism of the state and politics. The two things link up and cut across one another.

The finitude of man and his relationship with the world show through in '*mondialisation*'. In this way the worldwide human is condemned to derision at the end of every accomplishment. Religion dominated the human world, and this was how the divine discredited and destroyed itself. *Mundus est immundus*. Once worlded and worldly [*mondialisé et mondain*], God withered away. The stink of this decay still offends our noses. But already 'something else' was advancing, pushing away the rotting corpse, proclaiming itself superior to the divine, worlding [*se mondialisant*] in its turn. What? Economics (productive labour) and politics. Thus, the state, a worldwide monster, the coldest of cold monsters. And aestheticism. And technicity.

The idolatry of the state, the greatest fetish on earth after God, certifies for us the death of the divine. The *mondialisation* of politics and the state is pursued through fear and anger, hatred and revolt, in flows of blood, a path marked by monuments of pride and arrogance. It is accompanied by a radical critique of political alienation (Marx). The history of the state also contains a résumé of world history: the summary of practical struggles.

There are other worlds both imaginary and real (which their superseding shows to be simultaneously both real and imaginary): that of the imagination itself and of art, or that of philosophical abstraction.

The becoming-philosophy of the world, and the becoming-world of philosophy (Marx), already almost accomplished with the Hegelian system and the state that this justified, is perfected with the officialised philosophy of the socialist states, with the *mondialisation* of the state and politics. We thus live the exasperation and withering away of these inseparable abstractions: philosophy and the state, speculative representation and political representation.

We are also traversing the collapse of the aesthetic imaginary that reactivates outdated moments (the cosmic, the archaic, the divine, the maternal, the infantile) of the lived. Modern aestheticism alienates human living by subordinating to these moments. The abstract and the imaginary, when mixed together, exacerbate one another; they condemn themselves together to destruction and self-destruction. In terms closer to the empirical: the mass media signify the devouring consumption of a culture piled up and condemned to an end at the very moment of its victory; they also signify the worldwide enervation of an abstraction become palpable, of imaginary intervening in the lived to the point of confusion, of the political and the public tracking the private and penetrating it. This signifies both extreme fetishism and the profanation of fetishes, the sullying and deterioration of both the abstract sublime and the bewildered imaginary. Mass communications are mystificatory and go hand in hand with incommunicability. In the same way, the fetishism of language goes hand in hand with the destruction of language. The confusion of the private and the public accompanies their aggravated split, their clash, and their mutual destruction.

Need it be said that for a long time we have (to a high degree) suspended not judgement but irony?

By pursuing the most adventurous hypothesis, we have arrived at assertions. Do these depend on that hypothesis? Perhaps they break free from this after a certain articulation. In order to grasp the path taken by human works and their relationship, it is unnecessary to accept the death (and murder) of God in the literal sense. It is enough to admit that philosophy constituted itself against religion and also against the state. Each time that it boldly waged its combat, the struggle strengthened it. But it was unable to avoid compromise and worse than compromise: reconciliations, 'symbioses'. Philosophy was thus unable to prevail over its adversaries. It developed at the same time both against them and with them. Its fortunes followed the alliance with them, also reaching its own apogee. It was not even able to demonstrate their fate, accomplishment and end. In order to conceive this historical destiny, it was necessary already to conceive the superseding of philosophy, that is to say, philosophy as a work.

There has always been in philosophy ideology, utopia, myth (in the contemporary generalized and rather vague sense of this word, which denotes a certain form of illusion and no longer, as in ancient Greece, a concrete relationship between man and nature, perceived or transposed, by way of figures, images and symbols). A representation either disdaining or ignoring its presuppositions as well as its connection with praxis, distorted and mutilated reflection of the 'real' in its movement, philosophy was an ideology. An interpretation of the world aiming in vain to transform it by the force of spirit alone, the quest for a coherent purity in a 'world' that was contradictory to say the least, and perhaps chaotic, it was utopia. Containing a representation of the origins of man and a projection of this past towards future perfection, it was both utopian and mythical. The share of myth increased in the period of withering, precisely because 'philosophy' as such, above all after Hegel, appeared as a history, a concatenation, and the philosopher as a face. There is now a myth of the philosopher.

What ancestors, or what laggards of ill omen, could have written: 'the philosopher will be leader'? The truth is rather that the philosopher stands close to the Father, and the philosophical attitude to paternalism. Like the fleshly father, the paterfamilias, the philosopher begets; he educates with force and gentleness, with an iron fist (the system) or a velvet glove (persuasive discourse, rhetoric). Through his disciples, he summons crowds to him, and increasingly what he believes to be men as a whole. The philosopher is the spiritual Father. The disciples stand between stubborn repetition of formulas learned and little understood, and contemplation of the inaccessible model: the Master, and through him the True. They stand in the full flood of mimesis. This is how the true discourse, that of the philosopher, is transmitted from generation to generation (or would be transmitted, if the philosophical model were successful).

If the philosopher borrows from fatherhood something of its prestige and power, philosophy has rendered a similar service to paternity. The son is son of his father, philosophical discourse has repeated since Aristotle, thus setting aside woman, nature, society, that is to say, praxis. The Father contributes the form and stamps it on unformed matter, on empty and pure potential: woman. The Father possesses the Idea and ideas as part of his inheritance. The virtual and spiritual germ that he receives and transmits eminently contains the specific and social characteristics of human being: stable essence, entelechy, final cause and supreme reason. Philosophy, this final cause and reason, is the system (finally true). Thus philosophical fatherhood and family fatherhood have supported one another over the centuries; each of them theorized customs or norms that were debatable and are now past their time.

The Father did have his grandeur. In patriarchal times, progenitor and chief, he led a community that he served, and on occasion used and abused. This grandeur has disappeared, like that of the Knight or the Prophet, like many grandeurs. All that remain are traces: words and expressions, images, symbols, ethical models. These semantic traces are sufficient to maintain the role, in conjunction with some functional survivals. And yet the victimized or disdained elements – woman, child, society – have regained their 'reality', sometimes in exaggerated or illusory form. After the disappearance of the functional, forms persist (particularly in language) and institutions prolong what has historically dissolved. The Father, like the Philosopher, becomes institutional. Psychoanalysis contributes elements to the explanation and criticism of the myth of the father. But it does not deploy this as myth, and its critique is insufficiently radical. The sociological and political aspect is lacking, as well as the link with a praxis wider than the treatment of neuroses.

In this sense, socialism such as it is, and despite (or on account of) its most debatable and most defective sides, is indeed at the head of the progress. By proclaiming Stalin Father of the peoples, it has struck and discredited fatherhood far more than the most virulent anarchist proclamations attacking the family. By making philosophy official, by openly making philosophical reason raison d'état, and the philosophical system the political system (openly and practically, and not just in the abstract as Hegel had done), it has contributed to the death of the philosopher and the metamorphosis of philosophy. In the same fashion, it is leading art to destruction by self-destruction. It is clearing the way with the state as its bulldozer.

In the capitalist countries, philosophy is institutionalized only in the limited context of the university, culture and pedagogy. It is taught, and this teaching is left a wide margin of freedom, with the result that in certain conjunctures it offers a refuge to freedom. In the socialist countries, a philosophy is officialized that has been made obligatory. The end of philosophy is close, on condition that the point of Marxism, as radical critique, is sharpened and directed against the enormity of official Marxism as state ideology – and on condition that authentic Marxist theory, that of the realization of philosophy in the course of its superseding, is restored to the first rank.

Face-to-face, vis-à-vis, we have the myths of non-philosophical life, that is to say, the everyday, and the philosophical myth, that of the philosopher. On the side of the non-philosophical world, we discover an amazing trilogy: the myth of the father, the myth of adult age, the myth of entry into life. These three myths are three aspects of a single representation with its foundation long in the past, which has become abstract and phantasmagorical. The Father is the adult par excellence. He trains the adults who replace him. The adult is the man made, complete, achieved. He is, strongly and powerfully. He is made because he has made himself, accepting life as it is, with its limits, but fulfilling what can be fulfilled within these limits. He has put an end to the uncertainties and follies of youth; he is form stamped on this unformed matter, on empty and pure potential: life, adolescence. He has the fortune of being at the same time the classical type par excellence and (at least according to Péguy) 'the adventurer of modern times'. To assimilate this plenitude, he has had to enter into life as one enters the father's house by crossing the threshold, entering through the front door, leaving outside his errors and illusions, a well brought-up child or a prodigal son.[35]

In the face of these everyday myths that are all one, the philosopher proclaims himself Father, eternal adult, image of fully achieved man, announcing this, promulgating it, helping it to be born. He describes it and gives it a face, in two senses: in himself as human being, and in the system. He manages the entry into life, not of this or that particular child but of the human species.

The myths of philosophy and those of everyday life stand face-to-face. They reflect one another as each other's mirrors, and mirrors of a situation in the process of being superseded, precisely that in which the non-philosophical everyday and the non-everyday philosophy confront one another, render one another derisory, lead one another into the same slippage.

The diverse defenders of philosophy seek in vain to save themselves by clutching at science, art, or simply art criticism, occultism, whatever they can. 'The function of philosophy,' wrote Léon Brunschvicg, 'has lost nothing of its import and its effectiveness, because it scrupulously attaches itself closely to exactness, subtlety, the complexity of scientific development.'[36] In vain. The philosopher has lost all function, except when he becomes the promoter of official ideology and raison d'état. He has lost his essential function, that of radical criticism.

We can understand now the ever-more-frequent revolts against the philosopher and philosophy. The subtlety of Nietzsche, still philosophical, is increasingly remote. It was only a transition. Here is the virulent revolt:

> I turned away from philosophy when it became impossible for me to
> discover in Kant any human weakness ... Compared to music,
> mysticism, and poetry, philosophical activity proceeds from a diminished impulse and a suspect depth, prestigious only for the timid and

---

35 Cf. Georges Lapassade, *L'entrée dans la vie*, Paris: Éditions de Minuit, 1963.

36 Léon Brunschvicg, 'L'orientation du rationalisme', *Revue de métaphysique et de morale*, vol. 27, 1920, pp. 261–342, p. 340ff.

the tepid . . . The philosophical exercise is not fruitful; it is merely honourable . . . a *métier* without fate which pours voluminous thoughts into our neutral and vacant hours, the hours refractory to the Old Testament, to Bach, and to Shakespeare . . . The real problems begin only after having ranged or exhausted it.[37]

And then we have cynical revolt and parody. It is just as if it were possible to take one or another famous philosophical text and replace certain key words by others (for example, 'being' by 'bullshit [*connerie*]'), while the discourse preserves a sense (invariances) throughout this permutational game:

> Faithful to the Heideggerian theory according to which human bullshit has itself proclaimed what it is on the basis of the world and the ego, it is always by way of the density of a field of bullshit that my presentation to myself is made: this procedure presents, among its other advantages, that of avoiding the confusion between 'bullshit-immediate presence to self' and the 'bullshit-subject' whose revelation requires a mediation.[38]

A lighter parody, but equally destructive, can be found almost everywhere – as when, for example, the weekly magazine *Elle* reminds us how Chanel reinvented woman and inspired a whole new world of Chanelism:

> Thanks to Chanel, women and girls have obtained a philosophy.[39]

Philosophy and the philosopher had their grandeur and their beauty, like Beauty itself. Today, these figures serve to cover something that can easily do without it, but that cannot appear without rousing unease, horror or anxiety: everyday life, power, technicality, profitability, and so forth. No one needs philosophy or the philosopher anymore. The

---

37   Emil Cioran, 'Farewell to Philosophy', *A Short History of Decay*, New York: Arcade, 2012, pp. 47–8.

38   Georges Filloux, *Pour une dialectique de la connerie*, Paris: A. Devrue et Cie, n.d. [1964].

39   *Elle*, September 1963.

latter, alone in his reflection, sets himself up as a criterion of knowledge, or wisdom, or 'being'. 'We' know, however, that he is there. Like a watcher in a night deprived of any sacred character, a night without stars, a night without fears, as if in a vast warehouse.

The philosopher still claims to undertake unending research, bottomless fear, unlimited expectation, sustaining a double illusion. He no longer meditates, he reflects. He teaches philosophy; he discourses on other philosophers, for other philosophers. By *logology* and *egology*, he perilously approaches pleonasm. He does not really watch. If he awaits, it is with the same waiting, the same hope or the same despair as other people, those of the everyday [*les autres, les quotidiens*].

CHAPTER 4

Opening of the Testament: Inventory of the Legacy

From philosophy in general, understood as philosophical critique of the real, and from the Marxist critique of philosophy, we retain first of all the idea of a *radical critique*, without hesitation or compromise, of the existing in all domains. From this perspective, excesses of criticism (hypercritical points) seem less dangerous than failings.

We shall then be compelled, not to prove this attitude by philosophical arguments, but to render it effective by *theoretical acts*: by a critique of this or that aspect of the existent, a critique whose effectiveness can consist only in that it opens and indicates the possibility of a practical transformation of this 'existent', up until now unshaken or passing as unshakeable.

A number of concepts stand out from the totality of the philosophical tradition. Let us list these without claiming to be exhaustive: consciousness, knowledge, reason, freedom, world, man, form, content, beauty, truth, nature, logic, dialectic, alienation, creation, and so on.

What does the shattering of classical philosophy mean, as regards these concepts and their use? Does it signify that the concepts have lost points of imputation or application? In no way. If they all refer to *homo sapiens*, or man supposedly so, this *homo sapiens* does not disappear. These concepts, to which Marx added, while spelling out earlier virtualities, the particularly important ones of praxis (social practice) and appropriation (appropriation by man of external nature and his own nature), have entered the language. They have even penetrated to a certain point into praxis itself.

What the end of traditional philosophy prohibits is the attempt to systematize these concepts around a speculative principle, old or new.

What this event prescribes is seeking the meaning, the content, the limits of concepts, that is to say, their conditions of validity. In other words, the end of the old philosophy prescribes a primordial task: the critical inventory of philosophical concepts and their confrontation with the praxis in which they already figure as conscious elements, critical up to a certain point. For example, the concept of freedom. The confrontation will thus follow a double movement: critique of (philosophical) concepts by praxis, critique of praxis by (philosophical) concepts. This presupposes a clarification that bears first of all on this fundamental concept: praxis (social practice), a concept revealed by Marx but not completely spelled out by him, and rather obscured by subsequent Marxism.

This clarification must also bear on the instruments and means of theoretical labour: formal logic and dialectical reason, their relationships, their areas of validity and application. From research already made, it results that one concept deserves particular attention: the concept of alienation. What is its scope? What does it enable us to understand? What does it enable us to change? Is it the essential legacy of philosophy, the instrument par excellence of contemporary thought, the fundamental means of critical knowledge and the transformation of the existing world? Does it not also have its limits, and a confined area of validity?

Finally, a last point, philosophy, which does not bequeath us a 'conception of the world', that is to say, a system established to the point that it only needs perfecting in detail, does leave us a *project of man*. This project, or if you want to express it in more picturesque terms, this model, this sketch of human possibility, Marx began to extract from an enormous collapsing block: Hegelianism.

As far as capitalist society and the praxis of the bourgeoisie are concerned, economics and production in the narrow (material) sense of political economy play a privileged role. Economics and the critique of political economy thus move to the front of the stage in *Capital*, displacing the other aspects of praxis, relegating to second rank the wider notion (poetic, or rather poietic) of the production of man by himself, by his multiple works, in the course of his history. But the project adopted by Marx, and its realization by way of an economic transformation, only acquires its meaning by being related first of all to philosophy as a whole – to the notions of freedom, reason, accomplishment, and so forth – and then to the earlier project of a poet-philosopher, Fourier. In the theoretical ensemble known as Marxism, one 'Fourierist' idea – that of overcoming the division of labour – is at least as important right away as the discovery, in capitalist praxis, of surplus-value (the economic exploitation of the proletariat by means of money, which at the same time makes this possible and conceals it). Looking more closely, it is more important because it is initial and generative. This theoretical procedure is to be found in Marx's *1844 Manuscripts*. In order to understand alienation, Marx reconstitutes the path of dis-alienation. 'Fourier,' he writes, 'conceived labour levelled down, fragmented, and therefore unfree as the source of private property's *perniciousness* . . . which is to be annulled "as such" (Proudhon).'[1]

Fourier *imagined* the subsequent superseding of the division of labour, that is to say, his project was expressed in images, utopian dreams. As Marx notes in the text just quoted, Fourier imagined this superseding in terms of *agricultural labour*, conceived as labour par excellence. He dreamed the life of his phalanstery in terms of a return to man's natural origins. The superseding of the division of labour is thus presented as a poetic, or rather, poietic, project, founded on a posited and presupposed place between the original and the virtual, on the future reconciliation between man, 'nature', and natural operation on nature. The image of the past is projected onto the future; the memory of what man was before the division of labour is changed into a project of superseding. What remains to be shown, conceived and brought to conceptual level is the possibility of this superseding in industrial labour. That is what Marx did.

As economist and historian, Marx developed the full scope of the theory of the division of labour. Through this division, in fact, labour comes into conflict with itself. It becomes both simple and complex, individual and social, fragmentary and general [*global*], quantitative and qualitative. By being divided, it becomes technical and social, not without conflict between the demands of its technical division and its

---

1 'Economic and Philosophical Manuscripts of 1844', *MECW*, vol. 3, p. 294, emphasis in original.

social division, between labour in the general [*général*] sense, the particularities of social labour, and its singular (individual) characteristics. These contradictions stimulate social development, with its difficulties and misfortunes. Marx shows the successive separations of labour between the sexes, between town and country, between manual and intellectual labour, between the *technical* demands of the instruments and the *social* demands of organized production, between groups and classes. Philosophy itself is a product of the division of labour, like ideology in general, given that the representation of the world falls to specialized groups. Hence philosophical alienation, a particular and significant case of general alienation.

As for the superseding of the division of labour in industrial production, this presupposes first of all that machines take over technologically divided labour, and secondly a culture or rather a style of life that overcomes the social division of labour. This presupposes in turn the suppression of classes in society, leaving only those inequalities arising from irreducible differences between individuals and groups.

The idea of superseding the division of labour thus appears as a *theoretical* hypothesis that empirical observations have to support, and as a *practical* programme that analyses concerning praxis have subsequently to verify, and of course lead towards realization.

Marx took up the essential core of the philosophical project of man, showing its limits and also its defeat in the existing world. He criticized on the one hand the philosophical idea (or ideal) from the standpoint of the existing real (capitalist praxis), and on the other hand the existing real from the standpoint of the philosophical idea. Hence the project of a double superseding: that of existing praxis, so as to realize the philosophical project of the total human being, and that of the philosophical project, so as to retrieve this project from philosophical abstraction and realize it in a revolutionary praxis.

Classical philosophy came to an end as philosophy. It transmitted to us, outside of its perishable shells, a *kernel both rational and real*, that is to say, *realizable* under certain conditions: the figure of man.

We have to reconsider these indications that have been left aside for a whole century, that is to say, take up from its origin the incomplete spelling out of the philosophical project. Between the fundamental project and the radical critique, there is a reciprocity of perspective. Criticism opens an outlet; the project shows itself in this opening.

We must declare right away that the point here is not to question this kernel of Marxist thought by subjecting it to the demands of an unlimited research and an undefined problematic, uncertain in both its presuppositions and its conclusions, without foundation or end. Far from problematizing this kernel we are going to strengthen it, as it is also a question of superseding the philosophical dilemma: either undefined research or dogmatism.

Between all the changes that have affected social practice over the last century, some concern our proposal more directly. We retain those in which we can see a kind of warning: the urgency, in *praxis*, of having to transform this praxis or at least decide to do so. This urgency and these decisions consolidate, rather than undo, the theoretical kernel and fundamental project received from Marx.

Among the changes that matter to us here, let us emphasize first of all the nuclear danger. Despite technological precautions and political compromises, this persists and will persist for a long time – and with it the threat of death that hovers over all humanity. The differences between war and peace collapse; the boundaries between them are wiped away. A strange test: supreme alienation and perhaps a premise for total dis-alienation. Is this not the monumental and barbaric gate, the dangerous threshold, beyond which something other will be born? Through the danger on a planetary scale, philosophical representations of being and nothingness, of life and death, are reduced in fact to their state of abstraction. Life and death are fogged and mingled. They are 'lived' otherwise than in representation. Their conflict in life calls for superseding. Threatened at every moment, we are in a state of survival: we survive. We then perceive that the whole of humanity has always been in a state of survival. In groups or isolated, men struggled to survive by seizing from matter or from other men the means to avoid perishing. Life has not yet begun. Will history, according to the Marxist project, undergo a qualitative mutation and become time dominated by thought (whereas up to now technology has only dominated space)? Will we, with Marx, recognize what we call 'history', which includes the deep historicity of man, as the prehistory of man and the mixture with nature, human struggles still an extension of the struggles of species?

Whatever happens, the mutation will take place under the sign of mortal threat. This threat is accompanied by contradictory phenomena: a general (apparent) passivity, an aspiration (real, that is to say, entering into the real) for 'something else', a rejection of the fait accompli and of possible catastrophe. These phenomena only have their meaning in and through the risk that, threatening the whole planet, contributes to constituting worldness [*mondialité*] in praxis. With life and ruin mingling in a conflict that is hidden but acute, a new life needs to arise from this. The threat (and more than the threat: the constant actuality of planetary destruction) precedes entry into planetary life.

We cannot conceive of humanity emerging from the era of nuclear danger without a radical mutation of ideas and representations, of ethics and aesthetics. The questioning of man and the planet cannot but transform man and his relationship with the Earth that he occupies.

The aleatory intervenes and can be recognized in all domains. Each moment is seen as a gain, a chance. It has been won. It has a kind of gratuitousness. It is accepted as a reward or gratification. Will this dangerous game, this mortal game that man plays with the world and with himself, not create new participations of man in humanity and in the 'world'? Does it not create, in the threat that lies over humanity, a new image of the earth, of life, of the universe?

At the same gate, in the same opening, the possibilities of life and those of death press together. The dialectical unity of life and death, of being and nothingness, no longer presents itself as a speculative vision. The nuclear danger appears as the reverse image of the abundance made possible by technology, as also of the cybernetic automatism that seeks to super-organize society. It puts these in question. It tends to create, in the negative, the world unity that cannot but become 'positive'.[2] By this gigantic procedure we are already well beyond philosophers and philosophies.

One modification is our main concern: the recent consolidation, the crystallization (a word that falsely evokes transparency) of the

---

2   Karl Jaspers perceived some of these questions, as did Heidegger.

everydayness characteristic of modern societies. As for the appropriate label for these societies, societies that we observe around us and that we hear talk of when they are more distant, we can postpone this for the time being. Industrial society or technological society? Society of abundance or of leisure? Society of labour or of non-labour? State capitalism? Socialism? Civilization of the image? Era of the gadget, the jukebox, of nylon, plastic, the atom bomb, idols and 'celebrities'? We shall see along the way what justifies or refutes these labels.

At all events, this everydayness is being consolidated. Certainly, there was a 'life' in the past: the repetition of habitual gestures, eating, drinking, sleeping, working. For the majority of people it was a hard job to gain this life that was hardly more than survival. But this life of each day was enveloped by great cycles and systems: the months, the seasons, the years, life and death. Religion, the sense of the sacred, later morality, penetrated it and metamorphosed it. What contemporary sociology and ethnography call 'cultures' (applying to other societies a term that has acquired a precise meaning in our modernity, a procedure that does not avoid misunderstandings and anachronisms) transfigured life: their concrete 'systems' extended into the everyday. More exactly, they were not systems, cultures in the present-day sense (in which 'culture' becomes information, and is dispersed in its dissemination). They were *styles* of life, of works, of civilizations.

To understand this better, let us take a step back, though not too far. A century or a century and a half ago, every 'made' man had reached masculine maturity. He put away the dreams of adolescence as renunciation and resignation. He sought to realize himself in an everyday life tackled with experience and enriched by this experience. With adult age he attained a certain plenitude: a beloved wife, a trade, children to educate. The home was the symbol of this plenitude.

This was the end point and the meaning of a period of childishness and adolescence: apprenticeship for life. After this apprenticeship, maturity began. We recognize here the theme of the *Bildungsroman*, and especially Goethe's *Wilhelm Meister*.

Today, everyday life no longer realizes. It relegates to the rank of mythic images apprenticeship (life is learned quickly; it is enough to let oneself go, passively), adult age, fatherhood, entry into life.

Georg Lukács, eminent thinker that he was, conceived his *Theory of the Novel* without taking history into account. Goethe's novel, according to him, had as its theme 'the reconciliation of the problematic individual, guided by his lived experience of the ideal, with concrete social reality', whereas *A Sentimental Education* contains only 'the Romanticism of disillusionment'.[3] But something took place in the interval between these two authors, Goethe and Flaubert. What then, if not the beginnings of the establishment of the everyday?

Today, everydayness involves the split of 'real' life into separate, functional, organized sectors (structured as such): work (in a firm or office), private life (in the family, the place of habitation), leisure. The separation of these three domains can be read on the ground in human agglomerations as they have become, and as they are constructed. In the town and the city, these aspects of human life were formerly united (not without certain serious inconveniences). Today, in their separation, they are linked by common characteristics, constituting in this way the unity of the everyday. What are these characters that the separate sectors share by way of an implacably analytic praxis? At work, passivity, the inevitable acceptance of decisions taken elsewhere and handed down from above; in private life, the various conditionings, the manufacturing of the consumer by the manufacturer of objects; in leisure, the 'world' made into image and spectacle. In brief, everywhere passivity, non-participation.

Thus, everydayness is increasingly reduced to the repetitive (which is no longer that of the great cosmic rhythms and cycles, but that of linear time, mechanical gestures, and movements commanded by signals). In leisure time, by the intermediary of images, individuals and groups *imitate* (at a distance like abstract objects) 'celebrity' models. On its own level, or more exactly as a level, everyday life establishes and consolidates itself. It is *systematized*. It is subjected or controlled (in particular by the networks of circulation and communications, and by their technological demands).

For certain people, and it is no bad thing to emphasize this point, everydayness is simply the *residue* that persists when everything that

---

3 Georg Lukács, *Theory of the Novel*, London: Merlin Press, 1978, pp. 132 and 124.

is determined activity (functional, institutional) is removed. This residue would then have no particular interest. It simply has to be accepted as such.

To this we reply first of all that the functional and the institutional are not situated only in the higher spheres of the everyday. They enter into it. Bureaucracy, for example, is linked on one side to the state and on the other to everydayness. It introduces state forms [*l'étatique*], whose structure and activity it imitates, into the everyday. Besides, the separation of everydayness into sectors, this modern split in the human, is also functionalized and institutionalized. We encounter here the notion of 'residue', and raise a question that will recur several times again: is this 'residue' not what is most precious? We shall need to repeat this question apropos history, poetry, dialectics, tragedy and also the individual.

Everydayness raises new questions. And first of all, this one: do we accept it in its modalities, both strange (alienated) and trivial, inhuman and familiar, disjointed and monotonous? Do we submit to it as a destiny, or can and should we envisage a mastery of the everyday as a dimension of freedom, a radical transformation of man become everyday and defined up to a certain point by everydayness? There is a theoretical decision to be made here, a project to bring to light, a word to pronounce.

Should not the old watchwords, shining at the threshold of a thought that sought to be no longer speculative and purely abstract – Marx's thesis to *transform the world instead of interpreting it*, Rimbaud's injunction to *change life* – take on a new meaning, more precise and broader, in the face of the everyday established as such?

When he emerged from the spheres of speculation and began to explore praxis, Marx brought dialectical analysis close to the everyday; but the proletariat of his time was not yet immersed in the everyday. The honour of labour, the ethics of the trade, still veiled the triviality and humiliation of the everyday, which since then have borne down with their full weight on the working class (even if the material situation of the proletariat has improved in the major industrial countries). For Marx, proletarian *negativity* challenged bourgeois society as totality, and yet had to promote the everyday life of the proletariat in its positivity. Today, this challenge can take and has to take new forms, in particular because working-class confrontation is hesitant. A new problem has arisen. Knowledge of the everyday, of human poverty and wealth, do not precede the theoretical project of its transformation. This project is not deduced from knowledge of the everyday, as a consequence from its premises. Knowledge and the project of transformation go together. If one of them precedes the other, this belongs to the project and the challenge. We cannot forget that for hundreds of millions of humans, perhaps billions, the question is not to change everyday life but to reach an everyday life. But we do not forget either that Marx's revolutionary project only made sense for the advanced countries and the most advanced sectors of these countries. Thought only comprehends the everyday if there is unease and refusal, practical desire and will to change it. In order to know and understand it, we have to restore into a whole this reality that is both fragmentary and monotonous. We have to want, obscurely or clearly, to reconstruct a totality. Knowledge in act expresses itself in images, those of a metamorphosed life. At the same time, this knowledge has to pass by way of a praxis of transformation. The act that inaugurates knowledge and praxis is poietic: simultaneous creator of concepts and images, knowledge and dream.

Marx was unable to observe more than the first indications of an immense transformation. He noted the anti-natural, factitious, practically abstract character of the great modern cities, in which he saw at the same time how in the factories, the natural context of proletarian action, the working-class population was concentrating and becoming aware of itself. In the highly industrialized countries, the ancient conflictual relationship between town and country (which Marx defined as both a fundamental division of labour and as one of the first forms of the struggle of social groups and classes) is tending today to be resolved in an unexpected fashion. The town absorbs the countryside – though not without the resistance of those affected, or without convulsions. In a short time from now, in the most developed regions and countries, the rural population will undoubtedly have disappeared, making way for town-dwellers engaged in agricultural production with improved methods and industrial technologies. Agriculture is being aligned with industry, and steadily ceasing to constitute a distinct sector of the economy, almost autonomous on account of its technical backwardness. Cities and agro-cities will replace villages, reduced to an antediluvian, folkloric or touristic existence.

The urban phenomenon is identified first of all with the worldwide character of the results of technology. But this image is far too simple. By the process of growth, the city has itself shattered;[4] it is perhaps in the process of disappearing. This is a hypothesis not exempt from risk, not verified up until now, but seductive and fruitful, precisely as an extreme strategic hypothesis. Demographic pressure, industrialization and the influx of people devoted to 'services' (the so-called 'tertiary' sector, which includes the free professions and the bureaucracy as well as commerce) transform cities into enormous human conglomerations that no longer have any form. They are called 'cities' out of habit. The urban phenomenon is dislocated by its development. The city, by its immoderate growth, projects fragments and debris far and wide. It is surrounded by suburbs, and beyond these suburbs by bungalows and housing estates. Whether the bungalows are modest or luxurious, whether the blocks of flats are large, small or medium, they no longer have much in common with the city.

Throughout this time, the heart of the city deteriorates, is bureaucratized or simply decays. Will not the city be a social form almost as remote as the village? Human time and space change. Is the breakup of the city not symbolic of the end of ancient works and a new relationship (to be created) between man and his works? History, a history that we live without perceiving it (except in a trivial fashion: housing crisis, traffic congestion, nervous exhaustion, etc.), relegates to the past the magnificent forms that we still believe we feel around us. The magnificent image of the City [*Cité*], which still serves as an illusion to populate the human desert, must not wipe out history and actuality. When society and the state coincided with the city [*ville*], this was the preeminent work of praxis, the most perfect thing. But the state was free and not the individual. Urban democracy, still more in the Middle Ages than in antiquity, was the democracy of unfreedom. Free praxis

---

4   Cf. E. A. Gutkind, *The Twilight of Cities*, New York: Free Press, 1962; also *The Exploding Metropolis*, a collection of articles from *Fortune* magazine, New York: Fortune, 1958.

and consciousness do not recognize themselves in this perfect thing. The breakup of such a form cannot be accomplished without nostalgia. Must it not be accomplished? The preeminent work, the most perfect thing, dies and makes way for an absence at the heart of which men become things pure and simple – objects of multiple manipulations – and where, despite all this, the *means* of an immense novelty are accumulating without assigned goal.

Ever since its beginnings, competitive capitalism has sullied, eviscerated and mutilated towns, the magnificent legacy from the time when society and the City stood in close relation. At a given moment of history, town, society and civilization coincided in a unity. There was an urban 'system', concrete and practical. Later on, bourgeois society still projected itself on this terrain, with cities, monuments, state or cultural buildings. Subsequently, state capitalism and, more generally, industrialization under state aegis, brought the urban phenomenon to its end point: enormity, collapse. The city as 'system' terminates in a kind of explosion that leaves only the debris of what was great and beautiful. It is as if this supreme abstraction had to be reached in order to invent the concrete style of life, as if it was necessary to pass through the end of known forms to commence the unknown and one day definitively cut the umbilical cord that ties the individual to social constraints, both protective and oppressive for him.

It is in this practical context that the everyday establishes itself, and it is here that everydayness can and must change. The end of the city, the dislocation of what was the finest work and dwelling place of man, gives us notice to create new works [*oeuvres*]. The hard crystallization of the everyday gives us notice to reject illusory transfigurations (by art or image) and effectively transform the everyday. These two imperatives are connected and mutually reinforcing. It is here, in the debris of city and life, that there has to be poetic creation, or rather *it is not here*. It is elsewhere, in other forms, which remain to be invented by using the immense resources that are wasted today in monstrous pseudo-creations: 'conurbations', clusters, 'estates' of whatever size. What is currently called 'urbanism' is nothing more than an ideology (that of technocratic groups), designed, like any ideology, to mask real problems, propose false solutions, dissimulate the 'real', though not without revealing it involuntarily.

The idea of the end of the city seems far more productive and creative than that of its continuation or its 'modernization'. Especially as it does not lend itself to 'prospective' studies that are technologically and operationally useful.

It pertains to metaphilosophical thought to imagine and propose forms, or rather a style, that can be practically constructed and that realize the philosophical project, by metamorphosing everyday life. All means are suitable for the service of this new totality, at least in the most favourable hypothesis, that in which the project encounters forces capable of realizing it by changing the refusal to accomplish it into creativity.

Superseding of philosophy, connection of its themes with modifications (which some people will call 'sociological', but which in our view overspill and encompass what is called sociological research) in praxis: this is a first sense of the word 'metaphilosophy'. The project of a radical transformation of everydayness cannot be distinguished from the superseding of philosophy and its realization. Philosophical man and the philosophical project of man do not accept the everyday. Everyday man, non-philosophical man, is opposed to philosophical man and the philosophical project of man. It is from their contradiction, their confrontation, that the mutation of both will emerge.

CHAPTER 5

The Search for Heirs

Before 1848, romanticism – the Romantic movement – established a communication and a poetical–dramatic communion between groups disdained by bourgeois society: women, youth, 'intellectuals'. It inaugurated, at the heart of bourgeois society, an anti-bourgeois 'shadow society', mysterious and radiant, devoted to love and theatrical declamation. This lived utopia, this naïve and subtle revolt, carried with it the hope for a near end to bourgeois philistinism. In France, romanticism went further than in Germany (where it was content to dream about everyday life, as in Hoffmann's *The Golden Pot*,[1] or else escape into the depths of nature). In France there was a romanticism of the left, represented among other people by the first sociologists: Saint-Simon and Fourier. Marx borrowed certain elements of his thought from this subversive and critical left romanticism.

From 1850, and the defeat of the revolution of 1848, poetic thought in France embarked on a different path. There now appeared, confusedly but in depth, the link between recording and rejecting everyday life, between the themes of the everyday and the city, between these themes and a metaphilosophical exploration of the modern world. This connection is explicit in Baudelaire. The poet's ironic notes on philosophy in general and Hegelianism more specifically (in *Fusées, Mon coeur mis à nu*, etc.) do not go as far as the critiques of Marx or Kierkegaard, but they point in a similar direction.[2] What the poet turns his gaze towards is no longer natural beauty and eternal truth;

---

1   EN: E. T. A. Hoffmann, *The Golden Pot and Other Tales*, edited and translated by Ritchie Robertson, New York: Oxford University Press, 1992.

2   EN: *Fusées, Mon coeur mis à nu* is an 1851 work by Charles Baudelaire, translated by Norman Cameron in *My Heart Laid Bare, and Other Prose Writings*, edited by Peter Quennell, London: Weidenfeld & Nicolson, 1950.

what he listens to is not the divine word. He seeks poetry in what is fleeting and momentary, in the transitory, the everyday: fashion, the spectacle of the street, a Paris changing more quickly than a mortal heart, Parisian paintings. And yet the everyday, the source of poetic vibration, is intolerable. The city has these two aspects; poetry and horror. It is where the *fleurs du mal* grow.[3] It is pure facticity and factitious purity, art and artifice.

Baudelaire's most vibrant poems, the simplest ones, those in which he does not exploit the satanism of an abandoned Christian and powerless anti-bourgeois terrorist, speak the city. Does the great myth of the city derive from what man discovers here, or from the fact that the city begins to overspill the human scale? The one does not prevent the other, but the second event tends to cover over the first. Baudelaire reveals in the city a second nature, which imitates the first but in order and beauty. This second nature is made up of stones, water, mirrors, metals. It is beautiful, superhuman, inhuman. Where does the poet place himself? He dwells above the city, that giant presence, landscape of stone, monster of humanity and inhumanity. He is at the level of the church bells, listening to their solemn hymns carried by the wind. The city is both the place of the everyday and a refuge against the everyday. The poet, necessarily fallen into the everyday, rejects it. He goes elsewhere. Into an elsewhere that is here. 'Let us leave this country where action is not sister to dream.' Poetry becomes the country and the landscape of the poet. He does not seek to change life, but to transfigure it by means of this philosopher's stone, the Word, poetic speech.

Rimbaud says more clearly, proclaims more forcefully, what the philosophers do not say, what they will never say since they commit suicide (as philosophers) by the action of saying it. Beauty is lying and dying, truth is already dead. Life has to be changed. Love needs reinventing. The everyday is hell and the season in hell lasts forever. The city traversed by the immense shaking of forces, the holy city built in the West, tried one last time to assert itself as law and rule for society, as measure of the world. It made a supreme attempt to define itself,

---

3   EN: *Les fleurs du mal* is a collection of poems by Baudelaire, first published in 1857. There is a parallel English–French edition titled *The Flowers of Evil*, translated by Jonathan Culler, Oxford: Oxford University Press, 1993.

and to define man and human, around its unity and its diversity. This attempt – the Commune – failed, as the creation in Europe of a democracy tending towards socialism had failed in 1848. Rimbaud, after Baudelaire and like Marx, lived the defeat. Not only did he devote a great poem to the Commune, but three poems of his *Illuminations* are dedicated to the City, present and possible.[4] Rimbaud went on to find his own way, or rather his own byway. Poetry in him flared and then denied itself, refusing to degenerate into literature; for in literary success what sought to become the creator of a style of life becomes par excellence literature and trappings. Rimbaud is rebellion in the pure state, the rebellion of a child against the world that crushes him. And what is it that crushes childhood and the innocence of the child? Above all, everyday life (*Les poètes de sept ans*). Rimbaud, unable to change life, sought the alchemy of the Word: the magical transmutation of the everyday into poetic speech. He succeeded, but this success was a defeat. Nothing changed, except literature. Then he fell silent. He went away, having written: 'One doesn't leave'. Which means: no one ever leaves, since each person carries himself with him. The poet leaves only for silence and death.

In the early twentieth century a strange mutation took place. The simultaneity of these changes in life and thought, and more deeply in the perception of time and space, has not been sufficiently noted. Competitive capitalism was already over, without those involved being aware of it. The old logic had been shaken, lashed and entranced by dialectical thought for a century and a half. Around 1910, 'referentials' and frames of reference dissolved. The evolutionistic and continuistic conception of time and space became blurred, along with the coordinates to which it referred and the mechanistic conception likewise. The present was blurred as a point that past and future could be related to in a strict determinism. In the notion of *field*, which began to invade the domains of science one after the other, past, present and future coexist; and even the future, already present and proclaiming itself in the lines of force, tends to determine the actual instead of being

---

4   EN: Arthur Rimbaud, 'The Parisian Orgy or Paris Filling Up Again' in *Collected Poems*, edited by Martin Sorrell, Oxford: Oxford University Press, 2001, pp. 80–5; *Illuminations, and Other Prose Poems*, New York: New Directions, 1957.

determined by it. In painting, the horizon line completely disappeared, along with classical perspective and the three-dimensional space of this codified and systematized perspective. A system of sensations and perceptions, the visual system, collapsed. So too did another system, that built on tonality in music and song; tonality disappeared as a reference in new music (atonal, dodecaphonic, then serial). In mathematics, the systematized conception of Euclidean space retreated; this space was now only a single case in the indefinite multiplicity of conceivable infinite spaces. Number, as habitually known and systematized in classical arithmetic, was no more than a set or a body among an infinity of other sets. In physics, Newtonian space as systematized by classical mechanics and represented as an absolute gave way to relativity; the notion of a continuous and completely determined trajectory, this fixed and absolute foundation of mechanics, became cloudy at levels that were not those of the customary scales.

On close examination, we see that the classical concept of reason and the irrational was obscured and maintained now only by decree, in the institutional sphere. Looking still more closely, we perceive that the notion of a *work of art* begins to crumble. Was it not Mallarmé who offered his poems as fragments, 'fallen from an obscure disaster', of one immense poem, a great book that would never be written and could not be written? *Language* itself, at the moment when it would appear as system and structure, and thus move to first place before reflexive thought, was attacked by the *image*, a new reality, ambiguous and imaginary, with powers that were poorly defined and perhaps undefined.

In all domains, fixed and definitive 'foundations' have disappeared, including formal logic as a referential. We could even say that within praxis and everydayness, the old 'systems' codified and regulated food, clothing, housing and furnishing. These 'systems' were local, regional, national. Some who have studied their debris and survivals have called them 'forms of life'. In the early twentieth century, these shattered (a small illustration: women began to imitate masculine dress, and to dress as men). Sensation and perception were subject to new distortions, from the fact that their systematic organization at the current and everyday level disappeared. They were defined locally with increased precision: signs, signals, forms with clear outlines. To this finite and defined aspect, more discontinuous and more distinct than previously, that was integrated into everydayness, was added the unlimited, the undefined, perhaps the infinity of a consciousness no longer confined by any determined horizon.

Let us mention here, without insisting on it, this shattering of all partial systems (from which the most factitious, such as fashion, rescued themselves, as also did the broadest, those having an institutional or state guarantee, such as law and philosophy). This will be one of our great objections against structuralism, with its constant emphasis on 'systems'. On the other hand, let us insist on the fact that Marxist 'dialecticians' should subsequently have welcomed such a broad mutation and sought to account for it, whereas they challenged it in the name of philosophical materialism, revalorizing what was collapsing: realist painting, tonal music, non-relativist conception of space and time, and so forth.

Why this mutation? We can ascribe it to several reasons and causes: the end of competitive capitalism (this particularly influential and important 'system'), crisis of capitalism, imperialism, revolutionary movement or again: new technologies, electricity, aviation. These are only partial causes and reasons. There was something more as well. There was the breakup of all frames taken as reference in practice, from the city through to the nation, from the palpable that had been familiar for centuries through to intellectual (philosophical) schemas of the cosmos and the world.

The city, in particular, began to proliferate beyond its determined limits, to lose its heart, to expand into the suburbs, to empty itself of its palpable substance in favour of excrescences that laid siege to it. Its image cast a final flash of light with poets such as [Guillaume] Apollinaire, [Blaise] Cendrars, [Louis] Aragon (*Le paysan de Paris*). It kept the prestige of culture driven to its last refinements of facticity and abstraction, but it lost its sense of a second naturalness. It was faced on one side by lost nature, and on the other by what is beyond anything given and accomplished: Dream, Idea, Spirit.

In this connection, we may formulate an extension of the law of *uneven development* (a law indicated by Marx, and made explicit at the economic and sociopolitical levels by Lenin).

There is unevenness in the relationship of social man to his works: uneven acceptance, uneven 'consensus' or uneven rejection. Men unevenly recognize themselves in the works [*oeuvres*] that are offered to them for their self-recognition and acceptance. The realization of the human being in works (including the city, appropriated nature, art, knowledge) is uneven according to eras, classes and groups, sectors. The same holds for alienation. We may therefore speak of a law of uneven realization and uneven alienation.

We may also speak of the *uneven development of systems*. In the age we are talking about here (the early twentieth century), the agricultural or village community, which had previously been powerfully systematized, had long lain in ruins. Certain systems grew more remote but broader: religion, philosophy. Certain broke up: competitive capitalism, the traditional family, the 'systems' of perspective and 'tonality', 'systems' of clothing by sex and age, or of diet on a local and regional basis, and so forth. Others were strengthened: the state in particular. Others again were constituted or began to be constituted in everydayness: for example, the 'system' of prestige and consumption established around such goods as the motorcar – or the *technical and bureaucratic system* with superimposed controls.

God being dead, everything was permitted. The First World War brought proof of this. What Nietzsche had sumptuously pronounced, Tristan Tzara said in two little words: 'Da-Da'. Dadaism proclaimed the end of many 'systems'. It believed it was accompanying the end of all systems, now that the God system, the mainstay and support of the others, had disappeared. It believed it heralded the end of written discourse as a fixed system of reference.

In this explosion, what solid remained? What frame of reference? Only one: the everyday life organized by the bourgeoisie, which recommenced and consolidated itself after the war. An insufferable and intolerable frame of reference. How not to reject it? But where to head for? Towards revolution, which the bourgeoisie, based on its solid everydayness as well as on its state and its army, succeeded in halting in those countries that were (according to Marx) best prepared for it?

There was this in surrealism: rejection, revolutionary hope, disappearance of fixed frames of reference. Confusedly, without theoretical elucidation.

After the First World War (between 1918 and 1930), surrealism sought to realize the romantic ambition and resume the failed project:

the creation of a style of life, the reinvention of love. It also sought to constitute, within the bourgeois society that was re-establishing itself, a second society, that of revolutionary poetry, hoping that this would make the first society explode. At the same time, while the surrealists wagered and staked their lives on poetry, others equally naïve, equally 'authentic', philosophers, bet on philosophy.

What did surrealism invent? A new language? Power-images? An ideology, or a praxis embodying the theory of poetry? No. A gaze [*regard*] on the modern world, on the city, on Paris, on woman and women. An imaging or imaged gaze, if you like. A gaze, nothing more, and nostalgic rather than new. The surrealists drove individual rebellion against the bourgeois everyday to the point of absurdity. What they counted on was not so much poetry as the action of a revolutionary 'micro-society', neither secret sect nor mass party, an acting group, laboratory, anticipation, hope, centre of radiation and influence. Their revolutionary 'micro-society' had only a minuscule effectiveness, and the bourgeoisie knew how to absorb the scandals: alarming and amusing itself. The demand and thirst for a poetic totality remained unsatisfied. An original element in this poetic thought became a ritual. It was less a matter of changing 'real' life than of crossing 'the gates of ivory and horn' (Nerval) that divided the waking state from dream, our 'bit of reality' from a higher reality: the surreal.[5] The philosophical and literary temptation was there from the start: departure for the elsewhere of dream, abstract escape into the world of automatic discourse, escape into the 'world', this cosmic and cosmological aspect taken from German romanticism (Novalis more than Hölderlin).

Poetic speech and the judgement delivered on the everyday soon lost their authenticity. The creation of style succeeded to a certain point in literature; it failed in life, that is, in praxis. Poorly armed, attaching itself to philosophies (Hegelianism or psychoanalysis as conceptions of the world), sometimes evoking the end of philosophy without meditating on it, surrealism proved unable to tolerate the harsh political reality of the post-revolutionary period in Russia and

---

5   EN: Gérard de Nerval, 'Aurélia', Part I, in *Aurélia and Other Writings*, translated by Geoffrey Wagner, Robert Duncan and Marc Lowenthal, Boston: Exact Change, 1996, p. 3.

Europe: Stalinism, fascism. The confrontation between the poetic 'revolution', the real revolution and its defeats, and the fascist pseu-do-revolution, ended in the ruin of surrealism. It left a project in a larval state, unrecognized, little developed, mixed with impurities, but restorable on the basis of a reinvention of 'poetic thought'. This project could only be resumed in terms very different from the surrealist theses about the 'surreal', the primacy of dreams, the aleatory in verbal invention, automatic writing (a technique that might be worth recommending to a literary technocracy today; and besides, did not Antonio Machado invent a 'machine' that claimed to be surreal?).

How can the poetic project that underlies a line of poetry be redeemed after a century or more? How can it be melded with a phil-osophical thought of birth, freed from the one-sidednesses of philosophy? In our view, the project of a transformation of the every-day that would restore its lost riches meets these demands. As a project to restore to poiesis its full sense – production and creation – it stands in the line of poetry, while bound up on the other hand with the super-seding of philosophy.

After Marx, Nietzsche perceived the exhaustion and deterioration of classical philosophy, its incapacity in the face of new problems. It would be unjust not to give him his place. This is not a matter of forci-bly bringing Nietzschean thought into the concepts of Marxist thought, or attempting an eclecticism condemned in advance. But Nietzsche's work has reasons and resonances. One of these reasons, once again for him as for the poets mentioned above, was the tempo-rary defeat of the revolution in Western Europe, in 1848, and the necessity of a quest, an opening and an issue. After Marx, Nietzsche likewise condemned traditional philosophy, dogmatic or critical, to death, in one of the most virulent poems of *Zarathustra*: 'Immaculate Perception'. The faults and crimes of this philosophy? Nietzsche perceived, as did Marx, the analogy, hidden by controversies, between religion and metaphysics. Religious and metaphysical minds had in common, a little differently but with the same unpleasant fury, a contempt for life; they were the hallucinated of the late-world, those obsessed with the supersensuous. Philosophers, too, were slanderers. What philistinism in their resentment against the senses, their taste for pure ideas!

It is a miserable story: man seeks a principle through which he can despise men;—he invents a world so as to be able to slander and bespatter this world: in reality, he reaches every time for nothingness and construes nothingness as 'God', as 'truth', and in any case judge and condemner of *this* state of being.[6]

In the whole of philosophy, radical criticism recognizes a way of taking revenge on reality, ruining the conditions of man. It detects the symptoms of a discontent and resentment that find satisfaction in torture and destruction.

The history of philosophy is a secret raging against the pre-conditions of life, against the value feelings of life, against partisanship in favour of life. Philosophers have never hesitated to affirm a world provided it contradicted this world . . . It has been hitherto the grand school of slander. (1888)[7]

Today it is child's play to construct systems. What is needed on the contrary is to make decisions with a long range. There has been something morbid about the philosopher type. It is this type of man and thought that first has to be changed.

Philosophy has only constructed the figure of *homo philosophicus*, theoretical man. Would this be *homo sapiens*? Perhaps, but is it certain? Theoretical man sees himself as thinking and wise, and is perhaps crazy, a buffoon: the fool of theoretical purity, as a certain philosopher called himself God's fool. Nietzsche attacks with greatest violence the hero, the saint, the martyr of philosophy, Socrates. He played a leading role. He founded a human type: the man who finds more satisfaction in seeking a hypothetical truth than in life and living truth. Theoretical man is an optimist of theory. He gets pleasure from it, an artist in his way and yet an anti-poet because anti-life (anti-physical). Insatiable for abstract knowledge, he is at the same time vulgar, cunning, someone who by the use of concepts and reason has arrived at a strong

---

6   EN: Friedrich Nietzsche, *The Will to Power*, translated by Walter Kaufman and R. J. Hollingdale, New York: Vintage, 1967, section 461, p. 253.
7   EN: Ibid.

self-mastery that gives him ascendancy over more vigorous men, healthier than him, but who do not know where their sap and their strength hail from. The false health of Socratic man hides an underlying disease; his cunning conceals a great lack of naivety, innocence, spontaneity. His universal reason dissimulates the absence of freedom and free decision. He creates nothing except himself. He does not found a world. He makes a display of his wisdom among simple people who end up execrating him.

Starting from this critique of philosophy and *homo philosophicus*, Nietzsche's thought follows an original path. Nietzsche holds a great dialogue with Greek thought (germs of which can be found in Hegel and Marx). His discussion is not with Plato and Aristotle, nor with Democritus and Epicurus, it is with the pre-Socratics who meditated before the great split between poetry and philosophy, between creating and doing, between the decision that founds and the reflection that excavates or reexamines, between saying and discoursing. In first place among these pre-Socratic thinkers is Heraclitus, the poet-philosopher who is seen as obscure. For Nietzsche, truth is poetic in kind. It is offered and grasped in an action-thought that creates it by saying it, that speaks truth by revealing it. Truth grasps the person who grasps it. This double grasping transforms him: he is one thing and becomes another. He becomes what he is. This action is accompanied by poetic speech; only speech, which runs through discourse, can speak. Poetic expression is in no way exterior to thought itself. The principle of ontological repetition: 'Eternize each minute! Live each moment in such a way as to wish it eternal' – this principle, which seems passive, is active and creative. It is thus that Sigismond, in Calderón's *La Vida es sueño*, cries: 'Since life so short indistinctly weaves together truth and illusion, let us dream, my soul, let us dream once more.'[8] And he sets off for battle.

An active principle of this kind is (according to Nietzsche) the secret of poetry, the desire of the poet, absolute desire. It metamorphoses into poetry sensation and sensuous perception. The instant

---

8   EN: Pedro Calderón de la Barca, *Life Is a Dream*, multiple translations. The passage in quotation marks appears to be more of a summary of the sentiment of the play than a specific quotation.

becomes moment, eternity. Word becomes action. The act of this thought simultaneously reveals depths and detects possibilities. Poetic speech brings the bright horizon into harmony with the obscurity from which births arise. It seizes from the accomplished its secret, that of the possible. This inaugural poetic act does not involve a procession of arguments and considerations and consequences. It founds a style of life. Nietzsche sought this style both in a heroic creation, the super-man, and in the repetition of the Same, eternal recurrence, finally in their identity, the overman [*surhomme*] being he who offers the truth of eternal recurrence and consequently the identity of memory and image, knowledge and recognition, birth and resurrection. According to Nietzsche, this unity founds the present, acceptance of the present, the 'yes' uttered before life and inaugurating at last the genuine life: new birth, new innocence. If death bears within it life and life bears death, if sorrow contains joy and joy sorrow, if being and nothingness change places and meld each into the other, then the future is innocent and being rediscovers great innocence in becoming.

Shall we insist on Nietzsche's defeat? Yes. The idea of a new accept-ance of life, rediscovering the innocence of spontaneity, is a deep poetic idea. If it is true, as Marx said, that man is separated from himself and from his own life, this image has a sense. But the most poetic speech is not enough to change praxis, even if it says more than reasonable discourse does, even if it is good for it to have been uttered and if it indicates what is possible. In his turn, it collapses into litera-ture. It becomes discourse, in a world of discourse. And philosophical discourses imitate (badly) the speech of the Master. This speech does not found a style, that highest work; it strays into poems and tales and anecdotes. Is not the image of eternal recurrence again a philosophical saying? From Nietzsche let us keep the idea of a new alliance between poetry and philosophy, a unity that presupposes the radical critique of these two spiritual activities and their alienating separation. Through this project of a new unity, Nietzsche has more grandeur (a word that is somewhat ridiculous but useful) than the greatest modern poets and philosophers in the age of the withering away of philosophy, phenom-enologists, existentialists, historians of 'worldviews'.

To reply once again to those who proceed by dogmatic classifica-tion and class Nietzsche among irrationalist thinkers, idealists and reactionaries, it is enough here to recall the eminently poetic texts in which Marx proclaimed the unity of the original and the terminal, the ultimate reconciliation of nature and man, existence and essence, being and thought.[9] But we have decided here not to abuse quotations. If each assertion were accompanied by texts and references, then each paragraph would demand a chapter, and each chapter a volume.

Examination of Marx and Nietzsche as protagonists of metaphilosophy leads us to Heidegger. We shall find him along the way, as we did Nietzsche. What there would be to say about him will not be completely said, any more than about Nietzsche (or Marx).

Nietzsche and Heidegger: both thorny cases, and not because of the Nazi interpretation of Nietzsche's thought (a cheating one), or Heidegger's tendencies towards National Socialism. It would be easy to find the same tendencies in French work that is seen as important. Besides, the philosophical-political interpretation is out of date. It is not more valid for Heidegger than for Kafka, Joyce or Proust. The question is different. If we consider Heidegger, if we deem him considerable, we are faced with the danger of eclecticism. The 'Freudo-Marxist' eclecticism obtained by mixing philosophical ingredients can serve as a warning. None the less, the risk of a philosophical eclecticism along the lines that 'Freudo-Marxism' was and still is does not prevent us from giving a place to psychoanalytical research, or to Heidegger-style investigation. The only way: to define convergences and divergences differently from on the philosophical level. It is by no longer locating ourselves on the level of philosophy that we shall avoid philosophical eclecticism.

Let us clear away, at the start of this discussion, a misunderstanding that has major implications, as it puts philosophical terminology in question. When Heidegger praises the *thing*,[10] this thing is not the *object* (of any kind). The thing is slender and minimal, even in number, in relation to the swarm of indifferent objects. The *thing* is the jug, the ring, the mirror, the vase, works of handicraft rather than works of art, but still works, and in no way *products* (of industry or technical

---

9   Cf. Marx, 'Critique of the Hegelian Dialectic and Philosophy as a Whole', *MECW*, vol. 3, pp. 345–6.

10   Martin Heidegger, 'The Thing' in *Poetry, Language, Thought*, translated by Albert Hofstader, New York: Harper & Row, 1971.

operation in the modern sense). The knowledge of science and technology destroyed *things* as things, well before the explosion of the atom bomb; they reduced the thing to objective function and operation: those of an object. There are scarcely things any more, and their 'thingness' remains in the background, forgotten. To make the thing appear again, accordingly, means rediscovering materiality, in the sense in which painters and sculptors speak of the matter that they work, colour and clay, marble and its grain. It also means rediscovering the meaning of the thing, humble and sacred: the jug that pours water and wine, that is used for libations and offerings, that gathers around it, around table or altar, the living and the dead. Or again the wedding ring, this band of gold that unites (and imprisons, we may add with an irony that is foreign to Heidegger).

Heidegger thus pursues the restitution of the sensuous, or rather of the practico-sensuous, begun by Marx in the *1844 Manuscripts*, and taken up by Nietzsche. He pursues it in his own fashion, simultaneously conceptual and aesthetic. The *thing*, as work of creative activity, founds around it an activity: a praxis and even a certain universality of praxis. The words 'thing' and *Ding* mean a *matter*, everything that touches, concerns, gathers men and everything that is in question.[11] The same holds for the word '*res*' (*res publica*): the matter, the lawsuit, the case. The thing, as created work, creates a little world around it.

Hegel left a great deal of ambiguity in his dialectic around the concept of the thing. In the thing, man realizes himself; he also loses himself. He loses himself to the extent that he believes that things have a substantiality different from consciousness, to the extent that he satisfies himself in a certain thing. He realizes himself to the extent that, through all the imperfect and incomplete things, philosophies, the city, science, he tends towards the perfect and absolute things: the rational world, the reconciliation of subject and object, the Hegelian state.

On the one hand, Marx retained the first meaning of the thing; it is reification (*Verdinglichung*), loss of self in the *abstract object*, money, the commodity. On the other hand, he retained the second meaning: the product, the work. The abstract thing alienates; the concrete product realizes man (at least at a particular historic moment).

---

11   EN: 'Thing' is in English in the French text.

Heidegger did not cast light on the question of the *thing*. He added a new demand to questions already formulated. The more or less technological object, product of the scientific mode of representation, is emptied of poetry. The *thing*, as handicraft [*oeuvre artisanale*], was rich in poetry. The object is consumed. The *thing* creates around it a human microcosm. What is the conclusion? Heidegger confirmed an essential point of view: the relationship of man with the thing is an aspect of the more general problem, that of the relationship between man and his multiple *oeuvres*. Undoubtedly Heidegger's lack of the theory of alienation (of the double relationship with the object and the thing: presence and alienation, reality and reification) prevented him from answering its demand. Besides, the cult of the handcrafted thing, somewhat archaic, translates in Heidegger into a touching sentiment of the home, patriarchal and Germanic. We discover a similar sentiment with Gaston Bachelard, through his refined analyses of reveries on the elements, on space. For Heidegger, the Home is the dwelling: stable and sacred, profound and open. The image of the home (of the dwelling) runs through and inspires a wide-ranging reflection on 'building' and 'inhabiting', deeply connected with techne and poiesis. The home figures and symbolizes the individual being and his consciousness (*Dasein*) – or conversely; it is more than a symbol. It is bound up with serious questions. Being and authenticity have need of a dwelling. Language is to being what the home is to men. The image of the dwelling extends to reflection on thought, sojourn, site, situation.

For ourselves, here, it is the city, rather than the home, that offers a capital theme and a profound symbolism. Certainly, the city has always been made up of homes, as society is made up of individuals. But the space and time of the city have always been different from the time and space of the home, without abolishing the latter. There is a different grandeur, a different beauty, a different work, in the city than in the home. The relationship between home and city is rather like that of individual consciousness and praxis (though they should not be confused). Already for Hegel, the Greek polis [*cité*] was the most perfect thing, a grandeur and beauty destroyed by implacable becoming. What does the end of the city, carried away by time along with beauty, along with many past grandeurs, many ancient truths, what does this presage, what does it demand, what does it expect of us?

Let us assert at this point the validity of the Heideggerian line of questioning. Those who immediately protest that there is a contradiction between this assertion and the project of a metaphilosophy are requested to wait a moment.

In the *1844 Manuscripts*, Marx sought to redefine man and the human. In the wake of Feuerbach, he constituted an anthropology from the starting point of the sensuous, the senses and what has a sense (a natural, that is to say, 'material', sense). Man, as a being of nature, manages in the course of a long struggle to emerge from nature, to dominate it partially and to appropriate it (including the nature within him: his own nature). Man is first of all a being of need. Through want, through privation, through need, each is in perpetual relationship with objects and beings, including other humans for whom he is likewise object. Through labour, man (generic, anthropological) comes to replace the natural objects that satisfy his needs with produced objects. He thus produces new needs, and these needs change into capacities of production and satisfaction. Man, taken generically (generally), thus constitutes his human world, nature and society – though not without being destined to emerge from nature, to pass through the artificial.

To the long series of definitions of man by philosophers, Marx added a new one: the triplicity of need/labour/enjoyment. Man is not only a political animal, inhabitant of the city and citizen. He is not only reasonable or rational, using language and concepts. This triplicity encompasses the other aspects, showing their foundation and their truth.

Marx bracketed out a series of definitions of man and hypotheses on this paradoxical being, advanced by poets as much as by philosophers: man laughs, man invented wine and likes to get drunk, man often seeks his joy in the pain of passions, man is familiar with death and knows he is going to die, and so forth. If he does not reject these determinations, Marx either relegates them to second rank or neglects them. He emphasized *homo faber* without overly neglecting *homo sapiens*. Despite having a powerful sense of humour, he did not place too much emphasis on *homo ridens*. And though he showed the importance of leisure, he left aside *homo ludens*. He put death and the consciousness of death in brackets. Can we reproach him for this lacuna? Marx stood in the perspective of rational optimism; his thought reflected on life rather than on death, as did Nietzsche's. He vehemently repudiated an ancient definition of philosophy as apprenticeship for death, the wisdom of acceptance. For Marx, the beings of nature struggle and die; but nature is justified, since man is born and with him the human being, by way of history. Marxist rationality thus links up with Nietzschean thought in the justification of becoming.

But here is the important thing. The sensations and passions of man 'are not merely anthropological phenomena in the (narrower) sense, but truly *ontological* affirmations.' Moreover: 'Only by developed industry – i.e. through the medium of private property – does the ontological essence of human passion come into being, in its totality as well as in its humanity; the science of man is therefore itself a product of man's own practical activity.'[12]

Marx rejects in advance an anthropology that would be concerned merely with defining man and the human (by this or that: knowledge, culture, reason, society, etc.). If anthropological research is necessary, it is insufficient. It refers to an ontology – exploration of 'being' or nature – and this is because man, in his praxis, is not isolated from nature but multiplies his links with it. Contradictory links: conflict, struggle, domination, facticity, externality, return to, uprooting and rooting. Besides, knowledge of man does not set itself up above man but is born from him, in him, in praxis. It cannot therefore manage to hold man within a definition. It is he – the human – that defines himself, highly and perhaps infinitely complex.

Marx did not develop the notion of *nature* so as to confront it with that of *physis*. He drew it from French materialism, and not without criticizing the tendency of this philosophy to mechanistic systematization. He drew it also from German romanticism, and not without rejecting its irrationalism. Philosophies each criticized one another with the movement from one to the next: materialism became an abstract spiritualism of matter, and idealism was loaded with mechanism (with Descartes and his school, as with Kant and the physics bound up with his system). The notion of nature received from the philosophies contained a critique of philosophy, since this omitted the real genesis of man in nature and

---

12   Marx, 'Economic and Philosophical Manuscripts', *MECW*, vol. 3, p. 322.

from it, either explaining this by transcendence or conceiving man as being simply immanent in nature. Marx was content to reject metaphysis and view physis as the matrix of man, a rough and generous mother, a severe educator from whom man distanced himself the better to recognize her by dominating her and one day reconciling himself with her. If there is a 'transformation of nature into man' and at the same time 'becoming of nature through man', as the latter creates himself by labour, how and why is this possible?[13] Marx does not go further. He rejects the philosophical representation of nature. Taken in abstraction, isolated and fixed separately from man, nature becomes an object of contemplation: the being-other of thought for abstract thought: '*Nature as nature* – that is to say, insofar as it is sensuously distinguished from that secret sense hidden within it – nature isolated, distinguished from these abstractions is *nothing* – a *nothing proving itself to be nothing* – is *devoid of sense*.'[14]

It is certain that Marx would not have accepted any of the positions taken by later philosophy. He could not have considered nature as a 'region' of being, distinct from consciousness and without a profound (ontological) link with it. He would not have accepted that nature was the mere *residue* of the intellectual analysis operated on the sensuous and becoming, or forms constructed by the understanding. No more would he see in it a ready-made will, a wanting to live, a will to power, an impulse, an original life force or desire. On the other hand, in his thought, the Hegelian Ideal 'put back on its feet', identified more or less summarily with (material) nature, continues to symbolize the inexhaustibility of 'being'.

Marx seems to have thought that nature presents and explains itself in the course of the social action (praxis) that emerges from it and transforms it. And yet we may wonder whether reflection on the perspectives of this action, on the reconciliation between man and nature, on the appropriation by man of his own nature, does not demand a new procedure.

Nothing prevents us, starting from Marx, from viewing anthropology as insufficient (even if we accept its necessity) and making explicit

---

13   Ibid., pp. 305–6.
14   Ibid., p. 346.

the concepts of 'nature' and 'being', on condition that some precautions are taken, and that 'nature' or 'being' is never fixed outside of man and praxis, since it – praxis – founds through man and for man his double knowledge: of what there is outside and before him, and of himself. The question can therefore not be raised in philosophical terms, even though it continues the line of philosophy and extends the perspective of the philosophers.

Ever since Descartes, philosophy has swung between a metaphysics of the object, the in-itself, substance, and a metaphysics of the subject, consciousness, the for-itself. The philosophy of substance evolved towards materialism (considered as philosophy). The metaphysics of the subject evolved towards a theory of pure consciousness, of the absolute 'for-itself' (from Fichte to Husserl). Both these directions separated nature and being from the acting subject: from praxis. We can see in what way and to what extent philosophy in its decay has maintained this misunderstanding. Official Marxist materialism starts from 'matter', and believes it has reduced the abyss between object and subject by reducing consciousness to the status of a 'reflection'. Sartre starts from consciousness as consciousness 'of the other' (whether an object or another), and likewise believes he has bridged the abyss. Neither one nor the other has succeeded in doing this, but they are able to 'dialogue': they are on the same terrain.

Can we say that being and nature, viewed as progenitors of the human being, exist absolutely outside of him, before him and without him? Yes and no. Yes, as man is born from nature, the disfavoured son promised a brilliant destiny. Nature 'is' before he arrives, as is confirmed by the history of matter and biological life. These truisms are nowadays trivial, the daily bread of vulgar materialism. And yet, the answer is no if it is true that being and nature have as their destiny the budding, the birth, the accomplishment of the human. Lenin, in the wake of Diderot, wrote in *Materialism and Empirico-Criticism* that consciousness, as a property of matter, has to be accepted in the very depths of matter.[15] Is man the essence bound up with a primordial and original existence, nature, man beginning with what in him differs from

---

15   EN: V. I. Lenin, *Materialism and Empirico-Criticism*, Peking: Foreign Languages Press, 1972, p. 28.

natural being, in other words, thought? Right away we conceive his chance, his growth, his mastery over nature and over himself: appropriation. Is he only a stroke of luck, an accident, perhaps a monster? Then what happens to his chance with destiny? If we are unable to count on being and nature, are we going to wager on anti-nature? On facticity, culture, and – in psychoanalytic terms – on the reality principle against the pleasure principle? Unless another path can be discovered, beyond essence and accident, pure necessity and pure chance, beyond these philosophical concepts.

Starting from these notions, we can examine the work of Heidegger. He was right to question being and nature; he sought to answer on the basis of a reexamination of traditional philosophy, with the perspective of the superseding of metaphysics as well as of philosophical speculation. The investigation of 'being' supersedes the philosophy of the subject and the philosophy of the object, the metaphysical representation of the 'for-itself' and the 'in-itself'. Heidegger, by questioning being and physis, thus tends to supersede philosophy. Did he completely redeem these categories and concepts from the philosophical tradition? That is a question – *the* question.

In *Sein und Zeit*, Heidegger shows man and thought cast into the world, into dereliction.[16] Man escapes this by concealing his condition of being-for-death: in the 'one', in the inauthentic, in banality. Only the clear night of fear transcends commonplace care. From this point, Heidegger envisaged a new revelation of being. Would this creative unveiling sweep away the triviality of *Alltäglichkeit*, of everyday care? Undoubtedly. All the same, Heidegger did not envisage the metamorphosis of the everyday as a revolutionary work and project. He undoubtedly still dreamt of transcending it in risk and danger: in the absolute game.

Heidegger examined very widely the fate of technology, that is to say, a very contemporary relationship between man and his works [*oeuvres*]. He thus penetrated into praxis to raise questions for it. And yet, what he saw above all in industrial technology was one

16   EN: Martin Heidegger, *Being and Time*, translated by Joan Stambaugh, revised by Dennis J. Schmidt, Albany: SUNY Press, 2010.

aspect: the ravaging of the earth, the departure of the old gods and the death of God, the reign of mediocrity (technicians and masses). From that point, he could only describe these ravages, despite announcing in sibylline fashion the new unveiling of being, through technology and beyond it. He was rather too early to conceive technology – a question of dates. He did not discern its most troubling aspect: the simulation of life and thought by technological means, by machines. Heidegger was not able to observe how much this simulation converges with the 'real': the living, thinking, acting thing, represented as model. Is this not the most contemporary aspect of the relationship of man to his work, his *being-other*, this imitation that turns against its creator and tends to integrate him into it? Does man not cause his own image to arise from nature, like the God of Genesis, only for this image to stand up and confront him? Supreme accomplishment? Prodigiously deeper alienation? Or something else again? What is this technology? Servant, unleashed monster, a golem impossible to defeat? What will machinery be?

To answer this, reflection must press forward the line of questioning, think through to the end what it is that technology seizes, and technology itself, by taking it in thought to its ultimate consequences. That is what Heidegger attempted, but without having on hand all the facts of the question. He alone saw the essential thing: technology. Beside him, contemporary philosophers grow pale, ageing on the spot. Apropos, we can repeat what Marx said in 1843: the value of Germany lies in philosophical reflection; it is in this way that it is contemporary and present. Heidegger saw that this essential thing, the question of technology, shifted every 'problem'. While other philosophers continued to thrash around in 'problems', those of knowledge, of idealism and materialism, of the in-itself and the for-itself, Heidegger, for his part, described and perceived what was new and disturbing in praxis. Did he penetrate into praxis?

Heidegger's meditation contains both the best and the worst: the archaic and the visionary, the world of discourse and also poetic speech. Archaisms are his philosophical metaphors, the 'shepherds of Being', language as the dwelling (home) of Being. Forward-looking is the effort to conceive the essence of technology, to define the modern world. A world of discourse: the speculative struggles in the garden of

Greek roots, the studies on logos and *aletheia* that are very fine for their part. Poetic words: the exegesis of a poem (Hölderlin's admirable '*Dichterisch wohnet der Mensch*' – poetically man dwells) is a poetic work, a hymn to the glory of Home:

> But dwelling occurs only when poetry comes to pass and is present . . .
> Poetry first of all admits man's dwelling into its very nature, its presencing being. Poetry is the original admission of dwelling.[17]

We owe a certain recognition to the man who brought poetry back into the style of reflection, who recognized and declared poiesis superior to technology,[18] both this side of and beyond the narrowness that is content to act on men, to treat them in terms of *pragmata*, pragmatically.

Poiesis, Heidegger reminded us with luminous scope, was not originally a verbal art, a discursive imitation of nature, still less pure form imposed on verbal matter. In his initial and profound understanding, poiesis was grasped as production: as foundational and creative act. It was not only opposed to physis: 'Not only handcraft manufacture, not only artistic and poetical bringing into appearance and concrete imagery, is a bringing-forth, *poiesis*. *Physis*, also, the arising of something from out of itself, is a bringing-forth, *poiesis*. *Physis* is indeed *poiesis* in the highest sense.'[19]

Techne, likewise, in these dazzling beginnings of life and thought, does not simply refer to action but also to art in the highest sense: '*Techne* belongs to bringing-forth, to *poiesis*; it is something *poietic*.'[20]

Originally and deeply, poetry is truth and truth poetry: practical truth of action and production. Only later is there a separation of

---

17   Martin Heidegger, 'Poetically Man Dwells', in *Poetry, Language, Thought*, New York: Harper & Row, 1971, p. 227.

18   Gaston Bachelard also reintegrated poetry into philosophical meditation. But he allowed philosophy to be duplicated into philosophy of science (theory of knowledge, gnoseology) and literary philosophy (analysis and psychoanalysis of poetic images, reveries on the elements and space). He poorly perceived the rise of technology on the horizon. Despite the perspicacity of his perspectives on the new scientific spirit, on materialism and rationalism, a sumptuous nostalgia still governs his thought.

19   Martin Heidegger, 'The Question Concerning Technology', in *The Question Concerning Technology and Other Essays*, New York: Garland Publishing, 1977, p. 10.

20   Ibid., p. 13.

poiesis, physis and techne – indiscernible in a total act of 'making', effective operation on matter, discourse and verbal act, in short, the different aspects of a differentiated and contradictory praxis. But truth and poiesis have not lost, for all that, their connection and secret harmony. It is up to us to rediscover and renew it.

Let us get to the essential by trying to condense, prepared to revise this judgement in order to support and justify it. According to Heidegger, an inexhaustible Being appears in appearance, unfolds in becoming, is manifested even in the difference between being and thought. This inexhaustible Being, infinite and uncompleted, accomplishes itself in the finite and in the end of all that is finite; this Being sets out on a path towards an unknown terminus, opening dangerous paths for the beings that it launches in its adventure. Man, with his 'consciousness' and his thought, is opening; he is the very opening of being on its unfolding that arises from *physis* (nature). There is no grasping that does not supersede itself towards the possible, that is not open, that is not project. The adventure of the human being on the possible does not proceed without risk, without death and the acceptance of death, without the virtual annihilation of all 'existing' and everything accomplished. Being does not represent itself outside of the present, outside of presence. I do not grasp it in 'me', distinct from me. It is in me this opening of 'my' consciousness, perpetual starting point towards the other, towards the possible, towards the horizon. It is this nothingness, this void and this avidness, this basis and this uncertainty. It is 'this' but not only this; also that, the other, the world, and the site or situation of this and that in the world.

We can only have one of two things. One option: Heidegger's reflections are designed to define and determine this inexhaustible being. Knowledge or recognition of being changes the course of history: of its history and of man. It justifies and authorizes sovereign decisions, and will continue to do so. Being receives a name. This theory then falls again into the framework of traditional philosophy; there is a Heidegger philosophy; his fundamental ontology is hard to distinguish from metaphysics and 'ontics': the definition of being limits it, reduces it to a 'being [*étant*]', a new figure of the gods or dead god. The relationship of 'ek-static' consciousness to Being requires a name: faith, grace, summons, certainty, inspiration, and so forth.

The second option: Heidegger does not define being. In this case, where should we seek and find how this being offers itself while withdrawing, reveals itself while disguising itself, shines while obscuring itself? Why do we not recognize this movement, at least partially, in the practical alienation and dis-alienation of man, not excluding the economic, social and political forms of this alienation and dis-alienation? There is in Heidegger, as in Hegel, the image of an original 'being' from which emanate, while dispersing, a multiplicity of beings [*êtres*] ('beings [*étants*]').[21] Heidegger, more than Hegel, emphasizes the raison d'être of each emanation, each dispersion. Is this why there is no theory of alienation in his work? The notion of praxis makes it possible to situate alienations and dis-alienations in the real combats of men and man. But why should language, and not praxis, be the dwelling of Being, the place of revealing? And why language alone? Why not music or architecture, or any *presence* that is not alienated or alienating, reifying or reified? His investigations bear neither on the accomplished real nor on the ideal or what should be. They bear on the possible insofar as the possible appears, is discerned, is chosen as such, insofar as there is possibility and impossibility. They thus bear on the complexity and conflicts of a praxis open on the possible and the basis or foundation of the opening up of individual consciousnesses.

The 'shepherds of Being'? This metaphor comes from remotest times. Critias, in Plato's dialogue, says that men are the cattle of the gods, whom the latter guard and protect (with the implication that they also sacrifice and devour them). In Christian imagery, the pastor leads the flock; he is God, he is the priest, and the faithful are sheep (the little animals of the flock, Nietzsche comments). In Heidegger, this image is reversed. We (who? – philosophers? poets? meditators? men in general?) are no longer the cattle of Being. It is Being that commits itself to our guard; it trusts us and entrusts us with adventurous missions, chiaroscuro messages. We permit it to roam the paths of wandering, to cross deserts and forests, to gather in clearings and pastures, to refresh itself at springs, to find temporary dwellings. To end up where? We lead

---

21 EN: Heidegger distinguishes between *Sein*, 'being' and *Seiendes*, 'beings' – the latter being specific entities, and the former the more general question. In French these are frequently translated as '*être*' or '*Être*', and '*étants*'. Lefebvre is pluralizing the first term and comparing it to the second.

it where it leads us, in an adventure that is our own. Is this poetry? Yes. That is not an objection. But does this poetry not bypass the poiesis that calls us? Does it not return to philosophy? To a theology, a new mysticism, despite the proclamation that 'God is dead'?

This poetry conducts a dialogue with Greek thought in its nascent state. Now we can institute a wider dialogue, between praxis and praxis. On the one hand, we have the praxis of the City [*Cité*] at its apogee, carrying discourse to perfection, culture based on the written sign, concrete intelligence, 'dealings [*commerce*]' between men. On the other hand, we have our own praxis, that of the end (disproportion, explosion) of the *urbs*, that of operations of the understanding that have become automatic, that of signals and behaviours, a praxis that no longer finds its aim within its limits, but on the contrary its unlimited opening towards an undefined horizon, beyond this Gate of Death and the Possible, the danger of technology, atomic death.

Heidegger revealed the point to which our world has changed since Hegel: encumbered, saturated with facts, knowledges, technologies (even though technology was still far from having reached its worldwide end point). Worldness [*mondialité*] does not appear on a clear and free horizon, but by way of enormous entities (the state) and immense mechanisms [*dispositifs*]. Opening is thus more important than determination. There is nothing stranger than the transformation of the word '*Dasein*'. For Hegel it referred to determined present being, and for Heidegger 'ek-static [*extatique*]' present being, seized from itself in a productive way. Poiesis is opening, project. Marx opened the way. Let us keep to opening in Marx's sense: in praxis.

Heideggerian *Dasein*, presence to self, to the world, to the 'other' (and of other to self), is posited and presupposed at the foundation of individual existence. As relation with the other, it is defined by alterity: by the indefinable and undefined opening to the other as thing, as other person, as possible. Yet the 'ec-static' grasp, destined to supersede itself towards ever-new horizons, is scarcely more than an individual consciousness. This *Dasein* does not even have a sex. The Freudian theory of the *libido* (derived from the same sources as Heidegger's thought, in other words Schelling and Schopenhauer, also harking back to a certain tradition of Christian philosophy, St Augustine, Jansen, Pascal) is often richer and closer to the concrete than is that of *Dasein*. Beyond the Freudian opposition between the reality principle and the pleasure principle, projecting the superseding of conflict and the liberation of the pleasure principle, can we not conceive the renewal of Desire?[22] The project of a redemption of desire purified from the tares of the libido, freed from the constraints of culture and civilization, is poietic in the highest degree. Very different from the 'cathartic of the nothing' in *Sein und Zeit*, as a vision of the future revealing of being, in psychoanalysis this project becomes a certain practice, even if ambiguous and metaphysically interpreted. It is recognizable in a number of poets (Paul Eluard, René Char), who perhaps do not have the *Gründlichkeit* and *Heimlichkeit* of Hölderlin but whose words speak poetically the purity of desire, a human Desire freed from animal desire and social need, a desire recognized and recognizing itself, a desire desiring itself beyond the wished-for and the necessary. Poets proclaim desire, as in the same way do certain phrases of the most illustrious musicians.

Cast into the adventure of becoming, degraded into inauthenticity, prey to the commonplace, hemmed in by security, Heideggerian man is not the man of need, labour, enjoyment. In relation to labour as to sex, he remains in speculative abstraction. *Dasein* contains an essential description of the drama of consciousness. Heidegger expressly sought to avoid subjectivism. He did not start from a philosophy of consciousness. *Dasein* is not consciousness but its foundation philosophically grasped. Like all philosophical consciousness, it emerges only with difficulty from the individual. Being-with-[an]other, *Mit-einander-Sein*, is founded on the individual. When Heidegger speaks magnificently of man 'who opens his eye and his ear', who 'unlocks his heart and gives himself to thought', these moving images scarcely have more than an individual meaning. Only language transcends the private consciousness of the individual.

When he introduces the people or the nation, Heidegger accomplishes another '*transcensus*', and sometimes a dangerous one. For want of having grasped praxis, he can only remain within individual being or transcend it by hurling it into the abyss. This lacuna has other

---

22   On the possibility and difficulty of this 'dream', cf. Herbert Marcuse, *Eros and Civilization: A Philosophical Inquiry into Freud*, London: Routledge, 1987.

consequences. As has been remarked more than once, by both philosophers who follow Heidegger and those critical of him, his preoccupation above all with discerning the most general project of the sciences, and the human sciences in particular, his search to reveal and denounce the technological programme in favour of his fundamental ontology, leads him to leave the findings of the sciences aside. Or rather, for him there are no such findings. If he does not ignore the corresponding 'realities', he deliberately disdains sociology, economics and, of course, anthropology. He does not start with an anthropological research, like Marx in 1844, in order to detect its limits, on the scientific as well as on the ontological side (anthropology having also to leave room for political economy, mathematics, sociology and above all history).

An old distinction that played a major role for the philosophers is no longer significant or has changed its meaning. Philosophy contrasted quality and quantity. Hegel established a dialectical link between the two concepts (theory of the qualitative leap after gradual and only quantitative changes). Subsequently, with the withering away of philosophy, the two concepts were again disassociated and opposed. In Bergsonian philosophy, the quantitative relates to mathematics, it is abstract and constructed, while the qualitative is promoted to the rank of the concrete, the 'real', in isolation.

Today, however, mathematics has attained the qualitative (order, the aleatory, tactics and strategies in acts and decisions, etc.). As for the qualitative, that is to say, the immediate, is it not in itself abstract, and more abstract than quantity?

The domain of mathematics does not tolerate any limitation. The limits that philosophy assigned it, or still assigns it, have always been swept away. Mathematics advances. It tends towards totality, as is its right. No philosophy can forbid it, neither that of Hegel nor that of Bergson.

And yet 'something' escapes mathematics. From the mathematicians' point of view, this 'something' is simply a residue, the reduction of which they can always push further. Science rationalizes nature, said Émile Meyerson; but this operation leaves a *residue* that knowledge drags along with it, that it takes responsibility for.[23]

---

23 EN: Likely a reference to Émile Meyerson, *Explanation in the Sciences*, Dordrecht: Kluwer Academic Publishers, 1991 [1921].

Logico-mathematical reason causes an irrationality to arise before it. If we place ourselves in this residue, we discover that it is infinitely precious: an infinite in the finite that mathematical understanding can grasp. This is drama (of the individual, of groups, of humanity as a whole). Does not human 'reality' have this double determination, number and drama? The two 'aspects' are inseparable. Heidegger, however, dismisses number or perceives only its most derisory implications. He emphasizes only drama, and above all the drama of the individual being, on which basis he comprehends the destiny of man.

To perceive the impasse of Heideggerian thought, it is enough to compare his admirable texts on the work of art, and on Beauty as revelatory of the True, with the disabused note that follows the study of the work of art and the Thing in *Holzwege*. After Hegel, Heidegger glimpsed the end of art. This 'Epilogue' goes a long way.[24] It is impossible, Heidegger says, to evade Hegel's saying that art is now something of the past. Art thus ends up together with philosophy. But then what of Being and the truth of Being in Beauty? Where is the history of Being leading us?

If all *Dasein* has a foundation and raison d'être, there is no reason to reason itself. If what founds has no foundation, if the bottom has no bottom, if the world only has below it a kind of great game of Being, eternal creative child, then thought that seeks to supersede philosophy leads to a philosophy of play:

> If we hear the principle of reason in the other tonality and think about all we hear, then this thinking-about is a leap, indeed a far-reaching leap that brings thinking into a play with that therein being *qua* being finds its repose ... Humans are truly capable of playing and of remaining in play only insofar as they engaged in this play and thereby at stake in the play.[25]

A critical analysis that takes its starting point in the empirical – in praxis – reveals the starting point of play and the absence of poetry, their evacuation by technology, their reduction in everydayness to

---

24 Martin Heidegger, 'Epilogue to "The Origin of the Work of Art" ', *Basic Writings*, New York: Harper, 2008, pp. 204–6.

25 Martin Heidegger, *The Principle of Reason*, Bloomington & Indianapolis: Indiana University Press, 1996, p. 111.

childish games. The same critical description leads to viewing play as a *moment* among other moments, love, knowledge, and so forth. The theory of moments overcomes the opposition between the serious (ethical) and the frivolous (aesthetic), as likewise that between the everyday and that which is noble, elevated, superior (cultural). It reveals the diversity of powers of the total human being, powers that come to man from his being, and from 'being' (we can say, to avoid speculative interpretation: from Nature, from nature in him, from his nature). Restoring and rehabilitating the ludic in its authenticity and intensity, it grants this no privileged status, no ontological profundity. No more to play than to knowing or to fear, to desire or to repose.

The idea of a 'history of being' obliges us to reflect on the notion of history and its 'problematic'. Marx only left us fragments (in *Capital*) and sketches (in 'The 18th Brumaire of Louis Bonaparte') of the *total* history he envisaged. Can we suppose that it would have avoided the impasses of later historical thought? By tending to a deeper objectivity, it did not allow itself to be trapped in the bothersome dilemma between judgement of fact and judgement of value, between observation and subjective appreciation. It would have included a history of history and of historical consciousness, integrating the historian into historical time. In the same way, it would neither be reducible to a philosophy of history, nor to a history without scope. The later disassociations between economism (which falsely appeals to Marx) and the history of ideas seen as independent of economics, between 'event' and 'institutional' history, these disassociations that have given rise and still give rise to interminable controversies would have soon been settled if historians had understood the thought of Marx.

This deeper historical thought proceeds by a dialecticizing of the concept of time and of the unfolding of facts in time, starting from a global analysis and exposition of praxis (including, it goes without saying, the conflicts of peoples, nations, classes). It is now possible to conceive the integration into historical thought of the study of human needs, satisfactions and dissatisfactions, sensibility and the emotions. Several chapters of this history have been drafted or written.[26] Total

---

26 On the possibility and difficulties of this 'dream', see Marcuse, *Eros and Civilization*.

history would grasp the entirety of praxis by the extreme links and poles that are everyday life and eminent works. The total history of man can only consist in a history of total man, sense and sensibility, sensations and idea – this total man being always fragmented, always contradictory, in a totality always broken and resumed.

The history of the city would make a convincing contribution to total history. The city [*ville*] is a work of art.[27] The city [*cité*] is a work of art: continuous creation and action. We can generalize what Heidegger magnificently says of the Greek temples.[28] A certain traditional (and traditionalist) historical science has committed a great error by grouping together and exalting polis and *urbs* as one and the same type, seen as variations of the 'ancient city'. The agora symbolizes the Greek city, of which it is heart and kernel: a space sacred but open, empty and welcoming, place of assembly and sovereignty of the citizens. The forum symbolizes the Roman *urbs*, and beyond the *urbs* the Roman conception of space and time, society and civilization: a space isolated by prohibitions, a place where civil power protects itself with the aid of religion (augurs) against military leaders, an emplacement where state edifices accumulate and where institutional right is exercised.

However far one goes back towards origins (the Achaeans in Greece, the Etruscans for Rome), a significant difference can still be found. With the growth of cities this was deepened in some respects; in other respects it was later attenuated. Polis and *urbs*, each in its own fashion, produced in the course of their history a form and a formalism: the logos (with its political applications) that arose from the Greek city, the law that arose from the Roman.

Where was this difference born? How should it be understood? How should we follow its destiny? Chance, a fortunate coincidence? The political will of leaders, endowed or not with genius? Geographical, ethnic, economic, political determination? The question will arise later. We have to admit, at the birth of these two cities, a creation, a poiesis, which is also or already a praxis and subsequently develops

---

27   In a sense that the sociology of Georges Gurvitch makes precise and concrete. The notion of *œuvre*, as cement of societies and civilizations, runs through his whole work and is everywhere present. On the polis, cf. Martin Roland, *Recherches sur l'agora grecque*, Paris: Bibliothèque des écoles françaises d'Athènes et de Rome, 1951.

28   Martin Heidegger, 'The Origin of the Work of Art', *Basic Writings*, pp. 162 ff.

with this constituted praxis, which consolidates and metamorphoses itself in this. What did the creators found? Undoubtedly 'something other' than what they saw or believed. Certainly a *style* of life, of works of art. Perhaps a perception or a representation of time and space, whereas they simply thought of founding a city. The dialectical movement begun in this way makes it possible to tighten more closely the famous relationship, obscured by scholastic discussions, between masses, individuals and ideas.

Creation conceived in this fashion does not substitute an irrationality for the search for a rational determinism and a causal connection; by giving it a different name (for example, birth of quality or qualitative leap) it is brought into familiar conceptual frameworks; but nonetheless we find ourselves in the presence of a new, specific, original element. Either we note the creation, or the search for causal explanation makes differences and specificities disappear. As soon as we consider them, historical births force a structuring of becoming: we have to conceive this discontinuously, moving away from an evolutionary and continuist pattern in history.

Total history presupposes that new elements are introduced into the fabric of becoming (instead of the polarization between events and institutions): founding or foundation, project. These two notions have a philosophical origin, in the same way as those of praxis, appropriation, totality, need, and so forth. Notions that total history cannot dispense with – which in our view history cannot dispense with. Will we succeed in extracting them from philosophy so as to move them into history?

Foundation (creation and founding) as well as project can be represented on the basis of a philosophy of consciousness (a Cartesianism revised and corrected by Fichte and Husserl). All consciousness is act, intention, relationship with an 'other', object or goal. All consciousness, individual or social, projects and is projected. With the project, with the possible and impossible and their dramatic confrontation, consciousness disappears. All consciousness seeks to found, and searches a foundation for itself (no doubt in vain; how would it find another foundation than itself, in the abstract purity of its act?). It is thus possible to attempt to attain total history on the basis of consciousness and a philosophy of consciousness.

Jean-Paul Sartre, in the *Critique of Dialectical Reason*, seeks to conceive history and historicity in this conceptual framework. Yet it was not from consciousness that Marx started out. He started from physis, from 'being' and 'conscious being'. Still more: he rejected, in Hegel and Hegelianism, the superfluities constructed on self-consciousness. For him, the human being remains a being of nature ('material') even in his struggle with nature. Marx would be prodigiously surprised to see himself appealed to by 'structuralists', 'culturalists' and those philosophers of consciousness who cut man off from his foundation in nature. By putting nature 'in brackets', reducing it to an abstraction, denying it, the philosophy of consciousness risks letting an essential part of content and historicity escape. How are need and desire to be conceived (and thus the transition from one to the other, even if this transition involves reflective will, intention, discursive understanding, society and culture) without constant reference to physis? Is it possible to grasp the village and the city, people and nation, even social class, without thinking of the earth, the land, the territory [*la terre, au terroir, au territoire*]? Even the abstraction that separates from it refers to the native soil. How to conceive human works without reference to the matter that is worked, to the senses and sensibility in 'sensuous' activity? How to reflect on thought, without meditating on the difference between being and thought? Between *being* (living) and *thinking* (reflecting)? How to understand, on the basis of consciousness alone, that men make their history without knowing how? How to understand freedom without this double determination: mastery over nature, 'nature' freeing itself from its limits in man?

Claude Lévi-Strauss grasped perfectly well the interest of this question and nodal point. If the starting point of thought is the categories of analytic understanding, and it sticks to these, or if it starts from the intentions of consciousness and maintains itself there, then there is no more total history. There is not even history, as partial history (that of 'historians') is defined only in relation to a total history aimed at and viewed as possible. The analytic understanding grasps elements, decomposes ensembles into atoms of meaning and reconstitutes them into systems. It privileges invariances to the detriment of becoming (the synchronic as opposed to the diachronic). As for thought that takes its starting point and support in consciousness, this grasps individual motivations, impulses, effervescences, or those of 'groups', but never a historical process; in the project, it attains the subjective aspect and no more. The creative or foundational act essentially escapes it, insofar as it responds with an original and invented (created) relationship to a question raised by human groups in their relationship with nature.

According to structuralism, the fundamental operation is that of the *analytical* intellect that proceeds from the parts to the sum, from elements to the whole, from atoms to their combinations (whether material atoms or atoms of meaning). For this method, the grasp of the general is devoid of meaning. It is impossible. The general and the total are not operatory. For Lévi-Strauss, history that seeks to be total becomes so vague, and contents itself with such general representations, that it amounts simply to a kind of backcloth on which the objects of knowledge stand out: systems and structures. 'A truly total history would cancel itself out – its product would be nought . . . History is therefore never history, but history-for.'[29]

The structuralist negation of history has several arguments at the ready, of uneven importance and interest. Thus Lévi-Strauss is struck by the resemblances (homologies) between the most ancient cities of Egypt and the East and modern towns. The same monotonous grid pattern, the same mass of crowds, the same specialization of working-class, residential and administrative quarters. To this we can respond that the analogy of forms and structures conceals profound differences, that we are not entitled to omit the tremendous history of town and city, and that on top of this it is the end of the city that we see as the striking phenomenon, retrospectively and nostalgically illuminating the past.

The fundamental argument comes from the functional and operational identity attributed to human understanding in all latitudes and all cultures, which are seen as its constructions (more or less latent and hidden). Now this theory includes an ambiguity and an extrapolation. There is identity of the understanding insofar as the understanding is precisely the function of identity, that is to say, the logical function

---

29   Lévi-Strauss, *The Savage Mind*, p. 257.

constitutive of stabilities. But does this thereby include in it the whole of praxis, the whole of consciousness? Does it not postulate, by identifying the understanding with praxis, the elimination of becoming? Does it not omit the essential fact, which is that structures and systems are the mortal and the dead, the bones of the skeleton, the shell secreted by the living creature and abandoned by it on the beach?

Lévi-Strauss has a fine time with Sartre, whom he takes as interlocutor and target. By aiming at Sartre he has philosophy in general in view (which is not a problem for us), but also Marx and Marxism. There would be a lot to say, writes Lévi-Strauss, on the *supposed totalizing activity of the ego*, in which he sees only illusion maintained by the exigencies of social life. Here, Sartre is the target. But it is Marx when Lévi-Strauss goes on to say that philosophy and the philosopher are mistaken when they believe they have attained 'the being of change'. There can be no doubt that Marx believed he had attained the being of change, the essence of becoming – and this, not as a philosopher, but by dialectical concepts, conceiving capitalism and explaining it from its birth to its historical end point: 'Although in both our cases Marx is the point of departure of our thought, it seems to me that the Marxist orientation leads to a different view.'[30]

This is where they both are wrong. Neither Lévi-Strauss nor Sartre took his point of departure in the authentic thought of Marx, which they both neglected to reinstate. Both started from a philosophy: in one case a philosophy of representation and understanding, in the other a philosophy of the thinking 'I'. One took as foundation the categories of the analytical intellect, and the other took 'consciousness of self'. They come together in the same negation of total history, or in the same impotence to grasp this otherwise than in its partial aspects: Lévi-Strauss's provisional stabilities, Sartre's effervescences of consciousness. The former pursues this to its logical conclusion: he denies history. Sartre, obsessed by real history and desirous of a dialogue with official Marxism, seeks to conceive total history, but in vain.

Structuralism seeks to spirit away history, and by stopping it adjure it to cease being bloody. A good intention, but not one that depends on thinkers. Is technical, operatory, structuralist thought capable of

---

30 Ibid., p. 246.

replacing constraint over men with the administration of things? Would it replace struggles between human groups, nations, peoples, classes, by rational and planned organization? Would structuralism, in its own fashion, proceed towards the withering away of the state, by entrusting the question to technicians capable of 'structuring' it rationally? Unfortunately, technocratic ideology seems to be bound up with a state bureaucracy. The bureaucracy is the social force that permits technological and technocratic thought to enter into praxis. Together, in association, politicians and technocrats (whose strategic decisions are not motivated simply by technical reasons) replace the spontaneous self-regulation of competitive capitalism. They are better able to make use of precise technological mechanisms for controlling praxis. Can we then count on technological thought rather than a renewed democracy to realize the withering away of the state and the replacement of constraint over men by the direct management of things?

In the structuralist hypothesis, the historical, the historicity of human being, is simply a *residue* left by the analysis of systems, themselves constructed by the analytical understanding. Let us accept this – and repeat that we consider this *residual* as infinitely precious.

According to the programme of a total history, what comes into being and survives has a rationale, as Heidegger stipulates in *The Principle of Reason*. Everything: events, institutions, works of art, even crises and bloody changes. Splits and alienations also have their reason in the being of man and his relationship with being (nature). Splits and alienations have allowed something, made possible a further development (as Hegel already knew). The point of view of alienation would thus be defined and limited as an anthropological point of view. By limiting it in this way, we open it onto a broader horizon. It would be overcome, without disappearing, by total history. Nonetheless, on the path of dialectical thought, the reason of what has been generally appears only later, in development. For Heidegger, was reason not to be found above all on the side of birth, of the original? He seems to hesitate between raison d'être in the original and in the possible. For Hegel and Marx, necessity reveals itself to be freedom, or rather it changes into freedom, and this freedom, which is concealed in necessity and subsequently reveals itself, is the reason of history. There is a difficulty here. Do we encounter a contradiction between being and freedom? Shall we find another path, beyond the philosophies of being and freedom?

In order to understand total history, we must first of all *experience the presence of history*, writes Heidegger. And first of all we must detach ourselves from the 'historiographical representation of history', which grasps history as an object 'wherein a happening transpires that is, in its changeability, simultaneously passing away'.[31] No doubt. A history of actions, decisions, foundations, goes from the present to the past. It starts from an experience: the continuous presence of what was formerly founded in relation with the being of man, in praxis. But if language is the depositary of these presences, is it their agent? Is it endowed with a 'sovereign power'? We are scarcely beginning the dialogue with the present-past or past-present that has run through time up to now: with what founds and creates, what is perpetuated in us, with nature and being. Where will this dialogue lead us? To invent new words? Or a new praxis?

It is true that being and nature change for and through man. It is true at the same time that the history of man is not separated from nature, which has a history for and through itself. It is true that the human being, appropriating nature and his own nature, reveals and deploys, but also deteriorates, what is hidden in him as 'nature' or 'essence'. It is true that alienation and dis-alienation play a strange and complex game, that social man de-realizes himself in realizing himself, that he uproots himself in rooting himself, and vice versa. In order to rediscover nature, he passes by way of extreme abstraction and extreme facticity. By unfolding, developing, he destroys a part of that which was created; he keeps another part of it. He remains in the presence of what was founded. Linear temporality does not exhaust becoming, no more than does cyclical temporality.

The praxis that creates and destroys is also itself created and negated. Acts, decisions and words found modalities of praxis, which the latter verifies, reveals, unfolds, contests, which it dissolves by criticism in action, which it transforms, annihilates, overcomes. As soon as there is a margin of freedom – a new dimension in relation to nature, a relative

---

31   Martin Heidegger, 'Science and Reflection', in *The Question Concerning Technology*, p. 158.

independence in the interdependence between social group and nature – as soon as there is 'culture' or more exactly praxis, it was necessary to decide, to create. Creation had something arbitrary about it; the work of freedom delivered to chance and fate, destined to become great or mediocre. Men founded customs: cruel or kind, *styles*. Everywhere that there was style, or the attempt at style, it had to be founded. The notion of a natural and spontaneous transition from nature to what is no longer natural (the city as well as political construction or art) can no longer be maintained. This transition also had to be decided. There were leaps, creation of qualities, thus decisions and obscure wagers.

To illustrate this dialectical movement, creative act/created work, we previously took a fragment of the long history of one of the finest human works: the city. We observed a fundamental difference (dating from the foundation and founding) between the polis and the *urbs*. In this period, creation, saying and making were still not separated. Naming and denoting what was being born, in order for it to grow, was a single act. Religious solemnization and the rites of foundation were not performances, but ways of accepting the risks of the situation created, of committing oneself to maintaining the new work, eternizing it and being eternized in it. The sacred, before being institutionalized, well before becoming attitude and theatre, and justifying the private appropriation by those in charge of a work common to the people as a whole, accompanied foundation. The founder, the foundation and the founded were hard to distinguish. Let us go back again towards these sources; let us try to grasp better both the original unity and the splits that were effected within this unity. Splits both generative of history and produced by a history, episodes of the production of man by himself on the basis of nature, both alienating and productive.

After the great separation, each specialized activity went in its own direction: poetry wandering in the verbal imaginary disassociated from the rational, philosophy becoming fixed in formal abstraction, practical knowledge in fragmented science, practical action in the empiricism of current opinions and political power. Pre-Socratic thought stood within a concrete totality in which these differences germinated without yet producing themselves.

When Heraclitus symbolized the logos as an 'ever-living fire, in measures being kindled and in measures going out', exchanging itself with and against everything 'as gold for wares, and wares for gold' (fragments 30 and 90), these were not just words of rhetoric. The Heraclitean logos is act, measure, law; it coincides with creative and devouring fire, that of the hearth, the forge, of wild fires and volcanoes, that of the Sun that warms the Earth without burning it, not letting the Earth lose itself in icy darkness. Fire governs itself according to the reason that it bears within it: which it is. It is One and All, and wisdom knows the thought by which all things are steered through all things (fragment 41). Logos and fire negate and destroy, arousing and devouring according to rhythms that are those of nature, of the city, of thought. The same tension of a string kills with the bow and rejoices with the lyre. Tensions, and the harmonies that result from tensions, as in the bow and the lyre, are equally found in natural life as in the life of the city.

Heraclitus does not dream about fire or lyre. He reflects, symbolizes, that is to say, discerns an 'ontological' correspondence. He simultaneously perceives and conceives. As a poet, he does not operate on a distinct verbal matter. These specializations – artistic work on verbal matter, reverie on the elements, abstract use of symbol and concept – would come later. Heraclitus does not employ symbols and images different from those of coherent (logical) discourse and superimposing themselves on this. Myths and logos are not opposed; neither are reflection and action. In Heraclitus the emphasis is naïve and natural, his assertions are spontaneous and his humour is cruel. Indeed, is there in him emphasis or derision, assertion or negation, metaphor or hyperbole? The figures of rhetoric are not yet formulated as such. Heraclitus's reflection is act, even civic and political act. 'Those who speak with understanding must hold fast to what is common to all as a city holds to its law, and even more strongly' (fragment 114).[32] Logos, the law of the world, is also the law of the city, which unites opposites in it and forces them into harmony.

The later splits resulted from the division of labour, the separation between manual labour (left to slaves, peasants, artisans) and intellectual labour, between material production and the conduct of men.

---

32   Translated by Kostas Axelos as *Héraclite et la philosophie*, Paris: Éditions de Minuit, 1962.

Action is distinguished from production, and the production of works of art from the production of objects. With these splits, while artist is distinguished from artisan, each equipped with his own techne, the man who acts on matter is not the man who acts on men, who conducts commercial or political affairs. If (artisanal or artistic) work is gradually distanced from the product, at the same time action in the social (trade, education, politics) is distanced from production in general. The levels that will increasingly characterize societies by their existence and distinction, that is, the economic, the social and the political, sketch out the genesis of their differences at the heart of the Greek polis and its unity. Not that there is complete separation (this never took place), but rather superpositions and interferences characterized by the use of resources in goods and men on the part of society, in an aim set by such and such a group or individual that is 'representative'. In this separation, poiesis deteriorates into poetry: operation on verbal matter, discourse still inspired by images and symbols, but close to commonplace discourse and defining itself in relation to this. Poiesis forgets that it is also praxis: action on men by works and speech, education, formation, foundation. As for praxis, it establishes itself at the level of exchanges through discourse, through trade, through contracts. It forgets that it was initially poiesis: creation of a habited and habitable human world, dwelling of a truth in the community.

In Callicles' famous speech [in Plato's *Gorgias*] this split is certainly manifest with brilliance and cynicism. Callicles notes the separations, and knows how to take advantage of them. For him, empirical life is opposed to the contemplative life that claims to stand on the level of the soul, of Beauty. Practice no longer has anything in common with theory, or experience with poiesis. He deliberately renounces the quest for totality and the universal. He rejects theory, not on the level of theory in favour of another theory, but that of an attitude towards life. He wants results, efficacy. He is the man of praxis, or rather of an aspect of praxis. He is solidly established in the real, in usable particularities and circumstances. Philosophy, for Callicles, leads nowhere. It raises the problem of life only poorly, as life is defined only empirically, socially, politically, as a function of the result to be obtained. The philosopher seeks to be educator, legislator, man of universal logos and generator of the universe. But the philosopher does not know men. Knowledge of man is obtained only through (empirical) praxis. And it is praxis (empirical or political) that creates the state, a different state from that wished for by the philosopher, the social state which has nothing in common with the ideal or poietic state. Logos, for Callicles, is simply discourse, a coherent principle of action oriented towards the result, instrument of power far more than way of truth.[33]

With the separation of different aspects and levels of human life, there appear mediations and aspirations to rediscover the broken totality, attempts that are in part nostalgic, in part full of hope. We have discerned, at the lowest rank, life simply and empirically lived in social practice, labour, trade, family life. This existence is simply submitted to in relation to those who orient or dominate praxis. It is the domain of *opinion*; people imitate each other's opinions; they repeat each other with the same gestures and words. They also imitate 'leaders'. Naturally, each trade has its own gestures and words; everyone adds his own touch and his grain of salt to what has been said and done by others. Yet at this level, praxis is simply *repetitive*. At a higher level, it *imitates* and, without wishing to, without knowing, it does not repeat what it imitates, it creates something new:

> Men make their own history, but not of their own free will . . . And, just when they appear to be engaged in the revolutionary transformation of themselves and their material surroundings, in the creation of something which does not yet exist, precisely in such epochs of revolutionary crisis they timidly conjure up the spirits of the past to help them; they borrow their names, slogans and costumes.[34]

'Mimetic praxis' is imitation of other people, of leaders and ethical models that are on offer.

Far above this inferior praxis, certain men seek an effective action that consolidates the existing by eliminating incoherencies (contradictions) while subjecting it to their power. These are the men of political reflection and action, men of the state. Their decisions are of

---

33   Cf. Plato's *Gorgias*, 484c to 486c.
34   Karl Marx, 'The Eighteenth Brumaire of Louis Bonaparte', in *Surveys from Exile*, London: Verso, 2011, p. 146.

two kinds. Some strengthen what has been achieved by way of laws and institutions. Others, more rarely, change something, found something: a monument in the city, an activity, a way of living. It is at this level that groups and classes intervene. These 'bases' permit strategies.

Between the two lie attempts to formulate 'lived experience' beyond particularities and opinions, to put an end to incoherencies and attain an ensemble. The now disjointed totality seeks itself, projects itself in images, in symbols. Art in its way tries to 'totalize' praxis. Philosophy likewise. Philosophy is defined by the search for an autonomous 'theory', different from both religion and art, from science and from political action, despite being mingled with these modalities of praxis. An ever vain effort, always partial, always renewed, in essence unachievable because partial at the very start, philosophy is a modality of discourse aiming at a total and totally coherent discourse. It seeks to master men as knowledge, in order to master nature. It wants to orient them, insinuating its science and wisdom into them. It wants to arrive at this mastery by 'theory', by discourse employed otherwise than in pragmatic and empirical action. It projects a realization of man in the city or, if need be, outside and against the city. Relative to the circumstances in which the philosopher reflects, and which it 'reflects', it is no less propelled by a movement of its own: contradictions between its postulates and its aim, between real discourses and the total discourse, and above all between the philosopher and the non-philosophical world. The philosopher observes the non-philosophical world at these various levels: opinion (repetitive and mimetic praxis), political decision and political foundation. He contemplates it. He seeks to change it by putting an end to a separation that, however, is what constitutes this world as such.

The philosopher, from the time of Socrates and Plato, is fated to understand, to seek to understand everything, not to understand everything, and above all to be understood and seek much without accomplishing anything, on account of being deprived of the means of practical action.

Philosophy is destined to incompleteness and conflict: satisfaction/dissatisfaction, but also to promote an image (a project) of human realization and unrealization, satisfaction and dissatisfaction.

What does alienation consist in, in the human situation that is sketched out in the Greek city? It is multiple. Man is divided. The product distances itself from the work to become a thing. Society becomes an abstract thing. By political decision and the state, men (citizens) are led to aims that they are ignorant of, with those who lead them not knowing where they lead, and often not knowing anything, except that they have the political means to go in this direction. The result is that the means govern the ends, and that the 'citizens', these men of the city and everyday praxis, themselves become means and instruments. These are the alienations: economic (at this level, repetitive), social (imitative), political (instrumentality of men) and philosophical (split both combatted and confirmed by the speculative attitude).

Language, formalized by writing, receives during this period an ambiguous status, which is subsequently aggravated. More end than means in 'poetry' and literature, it is both (and in turn) end and means in practical conversation, in the experience of opinions. It is means and instrument in political discourse, in rhetoric and the art of persuasion (origin of dialectic), in sophistics.

The philosopher would like language to become, through him, both means (of act, of persuasion) and end (total and totally coherent discourse) – which involves certain difficulties.

Besides, oddly enough, what enables the philosopher to play his game is that the circle is closed. Completely a means, language once again becomes end: play on words, riddles, eristic. We could say that poiesis is perpetuated in intellectual work, which is individual work in a social framework, accomplished by an individual, himself divided (active life and contemplative life, body and soul, need and desire, etc.), but who tends towards the universal. As for the praxis of a society divided into masters and slaves, possessors and non-possessors, powerful and weak, it gives rise to the practical will and the 'will to will'. But the latter splits in turn into *good will* (to keep to the law, seek an ideal) and the *will to power* (ambition, appetite for power, will to dominate or possess).

Works conceived in this way, in a very broad sense, are based on an existing praxis and found a new praxis, more or less transformed. Between the old praxis and the new modified one, something more or less important has happened. Symbols, images, signs, have had and still have a practical efficacy. Words have been uttered in historic time, overspilling a discourse confined to giving proper form to the acquired and accomplished: creative words, introducing something new.

We thus pursue the analysis of this 'reality' that is so complex and rich: praxis. We discern in it the unforeseen and the predictable, determinism, chance, will. We also distinguish in it repetition, imitation (more or less passive or active), creative invention, sometimes striking, sometimes unperceived at first. Between these different things there is certainly no absolute boundary. Repetition, whether of gestures, behaviours or movements, mechanical movements, tends to establish itself outside of vital and cosmic rhythms, in the form of linear time and homogeneous space. Creation, unpredictable in invention and the consequences of invention, is in the extreme case genius. As mediation between the two, mimesis follows models, and in the extreme case identifies with or opposes itself to them: father, leader, master, idol.

Taken in its full scope as totality, praxis includes creation as well as continuation, revolutionary praxis as well as repetitive praxis, along with their connections. Within praxis, there is a difference between what is being born and what is continuing, between what founds and what is founded – a difference that corresponds, up to a certain point, to the familiar difference between qualitative leap and quantitative unfolding, between growth and development.

To resume the history of the city [*ville*], let us examine a medieval town [*cité*]. First of all a small market is established, near a ford or a crossroads, or a feudal fortress. It expands. And then one day there is a community, the beginnings of a town. Who named the city? Who gave it its laws? Who perceived its future? The person who *founded* it. Later, around its monuments and public buildings, people busy themselves, produce, exchange, talk, discuss. That is the praxis of the city. The monuments and buildings, churches, palaces and even empty spaces that are developed, squares and markets, are vital centres of this practical activity. They gather people organically; they impose rhythms and the nature of activity: commercial, religious, political. Monuments and institutions bind the city together and make it a whole. They were founded, and the city maintains them. At the same time, they have a certain beauty; they are eminent works. Around them time and space are organized in an original way, and also an image of man and the relations between men.

The act that pronounces and lays down a law, the decision that triggers a revolution or a war, the gesture and word that create a city or a nation, have unlimited consequences in praxis. However, they would not have been able to survive as events without a preliminary praxis, proposing possibilities. The 'verified' praxis, that is to say, renders real or unreal, true or false, absurd or effective, the acts and decisions, words and works; yet this notion should not be fetishized and fixed in the philosophical form of an immutable criterion of the true, necessarily pragmatic. On the contrary, it has to be dialecticized by reinstating all the modalities of creation into its concept, in order to become fully historical.

Among the conditions of merchant capital that appears precisely in these medieval cities and their environment, did there not have to be a reintegration of the formal logic invented by the Greeks, and legal formalism – the law of private property and contracts elaborated by the Romans? These forms came down the centuries. Did they not enable, as forms, the accumulation of a certain content: knowledges, technologies, wealth, which would lead around the sixteenth century in Western Europe to a vast and multiform cumulative process? Did not logic and formal law already contain, implicitly, the project of unlimited accumulation, by an internal dialectical movement stronger than the form as such?

Logic and law were empty forms. They constituted almost perfect *systems*, as susceptible to axiomatization as mathematics. They were bound up with identity pure and simple, the place of truth retained by the philosophers. But because they were empty, the logical form and the legal form could contain, pronounce and stipulate an unlimited number of equivalences, the former in discourse and knowledge, the latter in contractual exchanges between merchants and proprietors. And this was in praxis.

These forms, moreover, gave only the possibility of accumulation. This possibility appeared in its link with the form only after the event, after it was accomplished. How and why did these two systems, these two forms (logic, as form of accumulation of techniques and knowledges, and law, as form of accumulation of wealth in private property), *converge* in the city in the course of the Middle Ages? If we neglect these conditions (which also include the dissolution of the peasant community in which patriarchal egalitarianism was opposed to the accumulation of wealth and its investment, the conflicts between the urban bourgeoisie and the feudalists based on territorial domains [*seigneurie territoriale*], facts likewise characteristic of the European West), we fall into a philosophy of history and philosophical abstraction. Whoever says philosophy, says one-sidedness. Total history seeks the totality of these practical conditions of possibility, which are not at all speculative and abstract. Marxism, systematized as philosophy of nature and history, or even as economism, has so far given a poor answer to the question raised by Max Weber: 'Why capitalism in western Europe and not elsewhere, in China or in the Islamic lands? Is it not because a certain type of man appeared there, or a certain culture?'[35]

Marxists have not even been able to develop the very precise indications of Marx and Engels. Logic and law [*droit*], having survived the conditions in which they were formulated, are not simple 'superstructures' that disappear along with their 'base'. They differ from ideologies as institutions. Does this mean they are structures? Certainly: structures of the accumulation process. It would remain to explain precisely why and how these structures are structures, which refers us to a historicity deeper than the structures that it bears and contains, that it forms and dissolves. Who introduces them into praxis, transforming existing praxis? How? Who 'founded' capitalism, obscurely or in a striking way? In a total history, the oaths of the 'sworn communes' of the twelfth and thirteenth centuries, the struggles of the bourgeois against the territorial lords [*seigneurs*], the foundations and works of this bourgeoisie in its urban domains [*seigneuries*], its transformation into patriarchate and its decline, its replacement by a new bourgeoisie of manufacturing entrepreneurs, are equally important as techniques, facts about material production, or events that are strictly political. There were moments of creation, men and acts that founded something, that oriented the subsequent course of history and praxis.

---

35 EN: This does not appear to be a direct quotation, but is very close to the opening parts of *The Protestant Ethic and the Spirit of Capitalism*, translated by Talcott Parsons, London: Routledge, 1992 [1905].

So as to render more actual and concrete this notion of historicity, let us now take the most striking and recent example. Around 1905, after the defeat of the revolutionary attempt that took place that year, Lenin discovered the revolutionary possibilities of the 'peasantry'. He glimpsed the conjunction of these possibilities with those of the proletariat, and projected a political strategy based on this conjunction. Let us leave aside the (rather awkward) fact that Lenin took over, with his own manner and style, certain ideas belonging to those whom he was opposed to, and who were opposed to him: populists, '*narodniki*', the Left Socialist Revolutionaries. He even had the cleverness or dishonesty to take over a part of their programme: agrarian reform (which in itself was only a reform, and the meaning of which Lenin changed by rejecting the municipalizing of the soil, or its 'socialization', in favour of state ownership [*étatisation*]). We know that Lenin initially viewed the peasants as no more than a supporting force. Subsequently history went much further, as the revolution was continued in the so-called underdeveloped countries. As sorcerer's apprentice, Lenin triggered forces that went differently and elsewhere than he had intended. With him, history bifurcated. Lenin switched the points, with a very small change of direction initially, but increasingly large over time. To use another metaphor, he did not add water to the river, he changed its course, as the result of a *theoretical decision*. The social forces existed, on an economic base; they made certain actions possible. By giving these forces political form, by determining the strategy that the 'base' permitted, Lenin founded, created.

A total history (which would make room for all these elements, situating them in their relationships), would bring an end to the stagnation of historical thought, its retreat in the face of anti-historical ideology (structuralist philosophy in particular). It would include a history of human needs, even – why not? – desires and dreams. In this way it would take up the Marxist idea of the production of man by himself, with its double aspect: everydayness and eminent works, mimetic behaviour and invention, positive forming and creative contestation.

Outside of this total conception of historicity, the Marxist concept of 'superstructure', understood one-sidedly, degrades into the historico-sociological concepts of institution, culture, ideological representation. It is at the same time too narrow and too large; it does not coincide with that of work. In the same way, the concept of structure, perfectly legitimate in certain conditions, having its area of validity, is extrapolated into an ideology: structuralism. When extended into a general conception of operation and function, it no longer coincides with that of *form*. And finally, again in the same way, the concept of 'base' deteriorates into a simplistic economism, a rather crude material productivism.

These deteriorations correspond, in the majority of cases, to philosophical interpretations that are grafted onto a science, history or political economy, or onto a certain concept, by hyperbole, metaphor, extrapolation. Structuralism is a very elaborate philosophy of structure. Productivism is the philosophy, a very rough one, of a praxis that is historically determined but interpreted and made into ideology, with its materialist generalities, its ethics of labour, its realist aesthetics, its political concepts justifying the state.

At this point in the presentation, metaphilosophical thought can situate itself more clearly. It explores a 'totality', the modern world, in order to know the ruptures that break this totality; it seeks to perceive its levels and gradations, its critical phases, contradictions (such as the contradiction between the 'integrating' and totalitarian character of technological and political apparatuses in present-day society, and the explosion of systems and totalities: the city, the nation, culture, etc.). In itself, metaphilosophical thought attempts to reconstruct a totality, and first of all to reunite poetry, or rather poiesis, and philosophy, at a higher level than that of their ancient split. It seeks to be *action-thought*, reconstituted unity of understanding and practical consciousness.

CHAPTER 6

Mimesis and Praxis

Taking certain precautions in order not to extrapolate, not mistake a risk for a fatality and a hypothesis for truth, let us try to state, according to what we know today, the dangers and possibilities that technology conceals.

We may leave aside science fiction, a mixture of curiously archaic themes (telepathy, occultism, spiritism and spiritualism), vulgar themes (objects and machines that rebel against their human creator) and prospective themes (what to do in a society without labour?).[1] What we should look for are real discoveries of a scientific order, ideological interpretations, extrapolations, fabulations. Yet there is an imperceptible transition from one to the other, from science to science fiction (which has the incontestable interest of revealing the most threatening possibilities, by its combination of dramatic depictions of the future with ancient myths).

Let us simply consider the science that makes it possible to build *automatons*. This teaches us first of all that movement is analyzed into three types or levels: *spontaneous* movement (involving a qualitative modification and alteration), *mechanical* movement (involving the movement of a body in space, with greater or lesser use of energy, but always considerable, and transition to a final equilibrium in conditions imposed on the moving body), and movement endowed with a *self-regulation* (determining its own conditions of equilibrium in relation to an environment). Now, we can remark that the third kind of movement, which takes place in mechanisms constructed by human thought, reproduces the first as well as adding something to it. The

1   An allusion to the masterly Clifford D. Simak, *City* [1952], London: Victor Gollancz, 2011.

self-regulating movement has a spontaneity; it possesses qualities that it essentially preserves throughout the alterations imposed on it.

The automaton is no longer simply a mechanical machine. It moves of itself and maintains itself through changes and alterations. It preserves itself. It no longer transforms relatively enormous quantities of energy into mechanical displacements (as do classical machines, locomotives for example). It captures very small quantities of energy provided by its environment: by its milieu. It uses these to inform and govern the energetic processes it contains. It is constructed to respond to stimuli from this milieu by appropriate action, and adapts itself to this.

These automatons are increasingly complex, and there is no advance limit to their degree of complexity. Mechanical *complication* no longer answers the definition of *complexity*, as the latter is definable and even measurable. Information theory quantifies quality, or at least a certain quality. It allows a measurement of novelty and variety; subsequently, this measurement enters into the mechanisms. Automatons, already capable of adapting to disturbances in their *Umwelt* (environment) and containing complex autoregulations (homoestatic systems), are perhaps already capable of modifying their own programme and repairing themselves in case of accident.

The automatic machine is a machine, as it is constructed, breaks down into its component parts, and can be rebuilt according to a rule (doubly determined: functional and structural). At the same time, it simulates life and thought. To what point does this simulation go, and to what point will it go? To indefinitely approaching the living and thinking model? Reaching this? Even superseding it in certain aspects (calculating power, intellect or intelligence) while remaining behind in others (sensation, emotionality)?

The machine, like art and the artist before it, imitates nature, animals and man as organisms (living and thinking). It reproduces these on the basis of inert (material) nature, without the possibility of assigning limits to this reproduction. Perhaps the automaton will define and cross the steps and transitions between materiality that is in appearance inert, and thought that appears to proceed from itself alone (between what certain philosophers would call the in-itself and the for-itself).

Cyberneticians raise a certain number of questions for discussion. What indexes make it possible to distinguish an automaton from a living creature (leaving aside operations that would destroy their object, submitting it to radiation, etc.)? Are these indexes on the *physiological* level, the *psychological* level, or the *social* level? According to cyberneticians, it is only in terms of the memory of an automaton that this function can be correctly defined. Human memory differs from this, as it has gaps. The human being forgets (perhaps because he 'wants' to forget!). The memory of the automaton is correct and perfect.

In the same way are its intellect and its language, at least virtually. Automatons will 'speak' the universal metalanguage, reached by successive approximations (Algol, Syntol, etc., present-day machine languages). Human discourse differs from this by its imperfections: excessive and useless redundancy, spaces between morphemes (words), silences. In the human being, emotion that seems completely personal and draws it into illusions of subjectivity is simply disturbance, hesitation. The automaton also expects: it examines all possible combinations and makes the right choice. It is more intelligent than the human being. Shall we say that it can neither laugh nor cry? But it can; so long as the programmer has well defined laughter and tears, the situation for laughter and the corresponding stimulus. And tears likewise. Spontaneity? That is not a distinctive criterion, since the automaton rediscovers it in the only precise meaning of the term: that which moves of itself, containing and preserving the principle of its movement. Dreams? Imagination? Given that these terms are defined as a function of the possible and the aleatory, they can be attributed to the automaton. All that remains for man are the illusions of subjectivity, the gaps, the holes. He would be an inferior automaton.

And yet, if the automaton can be programmed to react differentially in relation to sexed beings, it is impossible at the present time to conceive it as *having* a sex. Would the distinctive criterion be biological? That is to say, in itself 'non-human'? We know moreover that the question of individual and psycho-physiological automatism is overlaid, or rather, complemented, by that of social automatism. Social controls, ready-made behavioural models, the influence of 'patterns', tend as we know only too well to robotize humans, into groups and by groups. The ability to code them onto punch cards proves this, as both result and effective cause. The question that is raised, therefore, is that of *hominization* (a term we borrow from [Pierre] Teilhard de Chardin, to show the determination of his theology[2]) of automatons, or the *robotization* of men. Has not the human being, in a parody of the God of Genesis, created the automaton in his own image, in order to summon it to him and recognize himself in it? This encounter, this association, this strange couple and its product, we could call the *cybernanthrope*. Are we already cybernanthropes?

W. R. Ashby, in *An Introduction to Cybernetics*, defines this as the 'science of control and communication in animal and machine' – like the art of government, he adds ironically.[3] The truths of cybernetics are autonomous. They 'do not depend on any other branch of science. Cybernetics has its own foundations.' It is to the actual machine (mechanical, electrical, nervous, economic) what geometry is in relation to the objects of our terrestrial space. It has as its particular object the domain 'of all possible machines'. It is thus in a position to indicate 'new interesting and suggestive parallelisms between machine, brain and society'. In particular, it brings a common language 'which enables one branch of science to utilize a discovery by another'.[4] Let us note the interest of these declarations by an eminent specialist, the discoverer of celebrated properties and mechanisms ('Ashby's quadripole'), on the autonomy of the principles of cybernetics and their totalizing character in relation to the particular sciences. Whether this claim is well founded or not, the aim of cyberneticians is certainly to constitute a total science of the *real*, not a particular one, by *realizing* mechanisms [*dispositifs*] (machines).

---

2   EN: See 'Hominization: Introduction to a Scientific Study of the Phenomenon of Man', in *The Vision of the Past*, translated by J. M. Cohen, New York: Harper & Row, 1966 [1923], pp. 51–79.

3   William Ross Ashby, *An Introduction to Cybernetics*, London: Methuen, 1965, p. 1. In this work Ashby presents, apropos homeostasis, the idea of autonomy and unity in a self-moving technological system, taking account both of changes in the 'environment' and of changes in the system itself; this makes it possible to connect the notions of automatization, autonomy and spontaneity.

4   Ashby, *An Introduction to Cybernetics*, p. 6. Cf. also pp. 101–2, the important definition of the homeostat (p. 201), and the proposition on systems of complex regulation.

According to Norbert Wiener, in *Cybernetics and Society*, apprenticeship is essential for man to attain maturity, both as species and as individual. Such apprenticeship, we would say, is mimesis: the mimetic repetition of gestures or behaviours which succeeded in a threatening situation, in the face of a danger. What is the essence of this apprenticeship? It has been revealed by machines, according to Wiener. Apprenticeship is a form of feedback, 'in which the pattern of behaviour is modified by past experience'. The principle of feedback means that behaviour is studied in such a way that the result, whether successful or not, modifies future behaviour. Apprenticeship is therefore a complicated form of feedback. Present-day machines are able to incorporate the result of their own behaviour. In so-called homeostatic systems, there is a reintroduction into the system of the results of its action. The information returns to it.[5] The performances of such machines thus reproduce very well those of the living organism and the thinking brain. They reproduce the path leading from matter to mind. This reproduction becomes an object of production and a produced object.

These propositions, recently vulgarized and extended to society by the inventor of the word 'cybernetics', are not recent. Before philosophy seized on them, science-fiction novelists had followed these hypotheses to their conclusion, sometimes very imaginatively. Several years ago already, Pierre de Latil drew from nascent cybernetics an 'image of the universe'. He described cybernetic animals, complete with their anatomy: robots capable of imitating animal life even in digestion and the appearance of sleep.[6] He described and analysed retroaction in the wake of the theoretical work of [Claude] Shannon and [Norbert] Wiener, simple or complex feedback as the principal

---

5   Cf. Norbert Wiener, *The Human Use of Human Beings: Cybernetics and Society*, New York: Da Capo, 1988 [1954], p. 61. This theory should enchant materialist philosophers. It draws on Pavlov's theory of conditioned reflexes (cf. p. 63). Otherwise, it curiously goes in the direction of a political Manichaeism (p. 178 ff.).

6   The governing machine appears in A. E. van Vogt, *The World of Null-A*, London: Simon & Schuster, 1948. On the robot that approaches man by imitating him, cf. *Pygmalion 2113* by Edmund Cooper, Paris: Denoël, 1959; and above all Clifford Simak's work of genius, *City*. Cf. Pierre de Latil, *La pensée artificielle*, Paris: Gallimard, 1953.

secret of organic nature, as revealed by automatons. The models of an image of the universe that is formed in this way borrow from Descartes and [Julien Offray de] La Mettrie (animal machines), Locke (the passivity of the mind), Condillac (the animated statue), [Jacques] Loeb (tropisms) and [Ivan] Pavlov (conditioned reflexes).

What is quite clear is that eighteenth-century materialism, devoid of dialectic, makes a return here. A well-known passage from Condillac's *Traité des systèmes* is not far from contemporary texts of the structuralist school. Condillac wrote here:

> To speak in an understandable manner, one's ideas must be conceived and put forward in the analytical order that decomposes and recomposes each thought . . . In fact, if I want to understand a machine, I shall decompose it in order to study each part separately. When I have an exact idea of each, and can put them back in the same order in which they were, I shall then perfectly conceive this machine, because I shall have decomposed and recomposed it.[7]

If we add to this text the concepts of 'functional' and 'structural', spelled out since Condillac's time, we have a very modern statement.

Here is the summary of a lecture given in December 1963 to the Société française de cybernétique by its president, Louis Couffignal, an eminent scientist and the introducer of binary numeration into machines (the calculus that reduces all numbers to combinations of 0 and 1). Cybernetic thought holds itself out as a general method. It proclaims a balanced, harmonious, human future. It gives a promising and almost utopian image of this:

> From the cybernetic method of thinking, we shall retain the following characteristics:
>
> - the primordial concern for efficiency, which presupposes the definition of aims and a total eclecticism in the choice of means;
> - analogical reasoning, generally realized by way of models.

---

7 EN: Étienne Bonnot de Condillac, *Logique*, Gand: Vanderketckhove, 1826, pp. 22–3.

The analogy between a living being and a human society leads to the notions of economic and enterprise function, defined as a human society whose activity is aided by material means. This predominance of the human element over the material element leads us to discover the importance of professional skill, an enterprise structure made up of self-organizing units, informational circuits, and the role of the government of the enterprise and of administrative organisms.

Analysis of the aims leads us to discover, right the way through, the role of the spirit of domination, undoubtedly bound up with the scarcity of the material goods necessary to human life. The advance of technology will make it possible, in a very short time, to suppress this scarcity; it will then be possible to assign to the whole of human economic activity the aim of assuring all people reasonable satisfactions. Professor François Perroux has formulated a 'planetary' economic policy of this kind, and an appropriate ethics. The cybernetics of enterprise functioning briefly described above offers a sure method for attaining this aim at the lowest costs.[8]

From this declaration we note the political indifference of technocracy, capable of making use of all means, those of the 'left' as well as those of the 'right', those of both democracy and monopolistic capitalism, to arrive in power and keep the commandment. The image of the 'governing machine' is therefore not just a theme of science fiction.[9] These machines would subject an already over-organized industrial society by way of institutions; they would group existing systems into a single system: the state, art, philosophy. They would consolidate structural equilibriums determined by operational demands (machines and technologies being clearly an integral and integrating part of these). With von Neumann's propositions having the force of theorems, teaching us that a complex (homeostatic) self-regulating system can control and even generate a more complex system, cybernetics transgresses an old philosophical presupposition, according to

---

8   EN: We have been unable to trace the exact reference, but Louis Couffignal was author of the introductory Que sais-je? volume *Le cybernétique* the same year (Paris: PUF, 1963).

9   Cf. van Vogt, *The World of Null-A*; also P. Dubarle in *Le Monde*, 28 December 1948; and finally Wiener, *The Human Use of Human Beings*, pp. 178 ff.

which the inferior cannot create the superior. The machine, now highly complex, tackles the problems of complexity, reserved up until now for philosophers.

Does von Neumann's theorem not apply to the totality of machines, objects, products, human relations, the living body and knowledge, to the great automaton that will be born from the ensemble of mechanisms installed? What has been designed and built by technology can move of itself, reproduce earlier movements of life to thought and produce them in itself. Why then should mimesis not be the first and last operation of nature and thought, simulating pure spontaneity, until the day when the subjective illusion collapses and mimesis turns out to be truth?

We can go still further. The automaton moves of itself and governs its movements. Are not automatism and auto-correlation a natural spontaneity basically identical to organization? If man has drawn from automation, from the general spontaneity that animates the universe, 'automatons or reduced models, minuscule duplicates of the automatic power of nature',[10] are we not on the road towards an automatic functional society?

Frederick Pollock, in his book on *Automation*, wrote:

An economic system could be maintained automatically in equilibrium thanks to the methods of feedback. As with any feedback, it would be a question of correcting oscillations while these are still minimal. This kind of automatism can only be effective if society has decided to put these formulas into practice. We can characterize the present situation by saying that machines can accomplish on the economic level almost everything of which man is capable, except purchasing the goods produced.[11]

Black humour this, and perhaps unintended. Moreover, why not construct robots that would buy and consume products? In fact, we rediscover a familiar idea here, in unexpected form: there is always a

10   Pierre Naville, 'Vers l'automatisme social', *Revue française de sociologie*, 1960, no. 1, p. 280.

11   Frederick Pollock, *The Economic and Social Consequences of Automation*, Oxford: Blackwell, 1957, p. 199.

residue that resists. Something irreducible! In this case, no more and no less than man as consumer!

Pierre Naville, in developing the article cited above into a book, emphasized the spontaneity of the automaton and the fact that social man can enter the automatism of society while preserving natural spontaneity, in other words without noticing[12] – or to put it differently, even with satisfaction: a satisfaction that it might be best not to disturb, particularly with the outdated theory of alienation.

Philosophy defends itself against this attack. Poorly. For Raymond Ruyer,[13] information 'is the transmission to a conscious being of a meaning, a notion, by way of a more or less conventional message and a spatio-temporal "pattern"'. M. Ruyer seeks to demonstrate that information and information technology depend on consciousness, presuppose it and do not challenge its (metaphysical) priority. There is only information, and thus an information machine, for and through consciousness. This philosopher seems to underestimate the importance and seriousness of the quantification of the qualitative, the measure of novelty. Where is this consciousness located? In the circuit of information. In this case, it is 'trapped'. From the start, or at

---

12   'It may be that the future will see the establishment of a basic dichotomy, both for industry and for the whole advance of the civilization bound up with it, between the maintenance of life and the creation of life,' Pierre Naville writes in his book *Vers l'automatisme social*, Paris: Gallimard, 1963, p. 105. Up to this point we can follow him, but not when he pronounces: 'It is perhaps its continuance, that is to say, its maintenance in the broadest sense, that constitutes its primordial aspect.' In our view, Naville is too quick to accept the convergence between two partial systems: social relations and technological relations in production (in the division of labour, cf. p. 112 of his book). Let us mention that the new Soviet generation, heedless of Marxist philosophy and its prohibitions, proposes above all to win the competition with the Americans. It is accepted that science has directly become a productive force, and that science teaching and the training of technicians needs to be reshaped. The proposal is to teach recent mathematics right from the start, along with machine programming and the general laws of biology and electricity. This scientific propaedeutic exactly corresponds to a cybernetizing and technocratizing of scientific teaching (cf. *Bulletin de l'Union des travailleurs scientifiques*, nos 2 & 3, Jan–Apr 1963, report of the international symposium on higher education, Moscow, September 1962). The task remains of combining traditional humanism with cybernetics in Soviet Marxist ideology – or alternatively of liquidating it.

13   Raymond Ruyer, *La cybernétique et l'origine d'information*, Paris: Flammarion, 1954, p. 7.

the end?[14] But then, what is the exact relationship of creative activity to its product, to its work? We know that this relationship no longer corresponds to the 'models' proposed by classical philosophy: subject-object, artisan-worked thing, value to something that bears or supports it. Not only can the dead take hold of the living, it may well be that the 'thing' is no longer exactly dead or exactly alive in the strict sense, but intermediate and transitional between these poles: that it is animated, imitates the living and thinking, which in turn imitates it.

Being and nature, becoming and action, would then be in no way given to man in a poiesis, nor even in praxis, but in mimesis. Truth would be discovered at the heart of appearance, in an unexpected fashion. Machines have taught men how far they proceed by disjunctions and dichotomies, binary oppositions, contrarieties, by 'yes' and 'no' in language and decisions. The machine reveals the truth of the structures of body and brain, of discourse, action and consciousness. Discovery of these structures in turn permits the unlimited perfecting of the machine. By imitating nature, it imitates man who forms part of this objective nature. Thus appearance and simulation – mimesis – would be at the same time real and bearers of truth. The appearance and imitation of thought and life would lead to the truth of life and thought. Man knows himself, recognizes himself, realizes himself in his work, his being-other: the machine. The other-being, his image, would also be himself. Information theory would contain a philosophical or quasi-philosophical conception of mimesis. Redundancy, the repetition of elements of the repertoire that is indispensable to all communication, makes for the intelligible form of the message. Information contrasts with redundancy, in the same way as surprise to the expected, diversity to repetition, disorder to established order, and the aleatory to the accomplished fact recorded in memory. Any message, simple or complex, any communication, would thus stand between the banality of the intelligible that repeats and is repeated, and absolute novelty, unintelligible simply by reason of

---

14   Ibid., p. 225, the conclusion of the book.

its excessive novelty, yet well defined by the disorder (equi-proba-bility) of signs used.

With the message occupying intermediate place between overly strict order and excessive disorder, between rigid form and the unformed, the privileged domain of mimesis is determined, between repetitive praxis that is necessary but insufficient, and the pure event. Mimesis is double. It reproduces an acquisition and aims at something inaccessible that it incompletely attains. The quality of information gained over the inaccessible that is too complex, chaotic and prolific, can be calculated. This makes it possible to quantify the complexity of any message, and even each new combination of distinct elements (objects, acts, atoms of meaning, etc.). Quantification accompanies the transition from the 'unstructured' to the structural. In the name of quality itself, it moves in a dialectic of quality from qualitative data to the quantitative system.

That would be the structure of all information, in other words every message. Information theory brings a concept of intelligibility. Redundancy (repetition of elements of the repertoire, always made up of distinct and discrete atoms of meaning) defines the intelligible. This definition has a very general scope, as it is possible to consider as a 'message' not only language and discourse, but no matter what inter-action between two natural or social 'beings', and likewise as a consequence relations between two or more things as well as sense perception among human individuals and relationships between them by way of discourse, images and symbols, the mediation of objects, the communication of acts and situations. The generality of the theory is shown by the fact that the fundamental magnitudes and equations present a remarkable analogy with those of thermodynam-ics or the theory of equilibrium and exchange of energy. Knowledge as constructor of mechanisms and machines in the wake of operatory calculations, and subsequently basing itself on these mechanisms and machines, has unquestionably made possible immense strides forward. Cybernetics is a science in full growth. The long opposition of Marxist philosophers who viewed cybernetics as 'mechanistic' and formal logic as 'idealist', has been unable to halt this growth. It only brought ridicule on Marxist dogmatism, and played a bad trick on science in the Soviet Union.

In this orientation, we see the dawn of a 'worldview' based on a linkage between structural linguistics, information and communications theory, and perception theory.[15]

At a time when the use of the word 'structure' is diversifying without always being made clear, when it is receiving ever new meanings, a new philosophy is also emerging: structuralism. Whether this actually is a philosophy we shall see.

We would first like to distinguish between structuralism in practice and structuralism as ideology, that is, as philosophy.

The specialist who dismantles and rebuilds a motor, who conceives it, repairs it or improves it, thinks structurally. He views each component part in terms of its form and its function. The set of parts is more for him than their mere juxtaposition or sum: it functions. Yet the motor breaks down analytically into these parts, each of which has its meaning in the whole that is built up from them. The parts as classified according to form or function: according to their differences and their relations of inclusion or exclusion. The technician who analyses and reconstructs functional systems is a structuralist in practice.

Structuralism as ideology, however, tends to become a logic, a general method, an anthropology, even an ontology. It links up with all sectors of knowledge, and presents itself as the link between the human sciences and those of nature. It also links up with aesthetic creation and sees itself as the link between the arts.

In a brilliant article which appears like a manifesto of the young structuralist school, Roland Barthes elegantly sketches the difficulty. He presents structuralism as a style (of activity, thought, life) rather than a philosophical doctrine. He speaks of *structuralist activity*.[16]

---

15   A linkage announced in 1956–7 in the periodical *Voies nouvelles*, nos 1 and 2: *Marxisme et théorie de l'information*. A passage in this article predicts the advent of the unknown philosopher who will accomplish this linkage, ironically acclaiming him. Has this philosopher arrived? Is his name Claude Lévi-Strauss? Or Roland Barthes? Or Abraham Moles? (Cf. *Information et cybernétique: Communications et Langages*, Paris: Gauthier-Villars, 1963; and A. Moles, *Théorie de l'information et perception esthétique*, Paris: Flammarion, 1958.)

16   'We see why it is necessary to speak of structuralist activity: creation and reflection here are not an original impression of the world, but the making of a world that resembles the former, not to copy it but to render it intelligible.' ('L'activité structuraliste', *Lettres nouvelles*, no. 32, February 1963, p. 74; 'The Structuralist Activity', *Critical Essays*, Evanston, IL: Northwestern University Press, 1972, pp. 223–30.)

What he says of it, however, immediately assumes a philosophical scope and tone. Structuralist activity is that of 'structural man' (meaning contemporary man, modern, not passé!). This structural man takes the real, dissects it, recomposes it. Yet he does not reproduce the real; he simulates it. Techne does not proceed according to poiesis, continuing physis, but according to mimesis. Structural man adds to the natural world a prefabricated world that does not copy nature, rather substituting for it intelligibility. This structural man is the man of technology and technicity, as technology is supposedly the essence of all creation. Structuralist activity is thus always bound up with a technology. It combines two fundamental operations: dissection (into discrete units, atoms of meaning) and arrangement [*agencement*].

Barthes thus defines at the same time the *subject* (man, the active intellect), the *object* (on the one hand the given real, on the other hand the constructed object) and their *formal* relations (analysis, technicality, disposition, simulation, intelligibility). Is he not proposing a methodology, an anthropology, a theory of the world (which is freighted with meanings and forms, but can be simulated by technologies), in other words a philosophy? unless it is simply a new mythology, bound up with the predominance of technology, its autonomizing in relation to the world and human being.

A philosophy of what? Implying what? Who is this structural man? What does he look like? That is our question. Even if it parodies a bit the thought of this new, structural man, we can say that he ostensibly prefers the prosthetic limb to the living one. Naturally, the prosthetic limb is useful and functional. It is incontestably more intelligible than the living limb, which it replaces for the injured person. It simulates this as well as possible. We cannot even rule out that it reveals some hidden structures. But can we not reply to our structural man that only the living limb has a meaning, that of life, despite not having the *finished* (and dismantleable) character of its artificial simulation? The living limb possessed this meaning before the construction of the simulacrum, as part of a living whole. Not only does it have functions and a form, it forms itself. It has a history and refers to a history, that of the individual and that of the species. Could life and its history be reduced to an unintelligible and irrational residue left by the construction of simulacra?

Still in a humorous mode, we can say that Roland Barthes introduces a *cool* style opposed to the *hot* style (tragic, bumpy, often impassioned) of dialectical thought, that of becoming. But is this new style really a style? Is it not something else, or quite simply an absence of style, a degree zero of style, which presents itself as a style?

The conflict that has blown up between the structural and the historical dates from the beginnings of sociology. Starting from the thesis put forward by Saint-Simon, that society constitutes an organic whole, Auguste Comte disassociated this whole and distinguished between social statics and social dynamics, placing priority on the former. For him, dynamics was subordinated to statics. This seeks the principles common to all societies, the laws of stable relations between the elements and the whole. Thus empiricism and positivism, from their beginnings, have not been content to observe given facts, accepting them uncritically, without a perspective of profound transformations – which would already be enough to mark this thought with a reactionary character. They set out above all to find invariances, definitive stabilities, conditions of equilibrium. They sought to reveal and formulate the laws of all societies, to make the society of their time conform to their laws and to do so against history. What becomes of history in such a conception? A series of illusions, errors or oscillations around the terminal equilibrium, except perhaps when the history of mind and knowledge is presented. This attitude is expressed in Comte's famous attack on Napoleon, a man of history. By a curious internal contradiction, positivism was a philosophy, even a philosophy of history, directed against history and historical thought.

This conflict, latent for more than a century, broke out when a society was established (contemporary American society) that did not have much history behind its actuality or its culture, and whose ideologists claimed to set up against the science of history a different science, empirical and quantitative sociology. A conflict of this kind also tended to break out because a society was heralded that claimed to have no other history than that of its technology (a society characterized in particular by cybernetics and automation, which has been given various names, none of which has particularly prevailed: industrial society, consumer society, affluent society, leisure society, mass society, technical society, etc.). In these conditions, empiricism and positivism reinforced by the use of new mathematical forms believe they have carried the day.

It is true that the conjuncture is favourable to them. Historical thought is uncertain, losing ground. Marxists, who should represent and deepen it, are lost in sterile philosophical controversies (between 'proletarian' and 'socialist' materialism and 'bourgeois' idealism, if not between 'proletarian science' and 'bourgeois science'!). They neglect the real theoretical questions.

Historical thought is then caught between bourgeois ideology and Stalinist ideology (or its sequels). One side wants to liquidate history or have it liquidated. The other side rewrites it for the purposes of propaganda, which has made no small contribution to a crisis of historical objectivity. If it is true that we are still in the age of 'world-views', and that such philosophical *Weltanschauungen* are not 'superseded' (whereas Marx proposed the superseding of classical philosophy by realizing it, in and through revolutionary praxis), why not a structuralist worldview?

The occasion is all the more favourable, given that structuralist thought proves flexible enough to envisage superseding the antinomy between statics and dynamics. And it does so by drawing inspiration more or less faithfully from Marxism. This is what Gaston-Gilles Granger attempts in distinguishing several forms of equilibrium and elaborating the notion of balanced growth or balanced accumulation.[17]

The structuralist worldview would then be defined as follows:

a) Structural or semantic reduction. The human being consists essentially of an (analytical) intellect. Man is above all a creator of forms and meanings. The rest, the 'content', is an irrational residue manifested only in the gaps and lacunae between forms, systems and structures;

b) [This intellect has an essentially classificatory and combinatory function. It breaks down ensembles into elements and reconstitutes

17   Cf. Gaston-Gilles Granger, *Méthodologie économique*, Paris: PUF, 1955, I, pp. 1, 4.

them. It prevails over the invariances that it attains or constitutes. The capacity to combine arrangements and permutations simultaneously determines intellect and the intelligible, instrument and object.

What does this reduction bracket out? A good deal. The concrete complexity of praxis, that of man and that of the world. Dialectics. Tragedy. Emotion and passion. The individual, certainly, and perhaps a large part of the social. And then history. All this falls into the residual, which has to bend itself to globalized technicality and disappear.

The source and prototype of intelligibility is situated neither in individual consciousness (the classic Cartesian position, continued in existential philosophy by Sartre), nor in 'being' (the classic metaphysical position, continued and transformed by Heidegger), nor again in praxis (the Marxist position). This source and prototype is situated in language.[18] The formal operation of the structuralist intellect is dichotomy. This separates, divides, classifies (into genres and kinds), determines formal differences, paradigms, conjunctions and disjunctions, binary oppositions, questions that it answers by a 'yes' or a 'no'. Leibniz already asserted, building on Llull's *ars combinatoria*, that the whole world (numbers and beings) arose from the opposition and combination of zero and unity.[19]

We have to recognize that this conception has received powerful support. In terms of calculating and translation machines, built effectively on the binary principle, structural linguistics, developments in pure and applied logic with games theory, decision theory, operational research, information theory. The definition of the intellect by separation, differences and dichotomy seeks to be functional and operational, which indeed it is. It undoubtedly corresponds to the fundamental

---

18   It is quite curious to see how this thesis has reacted to the teaching and understanding of mathematics since the publications of 'Nicolas Bourbaki' [TN: the pseudonym used by a group of French mathematicians, established in the 1930s, who set out to refound mathematics on the basis of set theory].

19   EN: Ramon Llull [Raymundus Lullus] was a thirteenth-century philosopher. Leibniz gave his theory of logic the name 'ars combinatoria'.

activity of technical thought. It thus links up with operationalism: a doctrine of efficacity, a praxeology.

It enables nervous and cerebral activity to be presented as an activity of distinguishing, of choice, of oppositions (in particular that between form and base), and consequently to connect physiological with psychological research, particularly that of the Gestalt theorists.

We know only too well, moreover, that the metaphysics of becoming (Hegelian and Marxist, or rather pseudo-Marxist) ended up forgetting that this becoming constitutes 'beings', and thus coherencies, provisional stabilities, precarious equilibriums, in a word, structures, before dissolving or breaking them.

This chair, for example, will certainly not be around for all eternity. It will come to an end, worn out, broken up, burned. Becoming will carry it away, is already carrying it away. While waiting to disappear, it has four legs, a back, a surface for sitting: a structure and a function. It cannot tolerate certain modifications without ceasing to be a chair, without losing its structure and function. As a stable object, it has a name and a concept: it corresponds to a sign that signifies its concept. It pertains to discourse and logic, despite remaining a chair. No one can say both that it is and is not a chair, until the painful moment when it ceases to be a chair, even though something remains of its form in the deteriorated object. The same can be said of every object, every technological arrangement, and even the Earth, Sun and solar system, not to mention each heavenly body wandering in space until destroyed by cosmic becoming.

Does restoring these considerations (stability, equilibrium, coherence) into cosmic and human becoming involve a depreciation or elimination of this becoming? Is consideration of stabilities, of 'things', necessarily a symptom of 'reification'? Must we remain with an evolutionism more or less complicated by the introduction of dialectical thought – contradictions, leaps, changes of quantity into quality? This is now our question.

Paradoxes. Language, logos, discourse become prototypes of intelligibility and 'privileged sites of philosophical reflection'[20] at the

---

20   Alphonse de Waelhens, 'Perspectives sur le langage', *Les Temps modernes*, no. 205, June 1963, p. 2279.

moment when in social practice, around us, language dissolves, deteriorates, retreats to make way for the image. Language is fetishized at the same time as it is threatened. Communication, and reflection on communication, become fashionable at the very time that each conscious individual complains of the absence of genuine communication, of solitude, of the avalanche of 'pseudo-events'.[21]

By combining into a synthesis, or rather a syncretism, the functionalist and operationalist contentions, the new philosophy of structure offers itself, whether consciously or not, as the worldview of technocrats. It presents its candidacy for this disputed post, again whether consciously or not. It designates an extensive, perhaps unlimited, domain of manipulations of men, of language, of objects. It wants to construct a 'world' for us, or rather a simulacrum of a world. It is rather like what today's housing estates, simulacra that are the present-day products of technocracy, represent in relation to both historic towns and possible ones. This philosophy is not free of a certain risk, that of a cybernetizing of social man, oriented from within and controlled from without by machines on the basis of what is most essential: language. Is man treated in this way anything but a simulacrum of the human?

Technocracy, today, needs an ideology that justifies it and makes possible the integration of the society that it seeks to construct. Now the *mondialisation* of technology and the technocratic conception presupposes a reduction and even a liquidation of the historical (seen as dead weight, residue, more embarrassing than picturesque).

With the reign of pure technicality and technocrats, with the cybernetizing of society, we would no longer have a future in this historical sense, a temporality in the customary sense. We would enter a kind of eternal present, probably very monotonous and boring, that of machines, combinations, arrangements and permutations of given elements. There would be no other events than the introduction of new technologies (which moreover could make great demands). Unless 'deviants', who would be pursued with barbaric cruelty, intervene to derail the system. Unless destruction and self-destruction one day put an end to this 'world'.

---

21 Cf. Daniel J. Boorstin, *The Image: A Guide to Pseudo-Events in America*, New York: Vintage, 1992, p. 7ff.

Historical thought, on the other hand, maintains that contents have as much importance and interest as forms, if not more. It says that forms and structures are made and unmade, dissolve or break up. It places on the same level, in time, the formation of structures (structuration) and their disappearance (destructuration). It shows, within structuration, the commencing dissolution or inevitable explosion. For it, the historic past is not reduced to a dead weight or a picturesque superfluity. Differences manifest themselves as they have always done within worldwide technology, due to the history of societies, groups, classes, peoples, nations. History continues. The seemingly irrational demands its integration, not into a philosophy or forms that reject it, but into a conception of man as a whole. In the absence of which it rebels. The theory of alienation denounces fetishisms, splits, mutilations of the total human being. It particularly denounces technical, technological, technocratic alienation, recently promoted to the rank of major human alienation.

And time? In the structuralist conception it disappears as becoming, genesis and formation; it is reduced to the order of appearance of more or less probable combinations, with a lower limit in pure repetition and an upper limit in unpredictable combinations involving the most unusual elements. The notion of temporality disappears into that of entropy (measure of the degree of irreversibility), between the lower limit of the immutable and immobile order, absolute cold, and the upper limit, the frenetically disordered agitation of molecules. The aleatory enters into the calculation and is envisaged as such. Along with time, it is history that disappears in the world, or acquires a new aspect, opening onto a kind of technological temporality without history, or with its only history that of combinations between technological operations.

Technological rationality, then, goes a long way. It challenge and undermines many theoretical and practical elements that seemed to form part of the definition of man, whether considered as *faber, sapiens* or *ludens*. It attacks time. This is far more than a matter of history considered as science of time, and heralds attacks on real (practical) time and its mutation into technological time, if this is allowed. It is scarcely a caricature of technological and cybernetic rationality (a rationality that, as we see ever more clearly, defines itself as understanding rather than reason) to say that for it, nature or what passes for nature scarcely counts for anything. It is an obstacle. It should be got rid of, the time devoted to these functions reduced or even substitutes found for them. Vital and cosmic rhythms? They are a kind of enemy to pursue in favour of a linear time broken into well-defined atoms (semantemes). Technological and structuralist thought is culturalist. Like culturalism, it deprecates nature. Like structuralism, it brackets it out. Nature is simply residual, and history likewise.

Man's relationship with his work would no longer be problematic. Man would no longer be lost in his work, but would rediscover himself in it; he would go from the machine to self-encounter. No more alienation in work and being-other. On the contrary: knowledge and mastery are accomplished simultaneously, by way of mimesis. Philosophy comes to an end. It arose from an illusion about poiesis. Man sought to produce himself by thought alone, whereas it was in a different way and elsewhere that he encountered himself, in the works of labour: the tool becoming machine.

And alienation? Inasmuch as we can still speak of it, it is found in philosophy, in ideology and in art (traditional, not combinatory and operatory), in the form of erroneous interpretations of productive activity. Marxism, inasmuch as it contributed something, overcomes itself. Dialectic falls, and bare materialism with an ascetic and misanthropic tendency (as denounced by Marx) returns to the surface. The discovery of technology, of the machine, of labour, opens up a new era, that of technology and machinery liberated from any obstacle, liberatory. 'Technology is the very being of all creation': structuralist activity, bound up with technicality, is defined by two operations: decomposition and arrangement.[22]

If robots converge with men, and man recognizes himself in this mimetic image, the spontaneity of the automaton, this is because man was already a robot. He did not know this. He is learning it. The nervous system and other biological, physiological 'systems' are self-regulating systems. The living body? A network of such systems, a complex homeostatic system of which Ashby's quadripole offers a simplified model. The brain? A complex and imperfect machine for

---

22   R. Barthes, 'The Structuralist Activity', p. 75.

recording, combining, disjoining and arranging. Thought? A succession of 'yeses' and 'noes', dichotomies. Action? A series of strategic
decisions in a complex play with 'nature' and other social groups. If
society can subsist, it is because it contains self-regulating systems. It is
because it is already a homeostatic system. In the new sciences of information and communications, the combinatory essence of the real, its
fundamental structure, is discovered and recognized. As for nature, it
does not even exist. It was also just illusion and myth. Still more: a residue. Mimesis turns out to be the essence of praxis; the appearances of
appearance or of appearing fall away: those of poiesis, those of transcendence, of subjectivity and subjective freedom, of temporality and
historicity, of nature as a whole. The robot is no threat to man, for the
excellent reason that individual and social man is already a robot, and
the threatening image of the robot is mere illusion. The figure of the
monstrous and untameable golem, rebelling against the sorcerer's
apprentice, would be simply a myth of the machine, and the myth of the
robotic inhuman a myth of man. The two entities, automaton and
human, meet up in a single category: the Cybernanthrope!

Marx's ideas on machinery are scattered throughout *Capital* and
the preparatory works towards this, but essentially in the second chapter of *The Poverty of Philosophy*. If there is a theory that overflows the
competence of philosophy, it is that of the tool and the machine taken
in praxis (in relations of production). As against Proudhon, the
philosopher of poverty, Marx establishes first of all the practical and
historical character of the division of labour. This was transformed
from the sixteenth and seventeenth centuries on, particularly from the
invention of machinery in the eighteenth century. It is unacceptable,
therefore, to weigh as Proudhon does the advantages and inconveniences of the division of labour, its good and bad sides, on the basis
of a general categorical definition.

Machinery is no more an economic category than the ox that pulls
a cart. Machinery is a productive force. The modern workshop, on the
other hand, based on the use of machinery, is a social relation of
production: a specifically economic category. Historically, it presupposes the market and the accumulation of capital.

Marx clearly distinguishes between the technical division of
labour and its social division. The technical division is constituted

and commanded by the productive forces, instruments and machines and their utilization. The social division is grafted onto this technical division and adds something to it: for example an ideology, professional narrow-mindedness. It is determined by the entire existing society. The automaton reduces labour to a few gestures. So it is liberating. Machinery, as such, is not alienating; on the contrary. It is simply its social use in class society, its insertion into contradictory social relations, that makes it a means for enslaving labour. In itself, having become automatic, it can take over all labour. It unites the total labour that was technologically divided and fragmented. Nothing less, but nothing more. It does not assure the full development of the individual. It makes this possible. The need for development grows together with automatism. The problem, therefore, is not to stop technology but to take it to its conclusion. Writing some time later, Marx did not go back on these predictions. Along with the power of the instruments of production, the role of material labour and human labour-time has to change:

> As soon as labour in the direct form has ceased to be the great well-spring of wealth, labour time ceases and must cease to be its measure . . . The surplus labour of the mass has ceased to be the condition for the development of general wealth, just as the non-labour of the few, for the development of the general powers of the human head. With that, production based on exchange value breaks down.[23]

It goes without saying that there were certain facts, events and conflicts that Marx could not see. How could he have supposed that the automatic machine would go so far as to imitate life and thought, and incorporate analytical understanding (though his ironic reflections on the internal automatism of the Hegelian system contain some shadowy presentiment of this).

No more could he foresee the extraordinary situation of modernity: technology bringing abundance and non-labour close and almost

---

23 *Critique of Political Economy.* [EN: Karl Marx, *Grundrisse*, London: Allen Lane, 1973, p. 705.]

imminent for an almost unlimited number of human beings, and this proximity provoking the planetary drama of a transition in which no one knows what to do with millions and billions of these human beings, peasants, workers in ailing industries, bureaucrats and others!

We rediscover here a familiar idea. For Marx, the revolution that with one bound crosses the gulf between blind necessity and the full freedom of rational man was to precede and permit the liberation of technologies through their mastery. But history has not proceeded according to the envisaged pattern. It is richer in inventions and difficulties than Marx's dialectic proclaimed, and dialectical thought cannot dispense with the idea of an unlimited inventive wealth of history.

Marx could not know, despite having proclaimed the process, that the law of uneven development would dominate a long transitional period. He could not know that the conflict between possible non-labour (the extension of leisure) and the demands of labour and (indispensable) accumulation would become one of the principal conflicts during this mutation. For the whole world – our world, our planet – finds itself facing the necessity of a gigantic labour and colossal accumulation in order to realize the conditions of non-labour. How can hundreds of millions of peasants be absorbed, when the production that is urgently needed demands fewer and fewer productive personnel? How are tens of millions of workers to be transformed into non-proletarians? Peasants are virtually suppressed and the peasant problem becomes acute, all the more so in countries and regions that are less developed, and where the demands of accumulation are more urgent. The proletarian condition is virtually superseded, but nowhere is this virtuality realized. Abundance is possible, but the spectre of hunger still stalks the planet. Leisure is close, and this closeness translates into an obstinate labour more oppressive and exploited than previously – to the point that all some countries in the course of development can do is manage their uneven development, guard against too great ambitions, reject the establishment of industries that are too advanced or too intense, that eliminate too many 'workers', and content themselves with backward means.

In the course of his research, Marx had to abandon the theorization (originating in Hegel and Adam Smith) of labour as the sole foundation, sole root and sole meaning of human activity. Discovering the automatic machine, he also discovered non-labour, leisure, and the demand for leisure (starting with the reduction of the working day). He also had to abandon the idea of overcoming the division of labour within this division, by permitting each person to change their labour as they liked, to exercise in turn and freely this or that productive activity, this or that occupation. This project, still visible in *The German Ideology*, disappeared before the full automatism of productive labour. From 1845 on, accordingly, Marx completely and definitively superseded the earlier communism with an artisan origin, ascetic communism. He conceived the socioeconomic conditions for a radical transformation of society in their totality.

And yet something of this still remains. If he eliminates liberation by way of change of occupation, he still imagines a future man who would choose in turn among creative activities that are determined and specialized: who would freely be painter, poet, sculptor, musician, philosopher. Freely in the sense of one day one thing, the next day another. Seeking to proclaim the concrete modalities of the future society, utopian despite his denials, Marx oscillated between this aesthetic view and the ethical view of a society constituted by the reciprocal free recognition of conscious beings. Did he completely escape the framework of the division of labour? No. Today machinery harshly reminds us of this, when it becomes machinery for making music, for painting: for art, and when ethical 'values' collapse, reduced to the state of compromised ideologies.

Much could be said on the pages that Marx wrote in the mid-nineteenth century, both for and against. In recent decades, a good part of the research of industrial sociology has been devoted to commenting on them, refuting them, amending them, extending them. Let us say by way of summary that today they strike us as amazingly 'prospective', especially when reinstated in their context. The machine, for Marx, was no longer what it was for Hegel: an instrument, a tool or a set of tools. It is already the automaton that overcomes the division of labour, or permits this to be overcome. Did Marx grasp the essence of technology? Yes. Schematically, the automaton makes possible non-labour.

We are now in this transition leading from the society of labour to the society of leisure. We are no longer, in 1965, in the society of labour, as some still believe, though we are not yet, as others claim, in the society of leisure. A difficult transition. A difficult mutation. The automaton has not yet made it possible to overcome the existence of working masses and classes. It demands from them ultimate efforts for the accumulation of enormous capitals and gigantic resources, for the construction of gigantic mechanisms. And yet, it is there. It functions. As a consequence, the number of 'manual' workers is dwindling and will continue to do so. The number of technicians, white-collar employees, bureaucrats, increases. And yet the 'labourer' is more exploited than ever (even if his material lot improves), more subordinated than ever, delivered to the demands of technological ensemble and automatic mechanisms, from the firm to the state. As for the bureaucrats, they are imprisoned in bureaucracy. The 'values' of labour are in full crisis, those of non-labour are hard to discover.

The automatic machine could well take over many 'things': all kinds of 'things' perhaps. The end point of this programme will be the automaton that maintains and constructs other automatons. For the moment, neither technological specialization and fragmentary labour for human individuals nor the gestures of the machine are abolished. Would the unskilled worker be available for the full development of the individual? What he is available for in bourgeois society is rather prefabricated 'leisure' activities, cinema, 'organized' holidays. It is not even certain that a 'polytechnic' training could give him the development desired. This seems more appropriate for labour in the fully automatic factory, in continuous flux, but is not without its problems. The automaton has not yet taken over technically fragmented productive labour, still less the totality of this productive labour itself. The de-skilling of certain groups of workers continues, and their exploitation – despite being concealed by technical rationality – gets worse. Added to exploitation (meaning an increase in relative surplus-value) are the control mechanisms at various levels, from the workshop and the firm to the state, and the remoteness from centres of decision.

The possibility that Marx perceived comes onto the horizon. The transition is nonetheless terribly difficult. In order to think the new possibility, we perhaps have to go further and elsewhere than Marx.

Already when we want to imagine a 'leisure society', we are stopped short by enigmas. Marx thought that every man would become a painter or poet, a musician or all of these. Even if we reject the 'theory' of innate aptitudes, the predetermined genius or stupidity of individuals, and accept the unlimited plasticity of the human brain, we doubt today that a man could become equally painter, musician, poet and scholar. Because encyclopaedic knowledge and total activity are needed? No. Because the abstract and the immediate are increasingly divided? Not only that. Because machinery and technology manufacture music and discourse and painting, automatically or nearly so, and we may very well imagine machines for listening to music or looking at paintings done by machines. The good programmer, with other gifts than those of the 'classical' musician and painter, will perhaps shortly replace the latter. Because making paintings (abstract or figurative) or music (traditional or electronic) does not seem to us an aim capable of giving meaning to life, occupying it. Because we see the entire art of the past being consumed, rather than new works being produced. Because art will be overcome as a specialist activity. Like philosophy.

Thus the evocation of human possibilities cannot arouse either euphoria or the ecstatic admiration that technocrats and official Marxists affect. Fortunately it gives a certain frisson, and actively disturbs a thought too easily optimistic and too assured of itself when it does not fall into anguished passivity. If on the one hand we have the proclamation of a future man prey to robots, his own work, we also evoke by contrast the image of a free man, boundlessly free, too free. How should we depict his figure? Like Marx in his time, we 'reflect' by 'reflecting' conditions hard to overcome. Like Marx in his time? No. It is harder for us. Marx could attribute to the proletariat an immediate negativity, determining and determined, destructive and creative. We have to open up the possible by theoretical decisions. And yet, there is mediation only in superseding: in the movement that supersedes. We are accustomed to a humanity formed by labour, in labour, for labour. In case we forget this, official Marxism and the ideology of productivist socialism remind us of it. How are the man and woman of non-labour to be represented?

The analytical understanding, to stick to Hegelian and Marxist terminology (the term 'understanding' or 'intelligence' imposes itself: for Hegel and Marx there is no analytical reason; reason for them is dialectical, and dialectic is rational), the understanding separates and divides. As a 'lantern with the head of an ant' (Éluard) it meticulously illuminates, with an immediate aim.[24] It breaks connections, and in particular the unity of contradictions. It determines and fixes what it has determined. After having distinguished and enumerated, the understanding reconstitutes sums and series.

These ensembles differ from dialectical superseding as determination by the understanding differs from dialectical contradiction. It is the Cartesian method, with its philosophical implications (general theory of the act of thinking, proceeding from the simple to the complex). This analytical understanding has its own laws: as a rigorous and operatory form, it links up both with formal logic and with the laws and structures of discourse. From logical and algebraic operations, the understanding moves on to arrangements, permutations and combinations of elements that operators manipulate. It advances along this line with no limitation of complexity. On the basis of distinct and discrete units (atoms of reality and meaning), it grasps ensembles and forms. We come back here to a particularly difficult question. How and why was this analytical understanding born? What are the relations between its formal laws and dialectical reason? How does the dialectical movement traverse and take up in it the analytical determinations?

The problem, left in suspense by Hegel, of the relationship between formal logic (in our definition, the general theory of stabilities) and dialectical reason, has constantly aggravated the difficulties of a philosophy reduced to varied reflections on questions of method. Marx skirted round this problem and bypassed it. Engels got bogged down in it, simultaneously asserting that the old philosophy handed down the legacy of formal logic across the ages, and that formal logic no longer had anything but a domestic use (trivial and everyday) in naming and discussing fixed objects.

---

24   EN: Paul Éluard, 'Nuits partagées/Shared Nights', in Mary Ann Caws, *The Yale Anthology of Twentieth-Century French Poetry*, New Haven: Yale University Press, 2004, pp. 178–9.

This problem recurs at the centre of Sartre's difficulties in his *Critique of Dialectical Reason*. He does not define either the domain or the level of logic, or the categories of understanding. No more does he manage to define the level and domain of dialectical reason. And this despite the fact that, for him, the 'practico-inert' is inexplicitly logic, the domain of the understanding and stability, while the agitation of the 'for-itself' and consciousness is the becoming of dialectical reason, now defined as a function of acts of consciousness, which does not define it in a satisfactory manner, either in itself or in relation to the logic of stabilities.

The chapter of Marx's *Poverty of Philosophy* mentioned above shows how, in praxis, a wide dialectical movement runs through the determinations of the understanding, fixed in 'things', tools and machines.[25] And this is of course without the human actors – inventors, organizers, labourers – being aware of it. These determinations are subordinated to those of the dialectical movement, carried away by them in becoming.

What then is happening today? The machine, the automaton, does not only (virtually) take over productive labour and the division of labour. The automaton takes over the whole of analytical understanding; that is to say, the understanding becomes automatic. Technology has always been operatory, as long as there has been technology in the modern sense, which does not coincide with the ancient meaning of techne (Heidegger). Today, every operation becomes technology, and every technology sooner or later becomes machine. Machines calculate, reason, translate, discourse. With operational logic, with games theory and decision theory, the science of the understanding seeks also to be a 'praxeology', theory of operational and real action.[26]

The understanding, therefore, does not only have an object – the world of stable objects – in which it operates effectively and acts

---

25 We can view similarly the first chapter of *Capital*, on the commodity. The commodity has a logical structure, and exchange values constitute a chain of equivalences (an ensemble). The relations of labour with itself and with the commodity are dialectical. (Division of labour: individual and social labour, quantitative and qualitative, simple and complex, fragmented and general, technical and social, etc.)

26 Cf. in *Futuribles*, nos 70 and 71 (supplements Dec 1963 and Jan 1964), the reticence about the unlimited claims of decision theory and games theory.

practically. It constitutes itself as totality. Totalized, it objectivizes itself, overdetermining the 'objectivity' of objects and the world of objects. It forms a block. It detaches itself from man and the human being. Either it draws and fixes them in the hardness of this block, or they free themselves from it.

We come to an alternative in praxis, which praxis has to resolve.

Either man is essentially constituted by the analytical understanding, with its operatory modes (the concepts of structure and function). Technological thought then prevails over dialectical thought. Its effectiveness is discovered at the bottom of all praxis, at the bottom of history, which, moreover, once recognized, it abandons to the past.

In this case the effective operation is defined as mimesis. Or, if you like, mimesis reciprocally defines the effectiveness of the technological operation. From the clay doll to the statue, from the hut made of branches to the analogical models that modern machines work with, mimesis has established and consolidated stabilities within the 'real'. In the chaos of phenomena, between the established order and inaccessible disorder, it intervenes and constitutes the world. Technology and art have imitated nature and man as natural being, each with its own means. Those of technology are stronger. Technology, mingled initially with praxis and poiesis (or with the poetic illusion), frees itself and becomes predominant. It relegates the other aspects of praxis to illusion or shadow. Analogy and simulation penetrate the real and even establish it. Objective evidence: the 'new towns' and estates, these simulacra of cities, perfect evidence for the disappearance of genuine 'inhabiting', in which people simply reside instead of inhabiting, in which the everyday presents itself in a clinically pure state. The 'theory of the real' is founded on mimesis. Objectification is basically mimetic. Still more: physis appears as mimesis. Supposed 'nature' imitates itself; repeating itself by spontaneously constructing increasingly ordered ensembles with elements that are initially in disorder, chaotic, dispersed and incoherent, once certain conditions favourable to stability (which partly escape us) meet together and combine. Nature, as we already observed, disappears in the face of technology and technical thought. Let man then accept himself as automaton, integrate himself into the general automization, individual and social! Enlightened about himself by machinery and mimesis, he can cease to believe himself a creative and transcendent god. The summit of reification bears within it the end of reification: the end of the opposition between the Thing and the non-Thing, consent to the spontaneity of that which moves of itself, the automaton.

Or in an alternative scenario, man frees himself from the automaton within him. He extracts himself from this and finally appears in his being. In the course of his history, man constitutes what we can call a block with a large part of himself, detaches it and places it externally so as to overcome it. Dialectical and poetical thought cease to be enclosed in technological structures, functions and operations. They finally shine with their brilliance. Praxis ceases to be the closed field in which obscure forces, now finally enlightened, struggle among themselves: mimesis, techne, physis, poiesis. Defined in its full scope by the Automaton, repetitive praxis becomes the terrain from which creative praxis takes flight, in other words a poiesis finally returned to itself. An enormous, gigantic reality has been established, consolidated, stabilized. It is made up of stabilities, taken to the point of self-correlation and self-regulation. Can this stable world serve as a springboard for advance towards a different world, which, however, will be nowhere but in this one? Which world? We do not yet know, but we do know that 'nature' or 'being' will form part of it.

Let us return to the fate of philosophy, and the relationship between philosophy and mimesis.

The problem of the relationship between logic and dialectic is resolved in praxis, whatever the side taken – in a praxis that verifies theory, and which this theory founds. Machinery, as product of the understanding, embodies it. Science, along with cybernetics, effectively becomes what Heidegger called a 'theory of the real', and even a theory of operatory, that is, effective praxis (praxeology). Perhaps it would be more exact to formulate the inverse of Heidegger's contention: the realization of man, by means of his analytical understanding, takes the form of a theory of the real that includes realizing or ordering praxis.

As *theoretical realization*, modern science – considered with the gigantic technological mechanisms it has established across the planet – puts an end, in its own way, to the split between the representation and the real. It realizes the essence of representation. Does it not thereby suppress the philosophical need, as Hegel defines this, born from the gap between the real and representations? Would this science, accordingly, and the mimesis that it presses forward, be what supersedes philosophy?

In philosophy which is *embourgeoisé* and withering away, the theory of knowledge has replaced ontology or the theory of being. It concerns itself with the supposed general forms of knowledge. Without taking account of the material at hand, or of the decoupage already effected on material and social nature, it arrogates itself the privilege of establishing the general conditions of knowing ('conditions of possibility'). Hegel strongly criticized, in the name of the philosophical (metaphysical) Absolute, this way of posing the problem of knowledge on the basis of the separation between being and knowing. He established that this split pertains to the (analytical) understanding rather than to dialectical reason. Either all knowledge already contains the absolute, and there is no need for a distinct 'theory of knowledge', or else it is irredeemably separated from it, and philosophy loses the right to speak of either a metaphysical absolute or a finished knowledge. Despite the Hegelian critique, the neo-Kantian schools in France, Germany and England have taken up the theory. This speculative effort, ashamed of itself, has sealed the distancing of the object in decaying philosophy, its loss in the In-itself, its volatilizing in empiriocriticism, its drowning in intuition and the philosophy of 'the lived'.

The germ of this process was there in the theory of knowledge right from its start! It took as its object pure abstraction, form without content, concept and category in the pure state. The effort to grasp this inaccessible form could only lead to proclaiming the nothingness of conceptual thought, the destruction of categories, adherence to irrational neo-mysticism. Bourgeoisified philosophy proved incapable of using the concept of totality (including its enriching negations: the partial, open, broken totality). It proved equally incapable of overcoming the crisis of this concept by using that of *worldwideness* [*mondialité*]. It would be derisory, however, to attribute this impotence to a weakness of the thinkers concerned, who never showed so much subtlety and refinement. And still more false to follow those who, accepting in philosophy the splits of the individual and the social in bourgeois society, maintain that the 'world' is not totality but plurality. Philosophers, in this sense, have even gloried in voluntarily ceding their place to the 'specialized sciences' of human reality, with their cleavages and their ruptures of level. With the real having become relative, metaphysics was dismissed (a good pretext to get rid of the philosophical problem, that is, the problem of philosophy, as well as radical critique based on the rehabilitation of the sensuous and the restitution of its richness, a critique whose philosophical name is 'materialist').

The reason for the failure is something quite different from a 'weakness of thinkers'. It lies in the situation of philosophy: decaying and sceptical in the context of bourgeois society, decaying and dogmatic in the context of socialist society. Its orientation towards knowledge was an illusory orientation that generated falsehood. Withering philosophy cannot manage to conduct itself critically towards its fundamental categories and presuppositions. It cannot free itself of fetishisms. It does not view the acquired culture as a moment to supersede, but views itself (not without reason) as an important element of this culture.

The 'materialist theory of knowledge' sought to stand from the start in an objective world. It left behind the implicit subjectivism or superficial objectivism of so-called bourgeois philosophers. It did not give itself the aim of a veiled deduction of categories, by starting from an unconscious acceptance of these very categories (within a vast tautology). It accepted human knowledge just as it is, in its historical reality. It not only proposed to establish the validity of knowledge, but also to explain errors as both illusions and dialectical moments of truth. In particular, in this perspective, it would not have been bad to show the dialectical movement in modern thought and knowledge: from metaphysical 'immobilism' that freezes 'beings' and categories to the conception of universal movement, and from this conception to research on relative *stabilities* (general problems of stability, and stability as a problem).

Here a new cleavage intervened. On one path, 'materialism' remained a philosophy, a system. Then it had to take up the theory of knowledge, starting from the thesis of a materiality posited and presupposed anterior to all knowledge: an insoluble problem. The dissociation of object and subject, being and knowing, made a paradoxical reappearance. Positing a 'being' or a 'matter' entirely external to knowledge led inevitably to ignoring knowledge as activity, grafting it onto being and matter as a double that is at the same time phantom-like and stuck in a place hard to locate (a 'reflection'), which determines knowledge as imitation of being without for all that defining it clearly as such.

On the other path, materialism was continued in the sense of Diderot and Marx: recovery of the sensuous as rich object of perception, critique of ideological abstraction. But then philosophy was transformed into radical critique: critique of (ideological) mystifications, critique of everyday life, critique of the representations that men make of their lives, along with attempts to justify and systematize these representations. This radical critique had to show that, in societies divided into classes, representations undergo the effects of a tendential law of polarization that converges or diverges them from their content, according to class interests. In particular when 'human life' is concerned, which the representations of praxis reduce to an abstract life, leading to the following result:

> As a result, man (the worker) only feels himself freely active in his animal functions – eating, drinking, procreating, or at most in his dwelling and dressing-up, etc.: and in his human functions he no longer feels himself to be anything but an animal. What is animal becomes human and what is human becomes animal.
>
> Certainly eating, drinking, procreating, etc., are also genuinely human functions. But taken abstractly, separated from the sphere of all other human activity and turned into sole and ultimate ends, they are animal functions.[27]

Hegel's *Phenomenology* already contained this striking theory of the *abstract animal*: man who, taking the abstraction and split of his activity (specialization) as reality and *thing* into which to absorb his consciousness in a seeming self-realization, becomes again animal – but an animal without spontaneous life, deprived of vital impulses and confined to the 'spiritual animal kingdom'.[28] A profound theory this, as

---

27   Karl Marx, 'Estranged Labour', *Economic and Philosophical Manuscripts of 1844*, in *MECW*, vol. 3, p. 275.
28   Cf. Hegel, *Phenomenology of Spirit*, p. 237ff.

much so as Marx's theory of the *abstract object* (commodity, money) that alienates and reifies activity. We glimpse in this the theory of 'theoretical realization'.

With the automaton, with 'theoretical realization', does knowledge remain in the air, without foundation, as philosophers fear in the absence of a theory of knowledge? Certainly not. The technological object guarantees its objectivity. It realizes this practically, in technological praxis.

Classical Western philosophy, we will say, broke the connection between subject and object right from the start. This then had to be reestablished, which was attempted on two levels: that of metaphysics, and that of theory of knowledge (the relationship between the two remaining ill-defined). Metaphysics did not succeed, as it borrowed its principles either from a hypostasis of the *subject* (the absolute 'I', the transcendental 'ego' of Fichte, Husserl and, in his own way, Sartre's 'for-itself'), or a hypostasis of the *object* (substance, the in-itself, matter). These hyperboles could not bring the separate terms into harmony, as they presupposed this separation. Nor did the theory of knowledge, 'gnoseology' or general methodology succeed any better. They shifted the 'problem', which became that of the relationship between the given and the constructed, the pure fact and scientific observation.

Today, the problem has disappeared because it has been resolved in scientific practice. A certain methodological and theoretical notion has acquired growing importance, that of *simulation*. We already know this. We find it here better illuminated and in a wider perspective.

The notion of simulation accompanies contemporary advances in microphysics, molecular chemistry, the construction of electronic machines, cybernetics. It is a very broad and powerful concept, susceptible moreover to a rigorous (axiomatized) definition.[29]

We presuppose an 'observer' external to an 'object', a given 'reality'. This scientific observer differs from the 'witness' or 'judge' – who, physicist or philosopher, or both at once, passively observed empirical facts or relationships. As *active* observer, he disposes of technologies

---

29 We draw here on the research of Abraham Moles.

and operations that enable him to apprehend the 'real' (the object) as ensemble of phenomena, dimensions, perspectives. These means then enable the observer to construct an object that 'reproduces' the initial object, initially posited as external and real. Constructive activity supersedes classical empiricism. This activity is not rational in the sense of classical relativism; it does something; it constructs not just concepts and representations, but the real. Effective *realization* plays the role of *experience* in the methodology accepted up to now.

Simulation thus includes the reproduction of a set of phenomena by technological mechanisms [*dispositifs*]. These means may be crude, little metal balls, wires and threads, as in the oldest 'models' of modern physics, or again painted paper, bits of wood. They may be refined, for example if the observer has several cameras available, or a perfected camera capable of grasping an object in the four dimensions of space–time and projecting an image in relief. Simulation or reproduction acquires its greatest effectiveness when the means it has available grasp combinations and sets of elements or distinct and discrete units (atoms of meaning, composition and arrangement).

All reproduction or reconstruction is necessarily incomplete. In its way, it breaks the unity of the 'real' that it reproduces; it varies it arbitrarily; it modifies and distorts its form (its 'gestalt'). So it is never complete and total. However, its uncertainties and weaknesses are conceived and perceived only as a function of the reproduced object, and its distance in relation to the constructed analogue. Each time a difference is noted, this observation makes it possible to refine the simulacrum.

It is essential to note that reproduction must itself be able to reproduce itself. Iteration or repetition plays an essential role. It is this that furnishes the practical criterion of validity. If successive reproductions differ from the first, there is said to have been a mistake. Study of mistakes makes it possible to define and classify the types of mistake, and to correct them. In fact, since the initial object is posited as external and by hypothesis inaccessible, it is in the course of successive iterations that the simulacrum is refined and converges with the 'model'. Repetition (as distinct from relationship to the object) thus plays an analogous role to that of the experiment carried out in defined conditions in the laboratory according to classic methodology.

Repetition verifies; difference reveals. Mistakes are always fruitful, making possible changes in points of view and mechanisms.

Simulation reconstructs and reconstitutes life and thought ever more closely. The Automaton simulates these. The procedure of knowledge and action *postulates* objective processes in the reproduced 'real' and a rational explanation of this real. And yet it does not claim to establish itself there and hold them. It *targets* them, by successive approximations in reproduction (by operations effectively accomplished on the basis of denumerable and measurable elements).

The notions of simulacrum and simulation thus include both a critique and a transformation of the concepts classically accepted by philosophy and the theory of knowledge (the gnoseology and methodology established by philosophers). The simulacrum, whether functional or structural, is neither true nor false in the old sense of these terms. It is not even 'exact' or 'inexact' in the customary sense. It is more or less *analogous* to the object. It approaches it to a greater or lesser extent, and reconstitutes it more or less completely. It is useful to emphasize strongly that the simulacrum is itself an object, the product of a 'positive and imaginative' act (Abraham Moles). In this sense, it overflows the concepts of analogy and resemblance, even though presupposing and enveloping these. It is a *creation*, but determined by an external 'model' (the methodology of the 'model' thus defined is modified, and this modification passes into the terminology; what is called *model* is not the *simulacrum*, but the *object*). The apparent and the real, the phenomenal and the objective, no longer have the relationships that they assumed in classical philosophy and theory of knowledge. They do not diverge, they converge. Being and appearing are not confused. They are not opposed. Appearing becomes the *apparition* of the (real) existing without there being *appearance* in the classic sense of a phenomenon detachable from the object, deceptive or illusory. Appearance is conceived as effective simulation, and bit by bit approaches the 'object', the substantial existent.

The true and the false are replaced by the possible and the impossible (the probable and the improbable). The possible does not offer itself as a third 'value' between the true and the false, or beyond them. It is *possible* to approach the object, indefinitely, by chance, by corrected trial and error. It is *impossible* to place oneself in the object.

We say here that with the construction of simulacra and automatons, with 'theoretical realization', scientific knowledge abolishes the theory of knowledge by making it useless. It establishes itself in a domain that it contributes to defining, that of mimesis: a domain that we have already determined on the basis of machinery (which the concepts of simulacrum and simulation make more precise) and information theory (analysis of any message).

In our view, these definitions converge. They fix the domain in question. They limit it. They do not yet say everything that it contains, everything that its contents mean.

The automaton takes upon itself knowing (science) as *theoretical realization*. In its own way, it suppresses the split between object and subject, between knowing and being, between the real and the representation. Having become practical act and reality, knowledge no longer demands a distinct (philosophical) theory. The automaton tends to capture and incorporate the totality of knowing and representations, thus freeing the human being from his objective part yet enabling him to draw support from this consolidation. He is himself the great automaton, the *abstract animal* in its full comprehension and full extension, fascinating parody of complete man, almost perfect simulacrum of the totality apprehended, experienced, reconstructed: reality and appearance unified. Is he not at the same time, in full 'synchronized' simultaneity, both realization and alienation? Which enables some people to say that he reconciles these, suppressing both as opposition and problem. And others (including us) to maintain that he drives the conflict to a paroxysm and heralds the great superseding.

In both perspectives, the philosophical problem of knowledge disappears. For some, mimesis is knowledge in action, known and recognized, realized, thus dispensing with a 'problematic' or a theoretical response to these problems. Even outside the automaton viewed as reality, 'structuralist' neopositivism responds as we know to the problem of knowledge by abolishing it: it defines the subject, the object, and the form of their relations. Philosophy disappears in the face of, or within, this philosophy of structure. The theory of knowledge collapses in the face of a theoretical knowledge that claims to express the real process of knowledge and thus incorporate itself into the real. In the other perspective, that which we opt for, we know ever more clearly that it is neither a question of knowledge nor of philosophical theory of knowledge, nor again of philosophy and 'problematic' in the philosophical sense. What the situation demands in fact are acts and decisions in praxis. Even if we term these acts and decisions 'poetic' (for example the decision to transform everyday life, and the actions that might follow from this), it is only a question of praxis, and it is only a certain praxis that is put in question. We take our stand *beyond* the theory of knowledge and philosophy.

And now, to continue this exploration of the field of mimesis, let us examine the famous 'problem of values'.

What is social consciousness in bourgeois society? (We can leave aside here socialist society, politicized or depoliticized according to representations little known.) Journalists say that it is public opinion. But no, moralists reply, public opinion is vulgar and uncertain and contradictory, manipulated by propaganda, bought and sold by advertising and the mass media. Opinion, from the time of Socrates and Plato, means the sum of representations that are false because unreflected and limited. Only the highest culture deserves the name of 'consciousness'. That is philosophy, the elaborated representation of the 'real' world, such as it is in life such as that is: true representation.

It is exact that the representations of the world and those of life are different. They are different and separate, like science and will, knowledge and desire.

There are those that deplore the fact that the will cannot stay the advance of science, the science that creates the automatic machine and chronic unemployment, space exploration and the atom bomb, that gives more power to the rich (individuals and countries) than to the poor (individuals and peoples). The representation of the will would be unequal to the will, and the representation of 'human things' inadequate to what these things are in reality. On the one hand, bourgeoisified thought recognizes that it no longer grasps 'things'. It denies that consciousness 'reflects' being. It is pragmatic. It says that consciousness is the condition of being, or the author of being, or the shadow of being. Which amounts to saying that the social consciousness of bourgeois society and the representation of life are 'something other' than 'real' life and 'real' being. As against this, socialist thought claims to be a *reflection* of the real. This philosophy of reflection also leads to pragmatism, but political and social, rather than individual, commercial and marketing pragmatism as on the other side.

To the extent that the idea of truth is abandoned, people cling to *value*. Axiology is separated from ontology, and for lack of the true maintains the good and the beautiful. Value insinuates itself into the fissure between 'real' and 'representation'. What is value? It is what is worth wanting. It is the 'valid' aim of will as will. An object of value is an object that one wishes to possess. A value is the representation of what one wishes to 'be'.

The bourgeois as such is disassociated. This disassociation forms part of his 'being'. He perceives himself as 'this or that': as individual, as man, as citizen, as paterfamilias, as boss or engineer, as aesthete, and so forth. Each 'as' is differently valorized. The bourgeois expects unification from will and supreme value. Will? His own, or that of a hero, a leader? Will? Or the 'will to will', will to the second degree?

The bourgeois individual will admit with a smile that his everyday life is on a low level. What do you want? Everyone has to earn a living. What do you want? You have to be a slave, serve the state, society, prosperity. What do you want? In order to live, you have to do things that you would rather not do. You would like to give your wallet to every beggar, but you realize this would be stupid. Life is hard, very hard, there are wife and children to feed, to educate, to establish.

But does this mean you are simply an animal, a machine, a robot, someone or something that 'reproduces' for want of creating, and persists in this reproduction? No. The bourgeois does not believe himself such. To those who believe him so, who criticize his 'system', capitalism, and wish to overthrow it, he replies humble and proud: there are values.

He possesses these values, masses of them. He creates and recreates them each day. When he can. Otherwise, everything would collapse. Previously, values were small in number, arranged in hierarchical order, sacred and consecrated. Today countless values have been created, invading even what seemed above all valuation: beauty, art, love. Invading them, shaking them and destroying them.

For centuries, as gold (we picturesquely say 'gold' here instead of 'capital', this abstract thing) broke down guild barriers and reduced peasants and artisans to the necessity of selling themselves, it proclaimed the value of liberty. And also of dignity. Replacing narrow and real liberties with liberty general and vague, abstractly available, money lodged the corpse of this liberty in the museum of values. Death spoke from its tomb; it spoke of the ideal. Regret changed into promise and hope. Crucified man made himself divine.

Each time a fragment of life was broken by the great pirate crusade of gold, and annexed to its venal domain, value sprung up on its tomb. Value was the glorification of life by itself at the moment of death. Value was also the triumphal cry of gold proclaiming its victory. By paying homage to the beauty that he subjugated, the victor glorified himself for having made such a fine conquest. Each time the bourgeoisie, through its philosophers and literary men, proclaimed a new value, this signalled the end of that value in the 'real'. When love is possible, love is not a value. Romanticism decreed the supreme value of love, which meant that love, increasingly rare, became dream, ideal, utopia, and that in reality every man was for sale and every woman could be bought. The bourgeois who bought women, the women who afforded husbands or lovers, consoled themselves because in the theatre, in the novel (and today in the cinema), people died of love and honour was thus safe.[30]

When André Malraux wrote about the *human condition*, it was because there no longer was a human condition.[31] When he proclaimed solitude and refusal, it was because there was no more solitude for the individual, caught in the mass of individual consumers, held by the throat in the demographic upsurge and the 'socialization of society', incapable of escaping, except in the dream offered the masses by a capitalist society that arouses this dream and assuages it in images. Solitude, this final pride, this final dignity, vanished. In modern cities or in the explosion of these cities and the housing estates that are their

---

30   The central theme of Norbert Guterman and Henri Lefebvre, *La conscience mystifiée*, Paris: Syllepse, 1999 [1936] [EN: This book is not translated into English, though brief excerpts appear in *Key Writings*, edited by Stuart Elden, Elizabeth Lebas and Eleonore Kofman, London: Continuum, 2003, pp. 200–30]. On Nietzsche, a part-mystified revolutionary, cf. the book already cited.

31   EN: André Malraux's *La condition humaine* is better known in English as *Man's Fate*, translated by Haakon Chevalier, New York: Modern Library, 1936 or *Man's Estate*, translated by Alistair Macdonald, London: Hamilton, 1968.

ghost, people have lost both solitude and social life; they find both promiscuity and the privation of 'private' life. The individual has survived as value, as abstract individual, the period when there still was the possibility of individual enterprise. Individualism presides over mass society, over-organized society, as a value. When philosophy (Heidegger in *Sein und Zeit*, then existentialism) started speaking of *authenticity*, there no longer was authenticity, except perhaps in the will for nothingness and rejection.

Values? The world of values? The philosophy of values? Axiology as opposed to ontology? It was in this form that the bourgeoisie became conscious of its life, sought to impose this consciousness and still does seek to. In bourgeois society, consciousness *reflects* life, despite the denials of philosophy. It reflects it because it does not create it. Consciousness is outside of poetry, and poetry is only a small sector of consciousness, a specialization (in the use of verbal material, that is, language as material). The sum of economic, political, moral, spiritual values, 'private' and personal, is what constitutes bourgeois social consciousness, even in the present period when competitive capitalism has disappeared. Mystified consciousness, but consciousness all the same. An inverted, broken, mutilated reflection. Consciousness, and thus meaning: meaning of what no longer has meaning. Life is no longer unique, and no longer tends towards totality. It has been broken into a thousand contradictory values. As supreme expression of alienation and fetishism, life has a thousand meanings. One can choose freely. It has a thousand meanings, but it no longer has meaning. And this is the point of departure for philosophical discourse on meaning and signification. Unicity is broken in the prism of fetishisms, and fragmented into a thousand specialized reflections. For this life to be understood, it has long been necessary for the mirror of value to be broken. The path taken by alienation and dis-alienation has to be reconstructed, following Marx in the *1844 Manuscripts*. The life that lies beneath each value has to be rediscovered, a life opposed to this value, the culture of values becoming the other pole.

In the course of this complex process, alienation and dis-alienation, the 'problem of values' arises. It is transformed, with each value becoming problematic. It becomes a reflection on values, a reflection more or less critical and apologetic. It is then that the philosopher takes over. As long as values impose themselves, they are 'unconscious' or 'pre-conscious'. When they pass into language and consciousness, they are already dissolving. It is the beginning of their end. The specifically philosophical 'problematic' always lies between the two: apogee and dissolution, reflection, discourse on discourse.

The problem of values is then formulated as a problem of the *value of values*. This expression can be taken in two senses: general value of values, or supreme value among values.

As regards value in the general sense, there no longer is one that spontaneously imposes or insinuates itself. Art, for example, is valorized at the moment when it is externalized in relation to everyday life and no longer intervenes. It was, and still is, 'art for art's sake', a second-degree assertion that envelops a second-degree alienation, in the wake of which art in the traditional sense collapses, undergoing a radical mutation that gives it notice to disappear in the face of the machine as producer of art (music, painting, etc.), or else serving the transformation of everyday life in an entirely new way.

As regards the supreme value, is this not technology itself? This is the end of values, except those supported by institutionalization or displayed by an ideology that is equally devalorized.

The path of alienation and dis-alienation has long since needed to be remade. But this critique, radical as it set out to be, was still philosophical despite itself. And this is where the great automaton is born. The abstract animal concretizes itself. It rises and grows. Irony and derision. It denies all values, threatens them in action. It supplants them. It is itself the superior value, technology, preeminent and (seemingly) final human work. It fascinates. It dominates social consciousness and incorporates itself into this. Like the grand automaton itself, its ideology (structuralism) also destroys values. What does the structural reduction bracket out? Emotion and passion, along with dialectic. Everything passes into the residual that is itself supposed to disappear into worlded technicality. Everything: values and supports of values, appearance and reality, drama and melodrama. Spilled out by the mass media, values lose prestige and force in favour of images. Art, massively consumed, is devalorized by acquiring a value that is not just aesthetic but social, political and commercial. The world of values erodes on all sides and collapses. Philosophy and philosophical critique no longer have a rationale. We can let the automaton act. It will get through the tasks that a still philosophical or overly philosophical critique proposes without accounting for them.

Value asserts itself as pure value, without base or foundation. Value is value. And so value dissolves into pleonasm, tautology, a robotic halo. Gold is relegated to second place in the hierarchy of great fetishes, but the new great fetish no longer directly arouses a fetishism. It recreates human beings in its image and renders them similar to itself, this being strictly speaking neither thing nor consciousness, but ambiguous. The automaton combines in itself spontaneity and constraint, self-movement and self-correlation. It establishes these simultaneously around it. The pleonasm, its halo, the fact that it is what it is and does not refer to anything else, as the thing does to consciousness and consciousness to the thing, is not seen by anyone for what it is. Caught in the mimesis that they have borne to first place, people can enter it with satisfaction. Art is art. Value is value. The state is the state. Signals are signals, behaviours are behaviours. And so on. The automaton thus reconciles in itself Master and Slave. Does it not force us to choose between a new slavery and a new freedom, between the new poverty and the new wealth? If it tends towards the greatest alienation by erasing consciousness of alienation, controlling even consciousness of alienation so long as this persists, the new consciousness will only be the more ardent, the more explosive.

Having thus determined the scope of mimesis and the importance of its concept (with implications that we are far from having exhausted!), we shall now turn back. As Marx did starting from the concept of social labour, elaborated by eighteenth-century thought, we shall retrospectively illuminate the past of human development and its contradictions by starting from mimesis.

In this way we shall add some features (nothing more) to the sketch of total history already proposed.

Formerly, when styles reigned, before cultures (or Culture), there were only few objects, few activities, few situations. And yet these were diverse. They formed part of very different systems: clothing, diet, furniture. These systems changed from one locality, region or nationality to another. What is happening in the era we are in now, where a monotonous and disjointed everyday has established itself as the generalized way of life? There are ever more objects, more activities, more situations. Quantitative growth is accompanied by an increased diversity. And yet old diversities have fallen away; the old systems have disappeared, having become folkloric and anecdotal. Technologies have imposed themselves that are similar to the point of identity: similar cars on similar motorways throughout the world, similar planes at similar airports. And then: masculinization of women, feminization of males, infantilization of adults, precociousness of youth, and so forth.

All these phenomena we shall examine under the sign of mimesis. A dual process pervades the modern world: *complexification and homogenization*. It is not easy, moreover, to see the relationship between these two aspects. Some people see only complexification and hymn the diversity of modernism. Others see only homogenization and fall into nostalgia for the past, for dead significations: into folkloric romanticism. We have to grasp the unity of the dual process, and perhaps the conflicts inherent to it. Complexification dissimulates homogenization, that is, mimesis. And yet it is not inconceivable that (qualitative) complexification may one day prevail over the reign of the homogeneous, within which diversity is only apparent.

At the dawn of our civilization, if we credit Huizinga, poiesis was a ludic function.[32] It stood in a ludic space, its own universe where things were connected by different ties than those of logic: 'Ancient civilization is now being understood anew in the light of this fundamental unit of poetry, esoteric doctrine, wisdom and ritual.'[33]

Primitive poiesis was both entertainment, social game, know-how, enigma and solution to enigma, the teaching of wisdom, persuasion, sorcery, divination, prophecy and competition, thus challenge. It is in this sense that the Greek poets, before literate poetry reserved for the literary public, exercised a social function, and philosophers were not distinguished from poets and musicians.[34]

At that time, play, knowledge, (religious) cosmology, poetry and political activity were not separated from one another. The men in

---

32 'Poiesis, in fact, is a play-function.' Johan Huizinga, *Homo Ludens*, Boston: Beacon Press, 1971, p. 119.
33 Ibid., p. 120.
34 Huizinga rather neglects music as unity of the cosmic and the human.

their assembly – citizens – reproduced in play the heroic and creative acts of the founders, gods and demigods inscribed in the practical memory of foundations (legend and creative activity being undifferentiable). The action that was played and sacred was more than the realization of an appearance, the performance of a fiction, the concretization of a symbol. Its participants believed that the action brought into play a higher order of things. And yet the participant realization kept the formal characteristics of a game. It was played, staged within the limits of a circumscribed space, like a festival, which means joy and freedom. A universe of its own, of temporary value, was marked out for its purpose. And yet, its action did not stop being exerted after the game was finished. It projected its splendour out onto the ordinary world, preparing security, order and prosperity for the group that had celebrated the Festival.[35]

In this way, mimesis was not yet distinguished from poiesis – at least in Greece. Mimesis reproduced the creative act, that of the (real or supposed) foundation. It became in its turn creator of gatherings, works of art, thought and poetry in the narrower sense of the word.

How did man (his reason or his understanding, we do not yet know) invent the wheel? Certain civilizations are marked by its absence, this being as little explained as its discovery, increasing the enigma. Certainly, we may think that the populations of sub-Saharan Africa who lacked the wheel had no need for it. Portage in the forests was more useful to them than carts (although some of them, settled and using fire to clear patches for cultivation, could have done with wheeled vehicles). But the Aztecs? Their ignorance of the wheel may be explained by their origins: oarsmen on the Mexico lake, warriors making war into a ritual. Besides, they lacked draught animals. Finally, they were ignorant of anything of the nature of abstraction or hypothesis, money for example. And yet the absence of the wheel is remarkable, particularly as they interpreted magically and mystically the heavenly movements and cosmic rhythms, remarkably represented as such. We cannot prevent ourselves from saying that technological and practical causes are not enough to explain the absence of the wheel. Perhaps they worshipped the sun too much, its circular form and movement,

---

35   Huizinga, *Homo Ludens*, p. 31.

to dare to inscribe it in a material object, palpable, tangible, usable. They did not profane the sacred and accursed form, that of higher powers that were favourable or threatening.

The forms of the city, from its birth to its explosion in the modern world, are reducible to two: the circular (radial-concentric) form and the grid form (square or rectangle divided like a chessboard). From the beginning, settlements and agglomerations took one or other of these forms. The circular form seems more spontaneous, for cities growing naturally around a fortified place, citadel, 'area', castle, crossroads, bridge, and so forth. It would be inexact, all the same, to maintain that the grid form followed the radial-concentric form as the reflected follows the spontaneous. On the contrary, the grid form seems older than the circular. Contrary to what one might believe, it preceded rational thought. Belatedly, the grid system proved practical, simple and useful for the construction of camps, new towns, colonies. Reflecting thought *imitated*. The grid pattern was adopted by the analytical understanding, for 'rational' reasons. And yet there is room to believe that it goes back to the origins of cities arising from a foundation. This form offers human constructions to the rays of the sun; it is oriented (towards the rising sun at the solstice, towards the place where a planet rises). A correspondence has been observed between the chessboard form and the strict orientation of the megalithic ensembles (at Carnac, for example).[36]

Rather than just a form of the city, the founders seem to have grasped an *imago mundi* and projected it onto the ground [*terrain*]. The circular city imitates the world, the Sun, the Moon, circular movement, stars and planets, the successive spheres. The grid city offers itself to the rays of the sun, which cut through its centre at the favoured and sacred moment of the solstice.

There is no doubt that the inventors of the wheel imitated the sun and its supposed movement. Before or after this invention, they constructed circular cities after the model of the wheel. The primitive network of roads, paths and tracks around the agglomeration fixes and

---

36 Cf. Pierre Lavedan, *Histoire de l'urbanisme, Antiquité et Moyen-Âge*, Paris: H. Laurens, 1966, on the Breton villages (Ile Tristan, Melrand), on the Italian Terramare (pp. 13–15), on Tell-el-Amarna (p. 95), and so forth.

imitates the tree. The roads around the city imitate the spokes of the wheel, which imitate the rays of the sun. The city itself appears at the centre of the world, its navel. At the centre of the circular city, as the hub at the centre of the wheel, rise the temple and the palace, seen as the pivots of the world.

The wheel, that of the cart, that of space, represented and appropriated in the city, was, it seems, the practical origin of the circle thought by reflection, as the practical grid marking of countryside and towns into a chessboard lay at the origin of the square and rectangle as formally (geometrically) defined. The wheel is thus found, not without multiple mediations, at the birth of both a number of material machines and the circularity of abstract systems:[37] the wheel of carts for transport and chariots for war, the wheel of torture, the wheel of time and eternal recurrence, the sphere of space and thought, the harmony of the world, the figure of perfection and thought for Parmenides. And likewise with the infernal circles of sorcery, accursed spheres, vicious circles; the wheel opened and determined a long period. It was as revolutionary as carved stone or Promethean fire. It defined a mimesis whose consequences are still not exhausted, in which the primordial symbol governs actions or series of actions that resemble it. Disjunction bound up with formal logic, discourse and structures of discourse, halts or sudden changes in material movements, today acquires a growing function in fact and thought, determining another form of mimesis.

Plato has preserved for us the traces of this primitive history in which mimesis and poiesis are mingled before being distinguished (in terms of the particular sciences, cosmogony, religion and technology were not yet differentiated). Among the various kinds of movement, philosophy discerned that of the wheel as a privileged one.[38] In rotation this movement is propagated, amplified, multiplied from the starting point of the immobile centre, and yet the movable form is maintained without alteration, whereas translation distorts. The

---

37   The notion of system (and perfect system) appears apropos music rather than philosophy, from the moment that the scale and its repetition in successive octaves (descendants in Greek music) is conceived. The octave is represented by a circle.

38   Plato, *Laws*, book 10, 893–4.

movement of the wheel symbolizes the movement of the soul and its relationship with the body. Still more: the soul of the world sustains and animates the world, as the hub holds together and moves the wheel as a whole. It 'leads the round' of all things, all states, from the sun to the moon and sublunary (earthly) creations. All movements of the cosmos imitate, closely or not, the soul of the world, more or less capable of its central and fundamental perfection:

> All that there is in the heavens, on earth and in the sea, the Soul leads them by way of these movements that are its own.

These immobile movements are first causes; the peripheral movements, those of the bodies, are both effects and secondary causes.

We know, according to the *Timaeus*, that the demiurge organizes the Cosmos by contemplating and imitating the Intelligible. The Ideas provide the eternal model that he reproduces by shaping the imperfect mass of the sensuous, temporal and perishable. The demiurge is in a position of mediation. Derived actions, and words that are not primary and creative, are also mediated and mediating. 'All that is said by any of us can only be by imitation,' declares Critias at the start of the dialogue, or rather the long monologue, that bears his name.[39] The text describes the ideal city, that of Atlanteans. According to Plato, this city reproduced the '*imago mundi*' by the action of the gods and divine men. It even reproduced two '*imagines mundi*', circular and rectangular, juxtaposing them on the island of Atlantis.

Plato admirably defines, under the name of *metexis* (participation), the original mimesis as we have conceived it: with two aspects, one facing an inaccessible aim that it seeks to grasp and incorporate (embodying it in a sensuous work), the other facing what is repeated and escapes into disorder, the chaotic and unformed. It is therefore a mediation, a participation that does not copy in the fashion of the potter when he reproduces a vase placed before and outside of him. It is an active and creative participation, despite Aristotle's debatable remark in the second book of the *Metaphysics*[40] *that contrasts the*

---

39 EN: Plato, *Critias*, 107b.
40 Aristotle, *Metaphysics*, 987b 11–13. [EN: This is actually in Book Alpha.]

Platonic metexis with Pythagorean mimesis. According to him, only the Pythagoreans believed that things and ideas imitate higher essences, the Numbers. But this is not the sense in which we have conceived mimesis-*metexis*.

Aristotle was no longer able to grasp the full profundity of the Platonic concept. The times had changed. Foundations and founders, myths, were now more remote. The predominance of logos in the praxis of the city, and action over men (*pragmata* and the pragmatic – in a word, business), acquired ever-greater importance, to the detriment of poiesis, creative action on things, reduced to the products of artisans and slaves. Aristotle similarly restricted poiesis and mimesis to modalities of discourse. Poetry was simply something spoken. The poet, like any artist, imitates an object of nature or a human action. As regards man, the poet imitates customs and characters, and what is permanent in him. The two verbs, *poiein* and *mimesthai*, thus sum up artistic activity, framed by nature and praxis, and limited by them. Poiesis and mimesis are defined in this way, but are separated, restricted and demeaned.[41] Systematic philosophy does not understand them. It reduces them to the level of logos and *pragmata*, associated with the practical and political life of the city, disassociated from foundations and fundamentals. For Aristotle mimesis has become a literary activity, a psychological and discursive function: imitation. The great images of the Soul of the world, the celestial spheres, the Earth and the Harmonies, have almost disappeared. Symbols dissolve, making way for signs, for verbal and written discourse.

It goes without saying that the historian can continue indefinitely to excavate the foundations of the Greek and Roman City. He perceives a historical process whose study he can deepen by going back to its origins or following its results. He will never come up against a barrier. No unknown power or occult force – mystical, theological, philosophical – will ever tell him: here, historian, you must stop. You will not go further. Here was the place of invention, creation! And yet, however far he goes back, however deep he penetrates, the historian will discover a form whose future no one in these distant times could divine. We have already remarked on this, and will further emphasize

---

41 Aristotle, *Poetics*, 1447a–1448 a; cf. also *Politics*, 1340a,18ff.

it here. The historian may attribute the thing (invention, creation, discovery?) to chance, determinism or will. It matters little. What is interesting for us is what had to come about. This necessity supersedes the event. The possible overspills actuality, and still more the past. Who knew at the time of their birth, who could know, what would become of the Greek city and the agora, of the Roman city with its pomerium and its forum? Without giving a magical-mystery resonance to this term, we have spoken, and will speak further, of a poiesis, a creation half-blind and half-conscious.

According to Pierre Lavedan, the Roman city derived from the Etruscans, and via them from the oriental city, essentially consisted of a sacred precinct, with gates that were likewise sacred. The foundation of the city was a voluntary act: Etruria did not have spontaneous settlements, which is explained when we understand that the Etruscans were conquerors who arrived from Asia Minor. The city and its foundation resulted from a religious system. When the site had been chosen, the founders – after taking the auspices – traced the contours of the city with a bronze plough, drawn by a pair of animals (male and female), a white bull and cow. The plough had to spill soil inwards. The furrow was interrupted for the placing for gates, where the founder raised the ploughshare with his hands. The pomerium (*pone muros*) was the space that the Etruscans, when they built a city, reserved on either side of the furrow of the precinct, where it was in principle forbidden to build. The pomerium represented the religious boundary of the city.

The sacred obligation coincided with technical and military requirements: to maintain a zone free of cultivation and construction in the vicinity of the walls. The foundation of the Etruscan city was accompanied by sacrifices in honour of the gods of Hades, sacrifices that included establishing the *mundus*. Bloody libations were poured and victims burned; the first fruits were laid down as offerings. The pomerium was only opened three times a year. In sum, the Etruscan and Roman city implied: a precinct not to be crossed, with the prohibition lifted for the gates; the pomerium, a forbidden space; the *mundus*, a sacred site, heart point and figure of the celestial vault, a summary of the world; the 'area', preeminence or citadel, a site inviolable because favourable to defence; and a site of meeting, the forum, likewise the object of prohibitions (particularly concerning the bearing of weapons). This city was well and truly a microcosm, characterized above all by prohibitions and sacralizations that were minutely ritualized and bound up with practical acts.

The Italic (Etruscan and Roman) city founded by ritual (*ritu*) seems to have been initially circular, with three streets, three temples, three gates, the number three being sacred and structural for this ritual foundation. Only later came the rectangular Roman city, with four regions determined by the intersection of two main roads, the *cardo* and the *decumanus*, drawn from north to south and from east to west with the help of a geodesic instrument (*groma*) that made it possible to point at the sun.

We emphasize here the circularity of the earliest Italic city and its consequences. The magic circle is above all the object of prohibitions. It is certainly not sufficient to explain the military and conquering temperament of the Romans by this constitution of their city. We may accept that it played a certain role, especially in the birth of their state and legal conceptions. Right from the start, power and property acquired a magical sense. The urban territory was the space in which the *aruspices* would examine the entrails of victims and influence the decisions of the magistrates, where magistrates with defined and limited powers could consult the *aruspices*, where neither foreign gods nor armed soldiers could penetrate, where it was forbidden to sully life by death. This was the native context of a state with a conception of law.

We could say that the space of the pomerium and what it contained (including the forum) was severely closed, but that time opened up unlimited possibilities for action: conquest, organization. Hence the importance of auguries. The Greek agora, on the other hand, was an open space, welcoming but determining a limited time for the assembly of free citizens who gathered there. This a posteriori interpretation arises from the fact that we know the consequence of this 'advent'. Sacralization and solemnization had immediate meanings and more distant significations common to all foundations, particularly the Etrusco-Roman. With the latter, they accompanied *inauguration*: the preparation by the augurs of the sacred perimeter, demarcation of the placing of gates and the day when the precinct would be traced, and so forth. By the solemnization of these moments, the decisions of the authorities became accepted and recognized facts, irrevocably adopted by the popular community. These founding decisions passed into praxis. The people confirmed the choice of the site and the wager on the future, thus they accepted the risk. By accepting the consequences of the inaugural act, those present committed themselves and their posterity to perpetuate the enterprise, to safeguard the nascent city. Sacralization changed the territory into the exclusive possession of the group, represented by the priests, and by civil and military leaders. It proclaimed the privative appropriation of the land, that is, the exclusion of foreigners, the rights of the participating citizens, the future of tensions and conquests.

Sacralization and malediction thus have a 'function' in connection with the birth of a city. We can say that they express and signify poiesis, by their transposition into a social language (words, gestures, ritual forms) – after which the social language permits imitation, mimesis. At the beginning, practical action bears within it expression and meaning. The emotion of the 'sacred' signifies this inherence of meaning. Later on, sacralization and malediction degenerate into official performance, corteges and processions, aesthetic forms and political and ideological uses (such as legends, folklore, etc.), leading on to pure and simple comedies and parodies in which no one any longer believes. Foundation and risks, acceptance and commitment, are remote. In antiquity, it took centuries for this split to be completed. Then the expression disappeared and the meaning of the gestures and acts performed fell away. Mimesis follows poiesis, but separates from it only slowly. Poiesis is characterized by the primordial unity of the elements that disassociate: technicality, world image, action on things and on the group, presence of the people, decision of the leaders, solemnity. It gives way to a gestural compromise, that is, one lived in a certain practice, between ritual and technical demand, between the mysterious power attributed to the founding decisions and practical cleverness, itself double, about things and men.

Jerôme Carcopino, an excellent scholar of Roman antiquity, recalls in his book *La Vie quotidienne à Rome* the ceremonial of foundation and its meaning:

The sacred orbit thus described in anticipation of the fortifications and walls to come, formed the abbreviated ground plan, the prophetic image of the future city ... From the pomerium the Urbs derived its name, its original definition, and its supernatural protection ... Although it preserved its religious character and continued to protect the citizens by remaining closed to gatherings of the legions, by classic times it had ceased to form the limit of the city.[42]

It had become symbolic. Carcopino shows the magical (sacred, accursed) function of the circle, and the formation of the symbolism on the basis of initial reality as well as its religious interpretation.

Further on, in this highly suggestive book, a relationship is brought to light between town, habitation and clothing. The Roman toga, from a word cognate with '*tegere*' (to cover), was the segment of a circle of white wool 2.72 metres in diameter. Its roundness distinguished the toga from all the varieties of clothing derived from the Hellenic himation. The Greeks expressed in their manner of dress their predilection for rectilinear architecture. They left in the piece of cloth in which they draped themselves the straight edges and sharp angles that it had on the loom. The Greeks, Carcopino continues, citing Léon Heuzey, drew admirable effects from these elementary forms, which pleased the simplicity of their taste and the cleanness of their minds. We may say in passing that the reader will not understand why the circular form is less simple and less clean than the square or rectangular form. The difference is elsewhere: in the context. The circle is closed in space and open to time. The rectilinear grid is open in space and closed to time. At all events: 'The Etruscans, followed by the Romans, who early on brought the arch into their system of construction, and who liked to raise their temples on a circular plan, likewise rounded the angles of their clothing.'[43]

This suggests an initial form, then its echo and repercussion in all familiar domains. There is no repetition. There is no imitation in the strict sense. Invention takes place in all domains – architecture,

42   Jérôme Carcopino, *Daily Life in Ancient Rome: The People and the City at the Height of the Empire*, edited by Henry T. Rowell, translated by Emily Overend Lorimer, New Haven: Yale University Press, pp. 12–13.

43   Carcopino, *Daily Life in Ancient Rome*, p. 154.

clothing, perhaps the diverse objects of everyday life – with the mind's eye fixed on the dominant and primordial form. These indications could and should be confirmed by detailed archaeological and historical studies. They still fail to explain to us in a satisfactory fashion the difference between the agora and the forum, between the Greek city and the Roman. Likewise the conditions in which the great forms of logic and law resulted from them. They simply put us on the right path. They show us a mimesis, created and yet creative, flowing and deriving from a poiesis.

The gods of ancient Olympus were in no way allegorical. On the one hand, they were attached to a location [*terroir*]; they depended on local cults. The most important were worshipped in many places, but never became completely detached from particular sites and definite events (rituals). On the other hand, they denoted human powers: love, courage, technical skill, aptitude for material or intellectual exchange, and so forth. They could thus preside over activities. They inspired works. Invocations and evocations were not reducible to words. Even having become symbolic, when written discourse and signs came to prevail, these divine figures and the specific sites that held them (sky, earth, sea, sex: Athens, Cyprus, Delphi, Olympus, Delos) lived on in the language of the Greeks. They influenced time and space, objects, acts, situations. Antique mythology reestablished the unity between man and nature that had been disassociated by the city, by abstraction, by the use of signs and numbers. It played the role of a living and lived mediation, both fantastic and practical, images and activities themselves both natural and social. It was thus far more than a system of significations or a combination of significant elements. It was a style of life, political and religious at the same time, with specifically 'pagan' features. Hence the creative power of this mythology, far above that of ideological illusion that might include 'beliefs', far above the magical illusion of taming nature by the use of divine names and gestures. 'Greek art presupposes Greek mythology, i.e. nature and the social forms already reworked in an unconsciously artistic way by the popular imagination' (Marx).[44]

Antique mythology gives us an admirable example of spontaneous poiesis, initial and primordial creation, in itself 'unconscious', followed

---

44   Marx, *Grundrisse*, p. 110.

by a mimesis that is itself living, creative, reflecting and extending the poiesis from which it derives.

On many occasions, we have employed the expression 'social language'. Does this forget that all language is social? No. By the added adjective, we mean to emphasize certain points in real language, real society, in praxis. This social language differs from soliloquy, and likewise from pure discourse (logic) and literary language. It is acted and lived as well as spoken. Gestures support it and comment on words. With partners who enter into a relationship, these gestures are often regulated on both sides, even ritualized. Context even becomes custom (for example the advocate's robe, the priest's surplice, etc.). Social language is both *mimicry* and *mimetic*.

We may assume that the ritual gestures go back to the most distant archaisms, and that ethnologists can follow their desacralization. Ritual gestures and words, it seems, were deemed to act on nature by way of a kind of supernature made up of occult forces and qualities. Reciprocally, an effective action on this supernature was obtained and sought by way of real or fictitious action on nature, first of all by way of gestures and phrases. The ambiguity of the 'sacred' and the 'accursed' serves as a starting point. A multiple ambiguity: the 'sacred' and the 'biological' have a primordial and obscure relation. Effectiveness is sought by way of a succession of words and gestures that are linked, isolatable, repeatable, both ambiguous and rigorous. Ambiguous in sense and rigorous in form. In this way a formalism is defined, within a confusion (sacred-accursed, nature-supernature), and even a totality (economic, social, ethical, etc.). It seems that the gestures best linked and founded, the best rhythmed, separate out from the others and constitute the best and 'purest' form. They are thereby profaned by their own action.

Paradoxically, this formalized and ritualized convention determines a *natural* that stands between raw nature and awkward facticity. By desacralizing, leaving aside both religious liturgies and the magical formulas of sorcery, these formalisms serve as it were as support and mould for the chaos of gestures and words in human relations. They give form to the unformed. By defining a natural, they define an agreeability, a charm, and thus a beauty, a perfection, a harmony. The most successful become exemplary. The philosophy that naturally links up with these social formalizations is Platonism. But outside of all philosophy, they enter into town planning, into civility, and consequently into civilization. This charm actualizes a mediation both fictitious and real between man and nature, between culture and biological reality. A kind of appropriation of nature by way of the social is accomplished, and of the social by way of nature; an appropriation that is incomplete, alienated, but which can always be said to be better than nothing.

Among these formalisms that have entered into everyday life and are incrusted in use by time, we can mention the rituals and forms of politeness, with their particular symbolism that has come down from the age of feudalism (the handshake and hand-kissing), their magic formulas (Good health! God speed!), offerings (a cigarette?). Initially, then, the idea or project of communication by way of contact, communion in the reciprocal and simultaneous gesture, in the mimed drama of the meeting. We may also mention the strange formalisms of justice and its apparatus, and the still stranger ones that govern the transfer of property (formulas of notarized 'acts'). These are systems of meaning established on the basis of forms that are all institutionalized, directly or indirectly, thus perpetuating the regulated and mimed acts.

These formalisms determine several particular kinds or types of mimicry and mimetism (thus mimesis), which we shall simply list: etiquette, ceremonial, the code of manners, hence mannerism and aestheticism, which confers on acts, objects and situations a parody of style. The form must always be capable of repetition; this is its solidity and rigour. However, it is never purely and simply repeated. It is adapted. The general must take account of the particular, and even of the inaccessible singularities of beings and situations. We evolve in the mixed zone of mimesis. Both constraint on nature and orientation of gestures, formalism can supply an ethics. Finally, it can either be charged with an ideology, or replace one. Things may lead to a dramatization, or even open onto the tragic. Risks and perils are dominated, in both fiction and reality, by way of a noble gesture; was not the nobility of the gesture, maintained in danger, mastering emotion, the wellspring of tragedy for the French playwrights of the seventeenth century? Is it not the secret of panache, display? An aestheticism that has become natural, or passes for such, is made into tradition and custom; in France it runs down the centuries, transmitted from one class to another.

Among the major forms that have come down to us and include law and logic, should we not count the strangest of formalisms, that of courtly love? Originally, at its birth, or its foundation if you like, a mad idea, the maddest of ideas and most delirious of projects: the unique love of one unique being for another. The impossible, conceived and posited as impossible, was at the same time posited as absolute possibility, as rationale of the palpable. The other being is known to be inaccessible, and the absolute can be attained only in the relative. The beloved being is doubly distant, in both body and soul. The lover commits himself to realize this impossibility, to bend all his forces towards the inaccessible, to live constantly in the desire for the absolute. To put an end to separation and split! Here, in his madness, the initial poiesis is evident. What mysterious cruelty, what strength, must one not possess in order to attempt this love? The great Western madness, creator of a limitless number of sensations, prevents us from dwelling in platitude. It has been until now the only style of this West, its grandeur. Along with its opposite: accumulation (of knowledge, of capital).

Let us now consider, under the sign of culture that has replaced style, the gaps and distortions characteristic of the great separation. We already know that the disassociations into separate sectors are accompanied by growing uniformity, common to all sectors. This is how it is in everyday life, labour, private life, leisure. Hence the other three elements of everydayness: objects, activities, situations, each follow their own course, but the same law of quantitative growth and mimetic uniformity applies in each sector.

The role of technological objects becomes predominant and determinant. The automobile, a technological object of use, comes to the fore and is transformed before our eyes, in our 'Western' society, into leading object. It determines important significations; it demands colossal investments, the transformation of towns, their evisceration. The automobile is the head of the 'system' in so far as there is a 'system' and not simply a succession of compulsions empirically undergone.

During this time, consumption is profoundly refashioned. Large-scale capitalism concerns itself with rationalizing the 'system' of

distribution in its own way. As distribution is seen as essential, rationality seems to extend to the entirety of economic activities. We have
gone further than studies that prospect the market, or act on needs by
way of advertising. The chain stores and supermarkets, according to
their apologists, represent the new *style* of consumption.

In the 'world of objects', thus presented in a total spectacle, in this
'objectal' chain store [*Uniprix*] world, everyday objects copy the technical object, a model in itself inaccessible.[45] The distance between the
everyday object and the high-tech is that between the electric mixer
and the missile. At their lower level, familiar objects are structured and
functional, like technical objects (that is, they require a double analysis
to be exhaustive, analysis of their structure and the operation of their
component parts; and analysis of the function performed by this
combination of elements). The mimetic character of the ensemble of
everyday objects, moreover, is accentuated as their very manufacture
becomes mimesis: with molecular chemistry and plastics, *moulding*
[*moulage*] replaces *assembly* [*montage*]. The object is produced by
direct reproduction.

These mimetic objects constitute a complete assortment, as seen in
the chain stores [*Uniprix*] and supermarkets, and possess a characteristic style or absence of style, the 'Uniprix style'. From furniture through to
cheeses, they are neither good nor bad, neither ugly nor beautiful: they
are useful. Do these objects form systems? Yes and no. Yes, in that they
constitute a vast system determined by the operatory (structural and
functional) character of the analytical understanding in action. There
are even partial systems, inasmuch as pilot-objects dominate, imposing
options (the automobile) or having consequences for everyday life (television). But these partial systems, unless they are institutionalized and
bureaucratized, are broken and integrated into the general system of the
object in our society. And we no longer know if there is a 'system', that is,
a rational coherence; for we know that there can be the appearance of a
system – a deceptive appearance, half fictitious and half real, an illusion
of rationality that invites a search for rationality and coherence, without
these ever revealing themselves except by reference to the absurd. For
example, in the state and bureaucracy.

---

45 EN: Uniprix was a French discount store.

Examination of small technical objects, gadgets, leads to perplex-
ity. The technical rationality of each does not extend to their ensemble,
which may well be quite absurd. It is with the ensemble of pseudo-tech-
nical objects (gadgets) and functional (useful) objects that high
technology and the leaders of society treat everyday life as a colonized
and underdeveloped sector of praxis. The chain stores and supermarkets are analogous to the old colonial trading counters.

Technical objects command rational *behaviours*. In relation to these
behaviours, the affectivity and emotionality frequently attached to them
are always absurd. Thus it is absurd to see the automobile as an instrument
of power, as opportunity for sportive play on the roads, as a companion
(spouse or mistress). It is lamentable that people become rude and abandon culture and civility as soon as they are at the steering wheel. And yet
these residues of emotionality and affectivity bring a little fantasy and variety to behaviour. Rational progress consists in their elimination. In other
words, behaviours tend towards uniformity. They are copied.

Under the sign of analytical separation and disassociation, a reign of
uniformity is established. This is more paradoxical than it might
seem. We know that complexity covers up homogeneity, that distinction veils argument. People *imitate*. Imitation is not an individual
phenomenon, a relationship between one individual and another. It is
a social relation: a form that produces conformity and a vast conform-
ist mentality. Attitudes have replaced autonomous activities, and
attitudes are mimicry.

Just as 'attitudes' and mimicry have replaced activities, in the same
way 'roles' have replaced perceived and experienced situations. It is
curious that psychologists and sociologists observe attitudes, behaviours, roles; they study them in an uncritical manner, thus confirming
mimesis and the reign of mimesis (that of the analytical understanding, discourse and rationality) without discerning the fundamentals,
and therefore without spelling out and explaining. They thus accept
without any kind of investigation, as an eternal requirement of society,
the general tendency to stereotype and the tendency to imitate the
idols and pantheon of the modern world. For us, on the other hand,
this ambiguous aim, this intermediary between reproduction and the
inaccessible, is what defines mimesis.

Can people be reproached, in the modern world, for wagering 'unconsciously' on mimesis, living by imitating and imitating to survive? No: they are free. Too free. Abandoned. Individualism dies and the individual triumphs; in this Pyrrhic victory, he no longer knows whom to blame for his failures and defeats. Individuation and massification do not exclude one another, as was believed in the 'belle époque'. On the contrary. The individual constitutes himself as such by borrowing a general image of individuality from other individuals, whose individuality he supposes to be complete and perfect. And the latter act likewise, conforming either to an external image, or to the image they wish to give of themselves, the image that is demanded.

David Riesman's analyses in *The Lonely Crowd* are interesting but insufficient: relative to a certain period of Americanism.[46] It is true that when there was still a living community, the members of this community corresponded, communicated and even communed with one another without having to imitate or resemble each other, except in appearance. They were fashioned (formed) by the tight conditions – limiting but 'formative' – of the community, of the style, of the organic unity (which was in no way a 'system'). In such conditions, individuals, despite being little individualized and knowing nothing of individualism, had characteristics and character. The age of community was also that of characters. A shadow or trace of poiesis remains in the very notion of 'character'. We know very well that character (good or bad) tends to disappear in the age of 'patterns'.

After the community there was, according to Riesman, the period of autonomous consciousness.[47] But was not this autonomous consciousness already commanded from outside, with an autonomy that was fictional as much as real, in other words, semi-real and semi-illusory? And when 'other-directed man' arrived, was the social orientation and social organization he accepts not demanded, claimed, at the very bottom of individualized consciousness, that of the lost and bewildered individual, unrealized and abandoned to himself, without an ethic to rebel against, without a palpable adversary, and without

---

46   EN: David Riesman with Nathan Glazer and Reuel Denny, *The Lonely Crowd: A Study of the Changing American Character*, New Haven: Yale University Press, 1950.

47   Of 'inner-directed man' [English in original].

God to play the devil against? This 'direction' that supposedly comes from without, which is what sociologists believe they observe, and actually do observe as the bureaucratic organization of 'industrial' society, comes in fact from within: from the uncertain freedom, emptied of meaning, that is devoted to freely reproducing, democratically copying.

Under the reign of mimesis, the individual tends to disappear. We do not say that he actually does disappear, still less that he would disappear by decree of implacable fate. We describe and explain a tendency and a tension. The individual is no longer anything but *residual*. With the dissolution of character, what is left is the *personage*: the man or woman who compose role, face and mask, gestures and words, 'as a function of'. A function of what is expected of him or her, a function of the demands of their 'status' or 'standing', the imperatives of career and hierarchy. This personage in flesh and blood does not have the clarity of the 'personae' of a novel, of the cinema, figures that are behind the times and too close to actual characters. The personage of today has no outlines except those he takes on by following what is beyond him. This real personage has little reality. He is no longer the 'persona' of classical literature, but a figure in search of an author, who finds no other author but himself, and whose own drama overwhelms him.

There is something very disturbing in the analogy or homology between the three following elements: the importance of the methodology of *models* and simulations in the sciences of today, and particularly in the social sciences; the importance of *patterns* in contemporary social life; and the importance of acting social groups that consciously or not count on mimesis: the bureaucracy and technocracy. The correspondence is such that scientific representatives of the technocracy believe they represent knowledge of the social real, by virtue of the fact that they use models and study 'patterns'. However, the uncritical character of this cognition (which is more a recognition) arouses attention. Positivism always bears with it acceptance. Science as envisaged in this way forms part of the 'positive' reality that it claims to know, and that it actually does know to the extent that it participates in it. As in Marx's time, however, the situation is turned upside down, and thought put back on its feet; it resumes its course by way of a procedure of criticism.

It remains nonetheless that the new sciences are *totalizing* (information theory, cybernetics, the methodology of models and simulations), and that the totalizing knowledge of conformities in relation to patterns, as well as the existence of social groups that live from this conformity and strive to gain power by totalizing activity (technocratic planning), deserves our attention. Structuralism tends to actually structure society. All the more so in that these groups possess not only theoretical sciences but also totalizing techniques in praxis: for example, punch-card indexes of the population.

Given the discrepancy between objects, situations and activities (or rather, between things, signals, roles and attitudes), mediations are needed between these disjointed elements, which each has its own uniformity. Language has always played the role of mediation (means, instrument, and something more: element and milieu of reflexive thought, in the sense that water is the element in which fish live). Today the mediation of language is supplemented by the mediation of the image.

Does the image provide a language, and to what extent can one speak of a language of images (or of sounds)? The abuse of language, of discourse seen as prototype of reality and intelligibility in contemporary reflection, forces us to pose this question. It is hard to give an answer. Certainly, people (photographers, filmmakers, editors and page-designers on newspapers, etc.) make use of images in order to say what they want to say. As image serves as a sign, it involves the relationship of signified-signified. And it is possible to speak of 'cinematic discourse' and its rhetoric (Gilbert Cohen-Séat).[48] There is in the image an expressive character and a signifying character, and among the images there are active symbols and signs. Finally, image as well as language lends itself to a 'lived experience' that is simultaneously individual and collective, acted and signified.

All the same, it is possible to wonder whether the relationship of signifier to signified is the same in the image as in language. Words and phrases signify generalities, and only with difficulty, by way of the

---

48   EN: This is likely a reference to *Essai sur les principes d'une philosophie du cinema; notions fondamentales et vocabulaire de filmologie*, Paris: PUF, 1958.

general, reach the particular and singular. Only *speech* (unique, living, poetic) unites the singular, the particular and the general in the universal, whereas the image designates or denotes singularity and particularity, reaching the general only by way of these. In 'lived experience', imaged or imaginary, and on an emotional rather than a representative level, processes are effected that discourse arouses only indirectly and by way of gesture, mimicry, costume, emphasizing the discourse and adding a substitute for living speech. Finally, a last point, the image seems not to lend itself to dichotomies, binary oppositions, syntagmatic contrasts and paradigmatic oppositions, which, according to the contemporary linguistics of phonemes and the operation of sentences, are what characterize discourse.[49]

As a consequence, we express some reservations about a forced analogy between image and verbal language (the same as between music and language) – reservations that apply also to abuse of the term 'world', if one may with caution speak of a 'world of the image' and a 'world of words', their superposition, interaction, unity and conflicts.

It is an exaggeration to define our civilization by the image. The term 'civilization of the image' is as equally true and false as a dozen others: civilization of the gadget, of the jukebox, of nylon, of technology, of leisure, and so forth. If it is abusive to draw a historical and sociological definition from it, there can be no doubt as to the importance of the image: from photography (in the mid-nineteenth century) through to television (mid-twentieth), the extension of the image has been prodigious.

The image seems comparable with the fact. It appears as a given, analogously to the sensation and perception of classical psychology; something objective, in short, a fragment of the real. Yet the image, whether a single photo or a succession of photos, is ambiguous and more than ambiguous. It is dream and memory, escape from the real without losing reference to this palpable real, without dissolving into a transcendent 'other world'. It floats between the real and the unreal (or surreal) without ever coinciding with any of these terms, which place

---

49   Cf. Roman Jakobson, *Six Lectures on Sound and Meaning*, Cambridge, MA: MIT Press, 1981. Also André Martinet, *Éléments de linguistique générale*, Paris: A. Colin, 1963, p. 33ff.

inaccessible boundaries on it. It always has several meanings and leaves people in a disturbed expectation, sometimes flattering and agreeable, sometimes painful.

There is thus, up to a certain point, a 'world of the image'. This is no longer the imaginary of old, based on symbols, their power of evocation and participation. It was in Romanticism that the magic of symbolisms cast its last rays, which were often blinding, before the great promotion of the image we are trying to understand. The imaginary of the image is no longer a magic. There is no longer the power and freshness of romantic poiesis, that of Hoffmann's *The Golden Pot*, or the poetry of Hölderlin that transported the reader into a dream, abolished distances, identified with ancient heroes. The modern imaginary is a social imaginary. It does not escape ambiguity. The projection and identification described by Edgar Morin[50] have no freshness, no power. They scarcely go beyond the bounds of a compensating and compensated unease. They do not transport.

What is most important, for our radical critical analysis, is that the image is *reproduction*, of someone or something: of a fact, an act, a real or fictitious event. Reproduction as such has no limits. A photo can circulate in millions of copies, a film can be duplicated as many times as needed; the number is determined only by cost. And yet, the reproduced figure (whether a classic painting, a car accident, Marilyn Monroe or the queen of England) is inaccessible as such. The image is located between the repetitive, as its lower boundary, and the inaccessible, a higher pole. At the lower boundary it falls into banality. Approaching the upper limit, it borders on the uniqueness of being and event, primordially and initially given. We recognize here the general definition of mimesis.

The 'world of words', discourse, is taken as true or false. It is certainly either quite coherent or quite incoherent. And the 'world of images'? It deceives or undeceives. It exalts or depreciates. It distances into marvellous remoteness and transcendence, or insolently intrudes into familiarity. This is its particular rhetoric. It only appears to *denote*, to designate this or that. And it *connotes*. To the extent that it escapes

---

50   Edgar Morin, *The Cinema, or The Imaginary Man*, Minneapolis: University of Minnesota Press, 2005, and *L'esprit du temps*, Paris: Grasset, 1962.

from ambiguity, it completely mystifies (with the illusion of objectivity) or demystifies (with the appearance of establishing a fact). It falls into banality or goes off into the extraordinary, the peculiar. In order to astonish, it is enough for it to approach the vicinity of the event, the figure, the fact: their uniqueness, though this astonishment does not last. Banality does last. A paradoxical consequence is that those works that make use of the image (films, photo exhibitions, reproductions) have little influence. What emerges is the star. The contrast between the ephemeral character of the work (even when repeated after being forgotten for a long enough period), the effacement of the author, and the importance of the star, the 'cover girl',[51] the model, deserves our attention. The star becomes a social stereotype, both effect and cause of a mimetism. The child-woman type existed among women and in men's representations; Brigitte Bardot crystallized it into a *model*. The woman who aspires to accomplishment exists in society, and Marilyn Monroe gave it a face. The good little girl who becomes a good wife and mother is here in front of our eyes in 1965. Comic detail: she emerged from the comic rebellion of the *yé-yés*; her name is Sylvie Vartan.[52]

Films pass; figures remain. Works live only through figures, models. Outside this crystallizing influence, moreover, the 'world of the image' is marvellously deceptive. There is in this dupery the ultimate reflection of poiesis, a very remote one. Millions of women in millions of images (cinema, women's magazines and romance novels) believe they are encountering the 'reflection' of their reality, their promotion, their beauty, their 'being', whereas all they have before their eyes, transformed into technologies, is the reflection of the oldest and most primitive procedures of femininity – of appearance, of seduction, to excite the nerves of the male. It is quite right that the social imaginary, one of the sectors of mimesis, should be also the domain of myths. And even more right that this has never been said – on condition, however, that we do not omit other sectors, including the ensemble of praxis and contestations, as well as poiesis.

---

51   EN: In English in the text.
52   TN: *Les yé-yés* was a nickname given to the English pop music of the Beatles era as in 'She loves you, yeah, yeah, yeah'. Sylvie Vartan was a pop singer of the 1960s little known outside France, married at this time to Johnny Halliday.

It is useful here, the better to situate and define the reign of mimesis, to recall that the majority of machines that enter everyday life are machines for *reproducing*, from printing through to moulding plastic. Mimesis thus becomes a technological process. It reveals the essence of the machine while the machine in turn reveals the social essence of mimesis. Records and record players, tape recorders, reproduce music, voices, discourse on an unlimited scale. Photography was already a reproductive imitation of objects and existent 'beings'. It is in this way, seen from another angle, that the world of the image is a mimetic world: mimesis become world. It is in no way surprising that in these conditions there should be 'models', 'patterns', directing 'other-directed man'[53] from *inside*, while *appearing* to do so from without.

Technological mechanisms [*dispositifs*] have thus run through different phases and made clear their mimetic nature in a short period of time. The automaton of the seventeenth and eighteenth centuries (the chess player that was a false automaton, artificial animals) imitated, with or without trickery, the living and thinking being. This was only the advance signal for what would follow. Mimesis and its reign were announced by these small toy automatons, the first works, still charming ones, of combinatorial intelligence. Then came photography, sound recording, cinema, the worlds of the image and of moulding (the key perfecting of mass production: change from production to reproduction). The place was prepared for cybernetic machines and mechanisms that imitate organisms, simulate discourse, and bring to life 'Mr Everyman, this natural logician' (Benjamin Lee Whorf).[54]

The 'world' of mimesis in general, and that of the image in particular, was bound to have a reaction on Art – and particularly on painting, as a unique image bound up with the uniqueness of object and act, thus with a poiesis. On the other hand, painting connects with the subjective side, with the gaze [*le regard*]. Now this pure gaze ceases to be a gaze. The pure gaze at a pure spectacle is lost as gaze. What gazes is the object. The signal-object and the image-object have dissolved painting and destroyed art. Modern painting, with a certain delay in

---

53 EN: English in the original.
54 EN: *Language, Thought, and Reality: Selected Writings of Benjamin Lee Whorf*, second edition, edited by John B. Carroll, Stephen C. Levinson and Penny Lee, Boston: MIT Press, 2012, p. 299.

relation to poetry but actually with a certain advance in relation to philosophy, has made this truth visible and palpable to us. By opening our eyes, it has revealed to us that there was nothing to see.[55] Obstinately, without letting itself be stayed by repeated defeats, we can say here, it has committed itself to reinventing presences: to attaining inaccessible presences, to rediscovering poiesis by denying mimesis. A labour of Sisyphus. But we shall see below how the mimetic gaze, whether it focuses on the other gaze or only on itself, becomes redundancy, tautology and pleonasm.

Certain sociologists have 'discovered' a modern pantheon [*Olympiens modernes*]. The historical fact that this should have been 'discovered', while pertaining as it does to contemporary sociology, does not lack a certain humorous aspect. The gods of today are well-known to everyone. They are 'commonplaces' of contemporary society, the dominant images, the perfect stereotypes, the preeminent 'patterns'. All that is needed is precisely to discover them as such, thus first of all to escape from them and grasp the banality of this imaginary transcendence. The modern pantheon differs radically from the pantheon of antiquity. What could be said of the old gods is that they presented human powers attached to particular times and places, stories, actions. The gods of today are no more than general representations, not presences. They are not as is too often believed, even by those who accept this pantheon when they imagine themselves to be reflecting it, the product of publicity and journalism. They are the products of modern society as a whole, of its way of producing and devouring. On an everyday life that is masked and dissimulated, because too painful, through a fictitious society that calls itself 'mass' (and not class), one of consumption and abundance (not penury), of leisure (not work), they extend the second degree of illusion, the dream of illusion. To attain the pantheon, it is necessary to *transcend* everyday life. Power, money and glory are not enough. A relationship with everyday life, and with people immersed in everyday life, must also be reestablished. It is necessary to become human, by way of some weakness, some

---

55   Octavio Paz, presentation of the Nieko exhibition at the Galerie de France, January 1964. We differ from him in that he refuses to acknowledge the 'social death of art' and its future mutation into the instrument of a metamorphosis of everyday life.

vulnerable side, some human suffering or misfortune *immanent* to the everyday.

If someone asks in what way 'socialist' society differs from 'capitalist' society in the respect that concerns us here, it is hard to find a response. The chemistry of plastic materials, the technology of moulding, the commercialization of products of this technology, are more advanced on the capitalist side. There are probably more tape recorders and individual cameras in service among the bourgeoisie than among the leading strata of socialism. The same holds for individual cars. The temptation to the 'commonplace' and identity seems identical. Both societies find themselves under the sign of mimesis rather than that of 'technology' in general. 'Combinatorial intelligence' rages on both sides, if seemingly more accentuated, more analytic, more dichotomous, on the bourgeois side – because it has not been corrected by a residue of dialectical thought, or because it is less subject to a naïve Manichaeism? What is certain is that the pantheons do not coincide. Neither Grace Kelly, nor [Maria] Callas, nor [Aristotle] Onassis, are part of the socialist pantheon. Nor the Aga Khan, nor Queen Elizabeth nor Farah Diba.[56] And yet, the socialist pantheon and the capitalist pantheon do have some common divinities: Picasso, the Kennedys, perhaps Pope John XXIII. Sylvie Vartan and Brigitte Bardot, if they were allowed to penetrate there, would take the proletarian real by storm – which is why they are so strictly prohibited from entry. A remarkable fact: Stalin, a socialist divinity, has become part of the bourgeois pantheon, likewise Khrushchev and [Yuri] Gagarin. And Fidel Castro.

Let us hope that the war of the gods replaces that of men. If we believe their horoscope and predictions, 'socialism' is already victorious. The bourgeoisie lacks strength. It would not have worshipped such a strong and cruel divinity as Stalin. What a power, that of socialism! The severity of God the Father is enough for the bourgeoisie. The capitalist pantheon, in its decadence, opens itself to the gods of the enemy. But what enemy? What socialism? One that needs divinities? That lives in mimesis, in the praxis of combinatorial and

---

56   EN: Lefebvre is likely referring here to Prince Ali Aga Khan, a socialite and jockey. Farah Diba married the Shah of Iran in 1959.

operational intelligence, below the level of revolutionary praxis, of renewed poiesis?

Having thus explored the domain of mimesis, we can return to the concept. Our argument is that it renders *transparent* (that is, intelligible, but not in the sense of the analytical understanding) a large number of social and historical facts that were formerly *opaque*.

Mimesis, as we can see, is not a phenomenon or a function limited to the individual, his psychological or psycho-social life. It is a modality of praxis. We distinguish it therefore from notions with which it might be confused.

Imitation is a psychological concept that presupposes extreme passivity on the part of the subject in the face of the object that he imitates from outside, as well as the one-sidedness and simplicity of the imitative act, since this is only defined at the sensory and perceptual level. Imitation is simple and copies an object (or a 'being') posited before the subject. As generally conceived, it reduces to 'psychological' or 'psycho-sociological' repetition.

Repetition, however, we see as the lower limit, the pole that makes it possible to define mimesis, but where this is erased and disappears. Our critique of mimesis, fundamental and radical, demands that the concept be fully restored or constituted. It cannot be reduced to imitation in the sense explained above; mimesis is active. It decomposes and recomposes the real. Structure is nothing but the operation or operatory protocol that, by analysing and reconstructing the object, yields a simulacrum of it (Abraham Moles). There is a structuralist and mimetic activity (Roland Barthes), analyzed by Lévi-Strauss in *The Savage Mind* on the subject of bricolage, with the result that this bricolage could be taken as symbolic of mimesis. The operation divides into decomposition and reconstruction, in the course of which what the object aims at becomes apparent: the intelligible, the simulacrum, or more generally perhaps description; does describing a landscape not presuppose that the writer has decomposed and recomposed it at the level of his discourse, introducing not so much his 'sensibility' as its own intelligibility? Are not the writer, the painter, the sculptor, who fail to discover the source of poiesis, in fact bricoleurs, arranging a 'reduced model' of reality and proposing this to those who view with amazement and admiration the relation between this reduced object and the external 'model', a relation of resemblance or dissemblance, analogy or distancing perceived as such?

Does a child imitate his father? Yes and no. He admires him, he follows him. He believes that he copies his gestures, his words. At the lower limit, he repeats what he hears and sees; he is close to pathological identification. At the upper limit, the model seems to him so inaccessible and transcendent that he abandons it as model; and a different morbid situation then lies in wait for the child or adolescent. In fact, the child who 'imitates' his father or mother constitutes himself in an alienated and often deceptive manner by way of this imitation. He starts from his situation as a child, from his needs, his gestures and his words; he refashions these and enriches them (or impoverishes them), equally on the basis of the image that he has of the adult. He aims at the 'world of adults' by way of representations and myths, the myth of the father, the myth of adulthood. In this way he becomes other than he was, other than he sees, not without alienation.

We can say that pure and simple imitation is a pseudo-mimesis, or that mimesis is a pseudo-imitation. Mimesis thus conceived envelops imitative activity in the customary sense of psychologists and sociologists, but it goes further. It shows its internal functions and structures.

The psychological simplification comes from Aristotle. Art (which for him is no longer poiesis) imitates nature (which is no longer physis). Mimesis is thus no longer anything but a modality of the spectacle.

Mimesis is not conceived in its double determination, which the (philosophical and psychological) concepts of immanence and transcendence, repetition and aim, copy and resemblance, express only poorly. If on the one hand it is close to repetition and recommencement (of what? of the acquired, the stereotyped, the redundant, the established: gestures, words, movements), on the other hand it proposes for itself a term that escapes it, but is not transcendent in the classical sense of this term in philosophy. Mimesis is ambiguous, or rather double. In it, and in this zone, activity partially manages to grasp the 'term', to incorporate it, to put the image to work and follow the model. Thus mimesis becomes creative and participates in praxis, without for all that being identified with a rediscovered poiesis. It encompasses what psychologists and sociologists call 'creativity', which must be carefully distinguished from creative power, from poiesis.

Conceived in this way, mimesis supersedes the psycho-sociological theory of individual consciousness (Tarde) and the sociological theory of collective consciousness (Durkheim). The mimetic is social, since it is a modality of praxis. But it opens onto individuals, because individual consciousnesses open onto it. It thus encompasses a multitude of familiar phenomena, such as the imitation of the upper classes by the lower classes (which presupposes classes, a hierarchy and a struggle, a latent conflict between mimetism and class consciousness).

Let us now fix the limits of the general theory of mimesis. It bears essentially on *forms*. By presenting it in its main lines, we have successively encountered the forms of the city, those of discourse and law, those of social languages and accumulation. Without the necessity of emphasizing it too much, it is clear that the theory of these forms is not exhausted, and likewise that these forms and their theory do not exhaust historical and social reality: praxis. We have only given one way among others of analysing praxis, by connecting it with a primordial determination, poiesis, and going on to show how it separates itself (incompletely) from this as mimesis.

Despite this notion having a relationship with those of *function* and *structure*, as also with that of *form*, we do not think that from this starting point it is possible to attain all the forms, all the functions, all the structures. We are careful here not to present a philosophy of mimesis, a system.

We refuse to erase the differences in mimesis, and particularly those between functions, forms and structures. We expressly refuse to reduce human 'reality', including the possible, to the theory of mimesis.

Can we not say that reality, that is, praxis, is described and analyzed in a new light? It contains forms, functions, structures. It can only be grasped conceptually at its various levels as an interaction of these three terms. Forms act on functions and structures, and vice versa. The elements in interaction and transformation can be neither disassociated nor confused. Systematization privileges one of the elements, driving it to the absolute, absorbing the others into it. It totalizes praxis, or rather, tries to totalize it. There were thus, and still are, real systems, constituted or maintained by a totalizing activity of praxis. This is how formalism, functionalism, structuralism are posited today, strongly and vigorously, but narrowly. It would be easy to show, in a case relatively close at hand and concrete, that of the city and its inhabitants, the motives and advantages of such systematizations, their limits, the aberrations that they lead to arrive in praxis, and finally their ideological characteristics. We reject such a systematization. When need arises, we have emphasized separation, which never goes so far as making a complete break between the elements of interaction. For example, between the aspects of everydayness, labour, private life, leisure, or again objects, activities, situations (or what corresponds to them). We have also emphasized the *uneven development of real systems*, their disappearance, their dissolution, their ruptures, their mutations, the replacement by new 'systems', in a word, their non-convergence. A process of this kind is masked by ideological systematization, precisely by driving theory to the absolute and consolidating in practice this or that 'system', these or those forms, functions or structures seen as foundations of a system.

The theory of mimesis thus constitutes – among other things – an analysis of praxis. It would be interesting to make a comparison between these analyses. It is possible to distinguish the dominated from the non-dominated sector in natural (material) facts. Does not mimesis establish a bridge (a transition) between the sector dominated by instruments and technologies, and the sector not dominated? Does it not mean the dominated sector embarking on an appropriation by man of his own nature, still uncertain and incomplete? It is also possible to distinguish what arises from determinism, chance, will. Is mimesis not a determinism that encompasses varied chances and envelops will, yet which increases the domain of will?

We have distinguished a mimesis still attached to an initial poiesis from mimesis that separates from this. Above all, we have emphasized a mimesis that becomes autonomous and automatic, which is sufficient for itself, or seeks to be so. On this account, it extends and grows. It becomes the general form of increase and accumulation.

One of the strangest stages in this process, which indicates the proximity of its conclusion, is the *Pleonasm*: in familiar terms, the round robin [*Tourniquet*]. Mimesis tends in this direction. Is this by a law analogous to those of physics, closer to those of thermodynamics than to those of entropy? Would it not rather be because logic, the formal kernel of mimesis, tends towards tautology and establishes itself around pure identity, $A = A$? The one does not rule out the other, and perhaps there is a relationship between the general (logical) form of stability and the physical laws that determine order and disorder, that is to say, precisely the conditions of the stabilities of nature.

Activities that acquire autonomy tend towards pleonasm. From the moment that art sets itself up as a domain of its own, above and outside everyday life, as culture and not style of life, how should it be defined? One may say: art is art. In the same way: science is science. Philosophy is philosophy. Politics is politics. And so on. This tendency is accentuated when we move to the *second degree*: discourse on discourse, will to will, love of love, poetry on the poet and poetry, quintessences of essences, and so forth. Critics have often pointed out this fact, though rarely following it through: paintings are made about paintings, painting on painting, images on images. This succession, which in the past sometimes seemed to offer art and thought an eminent dignity, that of reflection and purity, reduces them to tautological duplication.

We shall not dwell here on the *logology* and *egology* of the philosophers. We have mentioned these in passing. We shall also have the opportunity to return to the circularity of the processes by which social 'systems' arouse energies that may overflow them and manage subsequently to control and integrate these energies (feedback, self-regulation).

Let us emphasize the palpable figures of pleonasm. There are little figures and little pleonasms. The crowd attracts the crowd (very materially, by a spontaneous mimetism, at the entrance to a shop or a cinema, around an incident in the street). Success breeds success. The number of readers of a magazine provides an advertising theme. In competitions organized by newspapers, there is often a question on the number of respondents, often the decisive one.

There is also the mirror that reflects the mirror, for example the wife who reflects the husband and the husband who duplicates the wife. And love that reflects love (without a third term: world, rival, child, action). The pleonasm here is already more serious. It becomes important in our eyes when we consider woman, queen of the market, buyer, supreme devouring consumer – and supreme commodity, advertisement of advertisement, commercialized model. And it is the same woman who is duplicated with a real and an abstract existence, actual and symbolic: pleonasmic. Woman is woman. *Cherchez la femme.* [*La femme, c'est la femme. Cherchez-la.*]

Take a motorway, in Europe or better still in the United States. You come across restaurants and motels that straddle the road. People stop in their cars to watch the passage of others in their cars; and besides, motorways hide the landscape, bypass cities, are empty in an ever-similar way – everywhere the same cars, the same people, the same places that are abstract because denatured and the same moments. Parisians on their Sunday outings are on the right track, stopping on the roadside to eat, wash their car and watch the other cars.

Another disturbing figure of pleonasm is the enormous information apparatus known as the 'mass media', which produce fodder when real food is lacking. The machine for conveying news creates pseudo-news and pseudo-events, which the consumer cannot distinguish from 'true' or 'real' ones. [Daniel J.] Boorstin explains very well how this happens. A politician visits a town. A crowd turns out to see him. A million people are in the street, and four million in front of their television screens. The camera shows the figure of the great man stepping out of his car for fifteen seconds, and shows the crowd for several minutes. For the television spectators, the crowd serves as spectacle. If we suppose that all these people stayed at home to 'see better', there would no longer be anything to see. In this way, the 'world of the gaze' and pure spectacle contains within it the germ of its negation and self-destruction, at the moment when it sets itself up as self-sufficient: pleonasm.[57]

As C. Wright Mills writes in *The Power Elite*, the immediate experience of the mass media only leads to confirming their success. The further one goes into the experience of significations, that is to say, the more one reveals them, the more radical is the critique. Contained within narrow limits, the notion of signification can serve a neopositivist or structuralist systematization. For us, the 'world of significations',

---

57   Cf. Boorstin, *The Image*, chapter 1: 'From News Gathering to News Making'.

inasmuch as it is a question of a 'world', is a world without substance, without certainty, even that of uncertainties. It sways between safety and adventure, between stability and aimless wandering, between the banal and the tragic, without support, without end, without expression. But at a given moment, so to speak, the notion of signification turns against itself. If we go far enough, we reveal the elements of a radical critique not only of the mass media, but of the social praxis that the mass media express, that is to say, that they dissimulate by unveiling and veil by showing. The man of communications continues to communicate, even when there is no longer anything to communicate. Above all when there is no longer anything to say, he *simulates* communication, having destroyed its content. He becomes the automaton of communication as this is realized in the mass media. The man of signification, when he no longer has anything to express, signifies the insignificant. He simulates. He creates meanings out of thin air. He parodies poiesis. He reproduces himself.

It is in this direction that we could pursue the exegesis of *Superman*, *Mandrake*, and many other comics that invade the press. Radical critique respects the appearance that moderate criticism sticks to, but goes much further in its analysis. Beneath the sexuality on display, it shows the asexuality of the modern *hero*, his devirilization under the surface of the exorbitant (magic) powers that are granted him. This superman is nothing more than a robot. The automaton has no sex, or has only an external and borrowed one: a simulacrum of sex. It is transsexual just as it is transcultural. 'Is sex necessary?' an American writer joked. Not at all. It disturbs pragmatic rationality and effectiveness. It is a waste of time. Let us eliminate sex by a completely logical reduction. We shall attain Identity, perfect Coherence, supreme Equilibrium, higher Tautology, Pleonasm.

It could be maintained that this pleonasm consists in the fact that people find no other meaning to their life than reproducing and having an ever-greater number of children, whose life will have no more and no other meaning than their own. Life is reduced to *survival*, which *simulates life*. Have men ever lived? The myths of survival continue (the immortality of the soul). Survival masks life. Thus the meaning of life, and the search for this meaning, perish by self-destruction: the idea that life has another meaning than to be lived.

The honour of providing the most perfect model of pleonasm falls to the cyberneticians. An electrode is placed in the brain of a rat. This electrode affects a region that gives pleasure when excited. When the rat touches a pedal in its cage, it triggers the stimulus and feels pleasure. The experiment thus creates a 'looped' system. Only exhaustion and sleep prevent the rat from continuing, until it dies of fatigue, this scientifically perfected onanism that simulates and reproduces pleasure.

The 'looping' and self-excitation of pleasure is the symbol and conclusion of robotized man: in an optimistic version, one that does not suppress pleasure, which has become useless for stereotyped gestures and established structures. This is the palpable figure of the perfected automaton in a transsexuality that falls below sex and thus resolves the problem of sex, need and desire. The reflex, reflection of the behaviour that is reflected in it, replaces desire and even need arising from nature. The robot-man is caught in his systems unless . . . unless protest and challenge break the loop. Unless desire is one day regained. Unless man's domination over his works is poetically asserted.

The organization office that develops and creates and regulates offices is not a bad figure of pleonasm. In a more general way, bureaucracy the world over has three levels: counters open to the public, reception bureaus for difficult cases, and finally the hidden offices where decisions are taken. These decisions particularly include the defence and extension of the bureaucracy's interests. It has also acquired three very general dimensions: the organization of offices in the strict sense, the *system of knowledge* (Marx), that is to say, the hierarchy of competences and titles, the privileges of the mandarins, and finally the relationship to the state. Among the general knowledges that make up the privilege of the mandarin is knowledge of itself: knowledge of the functioning of the bureaucracy and its hierarchy, knowledge inherent in the mandarin and impenetrable (secret, mysterious) to people outside and the lower degrees of the hierarchy. Finally, the bureaucracy supports and maintains the state: the state consecrates the bureaucracy. This is the pleonasm, the vicious circle, impossible (in appearance) to break. At the state summit reigns the supreme tautology: 'The state is the state', or again, '*l'état c'est moi*', as power is power, and things too are what they are. And men likewise, rulers or ruled, governors or governed.

The pleonasm is approached by various routes. That of the analytical understanding, of logic and its implications, of mimesis. That of discourse and the 'world of discourse', where discourse imitates discourse, according to its forms and rules. That of bureaucracy and the state. That of the eye, of the pure gaze, or of objects that gaze. That of the image, a mediation that becomes sovereign. That of philosophy. That of technology. And finally that of everyday life, in which circularities are established according to the following pattern: vital rhythms, behaviour; reflexes; mechanical rhythms and gestures reflected in behaviours. This real or illusory substantiality is asserted by concealing from oneself and others the process of its tautological autonomization.

Would there then be only one pleonasm, the Great Pleonasm, the ultimate tautology in which rationality and absurdity are one and the same? This question anticipates a subsequent argument and will only be answered completely in the conclusion. If there was a convergence of these paths, if we were faced with the empty enormity of the Great Pleonasm, the perfect loop would be completed sooner or later. We would all be caught in the depth of a blind alley, on the perfect round-robin. But we have in fact already replied to this question in the negative, putting forward the law of uneven development (of systems, of autonomizations).

What happens in the vicinity of the pleonasm, which we may now assume is threatening but cannot be completely attained or actualized? The 'real' situation in this vicinity adds something to the old theory of alienation and its limit, reification. We find here second-degree alienations. This limit is the pure and absolute form. It differs from reification although it is analogous to it in its structure.

In this vicinity, in each sector, each system of what the sociologists call 'limited rationality' tends towards achieved coherence. It becomes closed. It changes into Identity. This is the success of the system. We are at the opposite pole of the contradiction. Everything here is true, transparent, clear. And so everything is false, apparent, illusory. Reality here can be defined by a finite series of questions to which the answer is yes or no. The operational determination of the real imposes itself. This is accomplished in fact on the basis of the pleonasm that defines the sector (language, mimesis, state, bureaucracy, etc.). This operational definition signifies that the operator manufactures the 'real' that he deals with and claims – or believes – he confirms. Everything in this context can be put onto punch cards. The technico-bureaucratic dream approaches realization. This accomplishment, carried out with handicraft means by specialists in fragmentary activities in their various domains, could be extended by machines to large numbers (of individuals, of determinations). Using electronic calculators, it would be possible to put large populations onto punch cards, onto matrixes, with their attitudes, behaviours, roles and functions.

We have been able to define logic as a general theory (abstract and formal) of stabilities, that is to say, of coherent forms, self-regulating systems. In this sense, by separating it from philosophy to which it was long attached, logic has enabled us to dominate the partial results of the sciences and to conceive the sciences (in particular those of 'human reality') as theories of the real and realizations of theory. Here we grasp the full amplitude of the logic of realization, that is, logic in realization: the constitutive tautology.

In this vicinity, the individual and history pass into the residual (which the boldest among the rationalists of technology driven to absurdity conceive as indefinitely reducible by way of new procedures). Likewise tragedy, dialectics, and so forth.

Fortunately, this dangerous region is also that of the self-destruction of autonomized powers. Fetishism of language and destruction of language go strangely hand in hand. Modern art posits itself as supreme *meaning, meaning of meaning* (in all *senses* of the term, that is: perception and sensuous organizations, directions, significations); and this is the moment when all arts and all artists practise a flamboyant destruction in and through their works.[58] They do so in different ways: through

---

58 Picasso remains the symbol of this perpetual self-destruction of the work, of technique, of painting itself. Does Picasso exist? No. There is no Picasso. What there is with him is the whole of painting, the whole history of art, reprised, used, destroyed in a supreme perpetual holocaust. In literature the line of destruction and self-destruction starts from Dadaism (Tristan Tzara). The first period of surrealism led through to Beckett, by way of Antonin Arthaud. Its apogee was Malcolm Lowry's

pure technique, through parody, through stammering, through heroic temptation to renovate, through silence.

The 'real' constituted by science and technology, with the blessing of art, leads to the consolidation of everyday life. But art cannot tolerate this everydayness, which it does not manage (as externality and cultural speciality) to encounter, transpose, metamorphose. In the general uneven development, the everyday is consolidated as a backward and underdeveloped sector, a substitute in the highly industrialized countries for the former colonized and backward sector. The everyday, as such, challenges art and culture, because they remain external to it. Likewise science and technology, because they create it and leave it far behind, after having subjected it to their structural and functional rules – which leads to disturbance, by this particularly tough 'real', the everyday, of the 'real' as a whole. The 'real' is duplicated and split more cruelly than before. On the one hand, it is what cannot be escaped, what brings satisfactions, what must be accepted, what should be grasped in a participatory and active fashion. On the other hand, it is what provokes an unbearable malaise, what must be defied or fled from, what can only impose itself on an imbecile passivity.

In 'mass consumption', and through the 'mass media', mimesis is reduced to the imitation of wealth, power, knowledge. It involves making the 'world' into a spectacle and the 'world of the spectacle', with the imitation of objects caught in the general spectacle, objects that are human beings. Spectacle and conditioning, images and stereotyped behaviours, go together. And yet, crude, clumsy, distorted by business and advertising, a kind of enormous ludic invention is attempted in this mimesis. Running through it, derisorily inspiring it, there is in 'mass communications' a vast and wretched spirit: play on words, play with violence and eroticism, games of chance and death. In this monstrous mortal seriousness everything becomes frivolous, everything becomes a game, although this game does not link up with invention. The critique of everyday life emphasizes the same tendency, which runs through the constraining banality of the everyday without

Under the Volcano (New York: Harcourt, Brace, 1947), where the self-destruction of the work and the artist becomes the theme of a work of art. In music, the line is marked by serialism, _musique concrète_, electronic and purely combinatory music, and so forth.

metamorphosing it. Are we saying that these games must be redeemed, pursued further and brought into convergence with the great poetic games? Are we remembering here and now that play is a moment? Are we asking if it has an ontological privilege, as Heidegger believed? No. We simply suggest that the self-destruction of autonomized powers presents an essential aspect of poiesis for our time. This destruction and this self-destruction are the poetic act par excellence, the conflagration that inserts itself in a striking and invisible way at the heart of our praxis, that which the powers in question divide up in order to seemingly dominate it. Under the sign of ever possible general self-destruction and the atomic danger, the self-destruction of these autonomized powers is beginning. Thus the tragic regains its place [*rang*]. Our poiesis is still tragic.

Criticism most commonly takes up an unjust and unjustifiable position, without being aware of this. It criticizes the present in the name of the past, the town in the name of the countryside, industrial life in the name of patriarchal life, modernity in the name of survivals, the division of labour in the name of what preceded it, harsh reality in the name of nostalgia and the memory of 'blue remembered hills'. Criticism never reaches radicality by limiting itself in this way. It floats indecisively between 'left-wing criticism' and 'right-wing criticism', tending towards the latter. We can observe in the works of Marx, and particularly the so-called 'philosophical' works of his youth, some traces of this hesitation. Yet Marx escaped from this. He took the 'real' in the grip of a double critique: in the name of the future and the possible, in the name of the past and memory. The former encompasses the latter and the latter links up with the former, but to the exact extent that the superseded subsists as past within the superseding.

Now, unless the contrary is proved, our critique links up with that of Marx by taking the reality of the twentieth century as its object. It does not set the past up against the present, but the possible against what obstructs it. It recognizes nostalgia only to the extent that nostalgia illuminates, that regret for a time before the division of labour proclaims that this separation can be overcome. The possible calls the past to it and gives it a (historical) meaning. The possible prevails in the order of reasons and will, the past having its place in the series of causes (determinisms). Thus criticism attains its full radicality and is strongly distinguished from any kind of 'passé-ism', although some people, particularly among technocrats, stubbornly dismiss in these terms everything opposed to their designs.

The complexity of praxis appears ever more clearly. It is polarized. It relates in part to repetition and the repetitive (redundant), in part to the combinatory (mimesis), and in part, finally, to destruction and creation (poiesis). The mixture is decanted. After a long period in which mimesis prevailed, a renewed unity is indicated in the fragmented totality of its moments. A vast bloc soon separates out, a partial totality, mimesis in praxis. Another dialectical unity, partial and open, poiesis in praxis, would attain the moment of a decisive promulgation. The predominance of mimesis would have served as intermediary, the aim of poetry being, across time, practical truth (Paul Éluard).

This horizon, both close and distant, is not however bright. It rises problematically. New themes are sketched, such as those of the relationship between *repetition* and *creation*. We have already considered these themes as metaphilosophical, in the sense that their elucidation must result from an investigation of praxis in its totality, and not from an ideology juxtaposed with the real and the theory of the real.

We have in mind a new unity of the totality grasped fragmentarily. This involves a unity in the difference between mastery and wandering, between domination and contestation, between safety and adventure. Thus between mimesis and poiesis: between achieved being and inexhaustible being, between absence and presence.

Human beings, individually and as a group, assert themselves both with and against nature, and such was poiesis, both with and against other men, such was praxis. Some cleared the ground for planting, invented handicrafts; others invented trade, industry, politics. Others again were conquerors. Sometimes certain peoples happily combined the various means of assertion (the Greeks, for example). Relationships bound up with domination – defiance, challenge, courage – always had two distinct terms, sometimes complementary, sometimes contradictory, one relating to nature, the other relating to men.

Up to now there have been three terms in play and at stake: nature, other humans, and autonomized technology (the automaton). The second term, the bitter struggle between human groups (peoples and classes) will attenuate after some explosive convulsions. In any case, we know pretty well the problems that this struggle raises. The third term will one day raise the most serious questions. It already does raise them. It faces man with his fundamental question, the *appropriation of nature and above all of his own nature.* Either poiesis will move to the front rank in the direct relationship reestablished between man and 'nature' or 'being', or else man will be caught by his own work: once again, the dead will have seized the living. This time, death imitates life; it caricatures it.

In social reality, mimesis has always been important by conferring importance on this or that. But it was profound and productive, when great symbolic images were offered for 'imitation'. It is in modern everyday life that mimesis becomes flat imitation of 'models' posited as abstract objects, 'patterns', stereotypes and images, the spectacular representations of the great of this world. By losing its depth, by becoming 'fact' with one or two reduced dimensions, mimesis ridiculously populates the everyday and modernity. In this modernity, what is not simulacrum? What is not simulation? A few 'moments'? A few dramas? Death? Even that gives rise to comedies, histrionics. It does not guarantee any authenticity. In this modernity, mimesis reduced to the clearest and most complete expression reigns supreme, even while machines take over and realize it materially.

Between man and nature, between man and his own nature, technology interposes a second nature. This second naturality is no longer the city, art, language or even the world of objects in general, but technology that is at the same time instrument, means, mediation, screen and disturbed, rather than diaphanous, milieu. Technology imitates nature and man, who imitate one another. And men seem to find satisfaction and happiness in this. The time of the masses. The time of buddies.[59] The time of pleonasm. The time also of protests, refusals, frustrations and an ever more generalized malaise: which cannot be challenged in mimesis, yet could be crystallized beyond cleavages of class and demands defined in economic and political terms.

---

59   TN: 'Copains' here is likely a reference to a French radio programme of the 1960s, *Salut les copains*, identified with *yé-yé* pop music.

Along the way we have encountered several familiar definitions of man: *homo faber, homo sapiens, homo ludens*. We have stressed the anthropology of Marx, despite the fact that his thought cannot be reduced to an anthropology: man is the being who founds a praxis, who acts and produces, who alienates and disalienates himself – loses himself, goes astray, rediscovers himself – in his works and his products. According to Marx this is *homo faber*, deepening the concept of this.

To the definitions and dimensions we have encountered, we added several others, resulting from anthropological research and a critique of anthropology, an elaboration that continues philosophy while contesting it and using concepts taken from philosophy.

Man is everyday. Man has to accomplish himself in everyday life: in an everydayness other than that which establishes itself around us.

Man is mimetic. He changes by imitating and imitates by changing. He imitates, imitates himself, by acting, by living pragmatically. He creates by imitating and imitates by creating. What does he imitate? The sun, the gods, the masters, celebrities, idols and finally machines. He parodies nature in facticity; he caricatures himself by copying human models, setting himself rules and norms for imitation: morality, philosophy, and so forth.

And yet, man is poetic. He is born from poiesis, with it. He dies far from poiesis, his homeland. He has to rediscover poiesis. With the recognition of poiesis as foundation of man, we go further than the opposition of the rational and the irrational, further than anthropology: towards nature or being, and towards the most distant possible, the horizon of horizons. The 'struggle against nature', however primordial it may be, does not exhaust the relationship of man with nature; this struggle is waged with technological means, with instruments. But the relationship envisaged is also unity, appropriation even in struggle and conflict. It is Poiesis. It is heralded in his works, with a share of uncertainty, unpredictability and the unforeseen.

And now, let refusal reject mimesis. Let restored desire lead to the theoretical decision to refuse – inevitably by way of despair in maturity or dissipation in youth. By way of unease and revolt. And by way of self-destruction.

In this sense, a theoretical decision can link up again with a revolutionary praxis (the political and social elements of which would come partly from elsewhere).

In this sense, poetry will have its chance. We shall wager on poetry, this residue of mimesis. In the very long term.

CHAPTER 7

Philosophy as Message

We shall now consider philosophy as a message. Not in the vague sense of a 'testimony', in which philosophy would be an angelic messenger of some kind of hope, but in the precise sense of this term in semantics and communication or information theory. In other words, we shall apply to philosophy the methods of semantic and semiological analysis. We shall ask the question 'What are the structures of philosophical discourse?', and try to answer it without dissimulating two intentions, two objectives: first of all, to use the concept of structure up to the limits of its zone of validity. And secondly, to determine and delimit philosophical discourse by defining it, or philosophy as discourse if you prefer – an approach that is indispensable in order to offer an objective balance sheet of philosophy in terms of what it has that is 'positive' (a 'positive' that may subsequently appear as negative, and vice versa), without abandoning anything of radical critique. The approach is equally necessary as a support for the metaphilosophical meditation that is born in the course of the superseding of philosophy, its contestation and (dialectical) negation. By superseding philosophy, in the course of this superseding, we shall say what philosophy was.

Along the way we have already introduced certain notions from semantics, semiology, information theory and structuralist thought. These notions are not new, and most of them are familiar. We shall find them again here. We shall be able to ask up to what point philosophy can be said to be a metalanguage (a universal language), or claim that it is the quest for this. Does not the philosopher sometimes suffer from a hypertrophy of signifiers, somewhat detached from the signified? Does he not seek to accumulate what cannot be accumulated? What are the roles of redundancy (intelligibility) and novelty (information) in philosophical discourse? What does philosophical discourse denote? What are its connotations? In the modification of philosophical systems, what can be understood according to diachrony, and what pertains to synchrony? Each concept can be of use to us in questioning the philosopher and philosophy.

As an effort towards system and totality, as a quest for meanings in facts and concepts, philosophy undeniably relates to semiology.[1] On the other hand, it is neither obvious nor certain that semantics and semiology exhaust philosophy or completely explain it. If philosophy is a system of meanings, is it only that? The application of semiological analysis to philosophy may well allow us to discern a residue, something irreducible, by way of which philosophy in general refuses to be completely contained in a system of meanings that is closed and given, a system like others; by way of which, therefore, every philosophy opens onto something other. Would this irreducible be a poetry or poiesis, or the 'project'? Perhaps. Would it be the alliance and reconciliation that is glimpsed with 'nature', with 'being'? Possibly. Perhaps philosophy in some respects, as pure discourse (logos), approaches in other respects forms that accept those elements arising from nature – symbols, expressive gestures, natural expressivity – which Saussure indicates as difficulties facing his method of analysis.[2]

Before embarking on this examination, let us pay some attention to *semantic reduction*. This is the operation by which the linguist distinguishes a language from speech and from the chaos of linguistic facts. Within this general phenomenon, two aspects are separated: language and speech. Language, in this sense, is what remains after speech is subtracted. Everything that does not enter into the system of signs is

---

1   Semantics studies changes in meanings. Cf. Ferdinand de Saussure, *Course of General Linguistics*, Chicago: Open Court Classics, 1998, p. 16. As for semiology, this studies the life of signs in society. It is concerned therefore with systems of signs and meanings, language forming a particular (specific) system but one relatively privileged in the ensemble of semiological facts. Cf. Saussure, *Course of General Linguistics*, p. 15ff.

2   Saussure cites the example of the Chinese who salute the emperor by prostrating themselves nine times on the ground. The signs of politeness, endowed with a natural expressiveness, are nonetheless fixed by a rule; and it is this rule, according to Saussure, that obliges their use, rather than their intrinsic value.

dismissed and bracketed out. By semantic reduction, language becomes a well-defined object extracted from the heteroclite set of facts. And it is an object that can be studied separately. Language thus delimited is a system of signs in which all that is essential is the unity of signifiers and signified, meanings and acoustic images. Language is a form, but a concrete one (as evidenced by writing). Semantic reduction thus contains dichotomous oppositions: that between language and speech (language is always virtual and speech always actual), between the signifier and the signified (the union of which makes up the sign), and between synchrony and diachrony (linguistics has first to study language in its functioning, as a system of signs used by a definite human group, with diachronic or historical study intervening only later, and subordinated to the former).

Let us consider the semantic reduction as given. It reveals a concrete abstraction: *language*. This operation corresponds to the phenomenological reduction of Husserl, by which reflection brackets out those aspects of the real or the idea that it does not for the moment place at the centre of its analytical or descriptive research. The semantic reduction also seems analogous to that which enabled Marx to reveal a concrete abstraction, the *commodity*, outside of the chaos of human acts of consumption, production and exchange, above the diversity of needs and goods. The analogy or possible homology goes a long way; like the commodity, does not language as such have an alienating and even reifying power which individuals and groups accept, use, or obscurely combat? Like the commodity, language is caught in dialectical movements; it is not dialectical in itself, it is a form, a structure, to be analyzed as such.

We propose (here and elsewhere) to dialectically reverse the semantic reduction, that is to say, to restore as closely as possible what it dismisses and brackets out. From the linguistic chaos, which is not praxis and study of which suspends praxis, we shall return towards praxis as a whole. It is possible to rediscover and recuperate the dismissed elements without falling back into the initial chaos: by *situating* these in relation to the revealed abstraction, language, discourse. This is rather like what Marx did in *Capital*: after analyzing the commodity as formal structure, he returned to the division of labour and the real groups and classes that constitute society. The reverse operation of semantic reduction, conducted starting from the latter, would enable us to take back speech, gestures, expressive elements, systems that contain natural givens. Instead of dismissing from language and discourse speech and linguistic chaos with their diversities (voices, mimicry, etc.), we rediscover these interactions. Do they return in the concepts, the categories? That is the question that immediately comes to mind. Yes, we can reply.

The intonations of speech that animate and diversify discourse, these particularities bound up with individuals, do nonetheless enter into classified and familiar generalities: the figures of rhetoric. It would be easy to show how Saussure indicates this movement in his lectures on general linguistics. His reflection follows a double movement: of reduction, and of return (layer by layer, element by element) towards what the reduction dismisses. In this way he posits simultaneously the principles of semantics, which presupposes reduction, and of semiology, which rediscovers the concrete dismissed by this reduction. The double movement has continued since then, with interdependencies and interactions between semantics and structural linguistics, on the one hand, and semiology on the other. In his *Essays on General Linguistics*, Roman Jakobson reintegrates the figures of rhetoric into language, without following this movement through to an end, since he restricts it to the two figures of metaphor and metonymy, even if these are particularly important.[3] As a whole, the studies and writings of linguists[4] and semiologists[5] complement each other.

We may well be able to determine places, zones, sites or situations that are occupied by 'systems', in relation to the marker and referential that is language in the full sense. And without fetishizing this. On the contrary: ceasing to take it as a 'structural' prototype of intelligibility and reality, while on the other hand not dislocating it or dissolving it,

---

3 Though Roman Jakobson does mention ellipsis, reticence, and so forth.

4 André Martinet, in particular: *L'Économie des changements phonétiques*, Berne: Francke, 1955.

5 In particular Roland Barthes. Cf. 'L'imagination du signe', *Arguments*, nos 27–8, pp. 118–20. Charles Peirce established the programme of a semiotics. Cf. also Emile Benveniste, 'Remarques sur la fonction du langage dans la découverte freudienne', *La Psychanalyse*, no. 1, pp. 14–16ff].

keeping a kind of respect for it, preserving in it its eminent dignity. On condition that we cease to take it as an end, and consider it simply as a *mediation* – something more than an instrument or simple means, but something less than the human essence. Without forgetting, finally, what has previously been stated so as to fully reintegrate diachrony (history) into synchrony, that is to say, the law of uneven development of systems, perspectives on the explosion or dissolution of structures, equilibriums, coherencies, self-regulations – which includes the idea of a collapse [*éclatement*] of philosophy as a system since the nineteenth century.

The topology and typology of 'systems' could thus be determined and located in an image of 'reality' both abstract and concrete.

That said, we shall try to answer some particular questions.

A) Should philosophy be seen as a metalanguage? Can it be taken as the quest for a metalanguage?

Ever since philosophy established itself, in fact, philosophers have always sought to find the common measure of all the works of man: aesthetic (literary, artistic), scientific, political, and so forth. They tried to elaborate a general language making it possible to translate, in its system, 'disciplines', 'sectors', 'domains', 'branches of knowledge', the most varied modalities of action. How is the decoding and deciphering of all these partial and divided activities to be accomplished? By philosophy, as general and clear language. The philosophical attitude postulates that this general translation is effected without betrayal (naturally) and moreover without residue. Philosophical discourse would thus become a common language, one that all specialized men can and even must one day use. Whether they adopt the standpoint of 'thinking thought' or 'thought thought', philosophers presuppose that their thought and their discourse attain the other attributes of human beings (will, emotion, passion, action, creation), and the very being of man – and that they exhaust these in the expression of substantialities or the explanation of meanings. Philosophers, in other words, each seeking to constitute their own system, believe that all other systems and activities are homologous to this, and are formulated in their *paradigm* ('substance—accident', 'subject—object', 'infinite—finite', 'in-itself—for-itself', etc.). By using the word 'paradigm' in this way, we distort the sense of the word somewhat, as it was developed by grammarians. For these it denotes a purely formal set of (significant) oppositions.

Secondly, we note that the philosopher reflects on words. Philosophy returns periodically to intuition, the philosopher taking a cure of immediacy. He seeks to brush aside the veil of words, go directly to things, plunge into the depths. For most of the time he proceeds on concepts and signs (signifiers and signified). He takes them either in isolation or in their linkages, but always in language. The philosopher accordingly changes language into an object. He reflects on it (even if he is essentially interested in objects, 'beings', the signified). His procedure is thus analogous to that of the linguist, the semanticist, the semiologist. The latter do indeed seek to constitute a second language, in which or with which they speak of the first.

The philosopher, all the same, wants to create his own language. He takes hold of common symbols: heaven and earth, light and darkness, surface and depth, and so forth. But he overburdens these; he overdetermines them; he makes them say something other than current language does. Does he create symbols and symbolisms? Only the detailed examination of philosophies, and the whole history of philosophy, would make possible a response. On the other hand, the syntagmatic connection sought by the philosopher differs from the connections of language only by its search for rigour. Philosophy would like to approach logic, algebra, geometry, the various forms of mathematical calculation, with their clear and evident order of reasons. On this point, and in this way, the philosopher attempts a metalanguage. And yet he possesses a paradigm of his own, which does not coincide with any of the linguistic paradigms, and sees itself as containing a privileged content, not a form or list of formally distinct and pertinent differences, determined by their opposition alone.

Philosophy as such, accordingly, does not escape a curious ambiguity. It both seeks and seeks not to be a metalanguage. It has this ambition, but fails to carry the ambition through. Who takes it up? The semanticist and semiologist? Certainly, but there is an abyss between the procedure that transforms language into an object and the constitution of a universal language. The inventors of machines for translating and accumulating knowledge are closer to metalanguage, along with pure logicians. And yet the machine languages that exist today (Algol, Syntol, etc.) are only steps on the road to this general metalanguage, and we do not know whether this can be realized or is only the horizon and ultimate limit of an indefinite research. We know from Benoit Mandelbrot that a language containing discontinuous signifying units (words separated by gaps, 'stops') cannot be totally deciphered. Absolute and total discourse, accordingly, would not exist. It would be impossible despite being dreamed as possible by philosophers and logicians.

At all events, in philosophy there is *discourse* (doubly systematized, according to connections as rigorous as possible and a paradigm as complete as possible) and *speech*. This speech seeks to be living, creative; to proclaim a truth or produce a satisfaction (happiness) among people, it makes use of symbols, it metamorphoses, it transfigures. In other words, each philosopher has a certain style. Inasmuch as philosophy seeks to be metalanguage, it fails. To the extent that it seeks to be something other than metalanguage, it lacks one of its aims: rigour, demonstration. As reflection (or reflect), philosophy seeks to be metalanguage. As proposition and projection (project), it belies this intention. As speech and style, it destroys it. By way of this procedure, the philosopher challenges the alienating and reifying power of language as such (a power crystallized and fixed by the semantic reduction). Philosophy thus establishes itself in the duality: discourse and more than discourse, alienation and dis-alienation. We rediscover here in a different fashion the aporias previously discussed.

B) By refusing philosophy the capacity to elaborate a metalanguage, is thought not condemned to impotence? How is it possible to move from one domain to the other? Do we not leave the results of the division of labour, the distinct works, simply juxtaposed? On the other hand, inasmuch as the proposition of a metaphilosophy has any meaning, does this new form of thought not consist precisely in semantics and semiology, which view language as essential to man, and linguistics as a fundamental science?

Let us remark first of all that the relations between 'sectors' in knowledge are not simply a matter of terminology. It is not enough to decode or decipher, to translate. That would mean posing the question in a formal manner that neglected the content, the movements of thought, the real interactions and interferences. When a discovery or an invention is made, and there is a productive encounter between different directions of research, something happens that is different from a new use of a word. We may maintain that a contradiction within knowledge, or indeed between thought and facts, finds a solution (provisional, relative). As far as vocabulary is concerned, each user must be able at any moment to release all the meanings of each word, and tie words to their accepted common use. Naturally enough, this demand is unusual, and more than one user (even in the social sciences where it is a fundamental condition) is unable to meet it; with the result that we have a kind of fiction or utopia. It remains nonetheless that semantics here depends clearly on diachrony, on history (on knowledge). For example, how to explain the meaning of the word 'atom' without recalling that it signified a simple and indivisible physical reality before going on to denote, through a remarkable reversal, a highly complex one? The semantics of knowledge may develop within knowledge, without depending on any kind of philosophy, provided that the entire set of movements of thought is taken into consideration.

The importance acquired by semantics and semiology goes hand in hand with the withering away of philosophy. Subordinating philosophy to these fields of research, asserting the relevance of philosophy as a system of interpretation of the world in relation to semiology, means accentuating this withering – even if analysis detects something irreducible in philosophy. Semantics and semiology, however, if they do not end up in a neopositivism that accepts and confirms the facts of language, and along with them the social faits accomplis, lead towards a reconstruction of philosophy. Structuralism hesitates and sways between scientism and worldview, between *how* and *why*, between super-science and *Weltanschauung*.

Metaphilosophical mediation seeks to be far more strongly challenging. It has radical critique as its foundation. It does not confirm any fait accompli, any existent. It grasps everything, 'things' and 'beings', works and activities, by their ephemeral side. It places itself in the movement of destruction, of self-destruction, of dissolution of stabilities (structures, equilibriums, feedbacks, autoregulations, etc.), thus in a restored historicity, in a diachrony put back above synchrony. It is not only death and the consciousness of death that resist structure, operationalism; it is ending in general, and thus becoming.

Here the line of argument takes a precise form. Metaphilosophical mediation (which proclaims itself 'meditation' rather than 'reflection', the word appropriate to philosophy) rejects the principle of immanence, formulated by Saussure[6] and accepted by the semanticists, semiologists and structuralists that have followed him. According to this principle, the study is situated within systems. The analyst must grasp each system from within. He places himself, according to Saussure, in the situation of the chess player, accepting the number of pieces, their rules of displacement, in short, the grammar of the game, and is uninterested in the material that the pieces are made of, whether wood or ivory. The notion of system is bound up with that of an internal exploration of this system that grasps it in itself, as communication and message, with its repertoire and memory. Metaphilosophy rejects and refutes the postulate of immanence, as a consequence of the postulate of system. But this is not in the name of totality. Such a refutation would be in vain, since totality conceived in this way can itself only be postulated, and postulated as the largest system (system of systems, systems of the world). That is to say, as philosophy of Totality. Metaphilosophy challenges the principle in the name of negativity. It introduces totality only with precautions: fragmented or broken totality, open and partial totality, virtual totality, and so forth.

Semanticists and semiologists leave aside praxis, or even defy it. They withdraw to the formal, non-dialectical character of language, and also to the fact that language is not praxis (discoursing is not acting or producing). It is true that language, like analytical understanding and formal logic, such close neighbours, 'is not' dialectical. To bring contradictions into language, it is sometimes necessary to twist it, to violate it, to inflict tensions on it. Structuralists reject praxis and dialectic along with history and historicity. They do not find there the solid ground that they desire, and that the semantic reduction

---

6   Saussure, *Course of General Linguistics.*

offers them. We think that by going further in the reverse movement to this reduction, that is to say, precisely by accepting it as reduction and rejecting its principle of immanence that fetishizes the systemic characters one seeks to apprehend, this will give a better grasp of systems, and still more so of the laws of systems. Is it not curious and significant that the most eminent semiologists (Roland Barthes) have hesitated before philosophy, confining themselves to studying one or other secondary 'system', for example fashion? In particular, we shall perhaps discover laws, those of dissolutions, of explosions. It is in this sense that we bring into consideration the unclassifiable or even (apparently) insignificant residual elements – Which amounts, in relation to semantics and semiology, to a kind of rehabilitation of the supra- and infra-linguistic, of nature as well as history. And also of the symbol, to which we do not unconditionally attribute 'depth' and emotional participation, but which resists being reduced to a modality of the sign or a kind of consciousness of signification, without for all that making language or concepts into simple *reflections* of more 'profound' realities.

A final point. Metaphilosophical meditation repudiates the characteristics and features (relevant or otherwise) of the System. It is not a new systematization that would recuperate certain significations of philosophical systems, or of philosophy as system, instead of letting these be lost. This is not the way, in our view, that it reprises, illuminates, continues philosophy after a radical break and an explosion of the latter.

C) What can recent information theory bring to the comprehension of philosophy, apart from a scientistic claim to supplant it?

Let us recall that information theory cannot pass for either a scientific theory of knowledge, or a substitute for the philosophical theory of knowledge. It likewise acts to dislocate this latter theory and render it useless. But it does represent a 'theory of the real'. Along with its complement, cybernetics, it contains a programme of realization. It accomplishes, in the domain of the social sciences, what the analysts of the natural sciences (Bachelard) and the critics of the philosophy of science (Heidegger) had foreshadowed. It does not study a reality; it constitutes it; it tends to produce it. It does not simply produce this or that object, this or that combination of objects, along the lines of regular science that is 'realized' in an object (the scales, the lever, the Atwood machine, the retort, the pendulum, etc.). It tends to be realized globally and literally occupy praxis. This is how it falls under the blow of a radical critique arising from praxis. This radical critique shows, for example, that at the very moment that communication is 'theorized', and a human reality is to be produced according to the schemas of communication, reality is attenuated and communication disappears. The same holds for language: fetishism and self-destruction.

Analysis of the message does nonetheless have a considerable importance. We discern here first of all the dichotomous opposition 'redundancy–information'. The agreement between linguists (Jakobson) and information theorists (Abraham Moles) is remarkable here. Redundancy, as we know, constitutes the intelligibility of the message. At the lower limit, repetition, there is no longer a message, and yet complete intelligibility. At the upper threshold, the excess of novelty and surprise makes the message unintelligible and also destroys it as such.

Let us now consider philosophy. The philosophical message is necessarily redundant. It refers to what is familiar and acquired: experience, concepts, symbols. It seeks to contribute, or rather to capture, what is new in 'the world'. We suspect that it oscillates between the lower threshold (repetition, rechristened for the occasion 'recognition' or 'return to the original and primordial'), and the upper threshold (named 'intuition', 'supreme knowledge'). But perhaps there is more. Does the philosopher not often confuse – in an eminent, or rather transcendent, unity – the intelligible and the surprising? Let us consider the Platonic Idea, Aristotle's pure act, the transcendent One of several other philosophers. These absolutes are inherent in relative truths and existences. They are repeated in each act of thought and each apprehension of the real. They thus constitute the redundancy (intelligibility) of the real: form of forms, unity of multiplicity. And yet, as sources of being and the diversity of beings, these speculative entities are deemed to bring the indefinite surprise, the decisive information always renewed by the intervention of the philosopher.

Can this frequent confusion explain the very particular tension of certain philosophical styles, where redundancy appears surprising? Here again, the philosopher places upside down something that should walk on its feet.

D) What can the famous distinction elaborated by Saussurean linguistics between the signifier and the signified contribute to the critical comprehension of philosophy?

We shall now examine, accordingly, the philosophical message as a sign charged with significations, that is to say, as a system of significations. Who makes these significations explicit? Someone who uses semiological analysis in a critical manner. This 'someone' does not form part of a transcendent mind that would judge the totality of the world or the world as totality, with the result that the problem and its situation in or before this totality would have a meaning. This 'someone' we call here by way of hypothesis: *metaphilosophical meditation*, implying a radical critique of philosophy as ideology, as utopia, as mythology – and yet one that extracts from philosophy as such the forms and contents, the theoretical kernels, that it has constituted and that survive it.

The philosopher drew signifiers from a collective repertoire, belonging to the general memory of men in society or defining this memory. These signifiers are of two kinds: symbols and concepts. Concepts come either directly or indirectly from praxis; they may indeed come by way of earlier philosophies. At all events, they are in the process of elaboration and belong to a history: for example, the concept of the state, or that of labour, or that of detachment (along with its opposite: commitment). It is in this way that philosophy has a relationship with praxis: it is partly born out of it; it returns to it and inserts itself in it; it has practical consequences, both false and true, illusory or real. It can claim to be invested and verified in praxis.

As for symbols, these are initially 'phenomena of nature': light, fire, stream, height, and so forth. Or else they result from a simple, elementary, archaic action of men on nature: path, hearth, home (Heidegger's 'dwelling'), and so forth. These symbols have first of all been lived experience, in an immediate vicinity with the real. At this stage, they were not yet symbols. Perhaps in archaic myths these signifiers (fire, path, star, etc.) had only a differential and combinatory role. Magic and religion (which philosophy follows) only overburdened their meaning by singling them out. The symbolism thus seems profound, though it is not profound. Psychologists or sociologists who believe in the inherent profundity of symbolism let themselves be misled by the distancing indispensable to the prestige of symbols, the specific 'distancing' (also an abused term). And yet, symbols only act and endure if they give the impression of 'depth' – poetic, psychic, philosophical – and only if they maintain this impression, or allow it to be maintained.

In this domain, however, appearance and reality are neighbours. For there to be a symbol, this symbol has to be accepted, so it has to have a symbolic power in a recognition that is 'reciprocal between subjects'. The 'depth' of symbols, illusory and real at the same time, comes from what they say and do not say, or suggest, or 'express'. They come to form part of the content despite not having a content. It is in this sense that they are not just words or signs like any other. They say and do not say; they reveal and do not reveal. Words such as 'the fires of love', the line from Racine: 'It is Venus herself fastened to her prey', or 'the standards floating in the breeze'.[7] Everyone knows what such things mean, and yet they do not mean very much. Inasmuch as they denote powers, capacities, the Greek myths form part of a symbolism that is still living today. By developing this analysis, we would manage to understand the double nature of symbolism: depth and combinatory, obscure symbolisms and logico-mathematical ones. We would resolve some questions arising from misunderstandings about this duality or double determination.

The signifiers of philosophy are the fragments of man as he emerges from nature, takes hold of it and appropriates it, yet does not succeed, accomplishes only a portion of himself, or fails. Man, and the human in general, seeks himself by way of philosophy that seeks his truth. They provide him with signifiers (repertoire, memory). The signified is man defined, situated in the world, in relation to nature. It is therefore man made, accomplished.

---

7   EN: Jean Racine, *Phèdre*, act I, scene III, in *Britannicus, Phaedra, Athaliah*, translated by C. H. Sisson, Oxford: Oxford University Press, 1987, p. 89.

Philosophical discourse differs from everyday language in that it is not learned by way of a practical apprenticeship. It forms part of culture: of what comes at the second degree. As discourse on discourse (on the symbols and concepts of everyday language), philosophical reflection is even the model of this second-degree knowledge that is inherent in cultural facts: poetry on poetry already known, painting on the basis of a painting, music on music, and so forth.[8] Is this not what Hegel saw as the twilight side of philosophy?

Philosophical discourse, accordingly, is made up of a large number of signifiers. What relationship is there between signifiers and signified? The specific problematic of each philosophy. Here, semantic analysis could be specified, diversified, qualified. It would indicate the motivations of each philosopher and rediscover circumstances, biography, context. Can philosophers not be classified into different types and species, into accepted classifications? For rationalism, for mysticism, for philosophical idealism in general, signifiers abound. Rationalism prefers to make use of borrowings from praxis, concepts, but not without adding to these some symbols cleverly drawn from the reserve (for example: the sun of intelligibility, the light of reason, clear ideas). Mysticism puts all symbols to work, mingling with them some concepts (identity, for example, boldly extrapolated from logic to contemplative or affective participation). What these signify, on the other hand, is feeble. For rationalism, it is the man of Logos, *homo sapiens*. For mysticism, it is the human before the absolute, or in the absolute. As for empiricism, its signifiers are poor and mediocre; it dispenses with them. Here it is man who is looking, observing, looking for clues. What is signified, on the other hand, is rich: it is empirical life in its diversity recovered in the name of philosophy. The abundance of signifiers gives a deceptive euphoria, which conceals disquiet and is disappointed by the poverty of the signified. Both empiricism and positivism, despite their poverty, have never lost their influence and have always reconstituted themselves (with variants: scepticism, pluralism, complete relativism). Why? In our hypothesis, because they make it possible to rediscover the palpable [*le sensible*] and the real, without, however, fully restoring these in their dignity.

---

8   Edmond Ortigues, *Le discours et le symbole*, Paris: Aubier, 1962, p. 198.

Can the gap between signifiers and signified not be viewed as a rather pathological symptom? There is a schizoid aspect to the philosopher, which grows with the withering of philosophy. The philosopher separates himself from the 'world', that is to say, from praxis. He performs an '*epoche*', suspending the real or bracketing out what it suits him to do. He 'reduces' the 'world' by a speculative reduction very different from semantic reduction.

Let us use the occasion to emphasize the analogy of reductive operations, the sterility of the one, which remains within philosophy (the 'phenomenological reduction' in the speculative line that runs from Descartes to Husserl) and the productiveness of the other. By '*epoche*' and reduction, the philosopher drives to their ultimate limit the troublesome consequences of the division of labour: separations, disassociation, the schizoid state. He hides these consequences from himself, strolling in the midst of a crowd of signifiers, amazed by their abundance, forgetting the signified which he encompasses in reduction. As a result of the technical and social division of labour, the intellectual generally thinks in terms of signifiers; he moves among them, he 'is' among them. Other men, and manual workers in particular, 'are' rather among the signified. The rupture and uncoupling in language – a social fact – is also that of social facts. There is a convergence between the analysis that starts from the commodity and the analysis that starts from language. We shall not press this hypothesis any further here. Let us be content to note that the philosopher drives the situation of the intellectual to its limit.

Marx's so-called philosophical works were designed to prevent the uncoupling and inequality of signifiers and signified. That is the 'sense', or one of the 'senses', intended by the rehabilitation of the *senses* (organs, directions, signification) in the *1844 Manuscripts*. Unfortunately, materialism of Marxist inspiration has simultaneously impoverished both signifiers and signified, ensuring their correspondence by this procedure of impoverishment. The stubborn philosopher has the choice between a philosophy that is poor and ashamed of its poverty, a materialism more or less dialecticized, which signifies above all *homo faber*, and a philosophy rich in signifiers but deprived in terms of signified, the good old idealism.

Modern philosophy struggles in its own way against this impoverishment, desiccation, and anguishing distortion between signifiers and signified. To effect this dis-alienation it turns to poetry, literature, physics, biology, and so forth.

E) What conclusion can we draw for the knowledge of philosophy as such from the distinctions that seem established in linguistics and semiology between symbols, paradigms, syntagms?

As far as syntagmatic connections are concerned, we have indicated that they tend, in philosophical discourse, towards logic pure and simple. The philosopher inflicts severe constraints on himself, as he lays claim to rigour: to demonstration. Logic tends to become the syntax of this discourse, which differs from everyday learned language in the same way as it differs from the discourse of dream or poetic speech. Philosophical discourse only becomes institutional in the same way as everyday language when a philosophy becomes official, as state ideology (a state that could be a church). Moreover: philosophy, vocabulary and syntax, can react on everyday language.

As far as symbolism goes, we have noted its origin, its importance and its nature.

There is a triple dimension in philosophy, starting with its *symbols*:

light and darkness
height and depth
rise and fall
nobility and baseness
good and evil
pure and impure
divine and demoniac
vision and hearing (speech heard and understood)
progressing and straying
vicinity and distance, and so on.

Likewise:

tree

fire
stream
horizon
sky
earth
sea
flower
mirror, and so on.

Then the paradigmatic dimension, the paradigm of *concepts* (arising from praxis):

practice and theory
need and desire
disquiet and serenity
attachment and detachment
work and rest
power and weakness
capacity and incapacity
cause and effect
agreement and struggle, and so on.

And finally that of *categories* (philosophical):

subject and object (subjective and objective)
infinite and finite
relative and absolute
partial and total
true and false
confused and clear
intuitive and discursive
empirical and rational
palpable and intellectual
causality and finality
determinism and contingency
necessity and chance
essence and appearance

reality and phenomenon
identity and contradiction
conflict and harmony
in-itself and for-itself
substance and accident
being and nothingness
actual and possible
space and time, and so on.

The seduction of philosophy arises from the fact that the philosopher can, with a great freedom of choice, draw from this reserve of paradigms whatever he needs for expression or formulation. The wealth of this reserve contrasts with the severity of constraints (syntagmatic, that is to say, logical). The philosophical operation thus contains several phases: drawing from the reserve (that is to say, from this or that class of signifiers), confrontation between the elements selected, elaboration under rigorous constraints (which eliminates certain combinations in the name of the fundamental demand for coherence). Each philosopher conducts these operations in his own manner, as a function of his problematic, which he receives from his predecessors or obtains from his age. This analysis (for philosophy as for praxis, several analyses are possible!) offers us three elements: one coming from the philosophy of the past (problems, concepts), the other from the philosopher's environment, and a third from the exploration of the possible, which he transmits to his successors (concepts, problems, projects).

The seduction of philosophy hides more than one trap. In its time of withering away, it becomes an intellectual game, a relatively easy combinatory, which facilitates the recruitment of philosophers and gives them the illusion of following the path of great creators, those who discovered an enlightening or productive combination, those who poetically employed a symbolism. How is philosophy taught? How does one penetrate into past philosophy, into philosophy in general and into each particular doctrine? By way of paradigms, and also by the syntagmatic connection, taking logical rigour as implicit or explicit reference. The paradigms of philosophy make it possible to conceive the internal architecture of each system: its own combination of symbols, concepts bound together with an optimum degree of rigour, categories that are legitimately or illegitimately postulated. They reveal to us the code with which the historian can subsequently decode (decipher) messages. The structural study of philosophies and of the conceptual architecture of systems is successful. Do its promoters clearly understand that this success seals the withering away of philosophy, by reducing it to the status of a dead language?

F)   What are the connotations of philosophical language?

Here we get into the delicate study of the figures of rhetoric, the use of symbols, of what philosophical discourse has in common with speech or written (literary) style. The straight line of (logical) discourse with its propositions (denotations) is constantly inflected by fine impulses: irony, reserve, embarrassment, reticence, euphoria, emphasis, depreciation, and so forth. Sometimes it is sharply broken off. Broken by what? By the introduction of an image or a symbol. By the arrival on the scene of a great classic figure of rhetoric: metaphor or metonymy, hyperbole or parable, prosopopoeia, redundancy or ellipsis.

Borgès, in 'A History of Eternity',[9] began counting the figures or quasi-figures of philosophical rhetoric. He listed them as necessity, reason, adjournment, relationship, consideration, format, order, slowness, position, declaration, disorder. It is clear that Borgès is mixing categories and figures. To this incomplete and confused list of stereotypes of discourse on truth (which we distinguish from discourse as such, and from true – poetic – speech that makes the truth of discourse), we would like to add:

emphasis and reticence
injunction and prohibition
praise and depreciation
extension and restriction
width and contraction
exaltation and abjection

---

9   Jorge Luis Borgès, 'A History of Eternity', in *Selected Non-Fictions*, London: Penguin, 2000, pp. 123–39.

superfetation and derision
irony and naivety
strength and relaxation
classification and derogation
diversion and avoiding
trust and disarray
eternization and temporization, and so on.

This list could be extended and completed. It already has a fairly precise meaning. Empiricism is a reticent philosophy, prudent and attentive not to exceed the signifiers that it draws from praxis. Scepticism was and remains a philosophy of reticence, reserve. Emphasis unleashes the philosophical mystic and releases him from constraints in order to speak and claim his beautiful soul. It enables him to free himself from constraints (coherence) and detach signifiers from signified. Systems with a strong denotation and poor connotation (empiricism, scepticism, positivism) make little use of rhetorical figures. On the other hand, connotation and figures play a dominant role in metaphysics in general, in idealism, rationalism and mysticism.

To this first list of figures, we can immediately add another:

assertion, negation, denial
use, rejection, misuse
knowledge, ignorance, misconception
approval, refusal, contestation
understanding, conflict, misconception
comprehension, externality, misunderstanding
trust, challenge, defiance.

It is important for our line of argument and our method to emphasize the triple grouping of these categories. Starting from dichotomous oppositions, they lead to the restitution of dialectical movements. Besides, they attain affectivity and ambiguity, whose role is incontestable but escapes dichotomies. The affective connotations, trials and errors of social communication and expression return into the research. The rationalism inherent in the fetishization of the discursive is corrected without being dislocated. It is here and in this way that we grasp again, starting from the reduction to language and discourse (semantic reduction), the 'realities' that this reduction brackets out, but makes it possible to order and situate. We thus have different, partially ordered[10] structures of dichotomies, and rigorous structures of pure discourse and logic (inclusions and exclusions, inherencies and non-inherencies). We may think that the old rhetoric has greater meaning than a repertoire of outdated and outworn literary procedures. Is it not one of those great forms handed down through the ages, which cross historical periods and modes of production, and which we have already met with logic, law? The forms of discourse and speech, the connotations of language, are as equally important as the forms of connection of concepts and those of exchanges and contracts. They differ from these. If this is the case, the forgetting of rhetoric amounts to a destruction of organized discourse; but its rehabilitation risks being accompanied by a fetishism of logos, the corollary (as we know) of self-destruction.

Philosophers certainly use metaphors. They insert them as they can into their syntagmatic connections (as rigorous as possible, each defining in his particular way the order of rigorous reasons, but always with reference to pure logic). From the classes of signifiers that they have available they take this one or that to substitute for another. Among these signifiers, certain are privileged due to their visual (light, idea, clarity, view or vision, perception, etc.) or auditory origin (hearing, understanding, listening, etc.). These are most frequently used in metaphorical substitutions. When the philosopher abuses them, when each page he has written contains too much 'clarity', 'light', 'illumination', 'perspective', 'darkness', he is close to a pathological state. The philosopher also uses metonymy. Sometimes he abuses it. Consider the famous declaration: 'I think, therefore I am.' If we accept it in the declarative mode, we are drawn defenceless into Cartesian thought. That is what generally happens to the student in philosophy. The semanticist, more demanding, will demand the exact signification of each term; in each case he will find several meanings.

We can go still further. We note that this famous formula is caught in a dilemma: either tautology and pleonasm – or else metonymy. Even

---

10 A term borrowed from the mathematical theory of lattices.

the tautology is double. When I say: 'I', the 'I' means 'thought' (Hegel). When I say: 'I think', I utter an initial tautology. When I say: 'I think, therefore I am', if this formula utters a definition of being, and if it defines being by and through thought, then it repeats the same utterance – unless I consider the formula as an extension, a substitution of the part (the 'thinking I') for the whole (being thought and defined by thought), or of the relative (the self that reflects) for the absolute (thought thinking and thought taken universally). In which case, the Cartesian formula constitutes a metonym. If it does not intend to identify 'being' and 'thought', it can only be seen as incoherent.

If the Cartesian formula is conceived as tautology, it is perfectly clear, rigorous, coherent. It is a deduction. But it is empty. The signified is not only analogous to the signifier, but identical with it: I think that I think. On the other hand, if it is conceived as metonymy, it is rich in signification but lacking in rigour. It floats between empty rigour and complete incoherence. What does it signify? The philosopher's claim to define being by thought (excluding will, emotion, action, etc.) and indeed define it by his own thought, by his 'thinking self'. Also the rationalist individuation of the rising bourgeoisie. And the pride and generosity of the honest seventeenth-century man who has won certain new virtues, those of the bourgeoisie in its finest era, without losing the older ones, those of nobility. And again a stoicism, a firmness full of strength and dignity, and so forth.

We observe a conflict between (logical) rigour and productiveness by way of the figures of rhetoric. At the lower limit, thought loses itself in repetition, pleonasm, tautology, redundancy. At the upper limit, it strays into paradox, surprise, leaps from one term to another, unconsidered substitutions: the abuse of metaphors and metonymies.

The importance of these figures must not justify the omission of others. The philosophical connotations are far too complex to be reducible to two figures and their opposition – all the more so in that we do not think that philosophy, caught in the completeness of its utterances and propositions, can be exhausted by the study of paradigms, syntagms, figures. In particular, symbols belong to a class of signifiers, thus to the paradigmatic reserve. They submit willingly or otherwise to the syntagmatic connections, to rigour conceived by the philosopher as the rule of his discourse (syntax, grammar). They can be used rhetorically, that is to say, they do not reject metaphors and metonymies, emphasis and reticence, irony and prosopopoeia. And yet they may disturb the continuity of philosophical discourse, and the transition by denegation from one philosopher and philosophy to others. The leaps of thought, the introduction of images and symbols, bring discontinuity and incoherence into this discourse. Sometimes (not always), do they not deliver its most valuable content? By way of signs, in the relationship of signifier and signified, a wide and imprecise project appears: the project of man. 'I think, therefore I am' *also* signifies the proposition of a consciousness that would fully think its content, that would dominate and appropriate both the external and the internal world.

G) Is the study of philosophy as system of significations confined to these generalities? Can it be summed up as an attempt at a classification of systems?

Certainly not. The semantic and semiological analysis of texts could be pursued in detail, in philosophy as well as in poetry, and still better than with advertising texts or fashion. We are scarcely approaching the specificity of philosophical language. In fact, we have simply established that philosophical systems constitute a 'corpus', to continue to employ here the terminology of the semiologists. Is it possible to conceive the breakdown of philosophical texts into signifying units, configurations of elements? No doubt. This dissection would involve the indexing and comparison of figures, metaphors and metonymies, reservations and reticences, emphases, prosopopoeias, euphemisms, ironies, and so forth. Also symbols, categories, concepts, with introductory texts. How do mirror and reflection, the tree, the seed, the flower, the horizon, the path, the flock, these solitary symbols that do not exactly form part of a paradigm, penetrate into philosophy, along with darkness and light (a Manichaeism latent in many systems)?

Research in this direction could eventually show that the connection of concepts and systems obeys the principle of economy,[11] of least

---

11   On the law of economy, cf. in particular André Martinet, *Élements de linguistique générale*, Paris: Colin, 1960, p. 182ff.

difference. Between 'consciousness', 'self-consciousness', 'for-itself', 'with itself (*bei sich*)', or again between 'being', 'substance', 'absolute', 'in-itself', are the differences not as small as possible? Are completely established paradigms not composed of symbols and concepts that, though different, are as little different as possible? Considering systems according to this synchronic connection, perhaps we would find a philosophy in each place determined by the least difference. Each system would differ as little as possible from the neighbouring doctrines, but sufficiently to be distinguishable. Perhaps we would even discover forgotten doctrines by positioning them in the ensemble of philosophy.

Taking the hypothesis to the point of paradox, we would keep only a single dimension of philosophy: internal coherence. We could then show, in the history of philosophy and the succession of systems (taking into account abandoned and forgotten doctrines), a *chain*, that is to say, a succession of significant units. Random elements intervene between them. We could even amuse ourselves by constructing the matrix of transition that results from the table of probabilities of transition from one state of equilibrium to another among possible states. In this formalization, those elements that have been seen as determinant (biography, historical and social context) would on the contrary be seen as simply the intervention of chance in the transition of the system from one state to another. It would be still more amusing to demonstrate that the System tends towards a final state of equilibrium (which occurs, mathematically speaking, when the 'Markov chain' is regular and the matrix of transition possesses at least one column made up of positive terms). This final state, naturally enough, would be Hegelianism!

We would thus develop the notion of a (philosophical) System to its logical conclusion.

We would particularly develop the idea of the *paradigm* in philosophy, considered as the most coherent discourse. We would show the role of formal rigour as constraint and condition of stability of systems, a role increasingly great through to complete systematization. We would go as far as showing in the philosopher's effort and the philosophical system an 'institutionalization' of the boldest subjective aspirations of an age. We would take account of the double role of circumstances (biographical and historical: *Umwelt*, the environment of the professional thinker). On the one hand, these stimulate aspiration and reflection. They pass into speech, given how speech dominates the discursive message, and to the extent that it does so. But at the same time, the coherent construction of philosophical discourse works against the inextricable interconnection of circumstantial (aleatory) phenomena in nature, society and the individual; it fights for the regularization of thought and the thought work, against the chances of subjectivity and praxis. Philosophy, considered as structure of communication, imposes a type of order: discourse, Logos itself. The philosophical game, or philosophy considered as a game, would thus have had its strategy. Theories and problems handed down from one philosophical generation to the next (from masters to disciples who accept the yoke of the master or free themselves from it) would thus play the role of filters, series, recurrent units, regular assemblages and associations of units forming the network of discourse. We would thus place philosophies and philosophers completely in the general rules of assemblage [*assemblage*] and composition that are those of every message, all discourse, any work considered as message and discourse. We would attain the specific rules of philosophical arrangement [*agencement*], in the formal context of the most general laws of arrangements. We would thus hold the broad lines of a science of philosophical *systems* and philosophy in general, considered no longer diachronically but synchronically.

We shall not go into this detailed analysis. Why? What has already been said here is enough for our purpose. Drawing inspiration from an ironic remark of Hegel against those who sought to deduce everything – even this pencil and its place in the universe – we deem it useless to pursue this level of detail. And then, what is involved is a game; we would play with the great Systems like a puzzle. Finally, this application of structuralism to philosophical systems would risk obscuring our purpose here. We also want to indicate that the triumph of structuralism marks its loss. As a philosophy of structure, revealing the structure of philosophy, it contributes to the superseding of philosophy at the same time as to its own criticism as philosophy and its superseding as one of the last forms of philosophy. By driving it to an extreme, using the concept of structure to the full, we turn

structuralism against itself, showing that it reveals deep contradictions that shatter its form and its formal theory. Philosophy as
discursive imitation of the universe, cosmos or world, finds its limit in
a theory of mimesis. The philosopher was the simulator of totality and
constructed in his system a simulacrum of the whole. He denounces
himself in the formalization that perfects this: in the general theory of
models, analogies and homologies, simulations, this theory of systems
which besides is embodied, if we can say so, in machines, and may be
entrusted to robots!

Beyond a certain limit, the structuralist analysis of philosophical
systems and philosophy falls into error. It defies history and the historical changes in praxis, extrapolating synchrony (the System and the
systematic character) to the detriment of diachrony. The development
of the theory reaches absurdity. It is absurd to systematize the study,
critical or not, of Systems. By escaping its limits and its area of validity,
analysis based on a preliminary reduction becomes unreason.
Philosophical discourse never manages to 'be' pure discourse. It is
never reducible to communicability and communication. Speech here
orients discourse (more or less), speech that seeks to change something and not simply communicate something acquired and
established. Philosophy was act, project. And thus image and poetry.
Thus history and historicity. If it exhausts itself, if it supersedes itself,
this is by redeeming and realizing this project.

Even in this exhaustion of philosophy as such, an irreducible
element is manifest, which to the structuralist understanding appears
as a mere residue but for us is what is most precious. For right down
the line we wager on this residual that the analytical and operational
understanding does not manage to exterminate, and that we name:
poiesis. We may say that philosophy is not completely suspended on a
timeless paradigm. Only a semantic reduction maintained at all costs
ties it to such a determination. Philosophies are not reduced to the
philosophical logos; it is barely probable that translation machines will
ever succeed in bringing them into a metalanguage. Something will
remain, as in poems. Philosophy will be irreducible because philosophical mimesis had an aim, inaccessible to it as philosophical
discourse, but which it opened towards: life, totality, universe (cosmos
or world). It aimed at this without being able to grasp it, and still less

so to realize it. And there intervenes in it more than elsewhere this irreducible element that it would be particularly interesting to study: the perpetual conflict between inertia (of what is expressed and language) and the demands of communication and expression, when there 'really is something to say'. Philosophical discourse, as arranged and structured discourse, makes manifest the limits of the structurally intelligible.

Conversely, the analysis effected by structural understanding on philosophical systems, as on any system, manifests the limits of systematization and discerns that which *already* supersedes this in any philosophical systematization. These remarks suppress nothing of the other criticisms that can be raised against fundamentalist 'semanticism' and structuralism, from various points of view. The significations are worn out and the signifiers remain without significds. Nothing is more empty and more disappointing than a 'world' of significations, of meanings lacking substantiality. Are not money and commodity, analogously to language, signs of signs, supreme signifiers and signified, in an economic and social 'structure' that language, including denotations and connotations, lets us see? Are the functions of language not more complex, more numerous, than communication theory suggests? Along with its function of social communication, it also has a function of expression, externalization, elaboration. By restoring movement into language, this is reintegrated into dialectical becoming, as Marx reintegrated the commodity into the internal conflicts and contradictions of labour. Let us remember once more that the fetishism of language, its destruction and self-destruction, go together.

H) Is it not quite dangerous, however, to privilege the symbolic dimension, to revive the aged concept of expression to equal that of signification? If philosophical discourse is analysed in a triple dimension – paradigms, syntagms, symbols – why suddenly erect the symbolic dimension above the others? Does not this amount to returning to an almost mystical theory of symbolic participation, a theory by which sociologists who believed they were explaining religion themselves converge strangely with religious thought?

If we leave symbolism aside, philosophical reflection is no more than a particular case of mimesis. It loses any connection with creation, with poetry or poiesis and likewise with praxis. It is no longer anything but concealed redundancy: discourse on discourse, repetition of the accomplished in representations issuing from empirical activity. The 'real' and 'true' that it aims at, that it never attains and that never give themselves to it, place it still more clearly in the zone of mimesis.

Image and symbol are 'facts' of nature, charged with a meaning designed to express the relationship between man (in general) and nature and being. We emphasize this double determination of the image and symbol in philosophy. A 'fact' (for example, the tree) in itself and in isolation, devoid of general meaning, is charged, in a context, with significations. Freed from the empirical, from immediate practice, the fact attains the universal. The philosopher expresses himself with images and symbols. Sometimes he says something that transcends him, and glimpses the superseding of philosophy. Is there not in certain pages of the philosophers a 'dream-thought'[12] that links the internal and the external, subjective and objective, and brings dynamism and movement to reflection?

In any case, image and symbol are not without danger. They lend themselves to rhetoric, as we know. They substitute themselves for concepts. They permit the abuse of this narcotic that is not the image but includes images: the signifier decoupled from the signified.

Philosophy has received a part of its stock of images from cosmogonies and mythologies. Several great philosopher-poets have introduced their images and symbols into this repertoire (Plato). Other philosophers have sought to dispense with images and symbols, but it would be curious to discern these in them through a fine-grained study (cf. Leibniz and the concept-image of 'harmony'). Finally, there have been great inventors of images, such as Augustine who was also a great rhetorician. This study restores to history (diachrony) its primacy over synchrony.

The inventory of Augustinian images and symbols is particularly interesting, as we rediscover here the long line that goes from Jansen

---

12 Cf. Gaston Bachelard, Introduction in *Poetics of Space*, translated by Maria Jolas, Boston: Beacon, 1994.

and Pascal to Freud, even to Heidegger. In the works of Augustine, the reader notes a profusion of *cosmological images*, charged with signifying the human condition: storm, wind, tempest, swirling currents, the abyss. The cross is the ship that makes it possible to cross the tumultuous ocean of life. The abyss (*mundus*) is rather terrestrial, with its opening and issue towards the divine. Certain images are borrowed from the desert: losing one's way, the void. Others are *physiological images*. Sin is a disease, an ulcer, an itch. Who is the doctor? Christ. What is the remedy? Grace. But the great image taken up by Augustine and launched into 'existential' thought by him is the image of the Voyage (*peregrinatio*). The soul takes the path of salvation or of perdition. It has lost, in the course of its wandering, the House of the Father, the Dwelling, the Home, the Native Land. It seeks the route to the heavenly City and eternal rest, which would also be a return to the lost homeland.[13]

The questions and answers above are clearly far from exhausting the study and debate undertaken. Let us try however to give an overall picture. We shall recapitulate the argument and sketch a history.

We take it as long since accepted that philosophy as such involves a double project, that of a *discourse* (total and complete), and that of a *representation* that designates the possible *plenitude* and even brings the *satisfaction* of real achievement. For all that, this notion of philosophy does not escape the 'desert of essence'. It does not yet become a whole philosophy, its essence along with its manifestations. The general project is perfected in the course of the philosophical history. It is made explicit. At the same time, it has revealed its truth: reflection on the discourse of naïve and common opinion, discourse on discourse. This character has steadily advanced to the foreground, displacing and supplanting the wider project that concerned man. To the extent that all discourse has a structure, it is likely that all philosophy increasingly consists of a highly structured discourse. We have been able to discover the general structure of philosophy and that of all particular philosophies. Within the project of a necessary and sufficient discourse, each

---

13   On the House and the Home, cf. St Augustine, *Confessions*, 12, 11, 1. On Wandering, 10, 11, 37 and 10, 5, 7, and so on. On the Homeland, 7, 10, 11 and 16, and so on. [EN: Lefebvre's references are to book, chapter and section, though the latter differ in the various editions.]

philosophy contributes its particular propositions. It proposes its figure of the human being, which forms part of a prospective inventory of the human situation or situations. Circumstances (biographical and historical), the immediate and more remote environment of the philosopher, his *Umwelt*, play a role (not negligible but still poorly defined) in the formulation of what he proposes.

Subsequently, however, the accidental and secondary aspects of philosophical reflection fall away. They appear as fantasies and ideologies bound up with individual situations, group attitudes or historical contingencies. They are the failed elements. General history, and the history of philosophy (inasmuch as it is possible to speak of a history of philosophy), effect a sorting. Those philosophies that are no more than ideology (in the service of temporary interests of this or that social group) disappear sooner or later. They are superstructures in the precise sense of the term, amplifying and dressing up these conjunctural moments of history into generalities. Other philosophies, the more 'profound', appear in retrospect insufficient as systems, allowing a part of the 'real' to escape. Their contributions, however, are integrated into the growth of culture, civilization, knowledge, praxis itself. The interest of these contributions forces reflection to return retrospectively over the entire work of the philosopher to reconstitute and locate it. This work then appears in full with its character of a systematized discourse, with an architecture, a structure, that gives rise to the history of philosophy (and the appearance of an autonomous history of philosophical thought).

In order to recognize the integrated elements – the 'moments' in this particular sense – we have to take up the periods mentioned and pursue the analysis under a different light. Socrates and Plato discovered that man (with the implication: man in his natural and social, thus historical, environment) does not simply make use of material instruments, tools, which in antiquity, moreover, he left to slaves; he makes use of concepts, ideas, signs; he uses logos. The correct use of discourse demands the subordination of occasional discourses – opinions expressed in diverse and contradictory discourses – to exact judgements, to concepts, that is to say, to coherent and rational discourse. The philosopher knows the laws of coherent discourse and masters them in truth.

The age of Socrates and Plato was also that when discourse recognized as mediator in social praxis was taken as a means in political praxis. If discourse is the site of truth, it cannot be the instrument of power. Recognition of discourse discovers this internal contradiction. Socrates died from it. Plato sought in vain to resolve it in the quest for a political truth and a politics of truth (the *Laws* and the *Republic*). Was this contradiction not also that of democracy in the Greek cities, that of Greek culture? Logos there became sovereign. Knowledge became specialized into the formal knowledges of logos (grammar, rhetoric, sophistic). At the moment that it was proclaimed as supreme form and end in itself, logos precisely fell to the rank of means and instrument of power, that of a commodity sold by rhetoricians, sophists, grammarians (the 'structuralists' of the age in question). The structure of Socratic-Platonic philosophy was determined in the face of the analytic understanding, because this understanding was already at work in this philosophy.

We recognize in this:

a) A great poetic image: the maieutic. Man is born from physis, with the risks of any birth. The birth of man, if it is to be successful, requires on the part of the philosopher a double investigative regard: towards the origin and the mythic past, towards the possible and impossible. As a project of man, the maieutic is unable to define man. It asks what he will be. It grasps him in the risk of childbirth.

b) [The theory of a technical practice: the rational use of discourse, the correct employment of everyday concepts, the effort to extract the true concept (idea) from the variety of opinions (*doxa*). The philosophical critique of *doxa* extends to the whole of the non-philosophical.

c) [A metaphysical systematization, constructed around a supra-sensible extrapolation, the discursive and conceptual abstraction elevated to absolute Idea. This Idea, as we know, is the principle of participation (*metexis*) or participant imitation (mimesis). But we do not know whether participant imitation is effected by the gaze, as the visual metaphor suggests: 'idea' = that which is seen. Perhaps for Plato it was music, the highest philosophy since it is both number and drama (*Phaedo*, 610), that made possible the best understanding of mimesis. On the other hand, with Plato, the Idea is the Sun of Intelligibility, through a hyperbolic use of a symbol.

What would philosophy retain from this? Culture and philosophy retained almost the totality of Greek culture and Socratic-Platonic thought. But they arranged its elements differently. Wherever there was the state, discourse remained an instrument of action, persuasion, intimidation. It would be cultivated as such. Grammar, rhetoric, eristic, sophistic, dialectic (understood as art of discussion and technique of advocacy) would form part of the initiation into a culture crowned by philosophy. The image of the maieutic, no longer a great poetic word, became a metaphor signifying education, pedagogy, the relationship between master and disciples. The use of the concept as such was generalized in the sciences, technology and praxis (without suppressing the diversity of opinions within this praxis, to the extent that there were differences: between both groups and individuals). As for the theory of the Ideas, it would remain a hypothesis of predilection for metaphysicians eager for eternity and depreciating of the palpable. From Plato to Hegel, the theory of the Idea would be the formal expression, effect and reason, of philosophical alienation.

One feature of the philosophical system was clarified by Aristotle. Although he reduced the scope of Platonic mimesis (closely linked, we believe, with metexis), for Aristotle the system clearly is mimesis: reproduction or imitative representation of the cosmos. Representation is defined as mimesis using a privileged tool: discourse. Art and technique, each in its way, imitate nature. The philosophy imitates the totality. He attains it because he, the philosopher (and not the demiurge or world mind, as with Plato), finds himself at the summit of the scale of intellects in the sensible: the highest of sublunary beings, the lowest of higher beings. The *cosmos* (which we shall distinguish from the *world*, which in its finitude opens onto the unlimited) is posited as finished, ordered in space, hierarchized. The philosophical system imitates the autonomous and automatic order, establishing itself according to its own laws and maintained within the bounds of the cosmos. It says what being *was* (emphasizing the past tense, which accentuates the accomplished fact of a cosmos in itself superior to the temporality of what arises and perishes in generation and dissolution). It is the pure (acting) intellect that is *poietikos*, the intelligible model creator of all intelligence and all being. This leads to a considerable difficulty, as noted by Léon Robin in his book on Aristotle.[14] This acting intellect must be at the same time immanent to logos (to discourse) and transcendent, because absolute Being. In 'modern' language, the acting intellect is both pure redundancy and pure information.

At the same time, Aristotle reveals in their pure (intemporal) form the laws of coherent discourse: logic, stable form of stability, matrix of discourse, technique and knowledge. Discourse and the discursive are finally posited on their own ground, elaborated as autonomous enti-ties. The form of discourse, logic, is bound up with dichotomous classification making effective use of the concept: genera, species, common characteristics and specific differences. This methodology is applied in the sciences as well as in practice. Biological in origin, it was generalized because bound up with logos. Science defines itself as 'science of the general'. For centuries to come, it would no longer be science of the particular or the (singular) individual, still less knowl-edge of freedom or freedom by knowledge. Logos dismissed myth and poetry (which would later take their revenge, however). Aristotle defined man with his place in the cosmos as a function of the most coherent discourse. Man, as political animal, lives in the city; there he finds his place, function, accomplishment and satisfaction. He is the object of political discourse, which establishes the constitution of the city. The subject is the man of state.

The structure of Aristotelianism thus comprises:

a) an image whose poetic (creative) character fades before the passive and cautious recognition of the finished and accom-plished: the cosmos. This image, however, is not lacking in scope. It evokes in its majesty an admirable order, cause and end of the cosmos. Critique and project become blurred, while poetry disap-pears. Everything is accepted, explained, and justified in its place;

---

14   Léon Robin, *Le système d'Aristote*, Paris: Vrin, 1960, pp. 204–5.

b) [a theory and a technique of the fully elaborated discursive form. The rigorous discursive form permits the mimesis (re-production and re-presentation) of all that is, in heaven and earth, in the cosmos, the city and the intellect. Logic, rhetoric, poetic, expound the order of perfect discourse;

c) [a metaphysics of substance (of being, represented as substantiality), unformed matter in some kind of intermediate place between the unformed (pure potential) and the inaccessible perfect form (pure act). The stars, pure lights, celestial fires, higher realms, become by metonymy intellects and intelligible, mediating forms. These elements of Aristotelianism would pass into culture and philosophy, where they would dominate for centuries. Much later, in the medieval town (new and original work in relation to the polis), logic would provide the form for the accumulation of knowledges and techniques in the West. It would connect with the form elaborated in the Roman *urbs*: law, the form of accumulation of capital.

Subsequently the split set in. Detached, the philosopher contemplated 'something' from afar, the cosmos broken up by the time of history (that of the city and society of antiquity), the temporal world still having an eminent form and order imposed by an internal and timeless but open law. Open to what? To disaster, catastrophe, dramatic end. A critique, based on the split between philosophy and real men, denounced the madness of men.

The philosopher seeks. He seeks wisdom. He thinks of the sovereign good. The good and wisdom are his own good, his own wisdom, which he offers without great hope to the mad, the alienated – an uncertain satisfaction and an incomplete plenitude that he attempts in the crisis of the unaccomplished City. Poetic speech regains importance and the philosopher sometimes turns poet, but in the fear and trembling of a truth little assured of itself. In its broken mirror, philosophy presents an image of what there is outside of it. For himself, as far as he is concerned, the philosopher only takes responsibility for his autonomous reason (stoicism) or his pleasure (epicureanism).

Each time that the philosopher and even the individual is constituted as such, in opposition (more or less illusory or real) to the surrounding praxis, he rediscovers this split and the options to which it gives rise: individual search for satisfaction in the personal autarchy of consciousness, or else in pleasure.

Augustine introduced into philosophy, or rather reintroduced (at the moment of the end of the city-states and the destruction of antique society), the time forgotten by the philosophers. For him, the spatial cosmos passed into the background, and the *world* came to the fore (with the implication of systematic depreciation of the *worldly*). The world is not set out in space. It is an abyss of darkness in time and a labyrinthine trajectory towards the sun. Augustine coined the Christian slogan: '*mundus est immundus*.' The *mundus*, as we know from Heidegger, who recalled its meaning, is the mouth of shadow, the hole, the abyss that is mortal yet open to the light. This play on words, '*mundus est immundus*,' deserves others. The Augustinian world is a fallen world, corrupted by original sin – yet in such a way that it opens towards God.

Riven by sin, cast into the shadows, the world has a double history: profane and sacred. The profane world will disappear with the irruption of the sacred. The time that constitutes the world and the worldly turns them towards divine transcendence. The theory of substance and the metaphysical idea weakens in the face of two discoveries. The first is that man is desire, infinite desire, desire for the infinite, but broken, with the result that his essence (his corrupted nature) consists in a triple desire, which imitates infinite desire without attaining it. *Haec sunt capita iniquitatis, quae pullulant principandi et spectandi et sentiendi libidine.*[15] Evil is a malady of desire. The symbols of disease and sullying are used here metaphorically, without scruple or reserve. The triple *libido* seeks in vain, in the worldly creature, the analogous of the divine infinite. This desire, like its failures, traverses temporality. More: it makes it. It is by way of the temporal deployment of the fundamental desire that transcendent God is at the same time immanent to the world. Disturbed and unassuaged desire can find peace and rest only in God. The problem of the reason and recognition of Logos is replaced by the problem of individual *remembrance*, obscure memory of the original (before the fall), gathering of scattered memories in unity.

---

15   St Augustine, *Confessions*, Book 3 [chapter 15].

> See how I have explored my memory in search of you, oh my God, and I have not found you outside of it ... It is here that I find you when I remember you and that I am happy in you.[16]

It is necessary to transcend that which comes from the senses and the natural light oriented to the outside, towards space, towards pleasure. *I shall transcend (transibo) this faculty of my nature.* The central theme of the *Confessions* is that memory imitates God, seeks him and has a presentiment of him. It is reprise and *tension* dominating the *distentio*, which constitutes time and the world and desire as broken totality. Each moment in the life of consciousness imitates and reproduces in its way the original failing, reproducing the distentio, this *alienation* that separates the earthly and worldly individual from the transcendent unity that, however, he bears within him. The distance of self to self, of memory to sense and thought, is also the distance of the self from the divine – a distance that is filled only by grace, which changes corrupted nature in its very depths and reestablishes desire. Salvation is therefore also return to the health and innocence of desire. Only the call of God, beyond memory, heralds salvation. Without God, desire cannot become desire for God.

Augustinianism contains:

a) an image, that of the (fallen) world. An image that Augustine intends as poetic, evocative of worldly dereliction, recreator of the lost unity and the path across the broken world towards regained unity and salvation. The Greek image of the world and its maieutic are replaced by the Christian image of purification and redemption by divine sacrifice. Rhetoric uses and abuses metaphors here. Metonymy is employed to present the end, death, rest as blessedness. This is not done without parables and hyperboles. Man as man is sick. Nature is not the generator of man, his mother and matrix, but the time and place of his 'worldly' perdition. The critique of the 'world' that systematically depreciates life, becomes adhesion to the hope of another world, beyond death. The 'world' and the 'worldly' are constituted as such by the act that transcends

---

16   EN: St Augustine, *Confessions*, Book 10, chapter 24.

them. It is in God that Augustine conceives the world and the worldly. The relationship with the world is accomplished in three stages: the radical negation and depreciation that discovers it as 'world'; the constitution of a higher existence in the wake of this discovery of the falsity, error and faults of the 'worldly'; then, in the extreme tension of the soul, the intervention of divine grace.

b) [a *theory on the structure of the human being*, as fallen and broken totality. Hence several disjointed structures. First of all, a *palpable* structure, naïvely and profoundly expressed: the five senses with their temptations, the entertainments that distance the soul from itself. Secondly, an *affective* structure: the fundamental desire and its breakage, the triple *libido*. Thirdly, an *intellectual* structure: memory reassembling the memories, and then, in a higher and already transcendent order, the supra-sensible unity that is intimated by way of the knowledge of pure ideas, such as those of number. Here Augustine catches on the wing St John's theory of the Logos (Word) embodied in Christ, whose metaphorical character is clear enough.

c) [a *rhetoric*. Augustine, a religious rhetorician, uses persuasive discourse and all the known figures with extreme cleverness. He offers an apologia for religion, making use of philosophy to depreciate the 'world' of which it forms an image. In the *Confessions*, he does not subject discourse to the demands of a thought founded on time (dialectical) that leads the existing to its disappearance. He uses it for the unconditional praise of an abstract thing: the Church. He is an advocate familiar with all the resources of dialectic, sophistic, eristic.

The importance of St Augustine in philosophy cannot be overstated. Against the image of existence in space (the cosmos) he sets up the image of temporality (the world). He posits the predominance of temporality (of becoming, of growth or decline, of rise or fall) over spatiality. Nothingness and the 'annihilation' (of the accomplished, the past, faults committed) enter into philosophy. With Augustine, the successive duplications of the 'self' lead him to view as a stranger both what he has been and what he is. The conscious being is defined by dereliction, error, the abandoning of *ek-sistence* (in Heidegger's sense).

In its rise, the soul becomes *ek-static*. It tends towards the veiled being that offers itself and flees, that calls and escapes. There is another world: that of truth and being, whose call demands detachment from 'worldly' life. Augustine founds, within the Christian interpretation of existence, a lineage opposed to the comfortable Aristotelian and Thomist lineage. This ties together the social, ecclesiastical and political hierarchy with the representation of a spatial hierarchy in the cosmos. The Augustinian line would thus lie at the origin of the majority of heresies, all the more so as it tends to depreciate institutions along with the 'worldly', and to designate in time the strength and anger of God dissolving what was established. The apologia of religion and the corresponding institution, the Church, returns against the author's intentions.

By introducing desire as an active foundation of consciousness, Augustine founds the line along which it is easy to situate Jansen and Pascal, then Schelling, and subsequently Schopenhauer, Freud and even Heidegger. It has been said of Hegel that he was Aristotle revised by Spinoza. It would be equally correct to say that Hegel attempted a synthesis between the cosmos and the world, between Aristotle's spatialized hierarchy and Augustinian temporality. Can Augustinianism not be seen as an alienated theory (philosophy) of alienation? But functional analogies or homologies in no way authorize us to combine the philosophies envisaged as successors to Augustinianism in a theoretical unity. The Freudian libido is no longer the libido of Jansen and Augustine, despite the identical name, despite functional analogies and even homologies in this or that philosophy.

Obsessed with what lay behind the world, linking philosophy to religion, a great rhetorician making use of philosophy to slander 'worldly' life and establish the transcendence of religion after having founded religion on philosophy, in the very long run Augustine made the perishing of philosophy inevitable. Yet the superseding of philosophy is something completely foreign to Augustinianism. For him, philosophy has the same content as religion, on a lower level. This makes it impossible to view Augustine as the initiator of a mental *structure* (thought founded on time, tragic dialectic, theory of the 'world' to be replaced by an ideal city, the city of God or the human city metamorphosed) that would extend very far and encompass Marx and

Marxism. Such an argument would reject the superseding and realization of philosophy by Marx, a superseding and realization that have nothing in common with the apologetic function that Augustinianism attributes to philosophizing thought.

More broadly than philosophies, 'worldviews' encompass these. The critique of philosophy leads a fortiori to rejecting the 'worldview' or *conception*. For example, the fact of extending maieutic to several philosophies, conceiving philosophies up to a certain point as maieutics and philosophy as a whole as a maieutic either avowed or disguised, does not rehabilitate the 'worldview'. Maieutic is not a conception of the world, but a project (uncertain, troubled, adventurous) of the human being, himself considered as launched in an (uncertain) adventure.

By pressing the reconsideration of philosophical history further in the same direction, we would be led to emphasize 'currents of thought', whether underground or visible by way of testimonies. These currents are not always represented and conceptually elaborated by leading thinkers. They are stimulated by images or image-concepts, vague and powerful. They have a long persistence, which shows that we are not dealing here with ideologies pure and simple, with 'superstructures' built on a well-defined 'base', but at least with syncretisms. These are remarkable cases, sometimes aberrant, and thus particularly interesting for the history of ideas (which we are not seeking to 'normalize', to centre around well-determined general structures, but on the contrary to divert from these well-traced paths).

The Paraclesian heresy, for example, has run down the centuries. According to this heresy, the incarnation of Christ did not save the world. The operation attempted by the eternal Father did not properly succeed. The world is worse than before, the corruption and tyranny of the Church being added to the secular powers that reign. The Word (Logos) is not enough for the salvation of the universe. The world, still in thrall to evil despite the sacrifice of Jesus, must be saved as a whole, and salvation of the individual soul is only a swindle. To lead the whole world into the age of salvation, justice and peace, a new incarnation is needed, that of the Spirit, the third person of the Trinity. The incarnation of the Spirit is prepared in the subversive actions that this Spirit inspires.

The Paraclesian heresy, bitterly combatted by the Church, runs through and animates mediaeval thought (directly or by reaction). It is particularly present in the work of a theologian who is relegated to the shadows by the official history of ideas, both ecclesiastical and secular, and who sought a synthesis of the philosophies of East and West: Joachim di Fiore. The nominalism of Abelard, who doubted concepts, words, discourse, thus the Word, and paid dearly for this challenge to official dogmatism, derived from it. Likewise did Franciscan poetry. Paracelsianism, preaching contempt for the official Church, the feudal 'world' and the hierarchies of its masters, justified the great peasant revolts. It probably influenced Catharism, a doctrine of the redeeming Spirit.

More subterranean still, the complete history of philosophy would discern the concrete modalities of perception of time and space, that is to say, of the social and natural environment (*Umwelt*). It would thus effect a conjunction and link between 'the lived' and 'representation', between praxis and theory. The history of representations would connect, at this level, with the history of the city and the town, in which representations of time and space are projected on the ground and transformed there. The history of ideas and concrete sociology would meet up.

Descartes? Here we discern first of all the fertile image. Man makes himself by knowledge, by reason, by their applications (techniques). The man Descartes, and men in general, are educated not by authoritarian education but by reading the great book open before them. Knowledge is a tree, with its trunk, its boughs and its branches. When the tree has reached its full growth, when it bears its fruits, the man who has cared for it and pruned it will attain plenitude. He will be master of the world. He will appropriate it for himself.

Formally, Descartes introduced into the methodical conduct of discourse the still recent techniques of mathematics. Aristotle was familiar with the Euclidean method (axioms, postulates, definitions, deductions), which he identified, not entirely justifiably, with a logic based on biological classification by genera and species (dichotomies). Descartes introduced algebra and the progressive construction of the complex on the basis of simple elements.

For Descartes, metaphysis deliberately starts from a hyperbole. There is the methodical doubt, inherent in the rational critique of what is finished in knowledge and the real. Then the hyperbolic doubt that shakes even the most certain experiences, even praxis. In the course of this doubt, the Evil Demon intervenes, a quite reasonable demon, not too diabolical, who arrives in his proper place and lets himself be tamed by Reason and the God of metaphysics. This Cartesian Mephisto, who appeared to him on the famous 'night of the stove', dissolves the unity of body and mind. He casts doubt on the external world, the body, perceptions, sensations, and so reduces thought to the pure act of thinking. By way of doubt and the disassociation of the physical (natural) mixture of matter and thought, metaphysics is inaugurated. It conceives on the one hand pure consciousness, the soul, the *cogito* or thinking substance (*res cogitans*), and on the other hand matter, body, extent and its automatic movements (*res extensa*).

We truly establish ourselves in metaphysics, *physics* being broken by hyperbole, absolute doubt, and the evil genius. The *homo* of the project is duplicated. Nothing can then prevent the abuse of metaphors and metonymies. By way of metaphor, the object is changed into space and the animal into a machine; in the wake of this abuse, there is no longer a place for the living. By way of metonymy, the absolute is defined by the thought that thinks it. It is 'duplex', after which matter and spirit, body and soul, the extended thing and the thinking thing, will pursue the broken unity. Fortunately, this rupture is not an act. Part fiction, part reality, and rather more of the former than the latter (the two fictions of hyperbolic doubt and the evil demon), it leaves the real man, the man Descartes, man in general, almost intact. And yet it corresponds in him to an accomplished rift. On the one hand, he is not materiality and yet is so to a certain point, and on the other hand, he is spirituality. Hyperbole and metaphor are not entirely without content and foundation. It is precisely here that philosophical alienation is located, which, moreover, reacts on the systematized ensemble. The split between flesh and spirit, inherent to Christianity, somewhat attenuated in the Aristotelian–Thomist distinction between matter and form, is aggravated: metaphysics seals it. It proliferates under the auspices of the divine demon, the evil demon. In later metaphysics, object and subject are hard pressed to meet, and still more to recognize one another. Metaphysics, proceeding in the direction of the pure subject (philosophy of consciousness) or pure being (absolute identity), exacerbates the opposition that it seeks at the same time to resolve.

Spinoza? An image of felicity, the Sage understanding everything, explaining everything, accepting everything, in the vision of the Whole (third degree of knowledge). Plus an extremely far-reaching formalization and systematization of philosophical discourse. Plus an absolute, quasi-tautological position, of divine Identity as cause of itself and immanent reason for the differences (modes and attributes) that it generates. Spinoza asserts the infinite infinity of Substance, after which, instead of discovering an infinity of infinite modes and attributes, he perceives only two: extension and thought. The identity of the divine substance (*causa sui*) is revealed in the common belonging of extension and thought that absolute knowledge contemplates. A fascinating vision, since the Same (identity, substantiality, repetition, pure 'consciousness') and the *Other* (difference, attribute) constantly pass from one into the other. We never know if we establish ourselves in perfect tautology or if we attain the genesis of the 'real' in totality. The mirror of philosophy offers thought its double, which itself duplicates itself, seeking desperately to attain unity, totality, identity. Pleonasm and metonymy seek to meet up. In the identity A = A, or rather, A is A, the second A both repeats and does not repeat the first. It is the same and it is not the same, since it is the second. The second differs as little as possible from the first, but it does differ. It we emphasize the Same in the Other, we grasp mentally only the general form of rigorous logic, clear and empty. If we emphasize the Other in the Same, we have the impression (illusion) of intelligibly creating difference and differences starting from Identity. Thus of mentally reproducing beings, and thought as thought of being and beings, from the starting point of Being.

Spinoza thus correctly elaborated the schema of metaphysics already implicit in Cartesianism. It is a formal schema, which tends to give itself a content and believes it does so by its own forces. It effects the formalization of thought and results from it. It passes from the form as perfected and decanted as possible – the form of coherent and rigorous discourse – to absolute assertions on the Absolute, by way of an extrapolation as little different as possible from pure formal rigour. Speculative alienation takes the form of a precise illusion, the illusion of creating with God, recreating the universe. The formal thought of the understanding believes that it passes from identity (tautological: repetition) to difference, by taking a difference as small as possible. It believes in this way that it can leap from deduction to creation, to production, to genesis. Or rather from pleonasm to metonymy.

Leibniz? To understand him, imagine that he seeks to unite the Cosmos and the World, space and time; that he turns at the same time both towards Plato and his conception of participant imitation, and to Aristotle and the philosophy of logos. His image is first of all poetic and musical, borrowed from the development of the theory of numbers, mathematics and physics, as well as from the music of his time: harmony and counterpoint. Descartes in his youth wrote a treatise on music, which already foreshadows the elements of his doctrine. [Marin] Mersenne developed the Cartesian theory of the unity of number and physical phenomenon, in a work on the 'universal harmony' containing several laws of vibrating chords. [Joseph] Sauveur would discover harmonics (1701) and [Jean-Philippe] Rameau give this discovery its theoretical extensions. Finally, Bach sought to unite the plenitude of the already well-established art of the fugue with the nascent theory and practice of harmony; by the late seventeenth century this unity was already heralded by the great French musicians, including Couperin.[17] We shall therefore try to understand Leibniz musically, and not according to the compromising metaphor of the watch or clock that would enable the divine clockmaker to harmonize the monads. Leibniz uses harmony metonymically, although without (apparent) rhetoric. Yet the apologia for God (*Theodicy*) is not devoid of emphasis. In his most general theory, which encompasses the partial points of view and perspectives, monads are 'vertically' harmonized by God. 'Horizontally', an immense counterpoint links their perceptions and thoughts in a giant fugue. The monads hymn the praises of God, who leads an eternal choir. The philosopher perceives the harmony along with God, in God. He contemplates it and attains it by contemplation.

The monad, moreover, is for Leibniz appetite and effort (*appetitus* and *conatus*). There is nothing inert about the monad, its 'matter' being

---

17   EN: Several generations of the family were musicians; it is likely Lefebvre means Louis Couperin or his nephew, François Couperin.

not an extended and thought substance, but the limitation of all finite reality. This 'real' given as will is integral to the analysis. The same holds for the content. Leibniz passes easily, by metonymy, from thought in act to the thought-object, and from this to will. Thus he brings new and decisive elements to the formalization. He attains a 'real' both continuous and discontinuous, by the double path of the continuous (differential and integral calculus) and the discontinuous. He reveals an aspect of the discursive understanding, combinatory and operatory, that was previously implicit. By an intuition of genius, Leibniz saw already in his adolescence that 'by the combination of the letters of the alphabet and the analysis of the words formed on the basis of these letters, it was possible to discover everything'.[18] The *ars combinatoria*, according to him, did not produce abstractions. On the basis of simple and discontinuous elements (distinct, discrete), he thus constructs the real. God calculates. Starting from *zero* and *one* (the same and the other), he generates the discrete number and the infinitesimal continuous (the series that mathematically guarantees the connection between discrete numbers and continuous functions, between measurement and combinatory order).

Leibniz's intellectualism claimed to make the discontinuous and the continuous converge in a perfect mimesis of the divine productive act. With him, the understanding seizes the real, decomposes it into primordial elements (atoms: zero, one), then recomposes it. He introduces intelligence into the real by a decisive victory over its resistance and opacity. Intellect is not added to the object from outside. By operatory and combinatory procedures, it makes a 'real' as real as the given or more so. Composition and arrangement are creation. And vice versa. Leibniz believes that he overcomes any dualism: that of extension and soul, that of object and subject, those of quantity and quality, finite and infinite, mechanism and finalism.[19]

The monad contains its own principle of movement. It moves of itself. It is therefore *automatic*. Laws are internal to it; the counterpoint of monads lets every theme and voice develop 'freely'. Yet the spiritual or immaterial Automaton is not transcendent in relation to the

---

18   Cf. Yvon Belaval, *Leibniz critique de Descartes*, Paris: Gallimard, 1960, p. 51.
19   Ibid., pp. 493 ff.

material or constructed automaton. God ensures their unity, not only that of the finite and the infinite, but that of the continuous and the discontinuous, creation and calculation, spontaneity and practical manufacture, by dismembering and arranging (by operations: arrangements and combinations). *Dum Deus calculate, fit mundus.* God handles substances, Minds or otherwise, like an engineer with his machines – though this is not without presenting certain difficulties.

Leibniz thus stands at the start of a broad current of thought that has a culmination and conclusion in our own day. This current of knowledge and speculation sometimes disavows its Leibnizian origins; it erases the traces of its progress; it frees itself from metaphysics in a quest to be technical and only technical, scientific and only scientific. For us, however, it is still philosophy and cannot deny its philosophical origins: in Leibniz.

Leibniz's metaphysics is supplementary to his formal theory. Transposition and extrapolation are still and always effected in the name of Substantiality, that is to say, by metonymy and hyperbole. In the Identity of Same and Other – identity and difference – pure Identity receives the privilege of ontological status. God, Being, is the Identity of zero and one, of unity and multiplicity, recurrence and event. It is the eternal and immutable truth. This Being posits itself, presents itself, presupposes itself, requires itself, such as it is, despite its infinitude, in the fact of reflecting thought. In the infinite of fixed monads, it does not emerge from itself. *Deus cogitate mundum.* The Spinozist schema of identity and difference (Same and Other) is reprised with new determinations, closer to the 'real' – or a certain real.

We shall not undertake here to rewrite the critical history of philosophy. It is enough for us to indicate certain lineaments of this. We are sketching a programme. We shall not continue it as far as Hegel, whose structural elements we know only too well: the Rose of the World, the apotheosis of logos, the great rhetorical figure of the Idea.

Our sketch has led us to use the notions of structure, a usage that in no way rules out tracing its limits, but on the contrary prescribes this. By giving free rein to a concept, the limits are indicated beyond which its validity changes into error, and its importance into ideology. The philosophy of structure has revealed to us the structure of philosophy; but the critique of philosophy, justified by this analysis, permits a radical critique of this philosophy of structure. As work of discourse, mimesis, and analytic understanding, philosophy must have a hidden structure. The concept of philosophy, spelled out and delimited in this way, has enabled us to define that of structure. And conversely. The superseding of the one leads to the superseding of the other. In the philosophies already mentioned, increasingly systematic as they are, we discern three components: a poietic image, a formal theory, and metaphors, metonymies or hyperboles that are specifically metaphysical. The image has almost always been neglected by historians who were concerned (and rightly so, since philosophers retrace the trajectory of philosophy) with discourse as such. And yet the poietic image contains the human project: maieutic in the line of Socrates, the sick man and his healing in the line of Augustine. The image borrowed from the given changes into symbol of the virtual. At the same time retrospective and prospective, it projects the future and projects itself onto it, with greater or lesser amplitude. In our view, there is a functional analogy (homology) between the poetic images in philosophical systems, even if these images and symbols differ to the point of opposition.

The formal part is methodological and gnoseological. It contains both a contribution to knowledge as such and a theory of knowledge as the most coherent discourse. The metaphysical element proceeds from a superfetation (metaphor, metonymy, parable, hyperbole, etc.). It swells to the point of hypostatizing as absolute truth this or that discovery of knowledge or methods. The customary history of philosophy, considered in isolation, amplifies this already inflated aspect. It sees this as the essential. It adds to the superfetation a new superfetation. Indeed, the metaphysics contained in philosophies was the most decrepit part: the ideology superimposed on concepts and projects. The image of man was its most stimulating and active element, but also the most obscure and obscured. As for the formal element, it is naturally integrated without too much difficulty in the cumulative growth of knowledge, in the technical perfecting of method.

CHAPTER 8

Metamorphosis of Philosophy: Poiesis and Metaphilosophy

Acquaintance with philosophy leads to circumscribing its concept. It tends to exhaust philosophy as such, and consequently to supersede it. It indicates, before and beyond this concept, that of philosophical discourse, something else: poiesis in its inexplicit connection with praxis. Mimesis appears here with a growing precision in its essential and limited function: connection and mediation between praxis and poiesis, between repetition and creation, between abstract identity and concrete differences, between discourse and speech. If mediation seeks to be totality, if it claims to dominate the terms that it links, this claim has only a certain time.

The fundamental contradiction (which has moved to the fore and become fundamental for us) is between philosophy and the non-philosophical world. In itself, this is only one of the contradictions of praxis. In terms of what we are concerned with here, this contradiction is principal, essential. Praxis, according to Marx, will resolve it, by actualizing philosophy in the non-philosophical world and not by renouncing philosophy and letting the non-philosophical world follow its course. We add here that this contradiction will be resolved by liberating the higher part of human activity from its lower part. Philosophy figured both in the higher part and in the wretched part. It thereby made a powerful contribution to the definition of man. Superseding it defines him still better.

To sum up, is not what remains of philosophy, in the direction of its superseding, in fact an *anthropology*? Every philosopher has discovered a feature, an aspect of man, and done so as a function of his own time, his experience, his environment: in existing praxis and its problems. Then he has one-sidedly expanded this feature, driving it to absurdity.

We shall not speak here of *philosophical anthropology*, but rather *philosophy considered as anthropology* (or philosophies as attempted anthropology). Nonetheless, this term immediately demands precautions and reservations.

First of all, anthropology takes man as the object of its study, and studies a definition (determination) of man as object. It leads to a closure rather than opening up horizons. For the theory of praxis, man defines himself in this praxis; his determinations are multiple; none of them is exhaustive. Moreover, it is not so much a question of describing, analyzing, exposing or explaining, in short, of knowing the human, but rather of creating him. And not only of leading or educating him in the name of an already established knowledge and definition. Any definition or determination is limiting. 'Total' man is not one thing or the other: *homo faber, sapiens, ludens, ridens*, and so forth. He *is* all this, and still 'something other' that is not yet said because it is not yet created.

Secondly, anthropology at the present time has taken a direction that is clearly structuralist and culturalist. It opposes culture and nature, defining (social) man by a culture. This anthropology of American origin has been transplanted into France by Claude Lévi-Strauss, even if he attenuates some of its paradoxes. Cultural anthropology emphasizes anti-nature (anti-physis), and the wager against nature in the cultural. The structure of society, of its varied communications and exchanges, is at least said to be independent of nature. This is true to a certain extent and up to a certain point, beyond which this truth changes into error and the concept into philosophy. We have given the concept of structure its place, a very broad one, the better to refute extrapolations. The relative independence of nature and culture holds perhaps for 'archaic' societies that, without having historicity in the broad sense of the term, have all the same changed by the constitution of styles of life, wisdoms. This appears to us as the mode of evolution of societies that do not evolve in the sense of accumulation, and that keep the primitive community as their 'base'. As far as these societies are concerned, between the thesis of the 'world of scarcity' and those of culturalist anthropology we take a more dialectical and more flexible position. On the 'base' of the tribal or peasant community, starting from a meagre social surplus product, privileged groups (which do not yet constitute classes, but can form themselves into castes: warriors, priests, lords, dignitaries, etc.) produce remarkable *works* in domains that the process of accumulation is bound to ravage. The sumptuary expenses of these groups were justified to the community to which they still remained beholden.

This age of scarcity was thus one of festivals, wisdoms, monuments, styles (style not ruling out cruelty, as there have been styles of cruelty, for example in pre-Colombian America). In these cultures and styles, a distance is established between man and nature. Man has a margin of freedom. He plays with 'his' nature, not against it. He investigates it without losing initial and vital certainties. Cosmogonies, mythologies, symbolisms, then a nascent philosophy that responds to his questions. At this time, the human was not yet detached from 'nature'. Capitalism, with the unlimited extension of the market and the power of money, was bound to accomplish this rupture, and only it could do so. Marx was alone in proclaiming a reconciliation between man and nature, by way of the accumulation of capital and the growth of industry, by way of the abstraction of science and concept, technology and culture. Without going any deeper, without saying in what way his notion of nature differed or did not differ from the Greek physis, without falling into the abstract lyricism of uprooting and rootedness, he explained that the split between man and nature was produced only by way of an indissoluble (dialectical) unity. And this was one of the strongest reasons for his rejecting metaphysics. According to Marx, with the accomplishment of the industrial age man's relationship with nature would turn out to be not instrumental but one of co-substantiality and co-belonging.

In sum, philosophy as such springs up with the beginnings of the process of accumulation (knowledges, techniques, goods and wealth): with its uncertainties. It reaches its apogee and its end when this process has taken shape and is approaching its term, despite hindrances. The industrialization process does not answer all questions. It suppresses many and raises new ones. Both necessary and insufficient, it renders interpretations useless and makes the transformation of the world (and its own transformation) indispensable. A new form of thought and action appears, a different relationship with nature.

Philosophy has too often destroyed or shrunk the notion and images of physis, especially since Descartes caught on this point in a conflict between the concrete unity that he detected (of body and soul), particularly in his *Passions of the Soul*, and the separation that his theory of Substance demanded. With Kant, another example of this shrinkage, 'nature' is reduced to the dust of phenomena informed by the categories and unified in a more concrete manner only in the work of art, by a transcendental finality. Metaphysis followed the lines of Christianity: a split always further aggravated, a disdain for the sensuous and the flesh, for the 'world'. The sense and sentiment of physis, during the domination of metaphysis, was preserved above all in underground currents and heresies: Paracletism, the doctrine of the Rosicrucians, the recall of ancient Dionysianism (Rabelais). On this side, traditional philosophy and metaphysical systems fit well enough into a structuralist and culturalist anthropology. But we know that this aspect of systems does not exhaust them.

The contribution of philosophy in general, and of particular philosophies, to an anthropology does not authorize us to define man outside of nature (for example, by culture and culture alone). A determination of this kind accentuates the abstraction and extrapolation (one-sidedness) of speculative philosophies. Anthropology, the study of man as such, refers us to an elucidation of the human relationship, in praxis, in history, with 'nature' and 'being'. It is not therefore a question of defining man and the human, but rather of dismissing those representations that claim to define him, leaving him free to define himself in praxis. This opens the path of freedom, which is closed in any other perspective. One problem remains. If man is the highest being in the universe, or one of the highest beings, how and why is this? Chance? Essence? Success? Does man contain the secret of the world, as opening and summit? How and why? Was it not on the contrary, as Louis Bolk's theory suggests,[1] a weakness

---

1 TN: The Dutch anatomist Louis Bolk first developed the concept of the human species's characteristically premature birth, subsequently known as neoteny

that gave the human being its chance, by a surprising dialectical reversal? Further research is needed. We are not afraid to recall that it was Marx himself who on this point explored the praxis he discovered in its amplitude and complexity. Marx's thought and method prescribe for us an investigation into the relationships between the human and the natural within praxis, in the most poietic (creative) part of praxis, as well as in the everyday and repetitive part. Before and beyond logos: before and beyond what historically has passed into philosophical discourse or has been brought into language by philosophers, in other words, the uncertain and deep regions of need and desire, of speech and images.

The philosophical project and image of man are not without contradictions, as we have noted in passing, which the supersession of philosophy overcomes after detecting them. For example, certain philosophers have defined the human in terms of need, lack, will; they have set this determination against reason and coherent discourse. Other philosophers, on the contrary, have appealed to pure reason and rejected desire along with the imaginary. Some have defined man by finitude, whether to deplore this as the mark of a tragic fate, or to assert that empirical satisfaction in limited existence can easily be determined. Others again start from unlimited desire, dissatisfaction, unease, even anxiety.

To supersede philosophy also means overcoming the contradictions between philosophies, by revealing the virtual unity across contradictory particulars. It means integrating the seemingly irrational into a reason set free from its abstract one-sidedness and from confusions with the understanding, a reason returned to poetic meditation and speech. It means showing action, work, knowledge in the service of need and desire so as to change them into concrete powers. Finally, it means revealing in man a dialectical movement of 'satisfaction–dissatisfaction', while superseding both one and the other.

This cannot be carried out without taking up the concept of *alienation* (without determining and consequently limiting it). Philosophers have used this concept more or less clearly when they sought to account

---

and further developed by a range of thinkers from Stephen Jay Gould to Jacques Lacan.

for splits and gaps (between the real and the true, between philosophical man and man living in praxis, between the infinite and finitude,
between desire and satisfaction, etc.). Philosophers by definition
decided against non-philosophical man and the world, viewing these
as alienated. By showing that there is also a philosophical alienation,
Marx united under the same concept philosophical man and non-philosophical man; he opened the way to the superseding of philosophy.
This does not mean that we have the right to abuse the concept of
alienation. This abuse, by hyperbole or metaphor, perpetuates philosophy within its supersession. The concept of alienation, like that of
totality, is less powerful than that of dialectical contradiction. It gives
us one aspect of total history, and one aspect only.

One of the most serious objections to anthropology is that, by
seeking to be scientific and *positive*, it tends to dismiss alienation,
whereas this negative, critical, non-operational concept seems to us on
the contrary essential for anthropology. It tends also to set itself up as
truth against history: as philosophy. Finally, it tends to accentuate what
there is that is finished and dead in the praxis studied: the structure.

The superseding of philosophy takes on a programmatic character,
but at the same time a concrete one. It continues philosophy while
radically transforming the philosophical attitude. It includes not only
the analysis of praxis, the presentation of praxis in the totality (real and
possible, closures and openings, levels and differences of level), but at
the same time the analysis of practical energy, the quest for social
forces capable of intervening.

This programme envisages the insertion of what it holds onto from
philosophy into (revolutionary) praxis. It has no meaning except in
these conditions – neither philosophy outside of praxis, nor philosophy of praxis. It overcomes this difference, as it also does the opposition
between 'being' and 'what should be' (*Sein* and *Sollen*), between fact
and value.

To sum up, we can say that the programme contains the following
articles:

a) *a critical inventory of moments*, from Plato to Hegel, discerning the
   propositional element (poietic speech, images, projects, utopias);
   formalization (logos); parables, metaphors, metonymies, in other

words, rhetoric and the connotations that made possible meta-physics.

It is impossible to *deduce* anything at all from philosophical *concepts* (including alienation and totality) as far as praxis is concerned. And yet these concepts can be used in the analysis and exposition of praxis. They figure accordingly in this inventory, as elements to retain.

b) *an explanation of the various philosophies* (considered as a succession of trials, projects and propositions concerning man and seeking to define him), thus of philosophy in general as *anthropology*.

c) [*a superseding* of the abstract, incomplete, contradictory charac-ter of the philosophical project of man (not only of philosophy as such, but of the man of philosophy), and consequently a super-seding from the anthropological point of view.

d) [*an exposition of philosophical alienation*, vis-à-vis that of real and non-philosophical man.

e) [*confrontation of the philosophical project with the 'real'*, with praxis, by 'cross criticism': of philosophy by praxis and of praxis by philosophical concepts.

f) [*a realization or at least an opening towards realization, in praxis, of the philosophical project* (revised and corrected). It is no longer a question of conceiving being, but of creating it, and first of all, medi-tating on the creative power released from the simulacra that this has constructed, abandoned along the way, preserved as supports.

The theme of superseding obliges us to reconsider the entire history of philosophy, and thus to rewrite it in a new way.

This superseding does not replace the contradiction 'philosophy—non-philosophy' with a complete coherence, a definitive reconciliation of the rational (philosophical) and the real (non-philosophical). It introduces meditation and action into a dialectical movement within praxis, a movement impossible to escape, between the realization of the rational and meditation on the real and the possible: on creation, that is, on poiesis.

Only the contestation of everydayness makes it possible to connect with radical critique on a new plane. A movement both double and single: impossible to understand the everyday without rejecting it, impossible to know it without seeking to transform it. Everydayness and its rejection put in question, fragment by fragment, the whole of the modern world: culture, state, technology, institutions, structures, established groups, analytical and operational thinking, the separations that these maintain, and so forth. This privileged contestation puts an end to the fragmentation of the ensemble. It reconstitutes it as a whole. It incriminates (though not in the same way) both capitalism as it exists and socialism as it exists, the (broken) totality of the existing. It brings to light correlations, analogies as well as differences. Moreover, this contestation that supersedes partial contestations is inevitable. Everydayness cannot be tolerated. It is insufferable, unacceptable. People conceal it, deny it, misconstrue it. No one accepts it. The critique of everyday life, and this alone, could thus combine the multiple contestations into a bundle; the new wealth can only be defined on the basis of the new poverty, that of an everyday 'privatized' of what makes for its wealth.

We can thus detect a generalized latent malaise, and also points of crystallization for discontent and rejection (art or what is already replacing it; questions of housing and urbanism; those of education and training, etc.). We can discover direct contestations (in the action of social and political forces) and also indirect ones (in the clumsy attempt to rediscover playful activity, for example). Partial groups (young people, women, intellectuals) take turns in aspects of contestation, and so of course does the working class. The totality of contestations and the contestation of totality, that is, negativity, are only reconstituted on the basis of the everyday.[2]

This general [*global*] contestation, linking up with the radical negation conceived by Marx, would be meaningless if there was a *convergence* of established systems and forms of the existing. This convergence would block the situation; it would put an end to becoming, not by the definitive promulgation of a single system (philosophical, state, ideological, moral, etc.) but by the totalization

---

2 'Production relations... are not changed until the various groups of workers start to have a real, day-to-day... control over the management of the enterprises, the working out and carrying through of the plans', notes Ernest Mandel, *Marxist Economic Theory*, vol. 2, London: Merlin, 1962, p. 644.

of existing systems. But we have tried hard to establish non-convergence. This is what the law of uneven development means, a very general law applied here to systems of significations and operations. First point: these are multiple. They cannot be reduced to just one. Second point: we have carefully noted the phenomena of destruction, de-structuration and self-destruction.[3] Third point: forms and systems close on themselves and consolidate, dissolve or explode with a certain independence from one another, thus precisely from the fact that each of them acquires autonomy and seeks to set itself up as absolute in the 'real' and above this 'real'. On top of this, if there is convergence, it is rather against the systems, in the forces of dislocation and contestation, in the negativity that asserts itself against their positivity and that contains the genuine positivity.[4]

Every system leaves a *residue* that escapes it, resists it, and from where an effective (practical) resistance can take off. In particular, the semantic reduction, which seeks to found a system, structuralism, turns against itself. It brings to light a residual element of primary importance, which is nothing other than time. Can human thought and action only grasp and realize discontinuous pieces, 'discrete' units or entities that they dismantle and reassemble operationally? Maybe. But time? This is said to be the common and general basis on which forms detach themselves. It does not intervene in the formation of these forms. It has neither importance nor interest. It is ungraspable: impossible to manipulate. But then, precisely, time punctuates the succession of forms, their connections. These are born in it. The residue manifested by this detour becomes the essential, better perceived and valorized after its reduction.[5]

---

3   The phenomena of destruction are not restricted to art and culture. Not only does automobile traffic threaten to destroy towns (without replacing them by a new creation), but cars are themselves an investment with rapid depreciation. Is it by chance that this production has become a key industry for capitalism, and the automobile 'pilot-object' a system of significations?

4   In a collection of texts published recently in France, Herbert Marcuse seems to overdo the closure of the real. He seems sometimes to think that men are entirely fashioned by moulds (by mimesis). A certain number of sociologists, in both America and France, share this pessimistic vision. Would Eros be the only fissure? (Cf. *Eros and Civilization: A Philosophical Inquiry into Freud*, Boston: Beacon Press, 1955.)

5   Gödel's theorem suffices to show that mathematics does not effect a closure. The circle closes neither on the side of its principles, nor on that of its consequences.

Do these residues come from transcendences thus manifested? Do they arise from a method of interpretation, a hermeneutic that would still be philosophy? No. The essence of each attempt at reduction (or rather the fact that it has an essence, as it tends to constitute a specific system, a 'world', a 'globalization': the state, technology, etc.) shows that what we have here is no transcendence. The diversity of residues and their residual character only have a meaning in and through the systems that seek to reabsorb them. The symbols themselves, as residues irreducible to pure signification, arise from physis ('nature', this residue displayed by culture and culturalism) and not from a hermeneutic. Expression and symbolism form part of the semantic field, itself conceived as a part of praxis.

For Marx, was not the proletariat a residual element of capitalist society, both beyond and outside it? Impossible for this society to dispense with it, despite its efforts. Derivative, thus by essence negative, and negative of its own negation, was this not how it attained for Marx the dignity of universal class? If it is not so for the moment, will it become so again? Perhaps, with new elements, in a new situation. It remains what is irreducible in this society. For the moment, we wager on the ensemble of these residues, the unease and discontent irreducible through and beneath the fragmentary satisfactions: everyday life, youth, deviance, underdevelopment, and so on.[6] A

There is accordingly a creative activity even in mathematics. Mathematics is a work. What residue does it display? Drama, which escapes number, but whose value is shown by the light that number casts on it, with the result that not only does number have to be taken into account, but also the will that it contains and dissimulates, the will to systematization and the specific nature of its failure.

6   In literature in 1964, to locate the question:

a) The 'nouveau roman' (focused on the object) displays a residue: the subjective, which is not or is no longer the bare object that fascinates writers. On the one hand, the 'objective' school extends to art the scientific notion of indefinite research. The research would tend to bring into existence an unknown reality, an anonymous substance. 'Nothing exists any more prior to the work, which is nothing but the investigation of something that previously did not exist.' (Cf. Nathalie Sarraute and Alain Robbe-Grillet, Cahiers Institut Solvay, 1963, pp. 437–47.) For us, that is the 'residue', hic et nunc. Genuine creation (poiesis) takes off from here.

b) Samuel Beckett best realizes today the destructive and self-destructive role of art. He indicates the residual in general: the unnameable!

c) Perhaps Michel Leiris has gone as far as possible in the pursuit of this ungraspable.

positivist sociologist would say: 'You're betting on the anomic'. Quite right!

The theory of residues takes up in modern terms a theme of romanticism. And so we support the thesis of a new romanticism with revolutionary tendency, or rather, one fundamentally revolutionary, reprising also certain essential themes of Marxism (negativity, contestation, radical critique). An important remark: this romanticism is not based on departure and escape; it does not offer itself as a method of flight; it does not posit the essential outside of the 'real', without for that matter ruling out the imaginary and the utopian. Even if we grant existential thought the point that Kierkegaard legitimately protested against 'the system' (Hegelian), we no longer have anything in common with Kierkegaardian existentialism. It remained philosophically directed against the philosophy of Hegel. It protested without contesting. It returned to religiosity and the worst metaphysics (the theory of Repetition, the God of Abraham, Isaac and Jacob rendering what they had lost to those who had lost everything in becoming and by death, and so on).

We end up proposing a *method of residues* (parodying the scientific method well known and little employed by scientists, the theory of which was provided by the empiricist philosopher J. S. Mill). Our method of residues contains a number of articles: detecting the residues, wagering on them, showing the precious essence in them, combining them, organizing their rebellions and totalizing these. Each residue is an irreducible to be grasped.

Poiesis, today and now, starts from the residual. Its first act is to gather together the residues deposited by the systems that stubbornly persist without managing to constitute themselves as totalities, to 'globalize' themselves. *Religion*, despite its efforts, has left and still does leave an irreducible: fleshly life, spontaneous vitality. *Philosophy* casts light on the ludic element that it does not manage to absorb, as well as the everyday (non-philosophical man) that it makes manifest by expelling it. Mathematics casts light on drama. *Structure* and *structuralism* indicate several realities: time, history, the particular and specific particularities. Technology and machinery point a finger, as it were, towards what resists them: sex, desire, and more generally the deviant and unusual. Mimesis displays poesis. The state bitterly opposes freedom and indicates it. State centralization (and even the necessary decentralization conducted by the centralized state, a curious parody) demonstrates the residual and irreducible reality of the regions. Art that has become cultural leaves a residue: 'creativity'. Bureaucracy in vain hunts out the individual, the singular, the deviant. Organization cannot exterminate spontaneous life and desire. As for everydayness, despite itself it opens onto the totality reprised and renewed by poiesis. This latter gathers together the irreducibles. Its strategy is based on multiplicity and heterogeneity, on the 'non-convergence' of 'worlds', on their gaps, dysfunctions, disharmonies. In a word, on their conflicts. Promoting a residue, showing its essence (and its essential character) against the power that crushes it and demonstrates it by trying to crush it, is a rebellion. Gathering the residues is a revolutionary thought, an action-thought.

This 'method of residues' is not utopian, neither abstractly nor concretely. The residues in question are there, *hic et nunc*. No more is it prospective. What it shows is not a deceptive image of the future, despite being turned towards the future and appealing to the possible (thus to imagination). It starts from the actual, without omitting the unforeseen and unforeseeable – those residues of rational foresight that always intervene, so that the new, different from what was thought and wished for, arises from a history. It is thus act and method in act. Wagering on the residues adds nothing to them. It is nothing by itself. It is not 'operational'. And yet it is decisive. It contains the idea that nothing is eternal, that nothing is completely durable. Not only are residues the most precious, they gnaw away and destroy from within, they explode systems that seek to absorb them. In this sense, the poiesis that takes hold of them must reveal itself as creator of objects, acts, and more generally, situations.

Metaphilosophical meditation, conducted in this way, would be a method and already a style rather than a definite form.[7]

First of all, it sees itself as *unclassifiable* in the accepted categories. Philosophers repudiate it, not without excellent reasons. Anthropologists, sociologists, psychologists consider it (bad) philosophy. It does not name itself. It would rather take the unnameable as its point of departure, in other words, the ensemble of residues, the disorder born of this factitious order, or more precisely of the multiplicity of factitious orders that seek to impose themselves. It arises from the pseudo-nothingness of residues that tenaciously persist between Forms and Systems, like seeds between building stones. Its point of departure is Non-value, that which does not have or no longer has value: everyday life, uncertain speech, the disturbed situation, ambiguity. And this is not in order to 'create' new values, caricatures of creations. It starts from the in-significant and its meaning.

In the course of this theoretical and practical gathering, the residual elements have to meet up and mutually recognize one another. They must therefore transform themselves: by converging, by struggling effectively against the systems that reject them and determine them by rejecting them. It is not a question of coalescing, or adding the residues to one another. Transforming the world now means metamorphosing them: each has to take back the dignity and strength of an essence manifested by the very fact of the attempt to destroy it, an essence that is conquered and surrenders with generosity. Will this not lead to defining a higher degree of human freedom? Metaphilosophical meditation, action-thought, thus renews philosophical reflection on freedom. The struggle for freedom, and freedom in history, acquire a different meaning (in the sense of palpability, direction, signification). And likewise totality. The duality of *moments* (moments of history that the human being abandons, moments of this being that constitute it as a totality) likewise acquires its full meaning.

Wagering on the residues by an inaugural poietic act, subsequently reassembling them in a praxis, directing them against the accepted

---

7   Noise was the residue of sound. This idea leads to taking a stand in favour of *musique concrète*, but no longer as music, but rather as means for the construction of specific places and times, contexts of a life to be created ('moments').

systems and forms, drawing new forms from them, that is the great challenge. That is the gauntlet cast in the face of powers and the established (existing) order. It is not yet the whole of metaphilosophy. We have so far given only a first approximation. We could also say that metaphilosophy sets speech against discourse (not meaning speech prior to discourse, archaic and folkloric: speech beyond discourse and the logico-philosophical understanding). Or again, it is the rebellion of poiesis against mimesis and their bitter struggle. Or better, the conflict between style and culture. The term 'rebellion' simply refers to the initiative and the starting point. The aim? Mastery (of speech over discourse, etc.), in other words, *appropriation*.

Technology extends the sector dominated and consolidated by man like a farmland extending over marshes. Beyond the polders and swamps there is the open sea. To get to the ocean, a boat is needed. Poiesis takes to the open sea. It is also conquest, mastery of what is not yet attained. But not in the same way as technology. It attains the appropriation by man of his own nature. It is in this sense that it defines itself by the practical relationship between man and nature: between man and his being.

We should not confuse poiesis (metaphilosophy) with spontaneity, though their movement is towards a retrieved spontaneity. Is there not a deceptive spontaneity, unconscious, that follows 'models' and lets itself be conditioned? We know that spontaneity is also the act of the *automaton*, which moves of itself. The automaton casts light on spontaneity. It is made possible by it and motivates its critique. It renders suspect a certain spontaneity (for example, that of a femininity of which one may well ask whether it is not 'pilot-robot' of cybernetic society: modelled, mimetic, conditioned by images and objects, etc.). Rediscovered spontaneity has passed through the test of tearing and split. It has revealed itself irreducible (residual) to models, behaviours, attitudes. It encompasses lucidity and action. It has perhaps a foundation or an ontological meaning. It does not react spontaneously towards this or that object, this or that stimulus, this or that image, but towards the ensemble, so as to modify and recapture it. This spontaneity higher and deeper than the elementary is reason and resultant of poiesis, residue among residues, fundamental rebellion. Not 'savage mind' but 'savage desire'.

Metaphilosophical poiesis could also explore the unknown aspect of love, sex, pleasure. Not by the paths of sadism and masochism, though by other paths than those of the 'normal', of accepted customs, including conscious perversities. For love is moment, and thus modality, of presence (to self, to others, to the 'world'). But it is perpetual creation (of presence, of joy and pleasure, or of pain, or the two combined), at the same time rift and totality always attempted and always broken. The aim today is either to deny love in the name of moral order, or (still worse) make love the foundation of the moral order. But it is precisely what is irreducible to the moral order: the residue.

Metaphilosophical poiesis would thus be poetry and truth. This truth would no longer have anything in common with that of philosophy (exclusive, prefabricated, constrictive, systematic), nor yet with the moral or political order. On the contrary: it starts from the disorder inherent in the always failed order of Forms; it bases itself on partial truths in order to *create* a truth. This metaphilosophical poiesis, therefore, does not consist in a certain way of *speaking* (of things, of people). Though it may also renew the way of speaking of them (of faces, homes, landscapes, and so forth). Though it may bring meaning to the insignificant (the everyday) by transforming it. It seeks to be more than poetic expression and description: to be creation.

If we want to locate it better in diachrony (history), let us return to the characteristics of modernity, its conflicts and problems, in a word, to the 'transition' and the actual situation of human being. We shall thus avoid the almost inevitable reproach of 'prophetism'.

From particular cultures (humanism and classicism, with their abstract universality; culture of peasant origin; bourgeois culture; proletarian culture; national cultures) we pass to world culture, which initially consists in the worldwide consumption and destruction of all past and dead cultures. And through this we proceed to the reconquest of Style. From ancient art and art for art's sake, we proceed to a radical mutation already under way: the death of an art external to everyday life, the fusion of art and everyday life in a metamorphosis of the latter. But we also move, along the way, from life grasped and organized by institutions and ideas (the sacred, culture) to a forsaken life, from rootedness (in the native soil, the city, the milieu) to an 'uprooting', from man limited but concrete to the man of complete abstraction. This seems to be a necessary stage: extreme abstraction, quasi-total alienation (to the point that no one grasps it as alienation, and the theory of alienation seems outdated, lacking object or effectiveness).

With the proletariat not having accomplished its task, the political and cultural revolution is paradoxically pursued within the 'inverted world' (Marx), that of the bourgeoisie, by the devalorizing of the bourgeoisie and the bourgeois way of life, by the dissolution of existing forms, by the decomposition of the individual, of consciousness, of language. Without the creation of a new 'style'. Incapable of opposing a style to the bourgeois absence of style, the 'socialist camp' compensates for this impotence by an exasperated philosophism. Systematized philosophy (which thus falls back towards Hegelianism or below this) becomes criterion, field, terrain and stake [enjeu] of theoretical discussions. Obsolete philosophy and Manichaean moralism have supplanted (for how long?) Marx's realization of philosophy.

Philosophy aggressively survives. It is aggravated in teaching and pedagogy, in scholastic and institutional continuations, in technicalized or non-technicalized culture, in philosophism. By becoming cultural – complement and compensation of technicality – philosophy becomes picturesque, an agreeable leisure occupation, like visits to museums and ancient cities: folklore.

A strange mixture that is found even in the solitary grandeur of a Heidegger. Philosophy drags along with it an immense folklore, bequeathed to the industrial and technical age from earlier times. The tradition of the rural world, ideas on nature of agrarian origin, the oldest of symbolisms, are all reborn in it. Compensation and consolation is sought in the face of the aridity of the signs and significations that proliferate but do not people the robotic desert of modernity. We know that the abundance of signifiers arouses a specific pathology. Philosophy conveys precapitalist representations and 'values', agrarian or handicraft, as well as their abstract negation. In Heidegger and also Bachelard, we find ideas and dreams about the home, the elements, the sacred. For these great meditators, and this is perhaps a trace of philosophism, the concern for comprehension wins out over the exploration of praxis; comprehension reveals itself in profound but archaic symbolisms. This remark enables us to take a distance from both Heidegger and Bachelard, not without making clear their prestige as thinkers of transition within the transition.[8] We may also meditate on the invasion of anthropology and ethnography into philosophical thought. A strange mixture: the meaning of 'nature' set against technology and the cybernetization of society, but in confusion; the search for 'roots', a distant prefiguring (perhaps) of the alliance with nature proposed by Marx. Unless it is simply a parody mimed in more or less picturesque fashion.

Here we again find our hypothesis, developed and supported. Philosophy pursues its globalization – along with the state, with technology, with art. Globalizations of real 'systems' are pursued, not without conflicts between 'world powers'. The alienated powers pursue their career. They will continue to the end of automatization. We do not say: the end of reification. An automatism is not a thing (in the sense included in the term 'reification'). The robot simulates logical thought (logos), to the point of attaining and embodying this. Mimesis constitutes a thing that is also non-thing (mixed), transition and intermediary between thing and non-thing. Hence our constant reservations about the current use of the term 'reification'. At the same time, we see in parallel the degradation of philosophy, the bureaucratic rotting of the state, the deterioration and devouring consumption of art, the robotization of technology. At the same time again, the radical critique of philosophy pursues its path, and likewise revolutionary struggle, the mutation of art into everyday life, and the effort to redeem creative (poietic) speech from cybernetized and mimetic discourse.

Metaphilosophical thought encompasses this fragmentary, broken totality, on route towards 'something else': towards a planetary totality that is totally new. Along with the globalization of autonomized and automatized powers, at the same time the true powers of the human

---

8   Yet they are closer to a metaphilosophical meditation than [René] Le Senne believing he can list the functions of the idea of God (*Le Devoir*, Paris: PUF, 1949, pp. 356–7), or Whitehead seeing this idea as the 'necessary metaphysical function' of an assessment of the world (see the conclusion to *Religion in the Making*, New York: Macmillan Company, 1926), for us to follow these thinkers who frequently inspire the philosophical and metaphysical vulgarization that survives philosophy.

being, his *moments*, strengthen and reassert themselves: play, rest, love, poetry, and so on. Already, if weak and divided, the party of supersession of philosophy and metamorphosis of the everyday constitutes a party, despite or against philosophical and philosophical-political parties.

Man is total. Being and (conscious) thought, or if you prefer, nature and praxis, recognize one another and encounter each other in their reciprocal shared belonging and appropriation. Not without conflicts. This totality can be attained neither by philosophy, nor by some science of human 'reality', nor again by the ensemble of these sciences. These sciences can be neither separated nor united. As soon as they are separated, they confront each other in a formless babel; and as soon as the attempt is made to unite them into a synthetic picture, they divorce and each goes its own way. Only a new thought, aimed at a totality that is determined neither as economic, nor as sociological, nor as historical in the usual sense of the term, and yet takes into account all these levels and elements of the 'real', can dominate the sciences. Only it can define – starting from the 'real', from 'facts' and 'results', but above all from absence and absences, lack and lacks, gaps in the real, empty places or the empty place, in short, from negativity and radical critique – the future (virtual, possible) totality. It is not inconceivable that, during this transition, metaphilosophical meditation may support for tactical reasons a new type of thinker: the 'nexialist'[9] capable of standing at the nub of fragmentary knowledges, programming research in this direction and contributing concrete solutions to this or that partial problem.

The debate thus engaged can only deepen. We must not retreat in

---

9 This term, borrowed from science fiction (van Vogt, *The World of Null-A,*), indicates the individual charged with foreseeing and organizing encounters between ideas and technologies that seemingly have nothing in common. He is not concerned with having people meet, but rather fragments of reality, knowledge and action. This does not demand any philosophical theory (on the 'encounter', or anything else), but on the contrary a liberation in relation to the fictional encounters imagined by philosophers or situated in philosophies. Meditation situated beyond philosophy does not coincide with 'nexialism'.

Some science-fiction novels go so far beyond today's reigning ideologies, raising the most topical questions, that we can expect that one day, not so remote, contemporary literature (Mauriac, Malraux and Robbe-Grillet) will be forgotten and these works will remain the only testimonies of our age.

the face of its depth, but on the contrary, expand this. It compels us to redefine socialism and communism, as perspectives (possibilities) of the historical movement. New elements have intervened since Marx and Lenin, which demand a redefinition. What are these elements? Technology, on the one hand, with the technocratic danger it involves. The state, on the other hand, and the necessity of reconsidering its enormity and its withering away (in the absence of which Marxism-Leninism collapses, leaving only a technique of rational planning and accumulation).

Marx's thought on socialism is confronted with the historical experience of a century. Illuminated in this way, it can be summed up in a few formulations; a process of accumulation constituted in Western Europe imposes a new situation on the world. Accumulation encompasses the two essential forms of wealth, the means of production and the goods produced. It includes on the one hand the accumulation of technologies and knowledges, on the other hand the accumulation of material objects that ensure the application of knowledges in praxis. The process of accumulation thus has form and content. It contributes certainties that abolish philosophy as vague and uncertain (thus abstract) research for truth in general. But it raises new questions. First of all, it has to be assured as growth by eliminating external obstacles and internal barriers. Secondly, it has to guarantee that the cumulative process will be in the service of the human being (social and individual). *Growth* and *development* must go together. The first aspect is necessary but not sufficient; the second aspect is indispensable but hard to realize.

The appropriation of 'nature' has two aspects: mastery of the external (material) world, and appropriation by man of his own nature (biological, physiological, social, psychological). This second aspect, appropriation, presupposes the first, but on this material basis a dialectical movement is not devoid of conflict. It would be impossible to warn too much against the automatization of the accumulation process. Since the death of Marx, in fact, the great novelty, as a consequence of the world historical situation (failures of the revolution; division of the world into two 'camps'; technological race, with its economic and social base in arms rivalry and the arms race), the great innovation introduced by history is this autonomization of the process.

On the other hand, experience shows that state capitalism and state socialism – despite their internal differences and specific tendencies – sometimes come dangerously close. The definition of socialism in terms of the absence of private property in the means of production, in terms of collective property, is insufficient. We need to spell out the modalities of the possession and social management of the means of production (self-management [*auto-gestion*], in particular).

Lenin was completely in the 'line' of Marxist thought and project when he defined socialism in 1917, after the October revolution. This definition was simple, no doubt a bit too simple, because it left aside fundamental theory and practical difficulties. Yet it was inserted immediately into praxis, and contained the essential: *soviets plus electrification*, in other words, economic (technological) growth plus democratic organisms capable of controlling it and verifying its orientation. Today, must we not redefine socialism as a function of these two aspects and their new demands: technology, democracy? Definitions in terms of the state (workers' state, people's state), in terms of economic growth alone, in terms of the power of the Party, have had their day. Would not socialism, in our days, be a dense network of organisms at the base (in production units and territorial units) plus an ultra-modern equipment in electronic machines? The base organisms would ensure the direct expression of social needs and more generally control over the summit, without which there is no democracy. The democratic character of planning would be guaranteed by this control, and economic growth subordinated to social needs expressed, rather than detected by 'specialists' or formulated by 'experts'.

The end of private property in the means of production would thus involve their social management. This management, bound up with the above double network (in production and territorial units), would simultaneously ensure, according to the fundamental Marxist project, the disappearance of the bourgeoisie as ruling class and the withering away of the state. Without a complex network, what would be the result of electronics, cybernetics and information theory applied to economic management? They would attribute exorbitant power to technocrats, manipulators of men and information. They would maintain the state with its prerogatives, aggravated by this power (even if politicians keep a certain part, and possibly come into conflict with technocrats). Today machines make possible the administration of things without resource to the active participation of men. Without machines and the electronic gathering of information, democracy at the base risks collapse into the inorganic, the promotion of incompetents. The two elements therefore form a whole. One is impossible without the other. Control of accumulation is certain, and the coherent (rational) shaping of praxis assured. A fundamental problem is resolved: taking technology away from technocrats.

This schema omits, for convenience of presentation, the inevitable contradictions between its elements. It makes sense only for the highly industrialized countries, which corresponds to a demand of the situation. The tendency to 'think socialism' as a function of countries that are little or poorly developed, and their particular social and political needs (notably as far as the state is concerned), has become preponderant. The Hegelian and Lassallean theory of state socialism, rather than the Marxist, has covered up the Marxist theory of the withering away of the state. We propose therefore a theoretical model that makes it possible to appreciate the distance that separates this or that country, in the general uneven development, from the possibilities and reality of modern socialism.

In the same orientation, we may mention the possibility of a political party, a site where the contradictions of praxis would be openly expressed, where options would confront one another – which would no longer be a place where contradictions are expressed and weighed only behind closed doors. This notion of the political party goes further than the customary democratic demands (free expression of tendencies, currents of opinion, etc.). Is it not the Marxist and Leninist conception of the party? Who could refuse it? Many people. Those who place tactics and organization above theoretical thought. Those who pin labels on ideas and people ('revisionist', 'dogmatic'). Those who have not had this conception, despite its necessity, because they think differently, according to empirical schemas, or simply obsolete schemas in their fixed dogmatism.

What we propose with this schema is simply a project, a 'model'. Its possibility is a certainty, but not its realization. We cannot rule out the hypothesis of a colossal miscarriage of human history (on the planetary scale). We must even, at certain moments, bring examination of this hypothesis to the fore, to assess its chances and risks. As *the most dangerous* (and extreme) *hypothesis*, we have to take account of it so as better to combat it. Neither planetary miscarriage nor nuclear annihilation can be ruled out as impossible. The miscarriage (for example, the definitive consolidation of the state) would arrive at the historical moment of success, with all the means of succeeding. The most probable, however, is a mixed period in which partial miscarriages and partial successes, failures and favourable tendencies, will be mingled.

If we now place ourselves at the level of individuals and their immediate ('interpersonal') relationships, what have we gained? A conviction. We have to dissipate the myths of everyday life by a radical critique. They cede nothing, in terms of influence and toxicity, to the great ideological and political myths. Myths of apprenticeship and entry into life, of maturity and adult age, of the Father – since the establishment of the everyday, these images are no longer anything but survivals. Today they mask the 'reality' of which they form part. They accentuate alienation and alienated reality by dissimulating it.

Alienation? This theory needs a sharper focus. Why? Because philosophy of traditional inspiration (what goes by the name of 'philosophy') has been unable to assimilate it. The concept retains its meaning only by freeing itself from systems. On the other hand, literature has seized hold of it; alienation, become a literary commonplace, has lost its critical import and trenchancy. At the same time, alienation has been transformed. In certain respects, it has worsened to the point of making protest – spontaneous consciousness and resistance – disappear. There are new forms of alienation. More precisely, the new alienation is an alienation of form and through form (by 'models'), by simulacra and simulation, by mimesis and the imitation of patterns, and so forth. If self-consciousness becomes alienating, this leads to a loss of consciousness of alienation, since what should dis-alienate itself by reflecting, instead sinks further into alienation. Some people go so far as to think that the alienation through which man emerges from nature becomes (second) nature for him. With duplication and reduplication (discourse on discourse; novels about novelists and novels about novels; world of image and mimesis, of copy and reproduction without limit, etc.), we have now long since entered into *second-degree alienation*, alienation on alienation whose limit is abolished:[10] generalized mimesis is superimposed on commodity and money without abolishing them. Alienation does not simply condition individuals. It does not weigh solely on classes. It involves the most diverse groups and society as a whole.

If ideological alienation has partially (very partially) dissipated, technological alienation has readily replaced it. We can extend to the theory of alienation the concept and law of *uneven development*. Yet alienation tends towards a kind of totality, never attained, since this would presuppose the convergence of all causes and reasons of alienated states; but total alienation is approaching through the disappearance of the consciousness of alienation.

Alienation has thus never been so real, nor the theory of alienation so important. And yet this theory has never been so ineffective, with the result that we have, as it were, to change the position and disposition of our batteries. We gain consciousness of the limits of the theory. This does not mean we have either to relegate it to the philosophical antiquities, or make it the centre of a philosophy, or eliminate it (in the name of an operational view of thought, or a so-called scientific philosophy). The theory of alienation, quasi-total yet never achieved as totality, remains the other side of the theory of total man, dis-alienated and realizing himself on the path of dis-alienation. But in this latter theory, the accent has shifted. It bears on *residues*, for example, and no longer on the general concept of alienation.

The concept does not have an ontological meaning (which comes back to philosophy). It would rather be an anthropological concept, subordinate to that of (historical) becoming by illuminating the contradictions of history, showing the detours of human 'realization', the succession of alienations, dis-alienations, new alienations. Which forbids us, as Marx thought, from substantifying, fetishizing, 'ontologizing' the historical outside of the human. As philosophical concept, alienation turns against philosophy and questions it, since there

---

10   By emphasizing reification, the Lukácsian school has committed a double error. It has defined alienation by its 'structural' limit, omitting the nuances of human non-realization. Moreover, it has overlooked analysis of new forms of alienation.

is – among others – a philosophical alienation. The theory of alienation signifies that philosophy sought to say what man is and what he
can become. It also signifies what philosophy did not manage to say,
still less do. What did it say? What man is and also what he is not: what
prevents *homo philosophicus* from acceding to being, that is, to realization. Philosophy sought to be praxis inasmuch as it indicated the path
of alienation, and consequently of dis-alienation. It did not manage to
act and insert itself into praxis, inasmuch as the philosopher was
himself alienated. Hence the split that situated it outside of praxis (and
poiesis) in order to reduce it to a particular mimesis. At the extreme,
the theory of alienation indicates in what way and how mimesis realizes (illusorily) human being, and loses it by alienating it. This theory
cannot dominate mimesis and designate poiesis, except from outside
and afar. It is not the highest theory.

As regards Totality, that is, total man, we detect the double aspect
of the situation where we are in the radical mutation that we are living.
On the one hand, total man is close. We are that, all that, already, here
and now: play, love, knowledge, labour, and so forth. 'Become what
you are!' This motto, one of the most poietic that any man has uttered,
prescribes the possible and detects it in the real. The goal seems close.
And yet it is distant. What do we have of these powers and modalities
of presence (to self, to the 'other', to the 'world')? What does the man
of today possess? Traces that are also germs, and that we have been
able, with this hope, to call residues. It is a narrow and difficult path
simply to supersede the fetishisms (of commodity and money,
discourse and communication) that accompany disturbing deteriorations and destructions, or to dominate the reigning mimesis and
subordinate the process of accumulation to man by appropriating it.
The passage from the possible to the real, from the germ to the act,
from the residual to the essential, cannot be accomplished by thought,
still less by a reflexive (philosophical) thought. It implies a praxis. Man
will be the supreme being for man. This has either not been said by
philosophers, or said badly, attached as they are to the transcendent
True, Beautiful and Good. But human being will only be the supreme
being for human being inasmuch as being ('nature', 'life', with their
multiple modes, attributes and powers) is for him the supreme goal
and meaning. And consequently inasmuch as man is the supreme

being for 'being'! – something of which philosophers have sometimes had a naïve and hesitant presentiment, but that only Marxism, superseding philosophy, has brought into praxis.

Perhaps exploration of this 'being' will supply some of the secrets of this 'world' or 'universe' whose appropriation constitutes poietic truth in praxis. Perhaps we shall be able in this way to answer, on a new level, various demands from philosophers that they have been unable to answer. There will be a kind of turning point – not, as Hegel would have said, in the concept alone, but in activity.

Are we then going to continue to philosophize, despite claiming to supersede philosophy? Not quite. We are going to grasp our praxis renewed by a poietic decision and say what it reveals.

Is this universe, our own, not essentially, if we may say so, approximate and relative? These terms do not mean the same as 'ambiguous' or 'uncertain', or 'ungraspable'. They go hand in hand with becoming. How could universal becoming create constant entities, with absolutely defined contours, destined therefore not to escape from themselves? No concept suffices to grasp this universe and the 'realities' that it totalizes. The most pertinent oppositions of concepts do not catch 'everything' in their grip. 'Something' always spills over. Nothing can be drawn without a wobble in the contours that gives the drawing life. Ruler and compass do not create. No line, no force, no volume, no circle and no real sphere are perfect and finished. Concepts and oppositions of concepts are always on the side of the determined, thus the finished, the terminated. Their negation contains their dialectical truth.

Negation, however, is first of all the approximation and relativity of well-determined limits. The universe is in-finite, negation of the finite. This negation starts with the inexactness of limits. Is this not why the residual, which determined concepts do not manage to reduce, has such importance? That which overflows concepts and conceptual grids seems at first, from a point of view beyond concepts, a mere residue; this residue is then manifest as what is most precious: the infinite in the finite, the inexhaustible creative power considered not ontologically or mystically, but in a concrete and historical fashion, in other words, poiesis.

Dialectical thought then appears in two ways: in the double

determination inherent to any apprehension (thus any concept), and in the 'overflowing' of every concept, the principle of supersession.

This universe would be 'approximate' from the standpoint of the rigorous form of discourse. This character itself could not be considered as a metaphysical definition.

It would be neither irrational nor absurd, nor in itself full of meaning. It would be characterized neither by meaning nor by the absence of meaning. Man would be neither its end nor its aim, neither its absence of end nor its absurdity. This universe would be neither world nor cosmos, neither oriented time nor hierarchically ordered space, but infinity in time and space, producing itself in finite time and space. It would be neither stability nor wandering, neither unformed not structured, but something other. Neither play, nor out of play. A universe of this kind could not be called either good or bad; it is doomed neither to success nor to failure. Neither causally determined nor determined by an end, nor undetermined. Between being and nothingness, between matter and spirit, between the In-itself and the For-itself, between the determined and the undetermined, these traditional concepts of philosophy, there would be the site of a *plasticity* without assignable limits, a domain shared up to now by three terms: praxis, mimesis, poiesis. Man and the human occupy this site. They fill it and give it a meaning, their own, by praxis and theoretical thought.

This universe pertains neither to the pure categorical nor to the indefinite problematic (neither philosophical dogmatism nor philosophy reduced to a set of problems without solution). According to us, it pertains to concrete questions and questionings, at the same time particular (specified) and general. The terms that are useful to us in thinking it ('mystery' and 'transparency', meaning and non-meaning, etc.) still bear an echo of their philosophical past.

Man finds himself called upon to create his dwelling. Not, as Heidegger says, the dwelling of Being in language, but the dwelling of man as 'human being', constructed by praxis. On earth.

In this attempt, which philosophy has accomplished for its part, with its own means (its essential means, discourse), it has failed as philosophy, like religion. It is no longer a source of invention. It has been unable to emerge from metaphysis. It falls back sooner or later into theology, 'every philosophy's spot of infection', with 'the further role of portraying in itself the negative decomposition of philosophy, i.e., the process of its decay', as Marx boldly and brutally wrote in the *1844 Manuscripts*.[11] It is only by emerging from the mode of philosophical reflection that the philosopher, having become a different man, will have his *historic revenge*.

The approximate character of the 'world' makes for its plasticity, opens it to action and motivates action (praxis). It is not approximate in the sense of classical philosophy and the theory of knowledge (even relativist). We do not have a universe of precise forms or 'beings', attained by successive approximations. We speak of a *double approximation*. Nothing has precise contours. Nothing is susceptible to rigorous definition (including the spherical form of the earth, for example, this prototype of stabilities and self-regulations). Nothing is completely determined or can be completely measured. Nothing is absolutely stable. Measuring instruments, the tools of knowledge (concepts) and those of action, are in the same box. Man is in the same general situation – which reestablishes correspondence and agreement between the 'real' and 'knowledge', rendering useless a theory of knowledge that strives to suppress approximation, to replace it by rigour, and which by this pretension opens up an abyss between 'concepts' and the 'real'. The theory of objectivity in knowing is replaced by a concept bound up with the very practice of knowing: the concept of *deepened objectivity*, including the double relativity of the 'real' and of 'knowledge'. Objectivity is always won, conquered and reconquered in this double approximation; it is always challenged.

The realizing and totalizing precisions that systems aim at are all the more disturbing if they succeed (more or less well, to a certain degree, almost, but 'really') in this approximate 'world', a world plastic because approximate. They are dangerous because they impose a form (almost finished, almost definitive) on the 'real', and hence constitute it by making it such as it is. By making it 'being'. Fortunately, we know that this systematic form always leaves a residue that gnaws away at it and breaks it.

---

11   Karl Marx, 'Preface to Economic and Philosophic Manuscripts of 1844', *MECW*, vol. 3, pp. 233–4.

Man creates in two ways, one more spontaneous, another more lucid and intellectual (analytic). This is not just a question of biological creation (having children) and social creation (works). Social man has spontaneously created, in a history that is steadily less blind, cities, peoples, nations. Subsequently and since, he has striven to 'consciously' create groups, towns, rational plans for these groups and agglomerations. This is not a matter of a difference between the contents of creative acts that are supposedly spontaneous, and forms that are reflective. We have tried to show that history and becoming also create forms.

There is no preestablished harmony between these modes of creation. One of the 'problems' of modern man is to link up with and if possible supersede, on the basis of analytical intelligence, the spontaneous capacity of creation. This 'problem' is manifestly apparent in questions of art and urbanism.

We can no longer believe in a harmony or convergence between man's creative capacities, but rather in their conflictual dialectical movement. Philosophical idealism posited and presupposed a divergence, attributing absolute primacy either to purely spontaneous creation (mysticism) or to (rationalist) reflection. Philosophical materialism posited, and still does posit, the natural unity of these capacities, without further investigating them. Metaphilosophical meditation is concerned with the conflictual relationship between the two modes of creation. It holds that mimesis imitates poiesis but also caricatures and parodies it. Mimesis, when it produces, does not reproduce poietic creation. It adds something else to it, something specific to itself: facticity, abstraction, autonomization, fetishism, pleonasm. The function of the creative capacities, therefore, cannot be easily grasped. We perceive the unity rediscovered or won which would supersede the tearing split in a redemption of poiesis, restored in the project after the trajectory it has pursued.

Thought and reflection are a certain manner of not *being*. Conscious and thinking being ('I', 'me', 'we', etc.) *is*. It *is* in the duplication (self-consciousness, reflection) of this manner of not being, of seeking to *be* (to seek 'its being'), on the basis of a 'being' that is both actual and open: body, historical situation, practical activity. If consciousness in a sense 'is', in another sense it is not, or is no longer. It seeks, and seeks itself.

What does it seek? It does not know in advance, and when it believes that it does know, it is mistaken. It errs (error and errantry), but on a path, that of praxis and that of knowledge. It is the negation of that which it was. Becoming conscious – something philosophers tend to overestimate on account of the philosophical attitude – is not taking hold of a reality but dissolution, loss, distancing in relation to this 'real' that is seemingly taken hold of. Consciousness is thus *finitude*: consciousness of self as limitation, consciousness of what finishes and what 'is' already finished. Consciousness is thus always critical. That is to say, always at a critical point. In a state of crisis. Once assured, rooted, securitized, it is lost. It *is* – and it is no longer! It is substantialized and goes astray. It repeats itself and disappears into misery. But surprises that are too frequent or too rich crush it.

Consciousness, the residue of everything that has been, residue of residues, would thus be in large part reminiscence, recognition, and this right through to the hope for resurgence and novelty. It hesitates between, on the one hand, repetition, redundancy, discourse, re-memorization, reflection, and, on the other, surprising adventure, discovery, poiesis sought intensely if not found. Meditation puts an end to certain useless torments of reflection. It converges with 'being' by rediscovering or creating it. Each 'human being' stands 'between two beings', a situation that is never linear, always double, in relation to itself, to others, to the 'world'. Each consciousness, precisely as what it is not, is a project of being (someone or something). It therefore 'is' essentially transition, passage, from one 'state' to 'another state'. In each of these states, it disappears. It is the project of rediscovering lost being or creating another being. It is thus project of totality, project of the world. Being is thus double, in the sense that it implies consciousness. And consciousness is double, in the sense that it implies being.

That said, philosophers have sought to define this 'being', either before, or during, or after consciousness, itself represented sometimes as act, sometimes as state. Metaphilosophical meditation refuses to define it. It recognizes the double determination of the 'real': the particular, the limit, the determined, the finite; the infinite, the undetermined, the possible, the universal. It refuses therefore to speak being, to posit the general, since and because *being is to be created*. Each being invents or reproduces, according to its finite power, an in-finite being. It moves between the lost being and the being attained, without either one or the other having to be determined in a general way; for they are always concrete. They are situations.

There is not, therefore, a philosophical problematic of being or consciousness. The 'problem' is always resolved in the act. It remains to investigate these acts by distinguishing *act of consciousness* (reflexive) from conscious act (*inventive and creative*). The act of consciousness has a role: inventory, shaping, establishment of the most coherent discourse. The conscious act differs from this. It has two characters: that of being conscious on the basis of a determined and open being, and that of inserting itself into a praxis in order to contribute something new to it. Thus the conscious act 'is' always transitory. It moves towards the other, the object, the act that modifies this object and appropriates it. It 'is' this act. There are, moreover, degrees of conscious act, degrees of freedom, so that the act of consciousness (duplication, reflexivity) 'is' everything that it can be.

We have already emphasized the double determination of *moments* (moments of history, periods, stages; constitutive moments of human being: love, knowledge, play, etc.).

We discover this notion of double determination everywhere. It permits and presupposes a step forward in the dialecticizing of concepts, the grasping of the 'real'. Dialectical thought that was external, reduced to a reflection, a Manichaeism, believed that it grasped entities and the conflictual relations between these entities. Yet no entity, no force, no 'being' is simple. All are double. Purely reflexive determinations, taken literally, are one-sided, because simplified. As we know, linguistics has displayed these dualities (connotations and denotations, signifiers and signified, diachrony and synchrony, non-signifying units and phonemes, signifying units and morphemes, etc.). These dualities do not correspond to dialectical relations; they remain formal. They are conceived as oppositions and dichotomies. However, they draw attention to the non–one-sidedness of everything that can be grasped. The forms themselves are double or dual. All the more so do form and content differ, as well as the contents themselves. This dual or double character cannot be identified with the ambiguity that results in certain cases and situations rather than being the origin of this. We express the generality of this fact by positing *the principle of double determination*. This will display the principle of the meditation we are trying to promote here.

According to the principle of double determination, the in-finite is in the finite, and the finite in the in-finite. Philosophy separates them; the philosopher reflected on them separately. Was this not the essence of metaphysics? The metaphysician stood either at the heart of the infinite (not without pretension) and the finite escaped him; or he stood in the finite, and the infinite seemed to him transcendent or ungraspable. We cannot think being either as finite (it is always and everywhere, here and now, in-finite) or as infinite (it is always determined, posited, situated, thus finite). This is how the legible truth presents itself. This is how the accessible unity, 'man-world' or 'praxis-nature', offers itself.

Freedom can no longer be thought of as either finite or infinite. It 'is' both, and as a consequence always between the two. It is first of all, as thought, negation of what the being was that delivered itself. In the course of this negation, the human being, as free, has his degree of freedom, of concrete negation; he chooses what he will be. There is risk, wager, quest in the choice. There is ambiguity even in a trenchant decision.

In order to act, the human being constructs forms. Between forms and contents, freedom seeks its way and its means. The forms both support it and imprison it. They enclose it in its work. There is thus a perpetual gap, always reborn, between freedom and itself. Hence the malaises, discontents, misunderstandings, disagreements, disarrays – ambiguities – that attach to freedom and the trenchant decision. These situations show that freedom is not foundation, it is founded on a foundation of being from which it separated in order to be (that is, to create, to become what the free being was and yet was not).

Human freedom involves a liberation in relation to needs. It has to detach itself from them, but only by multiplying them, intensifying them. It does not involve any liberation vis-à-vis desire. On the contrary: it restores this, or rather creates it as desire. Desire supersedes the conflict between essential (natural) needs and factitious needs, between determinate (and thus limited) satisfactions and the dissatisfaction that seeks to escape from these limits. It is the same as need, and not the same. It does not kill need; it starts from need, supersedes it and yet returns to the original. In and through love, for example. The nature that it rediscovers is prior to the birth of precise and localized need. Desire is infinite, infinitely vulnerable, yet it bears within it its certainty. Creation and re-creation rising back to the source, the heart of the new totality – is this not Hegel's Rose of the World? Hegel was mistaken in finding this flower in knowledge. Marx, in the wake of Goethe, rediscovered it in total life.

Culture stands at the level of needs (satisfied or unsatisfied). Style, poiesis, stands at the level of desire. Philosophy, for its part, does not find a place to stand. When it placed freedom at the foundation, it freed this from need and desire. When it took account of needs, it imprisoned man in satisfaction. It left aside desire, uncertainty and adventure founded on the relative stability of needs, but also on the lack of satisfaction brought by needs, always partial (need for this or that). Here, at the place and moment that we are, metaphilosophical meditation proves to be the restoration of desire, which encompasses the other inaugural and constitutive acts that we have traversed.

In the very name of philosophy, the philosopher no longer has any more than a philosophically recognized right: that of envisaging the realization of philosophy, that is, simultaneously its globalization and its withering away, its radical critique and its supersession.

The universal that we foreshadow here, in the name of an exploration of its enigmas that starts by denying the mysterious character of its 'secrets', this universal would obey only one law, the *law of the world*. The *law of the world* does not stipulate what the 'world' is or ought to be, but that there are worlds. That is to say, that the finite imitates the infinite according to its capacities, being infinity in finitude, with the result that the two determinations of praxis – mimesis and poiesis – were initially fused together before mimesis separated out, finite in the infinite, subsequently managing to dominate poiesis, infinite in the finite; with the result, finally, that each 'being' sees itself as a 'world', and each finite world must go to the end of its capacity, traverse it and prove itself in praxis through to its term and its end. A finite power only disappears after deploying all its virtualities, after trying to fulfil *everything*, to call *everything* to itself. Each power has to proclaim itself and wish itself and make itself totality: religion, philosophy, economy, state, art, and finally technology. Essence consists in this deployment, and totality in this global process. Each power tends from its side and for its part towards the great Pleonasm through which it supersedes itself because it loses itself in it as sufficiency.

In the course of this deployment, and only after this excessive and illusory proclamation, the negative that this 'world' always already bore within it gnaws at it, dismantles it, destroys it. Only an accomplished totality reveals that it is not totality. Each of the 'worlds', moments or powers, worlds itself or strives to do so. Accomplishment is at the same time defeat. The Earth as planet, stable sphere, wandering, is the figure (more than figure) and symbol (more than symbol) of the law of the world. It bears this and shows it to us.

As Marx saw, in this clarity that we seek to maintain for ourselves, investigation bears on 'realities' and virtualities that are in themselves neither economic, nor sociological, nor psychological, nor political, nor historical in a narrow and partial sense, nor philosophical. They are 'that' and yet 'something other'. That are sustained and encompassed by the creative capacity, inexhaustible presence of the infinite at the heart of the finite, of its life and its death. Metaphilosophical investigation bears on this poietic power.

The 'law of the world' (of what becomes worldly and worldwide [*mondain et mondial*]) can be uttered differently. We no longer have to choose between the determinations and propositions that philosophy distinguished, between which the philosopher chose for the needs of his reason. In a sense, up to a certain point, *all is total* or becomes so, or seeks to become so: every human fact (physical, biological, economic, sociological, etc.) and every human work (philosophy, religion, mathematics, the state, art, etc.).

In a sense, too, *nothing is total*. Nothing exhausts the totality. By placing itself within a particular entity (state, philosophy, mathematics, etc.), a residue is displayed, which becomes essential. Every fact, every work, presents gaps and voids in relation to the virtual Totality that never offers itself except fragmentarily: in relation to the infinite that never gives itself except in the finite, the contradictory and determined contradictions.

It is scarcely paradoxical to reprise here, on the planetary scale, apropos entities, systems and powers that substantialize (autonomize and automatize) themselves, and apropos those that reject automatism, the illustrious words of Anaximander, with which philosophy began:

> Whence things have their birth, thence they have their loss, according to necessity;

> For they give to each other justice and recompense for their injustice, according to the law of the world [*loi du monde*].[12]

Thus philosophy ends with the words that inaugurated it.

Strasbourg, August 1963 to November 1964

---

12 EN: We have translated Lefebvre's translation, which fits with his overall argument, rather than follow an existing English translation. For comparison, see Patricia Curd, *A Presocratics Reader: Selected Fragments and Testimonia*, Cambridge, MA : Hackett Publishing, 1996, p. 12.

Postface: Marxism and Poetry
Georges Labica

'Poetry must have practical truth as its aim'
Paul Eluard

Henri Lefebvre's *Métaphilosophie* has had an unusual fate. Written in Strasbourg in 1963–4, it was published by Editions de Minuit in 1965. Its appearance went almost unnoticed, and until now it has not been reprinted. Why such a silence, followed by such oblivion? Was the title to blame? Is metaphilosophy any more obscure than metaphysics or metalanguage (a term quite commonplace at that time), or again meta-psychology, which Freud risked at the end of the nineteenth century; metaethics (Lucien Lévy-Brühl); metamathematics; or metalogic? In the English-speaking world, the term 'metaphilosophy' has been used since 1940. In France, Lefebvre's word and his project were taken up by Kostas Axelos, despite other people's preference for 'post-philosophy', and a journal with the title *Metaphilosophy* has been published in the United States since 1970. Subtending all these approaches is the notion of an *after*-philosophy, as *meta*-discourse and *meta*-theory. I should add that many bibliographies fail to mention this book, and no scholar did justice to it until a recent thesis by a Korean academic.[1] And what justice, as M Dae-Myung No devoted no less than 900 pages to 'La philosophie politique d'Henri Lefebvre ou la politique de la métaphilosophie', with a confident handling of the material, near exhaustive knowledge and pertinent judgement that might well confound indigenous researchers.

In 1965, Henri Lefebvre (born 1901) had already published some

---

1   Dae-Myung No, 'La philosophie politique d'Henri Lefebvre ou la politique de la métaphilosophie', University of Paris III: Sorbonne Nouvelle, June 1997, unpublished.

twenty books, including *La somme et le reste* and the first two volumes of *Critique of Everyday Life*. In the field of Marxist thought, and well beyond it, he held an exceptional place, not confined to that of an initiator (*Le marxisme*, published in 1948, was and would remain the best-selling title in the PUF 'Que sais-je?' collection). The reason for this lack of interest, or lack of attention, I believe must be sought elsewhere, precisely in the conjuncture of the time. In 1965, *Metaphilosophy* found itself wedged, literally short-circuited, by the simultaneous publication of Althusser's two works, *For Marx* and the collective volumes of *Reading Capital*.[2]

The historical moment, which we will not dwell on here, saw the sudden transition from a humanist Marxism, challenging, iconoclastic and utopian, to a Marxism that proclaimed its scientific character and recited certainties. This transition was a double paradox, as it replaced one figure of Marx by another. The philosopher still inscribed in his time (that would be the sense of Lefebvre's metaphilosophy, referring both to his superseded predecessor, Hegel, and to the latter's perverse successor, Heidegger) made way for the scientist sure of his epistemological breaks and master of his concepts. But perhaps these are simply two sides of the same coin, in a two-way swing that history has accustomed us to, or rather thanks to which a certain history, that of Marxism, can obtain legibility: either Feuerbach or Hegel, materialism or dialectics, structures or human beings, science or philosophy, and so on.

But perhaps things are not so cut and dried. Let each protagonist of the time (some are still around!) reflect and question his own sedimentations. On the other hand, a change of this kind, beneath the appearance of restoring the combativeness and novelty of Marx's thought, could not afford to drape a new cloak over all these 'omissions' – individual, subject, desire ('tragic', Lefebvre would say) – which 'revolutionary romanticism'[3] or historicism (Gramsci) had, despite

---

2 EN: A complete translation of this work has recently been published by Verso; until now only some of the essays contained therein were available in English. Louis Althusser, Etienne Balibar, Roger Establet, Pierre Macherey, and Jacques Rancière, *Reading Capital: The Complete Edition*, London: Verso, 2016.

3 This is precisely what Lefebvre appeals to in *Metaphilosophy*: 'And so we support the thesis of a new romanticism with a revolutionary tendency, or rather one fundamentally revolutionary', p. 301. In 1957 Lefebvre wrote an article titled 'Vers la romantisme révolutionnaire' for the journal *Le Cercle ouvert* (1958), in collaboration

their weaknesses, the merit of pointing out. A similar condemnation of Stalinist dogmatism, on the part of both Lefebvre and Althusser, did not lead to the restless research of the former, with the risks of its lack of assurance, but rather to the comfortable intellectual sovereignty of the latter. What we should resolve to call a certain national spirit, more inclined, in the tradition of the eighteenth century, towards scientism than utopianism,[4] is certainly contestable here. It is true that, as things turned out, the PCF's opportunist jumble sale and inadequacies, prey to its notorious 'backwardness', were scarcely an incitement to adventures immediately perceived as regressions to the pre-Marx – idealist, anthropological or empiricist. Vis-à-vis the Althusserian flint, Lefebvre appeared only too friable, to the point of being effaced in favour of someone like Roger Garaudy, whom the performance of the famous central committee meeting at Argenteuil placed in the role of an alter ego for Althusser in responding to Lefebvre.[5]

This false reciprocity, which passed unnoticed at the time, sealed the eclipse of Lefebvre and the impasse placed on his *Metaphilosophy*. For the conjuncture would now open a new paradox, with the advent of May 1968: while the majority of its actors were inspired by revolutionary romanticism, those who challenged the PCF from within, petty-bourgeois, intellectuals and academics, rallied to the Althusserian positions. The 'revolution', which in principle could legitimately make use of two supporting currents, was going to sacrifice one. Or at least, obscure it, if only for the time being, since

---

with Guterman and Tzara; I owe this information to Alberto Suarez, author of an excellent dissertation entitled *Entre romantisme et modernité: Une philosophie en proie au possible (Henri Lefebvre, 1957–1978)*, University of Paris X, Nanterre, 1992. [EN: Lefebvre's essay was reissued as a book by Editions Lignes in 2011. The closest discussion of these themes in English translation is in the longest prelude of *Introduction to Modernity* – 'Towards a New Romanticism'. London: Verso, 1995.]

4   We may think of the French translation of Engels's booklet *Socialism Utopian and Scientific*, which offered a dualist interpretation to intellectuals already little inclined to dialectics – in Engels's own judgement. Lefebvre was aware of this, writing: 'What is quite clear is that eighteenth-century materialism, devoid of dialectic, makes a return here' (p. 166).

5   This session was held in early 1966, and caused a great deal of ink to be spilled: the goal was to arbitrate between contradictory positions on the question of humanism in Marx. [EN: See, among others, Garaudy's *Marxisme du XXe siècle*, Paris and Geneva: La Palatine, 1966; *Marxism in the Twentieth Century*, translated by René Hague, New York: Charles Scribner's Sons, 1970.]

everything leads us to think that today the scales are swinging back in favour of Lefebvre.

Before I go on to argue this, a further word on the genuinely emblematic character of the two men, Lefebvre and Althusser, who dominated French Marxism and were the eponyms of the two currents, always disconnected, even though (*nota bene!*) still today people say Althusserianism and not Lefebvrisme. It is hard to imagine two more different temperaments: on the one hand, Lefebvre the nomad, the adventurer, the beater of paths – investigating space, time, human relations, categories and concepts; on the other, the sedentary Althusser, a man of the study, who perceived the world through the keyhole of his office at the École normale supérieure, the controller or customs official. The one listens, changes, betrays, a disloyal investigator of the new; the other decrees, repeats and fixes the Tables of the Law, in the rigorous concern for doctrinal purity. Lefebvre took Althusser into account, read him, broke lances against structuralism, accepted the competition: Althusser, already in the preface to *For Marx*, committed the unbelievable injustice of ignoring Lefebvre, when he deplored the absence of Marxist theorists in France and formed the project, a quite personal one, of 'returning a little consistency to Marxist philosophy'. Althusser, the latecomer to theoretical struggles (twenty years after Lefebvre), offered himself the luxury of contempt towards his elder contemporary, something that some of his disciples would be sorry for later on. I am caricaturing a bit, of course, having loved and followed both of them.

THE METAPHILOSOPHICAL DESIGN

Lefebvre was, along with his friend and enemy Sartre, the last encyclo-paedist – interested in everything, and stimulated by everything, in the role, however, of contrabandist. He was, as he said himself – though in neutral terms, not explicitly – a 'man of frontiers':

> It is quite true that in the conditions of the modern world only the man aside, the marginal, the peripheral, the anomic, the one excluded from the horde ([Georges] Gurvitch) has a creative capacity . . . The

man of frontiers tolerates a tension that would kill others: he is both within and without, included and excluded . . . following paths that are surprising at first, then become routes and are eventually taken as self-evident. He travels along the lines of the watershed and chooses the way that points to the horizon. He may happen to pass by promised lands, but he does not enter. This is his test. He always heads for new lands, towards the horizon of horizons, from moment to moment, until he perceives the distant outlines of an unexplored continent. His passion is discovery. He can only proceed by going from discovery to discovery, knowing that in order to advance, he has to master a need to know that whispers to him to stop here and there, to excavate.[6]

But let this be understood: thought arises at the frontier where power and the will to power stop.[7]

Philosophy brings new concepts into Marx's doctrine . . . such as that of everyday life, a gain through which a frontier is founded, an edge, making it into a *metaphilosophy*.[8]

Here we have it. *Metaphilosophy* is an important book. Very important, Lefebvre himself emphasized, if my memory of our conversations on this subject is not deceptive. His most important? Possibly. In any case, a watershed book in his work, if we look at what came before and after. Not the most systematic, as Lefebvre had no system and was not even tempted in this direction, but certainly one of his most accomplished, perhaps the most accomplished, at all events the most synthetic and best organized. It gave form to what had come before, and paved the way for his great undertaking, the *Critique of Everyday Life*, the third volume of which, we note, was subtitled 'Towards a

---

6   Henri Lefebvre, *La présence et l'absence*, Paris: Casterman, 1980, p. 202. [EN: This book has not been translated into English, and nor have the majority of his more philosophical texts referenced by Labica. Exceptions are noted below.]

7   Henri Lefebvre, *Qu'est-ce que penser?*, Paris: Publisud, 1985, p. 49.

8   Ibid., p. 135.

metaphilosophy of daily life'.[9] Assuredly a centre of Lefebvre's work, but in his own style, between negligence and reference. The object of *Metaphilosophy* is clear enough to define. It is a question of taking seriously the last of Marx's *Theses on Feuerbach*: 'The philosophers have only interpreted the world, in various ways; the point is to change it'.[10] 'The revolutionary project', Lefebvre writes, 'has rebounded. It has taken back its full character: to change the world and life. We are no longer in philosophy, but beyond it'.[11] The task was to accomplish, in its full scope, the 'slogan' of André Breton that linked Marx together with Rimbaud.[12] To supersede philosophy. That is what 'meta' is: the after, the beyond, Marx's *verändern* and Rimbaud's *changer*. Lefebvre's *Qu'est-ce que penser?*, twenty years after *Metaphilosophy*, returns at many points to this 'little word' – 'meta' – to be found everywhere that 'something' pulled along in becoming . . . goes   beyond   itself: 'meta-phor,   meta-physica, meta-morphosis'.[13] Its extension is even considerable:

> '*Meta*'? The human being always goes *beyond* himself, beyond what
> is acquired, beyond consciousness and what escapes consciousness.
> Language only proceeds by *meta-phor*. Supersede? Overcome? It is a
> chance to attempt, an act, whether successful or not, but *necessity*
> consists in a transition or transgression of the 'real' towards some-
> thing other, towards a possible than may turn out to be impossible.[14]

This 'transition from philosophy to metaphilosophy', which Lefebvre

---

9   EN: Henri Lefebvre, *Critique of Everyday Life*. vol 3: *From Modernity to Modernism (Towards a Metaphilosophy of Daily Life)*, London: Verso, 2008.

10   Cf. Georges Labica, *Les thèses sur Feuerbach*, Paris: PUF, 1987.

11   See this volume, p. 63. All further references to the present book are given here in parentheses in the text.

12   Cf. André Breton and Paul Eluard, *Dictionnaire abrégé du surréalisme* (1938), under 'Marx (Karl), 1818–1883': 'Transform the world, said Marx; change life, said Rimbaud: for us these two watchwords are simply one': Paul Eluard, *Oeuvres complètes*, vol. 1, Paris: Gallimard, 1968, p. 756. Lefebvre, for his part, wrote: 'Should not the old watchwords, shining at the threshold of a thought that sought to be no longer speculative and vainly abstract – transform the world instead of interpreting it, Rimbaud's injunction to *change life* – take on a new meaning, more precise and more broad?' (p. 109). The expression of 'watchword' to describe the eleventh thesis on Feuerbach also occurs in Ernst Bloch, *The Principle of Hope*, Boston: MIT, 1995.

13   Lefebvre, *Qu'est-ce que penser?*, p. 96.

14   Ibid., p. 131; cf. also pp. 64 and 97.

tells us is very long-standing in his work, since it goes back to an article published in the journal *Philosophies*, in March 1925,[15] presupposes,
first of all, a critique of philosophy. This critique Lefebvre would arti-
culate, in the wake of *Metaphilosophy*, on the basis of three categories
that he saw as fundamental: praxis, poiesis and mimesis. The first is
taken directly from Marx, denoting the relations between human
beings and social activity, and cannot be separated from the historical, which includes the possible. The second relates to the appropriation
of nature around the human being and within him. Yet it is distinct
from and even opposed to technology, being the creator of works. Its
scope is that of 'total man', freed from the division of labour. The third,
which cannot be reduced to mere imitation, extends to all activity
that takes place according to a form and adding to this form. It is
'inherent in educability' and 'makes possible exemplarity, filiation
and affiliation' (p. 10). If it cannot avoid either formalism or conformism, it remains nonetheless a mixture or mediation between praxis,
representing one level of this, and poiesis, which it refers to. Philosophy
is 'a particular case of mimesis' (p. 272, already 67–8). Logological,
egological, tending towards the schizoid (p. 259), philosophy can take
its place among the 'pleonasms', those autonomized, 'automatic' forms
of mimesis (pp. 232–3). From then on, it turns its back on praxis,
which backs up its critique, and must definitively renounce an accession to poiesis.

In order for a 'power' in the Lefebvrian sense, such as religion, politics, technology, mathematics or philosophy, to arrive at the stage of
autonomization is the worst of outcomes; it amounts to forbidding
itself any creativity and substituting the product for the work. Analysis
of a process of this kind explains how Marxism was able to degrade
into its opposite, an orthodoxy that set up the economic 'as an autonomous power'.[16] Certainly Marx was careful to avoid this, emphasizing
that the economic was only 'determinant', but at places he left the door
open, and Engels still more so, for successors less careful of nuances
and desirous to dispose of a system.

---

15   Ibid., p. 146.
16   Lefebvre, *La présence et l'absence*, p. 196.

THE CRITIQUE OF PHILOSOPHY

The summit of autonomized power is the state. Marx demonstrated this, referring in his early writings to 'foreign powers' after the model of Feuerbach dismantling the hypostases of religion. Lefebvre would constantly return to this theme and deepen it – first of all, in the critique of philosophy, as philosophy is partly bound up with the state.[17] Between state and philosophy there is a historical connection. The state 'encompasses and perfects all partial systems, including philosophy' (p. 34). The collapse of the Hegelian system expressed the collapse of philosophy as theoretical system, and the collapse of the state as practical system (p. 18). Two hypotheses can be envisaged. If the proletariat breaks the state it establishes its dictatorship, which can only be provisional and heralds the withering away of the state, coinciding with the realization of philosophy, as 'there are concrete, simultaneous realizations of the formal aims of philosophy (freedom, truth, good, etc.) and of the formal representations of the modern political state: liberty, equality, fraternity, justice, etc.' (p. 19). If things do not happen in this way, if Marx's prognosis is not correct, then the state maintains itself and philosophy along with it, with its existing characteristics in aggravated form, as it is then in the service of the state, politics and the bureaucracy:

> Only a connection of philosophy with the state and the bureaucracy can assure it a certain effectiveness, and public honours for the philosopher. (p. 97)

In this way we reach the heart of the critique of Stalinism (p. 97). The attack on philosophy uncovers, on the one hand, as one path among others, but certainly a privileged one, the concept that governs the entire critique, that of *alienation*, to which Lefebvre remained indefeasibly attached from one end of his work and life to the end. *Metaphilosophy* is, in parts, the culmination of this, though Lefebvre still emphasizes its limits: 'immoderate use' of the concept leads to a

---

17 'The same holds for philosophy as for the state, which it has been in a relation of mutual support with ever since Hegel': *Qu'est-ce que penser?*, p. 19, also p. 130.

'mystical vision' (p. 58), 'abundant and fairly inoffensive literature' (p. 59), ignored by Heidegger (p. 127), at the centre of philosophy and ideology (p. 180), formal expression of the theory of the Idea (p. 275), *Metaphilosophy* exhibits the concept's positivity:

> Philosophers by definition decided against non-philosophical man and the world, viewing these as alienated. By showing that there is also a philosophical alienation, Marx united under the same concept philosophical man and non-philosophical man; he opened the way to the superseding of philosophy. (p. 296)

The bottom of the matter is that philosophy was unable to assimilate alienation (p. 312):

> The theory of alienation signifies that philosophy sought to say what man is and what he can become. It also signifies what philosophy did not manage to say, still less do. (p. 313)

And yet, which is the lesson of Marx: 'the path of alienation is also that of dis-alienation'.[18]

It is possible to distinguish in *Metaphilosophy* (and elsewhere) a double critique of philosophy. The first critique bears on classical or traditional philosophy, in fact all philosophy, inasmuch as 'meta-philosophical thought' (p. 53) intends to grasp it in its essence, itself enlightened by the 'crisis' that marks its 'dissolution' (p. 45). In this way, Lefebvre presents eleven 'aporias or antinomies' (p. 47ff.) that are characteristic of philosophical reflection, whether speculative or supposedly critical. The charge against contemporary philosophy is still more bitter, in that this 'continuing' philosophy represents an aggravated situation and 'finds itself either enslaved or floating, instrumental or inconsistent', incapable of waging theoretical battles (p. 21). The philosopher may well cling to science or art, or get bogged down in his own history, but he 'has lost all function, except when he becomes promoter of

---

18   Ibid., p. 103.

official ideology and *raison d'état*' (p. 98). Hence the many rebellions that philosophy arouses against itself.

> No one needs philosophy or the philosopher any more . . . He does not really watch. If he awaits, it is with the same waiting, the same hope or the same despair as other people, those of the everyday. (pp. 99–100)

Lefebvre is not generous! Besides structuralism, his bête noire, which 'ostensibly prefers the prosthetic limb to the living limb' (p. 173),[19] and cyberneticians of all feathers, who provide the most perfect model of pleonasm (p. 235),[20] he would later attack still more mordantly his most visible contemporaries – Sartre, Foucault, Lacan and Freudianism, Lévi-Strauss – in the 'Intermezzo' to *Qu'est-ce que penser?*[21] He would return to the charge in *De l'état*, to fustigate a certain Left Bank intelligentsia and its 'avant-gardisme':

> Philosophers, in a dying philosophy, symptomize the decrepitude of existing society; they contribute a bit to this themselves, let us say in their honour, while believing themselves to be renewing it.[22]

RESIDUES

What is philosophy guilty of, and philosophers in particular? Of leaving *residues*. The *residue* is certainly the newest and most original concept of *Metaphilosophy*.

---

19   See also *Une pensée devenue monde*, Paris: Fayard, 1980, p. 229 ff. The revolutionary conjunctural counts as much as the structural that seeks to dispense with history and dialectics, hence with contradictions. Lefebvre had himself dialectically associated history and structure, in defining his 'regressive–progressive method'; cf. *La vallée de Campan: Étude de sociologie rurale*, Paris: PUF, 1963.

20   See also p. 67 and the attacks on the *cybernanthrope*, a caricature of total man (p. 9).

21   See p. 118 ff. We may think of Nizan, who was Lefebvre's friend, and his *Les chiens de garde*, but here the charge is not aimed at the ideologists of the dominant class as such. Lefebvre is making a critical allusion to Léon Brunschvicg, a real Aunt Sally for Nizan (see p. 102).

22   Henri Lefebvre, *De l'état*, vol. 2, Paris: UGE 10/18, 1976, p. 375.

It is possible that Lefebvre borrowed this from John Stuart Mill, whose 'method of residues'[23] he appreciated, but he would confer on this a far more considerable extension. The *residue* is the consequence of the process of autonomization. It seeks to express precisely what is expelled: the singular and freedom expelled by the state, desire and subjectivity by cybernetics, drama by mathematics, speech by language, 'the non-philosophical (the everyday, the ludic)' by philosophy, and so forth (p. 12). It is precisely to metaphilosophy that the task falls of conceiving these residues, which are at least as 'precious' as that in whose name they are rejected by the closed worlds of powers that have become autonomous. The everyday is 'precious' (p. 56), insistently raising the question: 'Is the "residue" not what is most precious?' (p. 109). Did not Marx himself exclude *homo ridens* and *homo ludens*, focusing exclusively on *homo faber* and *homo sapiens* (p. 129)?

'Infinitely precious', too, are history and historicity, which both structuralism (p. 146) and globalized [*mondialisé*] technology (p. 178) cast aside.[24] 'Precious' again is complexity, praxis, dialectic, the tragic, emotion and passion, the individual, all treated as negligible quantities (p. 176). And is not nature itself residual, when the human and the automatic are associated to produce the cybernanthrope (p. 181)?[25] Under the reign of the understanding,[26] which only knows stabilities, residues multiply. Mimesis, which 'makes the world into spectacle',[27]

---

23 This represents, along with concordance, difference and concomitant variations, one of the four rules of the inductive method, described by Mill as follows: 'Subduct from any phenomenon such part as is known by previous inductions to be the effect of certain antecedents, and the residue of the phenomenon is the effect of the remaining antecedents': John Stuart Mill, *A System of Logic*, chapter 8, 'Fourth canon'. *Metaphilosophy* explicitly alludes to Mill.

24 Listen to the prophet Lefebvre against today's Fukuyamas: 'The *mondialisation* of technology and the technocratic conception presupposes a reduction and even a liquidation of the historic . . . We shall have no future in the historical sense, no temporality in the accustomed sense' (p. 178).

25 Cf. Henri Lefebvre, *Vers le cybernanthrope*, Paris: Gallimard, 1971.

26 The object of repeated attacks in *Metaphilosophy*; cf. pp. 25 (Hegel), 278, 187 (against technical rationality and cybernetics; against culturalism and structuralism, etc.).

27 This was the thesis of Guy Debord, a follower of Lefebvre in the Situationist movement. His book contains several themes present in *Metaphilosophy*, in particular that of autonomization and split. Cf. Guy Debord, *The Society of the Spectacle*, London: Rebel Press, 2004.

tends to eliminate the individual, keeping only a personage without reality (p. 218). Why, one may ask, this leitmotiv, this red thread that pervades Lefebvre's whole work? Because the residues, these rejects of systems and specializations, are truly irreducible. They are 'the irreducibles' (p. 11). The residue resists (p. 189). It manifests itself, becomes essential (p. 323). The critique of philosophy means nothing more than this. It consists in wagering 'on the ensemble of these residues, the unease and discontent irreducible through and beneath fragmentary satisfactions: everyday life, youth, deviance, underdevelopment, and so on.' (p. 300). This is 'the method of residues', which not only seeks to 'detect' them and 'reveal the precious essence', but also 'to unite them, organize their revolts and totalize them' (p. 301). 'Gathering the residues is a revolutionary thought', neither 'utopian' nor 'prospective'. It confers its 'style' on metaphilosophical reflection, whose 'unclassifiable' character comes from the fact that it 'takes the *unnameable* as its point of departure, in other words, the ensemble of residues' (p. 303).

As we shall see, this 'method' has its successors, but it is possible to mention, at its origin, the figure of Feuerbach, to whom Lefebvre refers only rarely. In fact, when he analyses the relations between philosophy and anthropology (chapter 7), and particularly when he asks, 'Is not what remains of philosophy, in the direction of its superseding, an *anthropology*?' (p. 291), he finds himself very close to the old master, who asserted: 'Truth is uniquely *anthropology*, uniquely the point of view of sensuousness, intuition, as only this point of view gives me totality and *individuality*.'[28]

Attention directed at these *residues* cannot be without radical questionings, and it is significant that these appeal to the same

---

28 Cf. 'Contre le dualism du corps et de l'âme', in Ludwig Feuerbach, *Pensées sur la mort et sur l'immortalité*, Paris: Pocket, 1997, p. 168. [EN: *Thoughts on Death and Immortality: From the Papers of a Thinker*, translated by James A. Massey, Berkeley: University of California Press, 1980, p. 128.] Claire Mercier, who translated and presented these texts, comments quite correctly, in Lefebvrian style: 'The ordinary discourse of philosophy does not reconcile man with himself, but aggravates the split, maintains and reinforces alienation . . . Philosophy can no longer continue to be what it is, it must become joke, poetry, anthropology that is to say, a practice of dis-illusion, dis-solution of transcendences, re-sensibilization of individuals without which no activity that is genuinely transformation (*Abänderung*) and not metamorphosis (*Verwandlung*) can take place' (p. 63).

constellations of concepts: sensuousness, individuality, totality, alienation, split, poetry, and so forth.

THE SUPERSEDING OF PHILOSOPHY

In this way, we already find ourselves in the superseding of philosophy, or rather in superseded philosophy. It is necessary, then, to return to it. Starting, as did Lefebvre, with the philosopher who pointed towards superseding, but did so only to abandon it, in other words Hegel, admired and detested for this (p. 21 ff.). The famous Hegelian term 'aufheben', 'one of the most important concepts in philosophy', precisely indicates and reveals the nub of the problem, and of all subsequent difficulties, given that it means at the same time abolish and raise, suppress and realize. 'Hegel inaugurates the critique of philosophy; he proclaims its end and supersession by denouncing the essence of philosophical discourse. At the same time as he prepares the succession (Marx), he constructs the perfect system of the understanding' – a system which we know is responsible for all ills, that is, for the residues.

Superseding, *aufheben*, or the eleventh thesis on Feuerbach, signifies for Lefebvre neither the pure and simple abolition of philosophy nor the continuation of traditional thought, even if renewed. It opens the way to a movement, a complex becoming, which no specification of classical philosophy can define. To the 'apogee of philosophy' that Hegel reaches (p. 17), to the desire to have every residue absorbed by logos-language (p. 31), to total speculative alienation (p. 23 ff.), we have to oppose Marx's project that 'the *becoming-philosophy of the world* gives way to the *becoming-world of philosophy*, revolutionary realization and superseding of philosophy as such' (p. 17). The union of philosophy with the praxis of the proletariat would make possible the provisional form of dictatorship of the proletariat, which represents the condition for the state to wither away – this being identical, as we know, to the withering away of philosophy and, well beyond this, of all autonomized 'powers'.[29] Paradoxically, Stalinism confirmed this

---

29   Cf. p. 18, cited above. This is a recurrent theme with Lefebvre, see also p. 83:

necessity in concrete fashion: 'It has contributed to the death of philosophy and the metamorphosis of philosophy' (p. 97). Praxis, which Marx took over from Hegel, shows the way of historicity, which refers neither to sociology, nor to psychology, nor to philosophy: the way of superseding, which would enable 'man to dominate his own works, to fully appropriate these works that are both nature in him and his own nature' (p. 38), in other words, to arrive at poiesis. Or more exactly, as this is Lefebvre's position, to rediscover poiesis and return to it, after it was lost and forgotten.

There was a time, in fact, when philosophical speech and poetic speech were not distinguished: they were both bound up with praxis, itself dominated by poiesis. 'The poet-philosopher knew the laws of the city. He could decide on them. He was political' (p. 63). The split, which Lefebvre would describe in *La présence et l'absence* as an 'immense silent catastrophe',[30] generated the mimesis that retains something of the earlier stage, at the very moment when philosophy separates out – 'fortunate ambiguity, the chance of a misunderstanding'.[31] In this we can read the possibility of superseding, of a 'new alliance' reunifying word and speech, concept and imagination, giving back meaning to the metaphors of the philosophers (Descartes, Spinoza, Leibniz, Kant) even down to the 'rose' of the 'powerful and ponderous Hegel'. The time in question was that of the presocratics 'who reflected before the great split between poetry and philosophy, between creating and making', first among these Heraclitus, but also Democritus and Epicurus (pp. 124, 150 ff.). The whole history of philosophy can be appreciated on the basis of this criterion of presentiment or intuition of the split, thus of the superseding.[32]

'A condition *sine qua non* is that the theory of the withering away of the state again returns to the agenda. If politics remains the key to the situation, this theory remains the key to Marxist political thought', and *La présence et l'absence*: 'To realize philosophy and supersede it go together; in the same way as do realization of the working class as self-determining political subject in full consciousness and its superseding, by making an end to wage-labour and labour in general' (p. 94).

30   Lefebvre, *La présence et l'absence*, p. 193, and the whole development in the adjacent pages.

31   Ibid.

32   Lefebvre gives a deliberately incomplete sketch, but a very suggestive one, of this history of philosophy on p. 273–96.

We find here the philosopher-poets of ancient Greece, but also Fourier, from whom Marx started out (p. 103). Nietzsche, above all, is present here, as he understood that man had to traverse the death of God/the Father in order to put an end to a divine cut off from praxis (p. 92). His approach to philosophy has to be taken up and extended to the economic and its history, politics and its state, and art, also separated out (ibid.). Nietzsche has the merit of having bad-mouthed Socrates' *homo philosophicus* and praised his predecessors (p. 123).[33] It is he who is to be credited with 'the idea of a new alliance between poetry and philosophy' (p. 125). Among his contemporaries, Lefebvre accords particular interest to Sartre, distressed at seeing in him an exemplary form of failure (p. 82). Despite 'striking intuitions' and 'the presence of the future and the possible in the project', this 'excellent philosopher', blocked by his Cartesian starting point and his reference to Husserlian consciousness (pp. 71–2), maintains the gap between lived experience and history – this lived experience, 'nausea', 'bad faith' being simply another name for the everyday. And Sartre leaves too many residues: the absence of history in *Being and Nothingness*, but also of nature (p. 79).

To Sartre, we should contrast Heidegger,[34] even if he too does not go far enough in the critique of philosophy, because he reflects on concrete *physis* and poetry, equally ignored by Sartre; because he does not confine himself to 'making', like Sartre, but takes into account production and creation (p. 79), Heidegger praises the thing (*das Ding*), not the object or the product; he rehabilitates it in the face of science and technology which have destroyed it. The thing is the 'work of the creative activity' that founds a praxis (p. 127). After the Marx of the *1844 Manuscripts*, after Nietzsche, Heidegger re-establishes the sensuous or the practico-sensuous in its richness. Questioning of being and physis tends towards

---

33   Cf. *La présence et l'absence*, where Lefebvre explains that Nietzsche's *Überwindung* is not the same as Marx's *Aufheben* (p. 95).

34   Today's readers may find surprising the rapid absolution that Lefebvre gives to Heidegger for what he terms 'tendencies towards German nationalism'. Yet to understand how he can close the debate in a couple of lines, declaring that 'the philosophico-political appreciation is out of date', it is necessary to remember the context of the time, in which militants were trained in a systematic class suspicion, the detection of traitors, and trials (Lefebvre himself did not escape this, neither in the role of accuser nor in that of victim).

the superseding of philosophy, and yet Heidegger halts before the meta-morphosis of the everyday, of *Alltäglichkeit* (p. 133). Attentive to 'drama', he missed mathematics and number, which attain the qualitative; he disdains the human sciences, and his *Dasein* does not even have a sex (p. 138 ff.). Finally, however, 'he alone saw the essential thing: technol-ogy', which makes for a shift of all problems and above which Heidegger has to be acknowledged as having placed poetry (p. 135). The critique of philosophy then receives support from both phases of the split. There exists a *before*, when 'play, knowledge, (religious) cosmology, poetry and political activity were not separated', that was the time of the Festival (pp. 204–5); and an *after* that sees the reign of mimesis ('that of the understanding, of discourse and analytic rationality') (p. 218), the philosopher contemplating in it his broken mirror (p. 278).

THE WATCHERS, THE CITY

The 'great separation' did preserve, all the same, some watchers charged with indicating the way to metaphilosophy, by preserving, having rediscovered it, the message from the beginnings of philo-sophical thought. Does this *Aufhebung* express, in Lefebvre, nostalgia for a golden age? Does it relate to an origin myth? At all events, it possesses letters of nobility that it simply inherits: Heidegger, to be sure, and his 'admirable studies on logos, aletheia, physis, etc. Which stimulates us to study in the same fashion praxis, techne, mimesis, poiesis, etc.' (p. 69). Nietzsche and his watchword of a return to the Greeks; Hegel, before them, and his fascination with Heraclitus; and we should not forget Marx, who devoted his doctoral thesis to Democritus and Epicurus, as well as Engels, who waxed eloquent on the 'marvellous dialecticians' that the Greeks were. Paul Nizan, among other examples, from the time when he and Lefebvre were still linked by a tie of friendship and engaged in similar theoretical struggles, and who wrote a book-length manifesto on *Les matérialistes de l'antiq-uité*.[35] An attitude such as this, nostalgia reduced both to its simplest

---

35   EN: Paul Nizan, *Les matérialistes de l'antiquité : Démocrite, Epicure, Lucrèce*, Paris: François Maspero, 1965.

and strongest expression, seems to me to signal the basic concern (wish, desire) for Lefebvre that philosophy should be (or again become) a work, that it should be productive, creative, in a word, open to all proliferations of life. 'The work does not describe, does not imitate. It metamorphoses.'[36] The superseding of philosophy means nothing other than this: 'The superseding of philosophy, that is to say, philosophy as a work' (p. 95).

In the same way that, with negative hindsight, the state was bound up with philosophy, so the latter, in positive projection, that is, once it is superseded, encounters its most explicit metaphor in the city. It is no accident that Lefebvre should take the city as figure in his critique of Sartre. For Sartre, the city has nothing to do with creative work, it is simply the inert (p. 81). But the city is 'the supreme work, the work of works'.[37] Like philosophy, the city has known its period of non-separation: 'When society and state coincided with the city, this was the pre-eminent work of praxis, the most perfect thing' (p. 111). Like philosophy, the city underwent a split, with a few vigilant watchers within: Baudelaire, whose 'most vibrant poems' (p. 116) express this, Apollinaire, Cendrars, the Aragon of *Le paysan de Paris* (p. 119), among others. And like philosophy again, the city perceives its own end: 'It is perhaps in the process of disappearing ... the urban phenomenon, by developing, becomes disconnected.' Now the idea of its end, as again for philosophy, 'seems far more productive and creative than that of its continuation' (p. 113). Lefebvre would certainly not have disapproved of Italo Calvino, who seems to echo him in describing his book *Invisible Cities*: 'I think I have written something like a last love poem to cities, at a time when it is becoming increasingly difficult to live there.'[38]

---

36 Lefebvre, *Qu'est-ce que penser?*, p. 42.

37 Lefebvre, *La présence et l'absence*, p. 211.

38 EN: The remark does not appear in the English translation: Italo Calvino, *Invisible Cities*, translated by William Weaver, San Diego: Harcourt Brace & Company, 1974. It was made in 1983 at Columbia University, and is cited in Letizia Modena, *Italo Calvino's Architecture of Lightness: The Utopian Imagination in an Age of Urban Crisis*, London: Routledge, 2011, p. 57.

POIESIS

It is time now to come to the word that, as we saw, focuses the entire problematic of *Metaphilosophy*: that of *poetry*. The association of poet and philosopher, already met with, sums up Lefebvre's ideal and gives a name to the object of his critical effort.

To the 'prose of the world', alienated thought, it is absolutely necessary to oppose 'the Rose of the World',[39] poiesis. From the presocratics to Octavio Paz,[40] the figure of the poet-philosopher remains the model. Lefebvre himself sought to conform to this, mingling strictly theoretical analyses with poetry.[41] For poetry is not distinguished from truth. *Metaphilosophy* repeats this proposition at several points, with a certain stubbornness. 'Originally and deeply, poetry is truth and truth poetry' (p. 135). The *before* of the split speaks for its *after*, which must be brought into being. 'Residue among residues . . . metaphilosophical poiesis would thus be both poetry and truth. This truth would no longer have anything in common with that of philosophy' (p. 305). Certainly, Lefebvre is not unaware that he borrows this maxim from a man who remained his friend throughout his life, Paul Eluard: 'The aim of poetry being, across time, practical truth (Eluard)' (p. 241); and we know that the phrase 'poetry must have practical truth as its aim' is to be found in several of Eluard's collections.[42] One rediscovered poem, titled 'Les philosophes', would surely not have displeased Lefebvre:

> Too long they have laughed, the laugh of an intact vessel, of money sure of itself, they laughed at some unfortunate words that the poor used in the way that people kill themselves, in self-defence: believe, love, dream.[43]

---

39 Lefebvre, *La présence et l'absence*, pp. 10 (Paz) and 103 (the presocratics).

40 Cf. Lefebvre, *Qu'est-ce que penser?*, p. 6.

41 This is the case with *La somme et le reste*, Paris: Méridiens-Klincksieck, 1989 (reissue), *Qu'est-ce que penser?* and *La présence et l'absence*.

42 Cf. 'Deux poètes d'aujourd'hui', in Paul Eluard, *Oeuvres complètes*, vol. 2, p. 143; *Poèmes politiques*, 1948, p. 198. We may also think of the collection titled *Poésie et vérité*, 1942. Eluard had himself borrowed the expression from Lautréamont; cf. *Poésies 2, Oeuvres complètes*, Paris: José Corti, 1956, p. 377), which he cites in *L'évidence poétique*, vol. 1, pp. 514 and 521.

43 Cf. Eluard, *Oeuvres complètes*, vol. 2, p. 795.

The concept that poiesis is designed to reinstate, and to which it pertains to metaphilosophy to give a new depth, is that of totality ('fourth aporia', p. 51). That is why, from the very start of this book, in relation to creative praxis, 'total history' is presented as the aim of poiesis, or better still, as 'a strategy: the gathering of the "residues"' (p. 11). Themes again connected: to this total history, 'the history of the city would make a convincing contribution' (p. 143). The modern world is a totality, which it is necessary to explore in order to know the ruptures that break it:

> In itself, metaphilosophical thought attempts to reconstruct a total-
> ity, and first of all to reunite poetry, or rather poiesis, and philosophy,
> at a higher level than that of their ancient split. (p. 160)

For 'embourgeoisified philosophy proved incapable of using the concept of totality . . . It proved equally incapable of overcoming the crisis of this concept by using that of *worldwideness* [*mondialité*]' (p. 191). 'Man is total' (p. 308); philosophy can only spoil this 'total-ity', both close and distant: it must leave room for 'a renewed praxis by poetic decision' (p. 314). This is the path that superseding/realization imposes: to give the lie to Adorno's observation, which Lefebvre cites here: 'Philosophy continues, as its superseding did not take place; the favourable moment was missed.'[44]

The critique of 'Marxist' philosophy, or of what purports to be such, not only the critique of traditional philosophy, represents this 'missing', and finally offers the 'favourable moment' at which 'only a return to Marx can return the acute and trenchant character of these blunted concepts' (p. 13). In particular, that of the *possible*, which Lefebvre places at the centre of Marx's thought: 'Marx thinker of the possible'.[45] May I simply suggest here the interest that the

---

44   This judgement is repeated three times in *Qu'est-ce que penser?*, pp. 66, 109 and 135. [EN: The remark comes from Adorno, *Negative Dialectics*, translated by E. B. Ashton, London: Routledge, 1973, p. 3: 'Philosophy, which once seemed obsolete, lives on because the moment to realize it was missed.']

45   The title of the final chapter of *Une pensée devenue monde*, p. 215. Michel Vadée would pay homage by adopting this as the title of his own book *Marx penseur du possible*, Paris: Méridens-Klinksieck, 1992.

comparative perspective of three philosophies would present, philosophies that, starting from different premises, grant the Marxist category of the *possible* the status of a principle for deciphering the real and a lever for its transformation: Ernst Bloch, Jean-Paul Sartre and Henri Lefebvre have in common the same project, in that for all of them *utopia* is in no way presented as a product of the imaginary or of dream, but rather as a dimension of reality susceptible to ensuring its superseding.[46] This is again the terrain of Marx's eleventh thesis on Feuerbach.

LEFEBVRE AS METAPHILOSOPHER

The problematic of *Metaphilosophy* did not remain isolated. In the copious corpus of Lefebvre's work, this is attested by a number of his books published after 1965 that can be called 'philosophical', in particular *Qu'est-ce que penser?*; *La présence et l'absence*; which is perhaps the closest; and *Une pensée devenue monde*. We get the impression that Lefebvre, who no more liked to quote himself than to multiply quotations from authors he was indebted to (p. 126), sometimes forgot his own *Metaphilosophy*. Thus it is absent from both *La présence et l'absence* and *Une pensée devenue monde*, apart from a rare allusion,[47] whereas it is explicitly referred to in *Logique formelle et logique dialectique*[48] and *Qu'est-ce que penser?*, in which Lefebvre asserts that the question 'What is thinking?' explains the aporias presented in *Metaphilosophy*, and that 'thinking' was precisely what the first Greek philosophers had glimpsed.[49]

---

46   Lefebvre himself confirms this in relation to Sartre (cf. above). He makes an allusion to Bloch in *Une pensée devenue monde* (p. 242), though he asserts that Bloch's principle of hope is not the same as the possible in Marx.

47   Lefebvre refers to 'a reconstruction of philosophical language, sketched out in *Metaphilosophy*', dating this book to 1964.

48   Preface to the second edition, Paris: Editions sociales, 1982, pp. 13, 45 and 53. Lefebvre spells out that 'neither logic nor dialectics can clutch on to religious or philosophical ideologies' (p. 3).

49   Cf. pp. 10, 59, 64 and 82. Here *Metaphilosophy* is dated to 1962 (p. 19). The historical sketch of philosophy in France since 1925 given in the 'Intermezzo' of this book should be compared with that presented by Althusser at the start of *For Marx*.

It sometimes seems that Lefebvre softened certain of his judgements. Thus *Une pensée devenue monde*, starting from a parallel made between Kostas Axelos, who privileged philosophy, and Althusser, who opted for science, marked a certain hesitation, when he asked 'whether Marx was not at the same time one of the last philosophers, in the classic sense, and one of the first metaphilosophers, if not the first' (p. 71); or in raising the question 'What was philosophy in Marx's time, and for Marx?' The eleventh thesis on Feuerbach is judged false here, on the pretext that philosophers 'always wanted to change the world' (p. 73),[50] and unjust towards speculative philosophy (p. 104). 'The strategic hypothesis' of the conclusion even appears regressive: 'We take up Marx's approach on the basis of philosophy . . . The philosophical continues. Is it on the decline? Is it rebounding? Does it keep a relationship with Marx's thought?' (p. 258).

Is Lefebvre rejecting, or at least qualifying, his own thought? I do not think so. Lefebvre never read the *Theses on Feuerbach* as the radical abolition of philosophy, but rather as the project of its realization by the abolition of the proletariat, consigned to the final lines of the *Critique of Hegel's Philosophy of Right* (an 1843 manuscript). And he says this often enough.

In fact, Lefebvre was mad about philosophy. The hazards of his career, which made him a professor of sociology, are entirely explained by the narrow conformism of the philosophical institution, which refused to give its label to someone who did not possess the requisite colours. He was mad about philosophy from the start, from 'the abortive philosophical renovation of the 1930s'[51] until the end of his life,[52] as can already be shown by the imaginary dialogue in *Qu'est-ce que penser?* (p. 64 ff.), a kind of modest confession, which lightly explains some essential themes. Here and there, in the same book, certain accents *à la* Victor Hugo should not deceive us.[53] Lefebvre cannot

---

50   The same judgement is made in *Qu'est-ce que penser?*, p. 28.

51   Interview with Henri Lefebvre by Michel Trebitsch, '1936. Arts et littératures', *Europe*, 683, March 1986.

52   Cf. [Patricia Latour and Francis Combes,] *Conversations avec Henri Lefebvre*, Paris: Messidor, 1991.

53   Cf. 'these poles, these obstacles, these dangers: the sudden collapse of the identical, which is lost in the heaven of transcendence – the chasm of non-identity – which leads to the abyss of absence, nothingness' (p. 74), or 'the chasm of becoming' (p. 104).

escape from philosophy, but only 'continue philosophy by radically transforming the philosophical attitude' (p. 296) while, to a great extent, keeping its problematic (p. 320 ff).

The contribution of *Metaphilosophy*, however, is not confined to the adoption of this position, no matter how fertile. It presses us to emphasize a number of other lessons, genuine weapons to counter the contemporary phenomena of broken weapons, intellectual resignations and the complacent announcement of all 'ends', in the sense of death, that serve only the perpetuation of capitalism, for a time triumphant and without competition. In a tradition (Judaeo-Christian) both austere and hypocritical, and continued by media ideologists among others,[54] how can one not raise one's hat to a philosopher unafraid, more than thirty years ago, to take as subjects of his thought (indeed!) the jukebox, nylon, plastic (p. 107), ALGOL, Syntol (p. 163), cybernetic animals (p. 165), courtly love (p. 217), supermarkets (p. 218), gadgets (p. 239), cover girls, Brigitte Bardot, Marilyn Monroe, Sylvie Vartan and the *yé-yés* (p. 228), plastic materials and injection moulding (p. 226), or the mass media, alongside harmony and counterpoint, Sauveur, Rameau, Bach and Couperin (p. 307), just to stop there. Hence likewise, Lefebvre's style, his *speech* (rather than *discourse*!), colourful, lively, striking, often lyrical, as it was in everyday life. And an explorer without borders, blinkers or taboos, one of the first in our country, if not sometimes *the* first, to read and write on Nietzsche,[55] Heidegger, as well as Marx,[56] Hegel[57] and Lenin.[58] A tremendous beater of new paths, ranging from dialectical

---

54   The most representative names can be filled in ad lib. They are certainly not wanting. Alternatively, one can follow the direction indicated by Jean-Pierre Garnier in his recent books, *La pensée aveugle*, Paris: Spengler, 1993, and *Des barbares dans la cité*, Paris: Flammarion, 1996.

55   From *Nietzsche*, Paris: Editions sociales internationales, 1939, to *Hegel, Marx, Nietzsche ou le royaume des ombres*, Paris and Tournai: Casterman, 1975.

56   In collaboration with Norbert Guterman, *Introduction aux morceaux choisis de Marx*, Paris: NRF, 1934, and *La conscience mystifiée*, Paris: Gallimard, 1936; *Le matérialisme dialectique*, Paris: Alcan 1939; *Marx et la liberté*, Geneva: Editions des Trois Collines, 1947; *Pour connaître la pensée de Karl Marx*, Paris: Bordas, 1948; *Le marxisme*, Paris: PUF, 1948; *Problèmes actuels du marxisme*, Paris: PUF, 1958; and so forth.

57   With Norbert Guterman, *Morceaux choisis de Hegel*, Paris: Gallimard, 1938.

58   With Norbert Guterman, *Cahiers de Lénine sur la dialectique de Hegel*, Paris: Gallimard, 1938; *Pour connaître la pensée de Lénine*, Paris: Bordas, 1957.

logic to rural life, the city and urbanism, everyday life and the state.[59] On these last 'fields', as Lefebvre preferred not to call them, we shall not draw up a bibliography. It would be too long.

A POLITICS OF THE EVERYDAY

We shall, however, make two remarks that speak also for tomorrow and the days ahead, whether they are joyous or not. The first consists in wishing for the arrival of successors, in these matters, along with the concepts that they advance – to give just one example, the 'state mode of production', even if we should welcome the audience encountered outside France – one example being the work of anglophone Marxist urbanists, above all David Harvey.[60] The second, which more strictly concerns our object here, metaphilosophy, seeks to emphasize that despite subsequent qualifications here and there, as mentioned above, this has not only maintained the exact presence of a continuous reflection, but in its most adequate trace has proposed the design of a politics to which we are still invited.

This politics developed first of all in the persistent work that marked a long phase in Lefebvre's life, the *Critique of Everyday Life*, begun in 1947, continued in 1962 with a second volume, and completed (?) in 1981 with a third, which we have already noted was nourished by metaphilosophical reflection. I would like to point out, as an exemplary case, that one of the approaches to everyday life in *Metaphilosophy* starts from the attention given to the nuclear danger (p. 105). We are dealing here with a new object that illustrates Lefebvre's method. The nuclear danger, for the first time and for a long time to come, places over the whole of humanity a threat of death. This is no longer a matter of representation,

---

59   Or communication: 'Mystificatory, mass communications go hand in hand with incommunicability' (p. 94); 'The man of communications continues to communicate, even when there is no longer anything to communicate' (p. 235).

60   Although in this field, far more clearly than in others, French researchers are scarcely behind their foreign colleagues; among the most recent offerings, cf. Catherine Bernié-Boissard, 'Actualités de Henri Lefebvre', *Espaces et sociétés*, Paris: L'Harmattan, 1994.

but of lived experience. 'Life and death are fogged and mingled'; men discover that they are 'in a state of survival', and that they have always been so. 'The dialectical unity of life and death, being and nothingness, has ceased to present itself in a speculative view' (p. 106); we are beyond philosophy. And it is precisely the consciousness of this phenomenon that creates the conditions of its superseding, which 'contributes to constituting worldness [*mondalité*] in praxis'. It is no longer possible now to think and live as before.

The modification that matters concerns everyday life, which in modern societies can no longer be equated with a 'style of life', something that, on the contrary, 'contains the split of "real life" into separate sectors' – work, private life, leisure. Between these sectors there is just one form of unity: passivity, nonparticipation, the repetitive, submission, the mimetic. Is everyday life to be treated as a residue – a notion that 'we encounter here' (p. 109)? Or rather is the world and life to be changed?[61] A notice of this kind, directly issuing from praxis, does not simply confirm that 'thought is also constituted by considering everydayness, excluded by philosophy';[62] it calls for resistance. 'The everyday and its rejection put in question, fragment by fragment, the whole of the modern world' (p. 298), which is 'intolerable, unacceptable'. That is why 'the critique of everyday life, and this alone, could thus combine the multiple contestations into a bundle . . . The totality of contestations and the contestation of totality, that is negativity, are only reconstituted on the basis of the everyday' (ibid.).

The everyday provokes the insurrection of the particular, the *levée en masse* of the residues. This is the politics set to strike at the heart of the capitalist world. Once dogmatisms of every kind are rejected, of every school and tradition, starting with Marxism, socialism can draw from this a renewed force, mobilizing and offensive. It will finally become, as Lefebvre liked so much to repeat, Dionysiac. 'The party of supersession of philosophy and metamorphosis of the everyday constitutes a party' (p. 307). Is it

---

61 It is precisely here that Marx and Rimbaud are cited (cf. footnote 12).
62 *Qu'est-ce que penser?*, p. 40.

necessary to say that the ranks of such a party are potentially more numerous and better identified today than they were in the 1960s? Think, for example, of the new political spaces that are opening up almost everywhere, and the constantly growing set of anti-systemic movements growing everywhere in the world. A strong analysis of this kind, like that of José Luis Rebellato, for example, intersects and brings fully up to date Lefebvrian positions, from the categories of the possible and of concrete utopia to social *microprocesos* and *microrealiziciones*, or the 'culture of resistance'.[63] It is not hard to imagine which side Henri Lefebvre would be on, at whom he would rail and to whom he would dedicate his enthusiasm. He would find himself in the party of the excluded, those residues that our societies of abundance proliferate ceaselessly, on the side of the wretched of the Third World, the Zapatistas, Palestinians or the peasants of Brazil. *Metaphilosophy*, by denouncing the moral trickery that creates the illusion that belief in technology could put an end to bureaucracy, whereas in fact it serves it,[64] goes as far as suggesting the political form of these combats:

> Can we then count on technological thought rather than a renewed democracy to realize the withering away of the state and the replacement of constraint over men by the direct management of things?
> (p. 148)

We know in what direction Lefebvre would extend this reflection today, when he defines 'the contract of citizenship' in terms, and with demands, that render the present-day 'consensus' derisory. The heretic, on the contrary, the iconoclast, the permanent dissident, persists and, in the last lines that he wrote, signs off by

---

63 *La encrucijada de la ética, Neoliberalismo, Conflicto Norte-Sur, Liberación*, Montevideo: Editorial Nordan-Comunidad, 1995; cf. chapter 3, 'Etica de la liberación y construcción de alternativas'.

64 As we have repeatedly seen, *Metaphilosophy* conducts a veritable trial of technology, which may seem very singular for a Marxist, in view of the praise and expectations this receives in *Capital*. In the meantime, 'progress' has given adequate proof of the 'damage' it can cause.

reasserting his conviction that civil society must reabsorb the state and politics, 'which would complete, democratically, the abandoned project of the dictatorship of the proletariat'.[65] It is up to us to remember this lesson.

Georges Labica, Summer 1997

---

65 'Du pacte social au contrat de citoyenneté', in Henri Lefebvre et le Groupe de Navarrenx, *Du contrat de citoyenneté*, Paris: Syllepse, 1991, p. 37; 'From the Social Pact to the Contract of Citizenship', *Key Writings*, edited by Stuart Elden, Elizabeth Lebas and Eleonore Kofman, London: Continuum, 2003, pp. 253–4.

Index